THE COMPLETE IDIOT'S GUIDE® TO

Pro Wrestling

Second Edition

by Captain Lou Albano and Bert Randolph Sugar
with Michael Benson

alpha books

Macmillan USA, Inc.
201 West 103rd Street
Indianapolis, IN 46290

A Pearson Education Company

Publisher
Marie Butler-Knight

Product Manager
Phil Kitchel

Managing Editor
Cari Luna

Senior Acquisitions Editor
Renee Wilmeth

Development Editor
Deborah S. Romaine

Production Editors
Tom Eader
Billy Fields

Copy Editor
Krista Hansing

Illustrator
Brian Moyer

Cover Designers
Mike Freeland
Kevin Spear

Book Designers
Scott Cook and Amy Adams of DesignLab

Indexer
Brad Herriman

Layout/Proofreading
Cyndi Davis-Hubler
Terri Edwards
Steve Geiselman
Brad Lenser
Donna Martin

Contents at a Glance

Contents

7 Post-War Wrestlers and the New Pro Wrestling 71

8 Sexy, Serious, and Supreme in Their Roles 83

Part 4: History of *WrestleMania*   181

16   2000: Setting Up the Main Event   183

17   How We Got Here   193

18   All the *WrestleManias*   199

Appendixes

Foreword

As you undoubtedly know, I rarely speak out. But when I was approached to write the foreword to this book on professional wrestling, I thought it would be an honor to add my voice to it—an honor to attach my name to a book that is a must for all wrestling fans. A book that takes you behind the scenes, behind the glitz and the glamour, and that tells you about the great people, the great talent, and the great athletes in the world of pro wrestling.

I know there is a stereotypical picture of the professional wrestler. Most people think we're a lot of fake people, nonathletic, and all show. But we're totally different from what you've been led to believe. For even though we're outrageous and outlandish in the ring, we're different outside. Outside, we're real people: well-rounded, very approachable good guys doing what we're doing to earn a living.

Sure, I take it personally when someone says professional wrestling is "fake." After all, like all wrestlers, I have my pride. You've got to have great self-pride to face millions of people every week dressed in nothing but your underwear. But we know what we do is real—real in terms of our athleticism, real in terms of our ability to entertain, and real in terms of our being able to capture the imagination of people everywhere.

By people everywhere, I don't just mean kids. For even though our primary audience today is kids who are enthralled with the world of professional wrestling, we've been able to transform everybody into a kid—at least at heart. We have been able to reach the masses because professional wrestling is, bottom line, fun.

To give you an example of how we've transferred the fanaticism of kids to their parents, earlier this season I had the chance to visit Mark McGwire in the St. Louis Cardinals locker room. I thought it was funny when he asked me for an autograph for his son, who was a wrestling fan and had made his father into one.

I'm the luckiest wrestler in the world to be in the position I'm in. Through wrestling I've had a chance to reach out to the masses—not those typical masses you think follow wrestling, but to football players, baseball players, even cabinet members who like wrestling because it's entertaining and fun. And to reach out because of the exposure we've gotten on the Turner Broadcasting System, which televises us five hours a week, creating the opportunity to make new friends and fans for pro wrestling.

So, to my fans, to Turner Broadcasting, to the WCW, and, not incidentally, to Lou and Bert for asking me to write the foreword to the book that every fan needs, I want to speak my piece and say, "Thank you for making professional wrestling what it is today—fun!"

—GOLDBERG, WCW Champion

BILL GOLDBERG defeated legend Hollywood (formerly "Hulk") Hogan for the WCW World Heavyweight Championship title on July 6, 1998. A former star nose guard with the Georgia Bulldogs and NFL player with the Atlanta Falcons and Los Angeles Rams, Goldberg switched to pro wrestling when he suffered an injury. The 6-foot, 4-inch, 285-pound powerhouse is known for his spear and jackhammer and for inspiring "Gold-berg!" chants in arenas throughout the country.

Introduction

The year was 1949, the place was Washington, D.C., and like every young man who had not yet found girls, I (me, Bert) found sports—or what passed for sports in that time and that place. I found that wonderful world where picturesque names such as Gorgeous George, Antonino Rocca, and Primo Carnera dotted the landscape: professional wrestling.

The defining moment for this then-young man and the world of wrestling was maybe when, as a 13-year-old, I somehow found myself first to get through on a radio phone line with the now long-forgotten answer to an equally long-forgotten sports trivia question and won two free tickets to an upcoming "rasslin'" bout between Gorgeous George and Primo Carnera.

It was ecstasy. It was joy. And it was terror. For how on earth was a 13-year-old boy going to get away with attending a late-night wrestling bout held across town—and on a school night, to boot?

But that problem was soon solved. My mother, who was normally so asportive that she thought Sugar Ray Robinson was my Dad's first cousin on his father's side, assumed that because one of the names on the card was Primo Carnera, I'd won tickets to a boxing match. Boxing was far more "presentable" than wrestling, and because it was a free show (after all, I'd won *two* tickets), she decided she'd escort me to it. Imagine her surprise when she found herself seated smack dab in the middle of a crowd of people, all looking like they were a few beans short of a three-bean salad. Many of her fellow female match-goers, women who were then known as "Hatpin Marys," were running around the arena trying to stab a wrestler or two. Suffice it to say, the whole thing did not live up to her expectations.

But that made no difference to her son.

I was immediately caught up in the moment—and *what* a moment! There was excitement going on everywhere around me.

That first wrestling bout I ever attended, however, was something of an anticlimax. Gorgeous George, of the thick red neck and flabby white hide that made a marked contrast with his golden coiffure, tried a couple of underhanded moves on Carnera. All he got for his efforts was a disdainful sneer from "Da Preem," as Carnera was often called. Then, grabbing one fish-belly-white leg out from under his adversary, Carnera lifted Gorgeous George aloft and slammed him back down on the mat, stepping down hard on the now prostrate George's abdomen.

The referee got down on all fours to pound the canvas three times. In two bats of an eye, the main event was over!

No matter. That was the beginning of a lifelong love affair with the sport/entertainment of wrestling, and it hardly mattered that my appalled mother didn't speak to me for the next two months—my punishment for having dragged her to the event in the first place.

To be sure, the intensity of that first wild infatuation with wrestling dropped off rather precipitously once I discovered girls. However, this book gives me the opportunity to revisit that once-intense love that dates back to those more innocent days—more innocent for yours truly *and* for wrestling itself. Professional wrestling since then has changed greatly—but, then again, so have I. And so has society.

Back then, when men were men and women were glad of it, wrestling was a clear-cut case of black and white: Good guys were always good; bad guys were horrid. And there was nothing ambiguous in between. Now, in the days of laser light shows and tortured wrestling characters, things aren't so clear. But it's all still the greatest entertainment extravaganza there is.

So, while this book pays tribute to some of the wonderful legends of wrestling's early years, I've also tried to make it a no-holds-barred look at the whole wacky, over-the-top world of wrestling—a world that would have made P.T. Barnum proud.

In this book, you'll find some interesting and helpful information:

➤ A history of wrestling, from its earliest days to the modern era of pay-per-view and multimedia events

➤ Biographies of some of the major wrestling personalities, from the stars to the managers to the promoters, who contributed to making wrestling the greatest sport/entertainment available today

➤ Insider information on the rules, the moves, and the magic of professional wrestling

➤ Advice on where to go to get started on a career in professional wrestling—and what you'll find when you get there

Here's a rundown on what's in the pages to come:

Part 1, "This Crazy World Called Pro Wrestling," illustrates the broad appeal of wrestling and gives you a brief overview of how the sport developed.

Part 2, "The Founding Fathers: Wrestling's Colorful History," provides you with the biographies of the greatest wrestlers of all time—yesterday, today, and maybe even tomorrow.

Part 3, "Today's Superstars," highlights four of the biggest superstars working in the ring today: The Rock, Stone Cold Steve Austin, Goldberg, and Triple H. In addition, you'll find shorter biographies of many wrestlers, managers, and valets who make up today's rasslin' roster.

Part 4, "History of *WrestleMania*," takes you to wrestling's largest annual event. Not only will we look at the action in each *WrestleMania*, but we'll also take an in-depth look at the build-up to and execution of *WrestleMania 2000,* which turned out to be the largest wrestling pay-per-view event ever.

Part 5, "Spelling Wrestling With Six Letters: A-C-T-I-O-N," brings you the rivalries, feuds, and grudge matches that have kept fans fascinated over the years. Plus, we'll take a look at the greatest wrestling matches ever held, of both yesterday and today.

Part 6, "All the Right Moves: The Inner (and Outer) Workings of the Ring," moves off into a whole 'nother direction: Here you'll learn about where the wrestlers go to develop their skills, where you can go yourself if you want a career in the sport, and some of the things you might expect to find after you've started your career as a professional wrestler.

Extras

In addition to all this, sidebars are scattered throughout the text. These will give you definitions of wrestling's colorful terms, insiders' comments, a few warnings, and reminiscences and anecdotes from sportswriters and wrestlers. Here's what to look for:

Wrestle Mania

Here you'll find anecdotes and insider information about professional wrestling, past and present.

Captain Lou's Corner

The author steps out from behind the page to pass along a comment, clarification, or colorful tale.

In Your Face

These give you short, sometimes scabrous quotes or observations about this wacky world and the people in it.

xxiii

Body Slam

Warnings! There are things that you, as a fan, should know—so read 'em and heed 'em.

Bert's Corner

The author steps out from behind the page to pass along a comment, clarification, or colorful tale.

Fighting Words

You'll learn definitions of terms drawn from the wrestling world in these sidebars. Because much of wrestling's language comes from the carney lingo called "kayfabe," you'll need these sidebars as your insider's manual.

Acknowledgments

Without them, we'd have nothing to say—so here we give our thanks to all the wrestling pros out there, from the performers to the promoters. And thanks to the federations, particularly the WWF, for their assistance on the project. A special thanks to Norman Kietzer and Vince McMahon for giving us access to the photographs that enliven this book's pages. Finally, thanks to our team at Alpha Books.

Special Thanks to the Technical Reviewer

The Complete Idiot's Guide to Pro Wrestling, Second Edition was reviewed by an expert who double-checked the accuracy of what you'll learn here, to help us ensure that this book gives you everything you need to know about pro wrestling. Special thanks are extended to Dean Miller.

Trademarks

All terms mentioned in this book that are known to be or are suspected of being trademarks or service marks have been appropriately capitalized. Alpha Books and Macmillan USA, Inc., cannot attest to the accuracy of this information. Use of a term in this book should not be regarded as affecting the validity of any trademark or service mark.

Part 1

This Crazy World Called Pro Wrestling

How many people do you know who can wear almost anything they want to work? Does anyone you know show up to work in a mask? Unless you are an M.D. or are into robbing banks for a living, probably not. But in pro wrestling, the work force wears—in addition to the scars of battle—masks, makeup, capes, tights, thongs, and all kinds of gadgets and plumage. And, like plumbers who bring wrenches to work, or lawyers who carry briefcases to their offices, the workers in pro wrestling bring their own tools. But in wrestling, those tools might include everything up to and including baseball bats, metal chairs, trashcans, barbed wire, and a whole host of other lethal-looking gadgets.

As Butch said to Sundance, "Who are these guys?" They are the players of pro wrestling.

Today's wrestlers get it on in style and with plenty of showmanship. In this part, we'll show you what it's all about.

Chapter 1

Muscle Mania and Mayhem

In This Chapter

➤ The method in wrestling's madness

➤ Soap operas of the canvas stage keep fans coming

➤ The fans—everyone is invited

➤ Appearances are deceiving

Traditional wrestling—the sport engaged in at the high school, college, and Olympic levels—can lay claim to being the oldest sport in the world. But that's not what we're talking about. Although modern pro wrestling has its earliest roots in the classical form of the sport, what we're interested in here is that body-slamming, headlocking, chair-throwing, slightly raunchy combination of sports spectacular and entertainment extravaganza. *That* is pro wrestling, and it appeals to, as The Rock would say, "millions upon millions of fans" throughout the world.

Today's pro wrestling—featuring superstars such as Stone Cold Steve Austin, Goldberg, and Triple H—has universal appeal. It draws its fans from all walks of life and all age groups, regardless of gender or nationality. In this chapter, you'll learn about wrestling's broad appeal—and why the fans love it.

Fans, Fans, from Everywhere

Arturo Toscanini, the dignified orchestra maestro of yesteryear, would watch televised wrestling matches and scream "Keel heem! Keel heem!" when one of his favorite wrestlers took a particularly nasty blow from an opponent. Former first lady Bess Truman said the thing she'd miss most about leaving the White House at the end of her husband's term of office was "wrestling on Thursday nights." And some of the celebrities who've turned out for the *WrestleMania* events include Pete Rose, Mike Tyson, Mary Tyler Moore, Robin Leach, Vanna White, Gladys Knight, Liberace, Pamela Lee, and Alex Trebec. Other self-confessed admirers have included Douglas Fairbanks Sr., Will Rogers, Peter Ustinov, Sean Connery, and David Letterman. What attracts these notables, and every other fan, is wrestling's *drama*, its spectacle, its sheer energy and excitement. Wrestling fans are diverse!

Bert's Corner

Some old-timers will say that today's wrestling is sports entertainment but that back in their day, it was a real sport, as pure as the proverbial driven snow, so securely on the up-and-up that it was locked in the upright position. But, as Ira Gershwin wrote, "It ain't necessarily so." Wrestling—pro wrestling, that is, not to be confused with the scholastic amateur version—has always been sports entertainment. For those historical revisionists, we offer the following evidence: The April 12, 1887, edition of the *Chicago Tribune* ran an article about pro wrestling's world champion Evan Lewis—who was known as Strangler long before the twentieth-century superstar—defeating the previously unbeatable Joe Acton. The paper reported: "Betting houses, having received word that Acton was going to lay down for Lewis, took the match off the board." That is, they refused to take any bets on it. The final straw, the paper said, came when one gambler eagerly offered to bet on the precise time of the finish of each fall. Other matches involving Lewis during that same time period were called by the *Tribune* a "cooked-up contest" and "a regular exhibition of faking."

Boob-Tube Brawls

Televised pro wrestling rules the airwaves today. The dueling TV broadcasts are *RAW is WAR/Warzone* and *Monday Nitro*, which run head-to-head on the USA and TNT networks. (Although as we go to press, *RAW* is scheduled to move to The Nashville Network [TNN].) These shows are produced by the two major wrestling organizations—the World Wrestling Federation (WWF) and World Championship Wrestling (WCW)—who together own Monday prime time. Their shows generate higher ratings than any other shows on cable TV, while, not incidentally, at the same time marketing their product, developing new major players, and building future generations of fans. The WWF show *Smackdown* on the UPN network is the first wrestling show on prime time broadcast TV in decades, and its high ratings have been given credit for saving the struggling network.

More wrestling is on TV today than ever before, thanks to cable. And then there are the major pay-per-view bouts. Wrestling is big, and as you'll soon see, it's big business, too. But savvy marketing is not the whole secret to pro wrestling's success—fans get caught up in the ongoing story lines of feuds between wrestlers and grudge matches between flamboyant characters. Today, wrestling is much like a soap opera, and fans develop strong attachments to their favorites.

Captain Lou's Corner

The two major organizations in wrestling today, responsible for most of the cable wrestling programming, are Vince McMahon Jr.'s World Wrestling Federation (WWF), headquartered in Stamford, Connecticut, and Ted Turner's World Championship Wrestling (WCW), out of Atlanta, Georgia.

Wrestle Mania

The WWF and WCW each have about one pay-per-view (PPV) telecast each month. Leading into the PPV telecasts, the regular Monday night shows devote time to developing story lines that culminate in the PPV face-offs. Because the PPV shows are always broadcast on Sunday nights, the Monday after is always dedicated to handling the big fight's results and setting the story line for the next PPV bout scheduled for the following month.

There are strong similarities between pro wrestling and soap operas, in the development of both characters and story lines. Wrestling viewers watch each show, week after week, getting drawn into the story lines of feuds and personalities, just like soap-opera fans. Viewers come to believe in the characters as if they were real people—forgetting the performer behind the character.

Plot elements between wrestling and soaps are similar as well. Friends and lovers become bitter enemies. Betrayal and fickle allegiances occur. Good guys take on the bad guys. It's all there. Sometimes the good guy can be a diamond in the rough, and the bad guy can be the one that you love to hate. Clever writers have been more willing to put shades of gray into their characters to make them ambiguous, and fans following the ins and outs of the now-convoluted plot lines have rewarded them by making wrestling one of the most popular forms of TV programming. If you follow The Rock, for instance, you know him as conceited and vindictive, but supercool in a razor-sharp sort of way. And you're not going to miss a single one of his matches. But even if you don't like "The People's Champion," as The Rock likes to call himself, you'll *still* watch—in hopes that his archrival, WWF owner Vince McMahon, will surface to do him in.

The Rock is wrestling's top star.

Beyond the Small Screen

Pro wrestling's popularity goes way beyond TV telecasts. Drop in at your local newsstand, and you'll see how big pro wrestling is—several magazines are devoted to the subject, plus many new biographies on the bookshelf. Toy stores and video game stores are likewise filled with wrestling products. And next time you're surfing the Web, you'll be amazed at the number of sites devoted to pro wrestling.

So what's the secret of pro wrestling's popularity? Well, I like to compare it to *Playboy* magazine, which treats college kids like successful businessmen and successful businessmen like college kids, so the magazine becomes a guilty pleasure for both. Wrestling, on the other hand, is too immature for adults, yet too risqué for kids, so both groups love it. And when you put grown-ups and kids together, you've got everybody.

Wrestling is a theater of violence—not a theater in the round, but theater in the squared circle, performed in a venue that imitates one of sports' most time-honored symbols: the boxing ring.

Sure, pro wrestling has many detractors. You know the type—the ones who turn up their noses at the hype and the vulgarity, who sniff dismissively that "it's not a *real* sport." Well, you just can't please everybody—and some people may never be able to let themselves go and just *enjoy* the show. Too bad, 'cuz they're missing one helluva *great* show. Real wrestling fans know that it isn't about scoring points, or even winning and losing— it's entertainment. That's the whole point. That's not so hard to understand! And 36 million people get the point, worldwide!

Bert's Corner

Monday night's telecasts of WWF and WCW matches garner combined ratings as high as 10.0—the highest-rated programming on cable TV, beating out most NBA playoff games. Pay-per-view telecasts pull in $300 million a year in broadcast fees alone. Thirty-six million people watch wrestling every week. Now that's *big*!

Wrestle Mania

Internet Web sites featuring wrestling are everywhere! And most have links to even *more* sites, so you can spend days digging up insider information, interviews, match results, trivia, photos, sound clips, and much more! Official sites include www.wwf.com (the WWF home page), www.wcwwrestling.com (for WCW information), and www.ecwwrestling.com (the home page for the Extreme Championship Wrestling organization).

Captain Lou's Corner

According to Hollywood Hogan, when wrestling's insiders went public, admitting that the matches are choreographed (never, but *never* call them *fake*), the fan base exploded. Now it's not just the 18-to-34-year-old male demographic, but also whole families who buy tickets to the events.

The Greatest Show on Earth

All right, so you've got a compelling cast of characters and story lines complete with cliffhangers and plot twists worthy of Indiana Jones. You've got the fan magazines (fanzines) and Web sites, not to mention all the peripheral products—T-shirts and big foam fingers and the like. You've got show-biz savvy in the staging of events, too. Take one of pro wrestling's most popular shows, *Monday Nitro*. Each week's live episode is held in a different city, but there are certain things—such as how the stage and the entrance ramp to the ring are set up—that stay constant, week after week.

The Whole World's Watching

The people who do research at Turner Network, which telecasts *Monday Nitro*, are proud of the fact that their wrestling series beats out 62 percent of all broadcast programs in prime time among men between the ages of 18 and 34—the key wrestling (and advertising) demographic group. But that's only part of the picture. One of wrestling's largest and fastest-growing groups of fans consists of women.

What's the attraction? Maybe it's the "hunk factor," as one 18-year-old fan called it in an interview for *USA Today*. Her favorite wrestler is Bill Goldberg, "because he's beautiful," she said. Others find wrestling to be a great catharsis for anyone who has ever had to put up with an overbearing boss or a rude store clerk. When The Rock "layeth the smacketh down" upon his evil boss, Vince McMahon, there's not a working stiff in the audience who doesn't feel just a little bit of vicarious satisfaction!

Wrestle Mania

Before the late 1930s, wrestling was almost exclusively a men's night out. Mildred Burke, former women's wrestling champion, was the first of her gender to enter the ring. She tells of the first match that she ever attended back in 1937 in Kansas City: "... in a crowd of 3,000 or 4,000, you'd see maybe six or seven women at the most—they were probably the wives of the wrestlers ...." Women didn't really start coming out to wrestling matches in large numbers until women began participating as wrestlers.

With their great size and physique, wrestlers are real-life action heroes. Throw in the fact that they can fly like birds and dive like kamikazes, and you can see why they are adored by kids. As I said before, it's not all white hats and black hats anymore. As society has changed, wrestling's heroic characters have changed to reflect today's moral ambiguity.

And the whole marketing thrust of professional wrestling has changed to reflect the changing times and its changing audience. It borrows from the energy of MTV videos and rock concerts with laser light shows and steam streams. It's total entertainment now, and the younger fans have responded by the millions. Wrestling has never been for the easily offended or for the faint of heart—but it has now become an entertainment that has something to offer to everyone in the family, youth included.

I Can't Look ... Wait, Let Me See!

Wrestling is not sophisticated. It plays to our basic instincts. It surely delivers on the promise of violence, with its repertoire of headlocks, dropkicks, and body slams. Nothing else comes as close to satisfying our fascination for the grisly and the gruesome as today's wrestling—not even a horror movie.

Wrestlers bash each other over the head with chairs, toss each other off 16-foot-high cages, and whip their rivals with barbed wire, baseball bats, or whatever else is handy. They slam their opponents' heads into turnbuckles, caskets, dumpsters, or anything else that's nearby. Everything has been tried—and will be again ... and again.

Granted, wrestling has come under fire in recent years for all its bone-crushing violence and its physical and verbal abuse. But it's all about *performance*! You need to come to a match with as much suspended disbelief as you would to any movie. But that doesn't mean it's *all* fake. It's like what retailing giant

Body Slam

As more young viewers have gotten hooked on wrestling, it has come up for some heavy criticism. The foul language, the nonstop violence, and the sexual innuendo have all been cited as bad examples for the kids. Still, as Bonnie Hammer, senior vice president of the USA network says, "My husband grew up watching it, and he wound up in Harvard Divinity School."

In Your Face

Is everybody pleased with wrestling's admission that some of the show is staged? Not at all. "If you print that kind of stuff, it ruins it .... People like to forget it's pretend," says Eric Bischoff, former wrestling announcer, sometime wrestler, and on-and-off chief executive of WCW.

John Wannamaker said when he was asked if he was wasting his money on advertising: "Half of it is wasted, half not. The problem is, I don't know which half." The same is true for wrestling—some of it's real, some isn't, and it's up to you, the knowledgeable fan, to figure out which is which.

It's a given: Pro wrestling is a great game of illusions. But there's one thing that's *very* real—the injuries. I, Captain Lou, know, because I've had almost every bone in my body broken at one time or another. My nose has been broken 14 times, and I've always hoped that whoever broke it last would put it back where it belonged. And my experience is not unique. Yukon Eric lost his ear in a bout with Killer Kowalski, as did Cactus Jack. He caught his ears in the ropes while battling Vader. Steve Austin was momentarily paralyzed by an Owen Hart piledriver and has been sidelined on and off ever since with neck problems. Bruno Sammartino had his neck broken during a bout against Stan Hansen. "The body gets beaten up," says Macho Man Randy Savage. Darren Drosdov was paralyzed from the waist down during a match on Long Island. And more than a few wrestlers have died in the ring.

Bert's Corner

In many states, professional wrestling is labeled "entertainment," not sport. Vince McMahon of the WWF was largely responsible for this distinction, removing wrestling from the jurisdiction of state athletic commissions that were established to oversee the sport of boxing, not wrestling.

Death in the Ring: Wrestlers Who Have Died During a Match

Gary Allbright	Eddie Baker
Jim Browning	Dennis Clary
Mike DiBiase	Eli Fisher
Masakazu Fukuda	Gino Garibaldi
Ray Gunkel	Owen Hart
Javier Hernandez (Oro)	Emiko Kado
George Kinney	Jack Lewis
Gordon McKinley	Buddy O'Brien
Mike Romano	Joe Shimkus
Mariko Umeda (Plum Mariko)	Tex Wright
Steve Znoski	

Seeing Is Believing? Or Not ...

So what's real and what's not? Well, first of all, the athletes themselves are real—very real! Pro wrestlers are among the finest athletes in the world. Thanks to their training, they're able to perform almost superhuman moves each and every night and withstand an enormous amount of sheer physical punishment. They're in good enough shape to be able to do all the right moves with near-perfect timing. They have agility, ability, and amazing energy. They take their injuries in stride, preferring to keep performing while injured rather than to watch from the sidelines. And they do it all under the watchful glare of the TV cameras.

But while you can call it entertainment and you can call it performance, don't even *think* about calling pro wrestling "fake." Those are real athletes, performing real moves, choreographed or not. To call them fake is to insult the level of training and dedication that these athletes bring to their line of work. And that could be, as it says on cigarette packages, "hazardous to your health."

Is it real? Just ask comedian Richard Belzer, who challenged Hulk Hogan to put a headlock on him. Hogan complied with a side headlock, which cut off Belzer's blood supply. When the Hulk let go, Belzer was out cold and dropped to the floor. Or go talk to *20/20*'s John Stossel. On the TV show, he challenged Dr. D. (David Schultz) and got his ears boxed, literally.

As the legendary TV personality and one-time wrestling commentator Steve Allen once said, "Wrestling is only as fake as your imagination is fake, as your daydreams are fake." The illusions are created through *real* athleticism, *real* showmanship, *real* hard work, and *real* training. As a result, the fans get *real* enjoyment. That's good enough for me!

Bigger Isn't Necessarily Better

Admittedly some wrestlers look like poster children for "Save the Whales," but pro wrestling also has its beautiful bodies. These wrestlers clearly have spent more time raising barbells than beer

In Your Face

Wrestlers have personas, and story lines are tailored around them. Says Stone Cold Steve Austin, "My character is a blue-collar-type thing. I gotta go out there and be unimpressed by authority. They tell me I can't do something, I go ahead and do it."

Captain Lou's Corner

The heat that pro wrestling takes for being fake is really unfair. Pulitzer Prize-winning sportswriter Red Smith once attended a "real" boxing match in the company of Lou Thesz (one of wrestling's all-time greats), and rumor had it that the fight was fixed. No one believed it until the KO came on a flimsy backhand. Smith said to Thesz: "Lou, I'll never write an unkind word about wrestling again. At least you guys make it look like a contest."

bottles. In tights, with well-oiled bodies, these athletes are appreciated by both men and women as ideal specimens of manliness. And let's not forget the female wrestlers and valets. Va-va-va-voom! They bring a whole new dimension to the concept of "feminine pulchritude."

Keeping the Tradition Alive

Like competitive sports, professional wrestling keeps its history alive, with generations of fans and players passing along its heritage and lore. Younger fans learn from their fathers (or mothers, for that matter) that Gorgeous George was yesterday's version of Hulk Hogan. Bill Goldberg is today's version of Bruno Sammartino. And so the comparisons across the years go on.

The Least You Need to Know

➤ Millions of people from all walks of life follow pro wrestling on a regular basis.

➤ Wrestling combines the compelling characters and story lines of soap operas with the variety and excitement of a three-ring circus.

➤ Although wrestling is not considered a sport in the true sense of the word, its performers are real athletes—some of the best in the world. They perform real moves, suffer real injuries, and provide real entertainment.

➤ There are as many different types of wrestlers as there are types of fans—everyone can find a favorite to cheer for, or somebody they can love to hate.

➤ Wrestling's rich history and tradition have been passed down from generation to generation of fans.

Chapter 2

A Brief History of Wrestling

> **In This Chapter**
>
> ➤ Wrestling comes to America: Greco-Roman and catch-as-catch-can styles
>
> ➤ Promoters and pretense: the carney contribution
>
> ➤ Wrestling becomes rasslin'
>
> ➤ The first showman

Once upon a time, wrestlers wrestled—I mean *really* wrestled. Some historians have traced the sport's ancestry back to the ancient Egyptians, and then on to the Greeks and the Romans. I mean, wrestling goes *way* back, before the Great Flood!

But that's not the type of wrestling we're talking about here. We're talking about the body-slamming, head-bashing entertainment called professional wrestling—a form of entertainment that is as American as baseball, basketball, and apple pie. And *that* wrestling has a history all its own, as you'll see in this chapter. (And, like baseball, wrestling has caught on in other countries as well—particularly Mexico and Japan.)

From the Old World to the New

Old World wrestling was of the Greco-Roman variety, which had certain rules: No holds were allowed below the waist, and when one of the combatants hit the ground, it constituted a *fall*. In contrast to this "long-hair" variety was the more commercial form of wrestling, such as the matches that used to be held in old German beer gardens. Although *scientific* in nature, the main idea of these wrestling exhibitions was to sell beer.

The longer an exhibition match lasted, the more beer the beer garden sold. And so, the two wrestlers would lock the other in each other's arms and stay in one position for 30 minutes, 40 minutes, or more. Finally, when the wrestlers got thirsty, one would be thrown to the ground with a mighty thud, and they would rest and drink for 30 minutes or so. And so on through the long, wet night ....

The Carney Connection

When wrestling was brought to American shores by German and Irish immigrants, it was given a New World twist. Beginning in the post-Civil War period, wrestling bouts were staged at country fairs or touring carnivals in "At Shows" (short for Athletic Shows), where wrestlers with colorful costumes, equally colorful nicknames, and fictionalized biographies would wrestle each other or accept challenges from all local comers.

Fighting Words

Old World wrestling is called **scientific**—meaning that it was based upon specific holds, moves, rules, and skills—to distinguish it from the choreographed, entertainment-oriented style that has developed into modern pro wrestling.

Wrestle Mania

According to wrestling writer Joe Jares, "Vermont was, in the early 1700s, America's first hotbed of wrestling. Most popular was the Irish 'collar and elbow style,' in which each wrestler would start by placing one hand on his opponent's shoulder on or near the collar line and the other hand on the arm just above the elbow. 'Just step down and finger me collar, I doubledang dare ye,' was a typical challenge."

The carney At Shows featured wrestlers engaging in exhibition matches or challenging all comers from the audience in time-limit contests for money—say, $25. The challenger could win in one of two ways: by pinning the star or by managing to stay in the ring with him for 15 minutes.

Hookers and Hoaxes

The carneys employed all sorts of tricks to avoid paying money to the local heroes: They paid an operative to hide behind a curtain at the back of the ring, ready with a baseball bat to take out the challenger when he was maneuvered into the curtain; or they employed *hookers* or *hooks*, wrestlers who, using crippling holds, put an end to the challenge before the local could *sting* the carnival. If the local was good enough to stay with the carney wrestler, the hooker would maneuver him into a backdrop, where he would be whacked on the head with a two-by-four by a confederate, ending his daredevilry and preserving the carnival's money.

Barnstorming Brouhahas

At approximately the same time that carnivals traveled the highways and byways of nineteenth-century America, wrestling barnstormers were traveling the back roads, working by hook and crook to shake money out of the rubes. They promoted money matches for themselves against the local strongmen wherever and whenever they could find them, making side bets with the townsfolk on the outcome. There was a lot of connivance, sometimes with the willing assistance of the local hero, to make sure that the underdog always won—and, if done convincingly, the two could stage a rematch and sting the marks all over again. The barnstormers' bottom line was money, not victories.

Homesteading: Wrestling Comes Home to Roost

From the carnivals and the barnstormers, it was but a short hop, skip, and pin to the next stage in wrestling's development: matches held in small halls and saloons, much like the old German beer garden experience. Advance men hung up posters announcing the coming of the matches and stayed in town to *homestead*—that is, to promote wrestling. With both the traveling carnivals and the barnstormers spreading the popularity of wrestling and carrying it to the masses—particularly the European immigrants, who had long been interested in the sport in all its forms—wrestling was on the threshold of becoming Americanized.

Bert's Corner

In the old days, there were three classes of wrestlers: The hooker was the most proficient, an able wrestler with wrestling knowledge, ability and strength, and a bag of old carnival hooks in his repertoire; the shooter was a scientific and competitive wrestler; and the journeyman, the largest group, was a performer who could wrestle just a little.

Captain Lou's Corner

Besides George Washington, Abraham Lincoln, and Teddy Roosevelt, other presidents who wrestled included Zachary Taylor, William Howard Taft, and Calvin Coolidge.

Presidential Power

Three of the four faces on Mount Rushmore were wrestlers: George Washington was the champion of the colony of Virginia, and Teddy Roosevelt wrestled at Harvard. However, the most famous of all was Abraham Lincoln, a giant of a man who, at 6 feet, 4 inches, was taller by far than most of the men of his day and age. In fact, stories and storytellers have it that Lincoln was engaged in a wrestling match when couriers came to tell him in 1860 of his nomination for the presidency by the Republican convention.

Wrestle Mania

By the 1880s, Greco-Roman wrestling was all the rage. It was a style developed in Europe in the 1860s and in the United States a decade or so later. But, in truth, the Greco-Roman style of this period had little similarity to the classic style of the early Greeks and Romans. To score a fall in Greco-Roman wrestling, a wrestler had to throw his opponent so that his two shoulders touched the mat simultaneously. Neither tripping nor holds below the waist was allowed. This form of wrestling, called "long-hair" wrestling by some of the older wrestlers such as Lou Thesz, persists today in a modified form as an Olympic sport.

Wrestling's early days were marked by interminable bouts, including one in 1881 between William Muldoon, who claimed to be "The Champion," and Clarence Whistler, "The Wonder of the West," at New York's Terrace Garden Theater.

For nearly seven hours, the two huffed and puffed as first one and then the other got down on the carpet and attempted to turn the other over on his back or locked hands behind heads in a Greco-Roman match marked by constant cries from the audience of "I want my dollar back!" and "Get up and do something!"

Finally, at about four o'clock in the morning, with most of the spectators at the theater bar in the outer lobby, the proprietor ordered the lights turned off to save money, and the crowd, which had foregathered at nine the previous night, trudged out of the theater, "swearing and growling" as no winner was proclaimed, according to *The New York Times*.

Professional Wrestling's Roots

Wrestling's roots were so solidly embedded in the European culture that most of the first wave of great American wrestlers was made up of first-generation Americans of European descent, most from small-town America: Martin "Farmer" Burns, William Muldoon, Ernest Roeber, and Evan "Strangler" Lewis. They combined Greco-Roman with catch-as-catch-can wrestling, the latter initially popularized by Frank Gotch and Tom Jenkins at the turn of the century. That style allowed wrestlers to grasp any part of their opponent's body, and falls were scored whenever both shoulders of a wrestler touched the floor at the same time.

Captain Lou's Corner

The earliest recorded championship match in the new world was held in 1871: A match for "the championship of the United States and Canada and $2,000" was staged in Titusville, Pennsylvania. Major J.H. Mc-Laughlin threw one Nathan Dorrance. McLaughlin proclaimed himself champion and issued challenges to other wrestlers to wrestle him for the title.

The immigrant experience continued with the second wave of American wrestlers, most coming from mid-America, with wrestlers such as Frank Gotch, Tom Jenkins, and Dan McLeod joined by "The Russian Lion" George Hackenschmidt, who had won international tournaments in Europe and came to the United States to defend his title. Gotch and Hackenschmidt put on two of the most celebrated bouts in wrestling history—and two of the most controversial.

Gotch Gets the Lion

The first bout, for the supremacy of the wrestling world, was held at Chicago's Dexter Park Pavilion in 1908. It was generally believed that Hackenschmidt's bear hug and inside trip would be more than enough to make Gotch submit. However, "Hack" was unable to get Gotch in his grasp all evening—and later complained that Gotch had slathered himself in oil to make him all but impossible to grab. His inability to grab Gotch, coupled with Gotch's continual roughhousing and fouling, finally drove Hackenschmidt to quit after two hours and three minutes. The referee had no alternative but to disqualify Hackenschmidt and to award the decision and the title to Gotch.

For the next three years, Hackenschmidt campaigned for a rematch, finally getting one in 1911 at Chicago's new Comiskey Park in what was billed as "The Match of the Century." Once again, foul tactics reared their ugly head—this time, however, it wasn't during the match itself, but beforehand.

It seems that Gotch and his entourage had planted a hooker, Ad Santell, in Hackenschmidt's training camp. Three weeks before the match, Santell purposely injured Hackenschmidt's knee but made the injury look like an accident. The injury was so severe that Hack walked with a limp for the rest of his life.

With but one leg, Hackenschmidt tried to call off the bout. But the promoters, who had already spent the advance ticket money, pleaded with him to keep his injury a secret and go ahead with the bout. "The Russian Lion" agreed, but only if Gotch agreed to let him win one of the three falls and carry him to a face-saving end. Gotch double-crossed him and pinned the helpless Hackenschmidt in two straight falls.

Wrestle Mania

In what may have been the biggest upset in wrestling history, "The Peerless" Frank Gotch, thought to be unbeatable, was defeated by Fred Beell when he won the third of three falls after throwing Gotch out of the ring—Gotch struck his head on the floor. Beell pinned him to take the American Heavyweight Championship on December 1, 1906, in New Orleans.

The End of the First Golden Age

The press got wind of Gotch's duplicity and not only turned its back on the match, but also on the sport itself. That, and Gotch's retirement two years later to give wrestling exhibitions with the Sells-Floto Circus, spelled the end of wrestling's first golden era.

Sometime in the mid-1920s, a promoter named Toots Mondt, taking his cue from vaudeville, decided that enough was enough—sometimes too much—and installed a time limit in all matches. He also introduced the flying drop-kick, to make wrestling more exciting for the fans. But the sport's resurgence in popularity can be tied, like that of any form of entertainment, to its superstars. By the 1920s, wrestling had one: Ed "Strangler" Lewis.

The Strangler

Paul Gallico, the famed sportswriter, labeled the 1920s "The Golden Age of Sports" and placed five superheroes in the decade's pantheon of greats: Babe Ruth of baseball, Red Grange of football, Jack Dempsey of boxing, Bill Tilden of tennis, and Bobby Jones of golf. Had he but added a sixth, it would have been Ed "Strangler" Lewis of wrestling. In fact, Lewis even looked like Ruth—fat and balding, with a big chest and small, toothpick-thin legs. But nobody, was ever better than Lewis in the long history of professional wrestling.

Strangler Lewis puts a headlock on Hans Kampher.

(Source: Norman Kietzer)

Born Robert Fredrich, Ed "Strangler" Lewis derived his ring name from an earlier version, Evan "Strangler" Lewis, as well as his signature hold, the strangulation submission. After winning bout after bout with a monotonous regularity—usually ending the match with his signature strangulation hold from which no opponent could escape—and creating an undercurrent of displeasure among the fans, Lewis and his brain trust—manager Billy Sandow and promoter Toots Mondt, who, along with Lewis, were known as "The Gold Trio"—decided that it was necessary to "do business" (agree to lose once in a while) to keep wrestling fans interested. But even though he was to "lose" the title four times—in a career of more than 6,200 matches in his long career he was to "lose" only 33 times—The Strangler would win it back an equal number of times.

One of The Strangler's greatest matches took place in Madison Square Garden in 1933, when an aging Lewis defended his title against Ray Steele. On this night of nights, the crowds were lined up around the block to see Lewis finally get his from the challenger, Steele. The bout began with the two circling each other—Lewis, by now fat, 50, and balding; Steele, the body beautiful and weighing a trim 220. But almost from the start, it was no contest. Steele could do nothing with The Strangler. The fans, yawning at the lack of action in this scientific bout, began to stamp their feet. Realizing that he was hopelessly outclassed, Steele finally resorted to punching Lewis, and the referee disqualified him 20 minutes into the match.

Wrestling Becomes Rasslin'

By the time Lewis's career had wound down, the feverish '20s had been replaced by the troubled '30s. And the American Dream had become a nightmare as bread lines took the place of the boom-and-bust atmosphere of the previous decade.

Depression-Era Depression

Like all other forms of entertainment, wrestling struggled for its very existence during the '30s—people without enough money to fill their bellies with food had very little extra to spend on frills and extravagances such as entertainment. Still the sport labored on, with wrestlers such as Dick Shikat, Jim Londos, and Gus Sonnenberg passing the title around like a parcel nobody wanted. But then again, wrestling was a sport nobody wanted either—especially in its interminable, never-ending matches that produced thousand-yard stares in its fans.

Wrestle Mania

Despite the Depression, Jim Londos became a big draw, pulling in gates of $70,000 in Yankee Stadium versus Ray Steele in 1931; $60,000 in Fenway Park versus Ed Don George in 1934; and $86,000 versus "Strangler" Lewis in Wrigley Field in 1934—the largest gate since Gotch and Hackenschmidt in 1911.

Wrestling Goes to College

And so promoters such as Toots Mondt tried several innovations to lure the fans, including putting a time limit on the matches of 10 to 15 minutes in an effort to liven up the sport, much as baseball introduced the "lively ball" in 1930 to increase that sport's offense. Promoters also started scheduling novelty bouts—women's wrestling, tag teams, and even mud wrestling. Other innovations of the era included the introduction of "character" wrestlers and good-guy/bad-guy opposition.

While this was going on, the wrestling promoters divvied up the United States into what came to be called "territories." These early wrestling promoters had no more legal right to control a territory than a claim jumper, but they agreed among themselves to respect their territorial boundaries. Their ranks were filled with boxing promoters such as Jack Curley and Jesse McMahon, ex-wrestlers such as Toots Mondt and Ed "Strangler" Lewis, and promoters such as Jack Pfefer, who came straight into wrestling with no previous career stops along the way.

Most of the promoters formed an organization in 1948 called the National Wrestling Alliance (NWA), which covered the entire West Coast from Seattle to San Diego and included Texas, Okla-homa, Kansas, Missouri, and almost the entire South, plus Mexico, Australia, and parts of Japan and Canada. But the NWA was an organization in name only. It was really a loosely knit confederation of promoters, most of whom were, in the words of Lou Thesz, "hypocrites and lowlifes who'd stage a dogfight if they thought it would draw money."

In his book *Hooker: An Authentic Wrestler's Adventures Inside the Bizarre World of Pro Wrestling* (at www.twe-online.com, go to the Official Lou Thesz Web page), Thesz recounts one NWA annual meeting in which the membership had listened to a report from "some self-important judge from Texas who'd been brought in to mediate an internal dispute between two Texas promoters." As Thesz reports:

> The judge had obviously resolved the matter in a way to fatten his own pockets and, at the end of his report, one promoter stood up and said, 'Well, this guy looks like the type who'd steal a hot stove and come back

In Your Face

Along with Mondt's innovations, several other ways to draw in the crowds were devised during the depressed 1930s: tag-team matches, women's wrestling, novelty acts, gimmicks, and, not unimportantly, the introduction of "character" rasslers—the opposition of good guys versus bad guys. All these were enough to allow wrestling to survive, but prosperity would have to wait a while.

Captain Lou's Corner

Bronko Nagurski had not only led the Chicago Bears to four NFL championships, but he had been all-pro for four seasons. However, finding that George Halas, the owner of the Bears, "threw nickels around like manhole covers" and that his efforts weren't being adequately rewarded, Nagurski opted instead for a wrestling career and became one of the biggest attractions of the 1930s.

the next day for the lid, so I suppose he'll fit right in with us.' A lot of people laughed at the remark, but some members got indignant, as always happens when someone hits too close to the truth.

Captain Lou Remembers

Herman Hickman, one of the greatest linesmen in the history of college football, went to the same school I did: the University of Tennessee. He once told me how he got into professional wrestling: "In 1932, money was a scarce item, and there weren't many jobs floating around even if you did weigh 230 pounds, had made the All-American football team, and could recite a conglomerate of verse. So, when Rudy Dusek, the oldest and the mastermind of the wrestling Dusek Brothers, undertook to sell me on the idea of becoming a professional wrestler, he did not find it difficult. He mentioned something about the possibility of making $1,000 a week and becoming champion of the world. He could have got me for less than half of that, and he did."

To recruit performers who would draw customers, wrestling promoters began to seek out former collegiate football stars in an attempt to capitalize on their names and popularity. The first of this new breed was Wayne "Big" Munn, a lineman from the University of Nebraska back in 1920. By the 1930s, Gus Sonnenberg of Dartmouth and the University of Detroit, and Bronko Nagurski of the University of Minnesota and the Chicago Bears left the gridiron for the wrestling arena. But the addition of Nagurski, Hickman, and the rest of the collegiate greats was not enough to turn wrestling's fortunes around. The Great Depression followed by World War II kept Americans busy with more important matters. Wrestling's popularity did not surge again until the late 1940s, thanks to a newfangled household appliance called television.

Gorgeous George

Television and professional wrestling were made for each other. Professional wrestling offered an almost made-for-television format, tailored to the dimensions of the TV tube. And, in a symbiotic relationship, television offered wrestling an entirely new group of fans and fans-to-be. Soon wrestling was being offered up from arena and studio alike almost every day of the week—and served on Fridays more times than fish. But the wrestling boom of the late 1940s and early 1950s wouldn't have been possible had it not been for one man: Gorgeous George.

With Lana Turner-type bleach-blond hair and a bag full of gimmicks—including marching into the arena to the strains of "Pomp and Circumstance"—Gorgeous George always put on a show: having his formally attired valet spritz the ring with an atomizer filled with perfumey disinfectant called "George No. 4"; wearing his fur-trimmed robe; and giving away gold "Georgie Hair Pins" to the crowd. Gorgeous George became wrestling's biggest-ever draw. The man called "The Human Orchid" became wrestling's poster boy and set the stage for wrestling's all-new direction: show biz.

From that point on, wrestling became "rasslin'" as hordes of masked men, high-stepping Germans, monocled lords, Indian chiefs, Arab chieftains, and all other manner of gimmicked-up "rasslers" followed in Gorgeous George's wake. The second golden age of wrestling had begun.

Soon, however, television, which had used wrestling as mere filler, found other programming. Wrestling continued for the loyal few until the 1980s, when promoter Vince McMahon found a way to use the media to his own advantage, and pro wrestling roared into its third golden age—one that it is still enjoying.

Bert's Corner

Originally seen at the L.A. Olympic Auditorium, Gorgeous George's fame spread throughout the country as his bouts were kinescoped and shown in more than 50 TV markets. His persona became the butt of jokes by Bob Hope, Jack Benny, Red Skelton, and others. He even made an appearance on *Queen for a Day.*

Body Slam

Gorgeous George handled himself inside the ring better than outside. Though known to light his cigars with $50 bills in his heyday, George died broke in 1963 at age 48.

The *WrestleMania* Era

The one moment that defined the WWF's success, cementing its position at the top of the wrestling ladder, was *WrestleMania*. In truth, Vince Jr. had actually been thinking about it for a long time as a new way to put the WWF on the map. The idea worked so well that, more than 16 years later, *WrestleMania* remains by far the most popular annual wrestling event. We'll take an in-depth look at *WrestleMania*—including yours truly's involvement in the very first one, in Part 4, "History of *WrestleMania.*"

Today's Wrestlers: Crossover Appeal

Today's wrestlers are so popular that other forms of entertainment are competing to use wrestlers. Wrestlers make CDs and perform on television shows and in the movies far more than ever.

Wrestlers' crossover appeal is not limited to show business. Ever since Jesse "The Body" Ventura, a former WWF star, transformed himself into Jesse "The Mind" Ventura and successfully ran for Governor of Minnesota, the sky has become the limit.

Show Business

The Rock created quite a stir when he hosted NBC's *Saturday Night Live,* and that episode garnered the show's highest ratings of the season. The Rock also has a starring role in *The Mummy II*. Stone Cold Steve Austin is a regular on *Nash Bridges*. Chyna now has a recurring role on the sitcom *Third Rock from the Sun*. Mick Foley has appeared on the show *Now and Again* and does commercials for Chef Boy-R-Dee. Goldberg is in *Universal Soldier II*. Sting was in a TV movie opposite the beautiful Daisy Fuentes. Obviously, it is only a matter of time before a wrestling superstar wins an Oscar; although I have a hard time imaging Stone Cold saying, "You like me! You really like me!"

Politics

Jesse Ventura was born as James George Janos on July 15, 1951, in Minneapolis, Minnesota. Of Slovak/German heritage, he grew to be 6-foot-4, 250 pounds. After some time at a local community college, he enlisted in the Navy and served in Vietnam as a SEAL. From there he went into wrestling. He enjoyed moderate success as a wrestler, working for the WWF as Jesse "The Body" Ventura, but he was forced to retire because of a heart problem. He was moved to the broadcast table, where he spent years as the WWF's quick-witted color commentator and foil for the federation's then-announcer Vince McMahon Jr. It was here, behind the microphone, that Ventura gained superstar status. He even starred in a couple of action films during the early 1990s. After a falling out with the WWF, Ventura spent some time as an announcer for WCW before making the move to politics. He successfully ran for mayor of Brooklyn Park, Minnesota.

Even this local success was considered extraordinary. Gone were the days when wrestlers were tainted goods when they tried to move into more "respectable" fields. On the contrary, some voters were pulling the lever for Jesse because he had been a wrestler. Those who didn't approve of his wrestling career or who didn't care were still impressed by his clear thinking and clear speaking when it came to the political issues that they cared about most. When Ventura announced that he was going to run for governor in 1998, even his staunchest supporters had trouble taking him seriously. And, as late as the eve of the election, Ventura was predicted to finish a distant third in a three-man race. When they counted the votes, the whole world was shocked and amazed—a wrestler had won!

Ladies and gentleman, the Governor of Minnesota, Jesse "The Body" Ven-tur-a!

Now that Ventura has become a political force on the national level, other wrestlers are throwing their hats into the political ring, although it is doubtful that they'll achieve Ventura's success. Jerry "The King" Lawler, the current color commentator for the WWF, unsuccessfully ran for mayor of Memphis. Former WWF world champ Bob Backlund is running for Congress in Connecticut but is not predicted to do well—even if he put every voter into his patented crossface chicken wing! So, it remains to be seen if Ventura's political success was a fluke or merely the beginning of the great wrestling/politics connection.

The Least You Need to Know

➤ One of the oldest sports in the world, wrestling became Americanized through carnivals and barnstormers after the Civil War.

➤ Wrestling's high point as a sport came with the two Frank Gotch/George Hackenschmidt matches.

➤ Ed "Strangler" Lewis became wrestling's first superstar and arguably is still the greatest wrestler in history.

➤ Gorgeous George was wrestling's first showman and changed wrestling forever.

➤ Wrestling is so popular today that the performers are using it as a springboard into other forms of show business and politics.

Chapter 3

The Glue That Holds It All Together: Organizations and Federations

In This Chapter

- The organizations that make wrestling work
- The history of promotion
- Tele-savvy promoters: *WrestleMania,* cable, and pay-per-view
- Hardcore style: ECW

Although the wrestlers are the stars of the show—the players, if you will—the promotions that stage the matches are the basis of wrestling, its very fabric. The organizations and federations are the ones responsible for promoting wrestling, publicizing it, and plotting its course.

Today there are two major organizations on the professional wrestling landscape—the World Wrestling Federation (WWF) and World Championship Wrestling (WCW)—while several smaller ones survive and thrive. This chapter gives you an overview of modern promoters and their world—how they came into being and how they grew.

McWrestling: The McMahons and the WWF

Even though wrestling's cast of characters always seems to be changing, there has been one constant throughout the years: the McMahon family. The patriarch of the McMahon clan was Jess McMahon, a boxing promoter who turned to wrestling. A debonair, handsome gentleman of indeterminate age, Jess had co-promoted the heavyweight championship boxing match between Jess Willard and Jack Johnson in 1915 and then joined Tex Rickard in bringing big-time boxing to Madison Square Garden. From there it was an easy transition into promoting wrestling bouts, first in the Garden and then throughout the East Coast.

Into the Second Generation

His son, Vince McMahon Sr. (actually Vincent J.) ran something called Capitol Wrestling out of Washington, D.C.—a territory that covered the Eastern seaboard from Virginia all the way up to Maine and as far west as the Alleghenies, about the same region covered by America's first coaxial (television) cable. The near approximation of McMahon's territory and the area covered by the coaxial cable gave McMahon a huge advantage in selling his local wrestling bouts to the fledgling TV medium, which was desperately searching for programming to fill its screens.

Vince Sr. teamed up with the old promoter, Toots Mondt, who controlled the talent just as Vince controlled the TV access. Together they became the most successful wrestling promoters of the late 1940s and early 1950s. Capitol Wrestling's territory was so large and its operation was so successful and lucrative that the two men didn't need the National Wrestling Alliance. And so they went on their merry way, as strong a single entity as the NWA was as a coalition.

Captain Lou's Corner

I first became associated with Vince Sr. in 1952, when I started wrestling. I would drop in at the Franklin Park Hotel in Washington to visit all the time—and to receive my bookings. Well, one time during a drop-in visit, I met this little kid who was then about 11 years old. The kid kicked me in the leg. That handful would one day grow up to be Vince Jr.—and he remains a handful to this day.

Capitol Wrestling's Rise to the Top

One of Capitol's first great attractions was Antonino Rocca, the Argentine acrobat whom they imported in the late 1940s. Then they brought in Gorgeous George from the West Coast, and he caused an instant sensation—he was, after all, a made-for-television celebrity. McMahon and Mondt carried on a "Cold War" with the NWA throughout the 1950s, but in 1961 the war heated up over a new wrestler on the scene, "Nature Boy" Buddy Rogers.

Rogers, the biggest draw since Rocca and Gorgeous George, had won the NWA World Heavyweight Championship belt from Pat O'Connor at Chicago's Comiskey Park in 1961. But soon thereafter, the NWA found that its champion had gone over to Toots Mondt, who had taken over Rogers's bookings and was using him exclusively in the McMahon/Mondt eastern circuit. Only on rare occasions would a magnanimous Mondt consent for Rogers to wrestle for NWA promoters, allowing barely a handful of dates each month.

Former champion "Nature Boy" Buddy Rogers with Jimmy Snuka.

(Source: Norman Kietzer)

Things got so bad that Sam Muchnick, then head of the NWA, was heard to mumble aloud to anyone who would listen, "Toots controls Rogers now, and he's seeing to it we can't even use our own champion." Muchnick persuaded the venerable Lou Thesz, who had first held the world championship back in 1937 and five times thereafter, to take on Rogers and bring the NWA belt back home. But even though Thesz was to beat Rogers in one fall in January 1963, the East Coast circuit continued to recognize Rogers as "champion."

Four months later, in May 1963, McMahon and Mondt formed the World Wide Wrestling Federation (WWWF). And although it was not precisely "worldwide"—it covered only the Eastern seaboard—it was an impressive territory with an impressive-sounding name.

Shortly thereafter, the McMahon-Mondt tandem came to an end. Mondt, who had been on the scene since God knows when—and even God wasn't sure of the when—decided to pack it in and sold his interest in the WWF back to Vince McMahon Sr., who then resold that interest to Gorilla Monsoon, Phil Zacko, and Arnold Skaaland, keeping a majority interest in the new entity for himself.

A New McMahon Twist

In 1983, Vince sold his interest in the WWF to his son, Vince Jr. (Of course, as Vince Jr. says, "I'm not a junior—my father was Vincent J., and I'm Vincent K.") What followed was a nationwide wrestling blitzkrieg—a take-no-prisoners war of expansion that would radically change the world of professional wrestling.

Bert's Corner

When the organization known today as the World Wrestling Federation was first formed, it was known as the World Wide Wrestling Federation, the WWWF—quite a mouthful. A few years later, one of the W's was dropped, and it became the WWF.

Vince Jr. was able to voyage, Columbus-like, into the territories of other promoters because of the dawning of cable TV and the production values made possible by another innovation, videotape. His theory was that what worked in te Northeast could be exported and made to work nationally—and internationally. So, he declared war on the other promoters and invaded or purchased their territories.

While he was carrying out this scorched-earth policy, Vince Jr. was vulnerable: "We did it all with mirrors, it was all cash flow. Had those promoters known that I didn't have any money, they could have killed us."

But the point is, they *didn't* know. And even if they had, it's doubtful that the disorganized organization known as the NWA could have held Vince Jr. off. Rather than banding together to repel his invasion, they bickered among themselves and kept their heads firmly planted in the sand while Vince Jr. planted his WWF flag across the country, changing the face of professional wrestling forever.

Wrestle Mania

"My dad would never have sold me his end of that company, nor for that matter would the other stockholders have followed if they knew what I was going to do," Vince McMahon Jr. said. "He just thought I was going to continue to operate in the Northeast and respect the other promoters and their territories .... He said, 'Oh, my God, now you've just angered half the promoters in the business.'" But Vince Jr. had his own plans, so after he bought out his dad's partners, he began syndicating his television programming into Los Angeles, then St. Louis, and then throughout the country.

WCW: Wrestling Takes a Turn for the Better (Ratings)

WrestleMania made the WWF into the largest wrestling promotion of all time, not just with the publicity—which McMahon played for all it was worth—but because its coverage established the WWF as truly worldwide.

Now McMahon was able to continue his on-slaught against the other promoters, using television as his primary weapon. This time around, instead of TV using wrestling, as it had in the 1950s, McMahon used TV. The new cable channels were scrambling for programming that McMahon was able to provide, even if he had to buy up the air time to shut out the competition.

As more promoters folded up their tents and faded into the sunset, the WWF filled the void with its shows, which were now telecast on every newly minted cable channel. The notable exception was ESPN, which carried wrestling from Jim Crockett's NWA circuit.

Crockett was the only promoter left to carry the NWA banner against the WWF—all the others were on their last legs or had rolled over under McMahon's steamroller. Crockett's organization, known as Georgia Championship Wrestling, became, by default, the NWA.

Turner Tries to Take Charge

It looked like McMahon held all the cards and could dictate terms to television networks, most of which were so eager to keep their wrestling programming that they jumped at his every whim—all, that is, except for Ted Turner of the Turner Broadcasting System (TBS).

Rumor has it that Turner was upset with Vince Jr.'s demands for time slots or that he was upset with McMahon for buying some of Crockett's talent. Whatever the case, Turner decided to declare war on McMahon and bought Crockett's promotion. According to McMahon, Turner called to gloat about his new acquisition, announcing that he was now in the "rasslin' business." "Good," said McMahon, *"we're* in the entertainment business." And he hung up.

Captain Lou's Corner

Vince McMahon Jr.'s war on his competitors was decimating. Of the 20 regional promoters operating throughout the country in 1984, fewer than 5 remained by 1989.

Bert's Corner

Wrestlers switch from one organization to another almost overnight. I'll never forget the time that the late Ravishing Rick Rude appeared on both Monday night shows on the same night. He was on *RAW* with a beard, which was videotaped, and on *Nitro* live and clean-shaven. If you're tracking a wrestler and can't find him, make a quick check on the Internet to see if he has changed organizations.

Body Slam

Crockett's stars in the old Georgia Championship Wrestling were every bit as good as those in the WWF—Dusty Rhodes, Ric Flair, and others of equal stature—but the trouble was that nobody outside Charlotte knew them. The WWF's monopolization of cable kept them off the tube. Crockett soldiered on anyway, losing money hand-over-handstand.

Although Turner had bought Crockett's business, he hadn't bought the NWA name—at least, according to what remained of the loose alliance of regional promoters from the territory. The NWA sued Turner for his use of the NWA initials. That made no difference to Turner—he just changed the initials to WCW, as in World Championship Wrestling. After all, it was already the name of his number one TV show on Saturday nights.

It now turned into all-out war between the two moguls. And although Turner lost money for the first eight years, he never blinked. Having accomplished his primary purpose—preventing McMahon and the WWF from monopolizing cable TV wrestling—Turner was also creating his own programming for his coast-to-coast superstation, TBS.

With the ascendancy of Turner's WCW by the early 1990s, McMahon was suddenly in a dogfight, with his position as top dog threatened. By the mid 1990s, much of McMahon's top talent had defected. Hulk Hogan, Randy Savage, Kevin Nash, and Scott Hall all switched from the WWF to WCW.

With Turner buying up the top talent, McMahon cast *himself* as his promotion's lead bad guy and started a feud with new star Stone Cold Steve Austin. (Previously, McMahon had worked as the announcer on his own TV shows, and it was never acknowledged on the air that he was also the owner of the company. Now all of that would change.)

During the next few years, Vince's son, Shane, and daughter, Stephanie, became part of the act. Even Vince's wife and business partner, Linda, performed in front of the camera. This was talent that Turner simply couldn't buy. The McMahons, as they portrayed themselves on the air, were no Ozzie and Harriet Nelson. Keeping in tune with the soap opera feel of wrestling's plot lines, the onscreen McMahons were as dysfunctional as they come. This family affair has struck a responsive chord among the fans and—along with the great young wrestlers brought into the fold—shot the WWF, and its Monday night *RAW is WAR* show, back to the top.

Today the war between the two pits Turner's money—now merged with the Time-Warner empire—against Vince's ingenuity. And although Turner can always outspend Vince, Vince can always fight back with new ideas, newfangled plot lines, and outrageous gimmicks. In the past, McMahon has cut deals right and left to keep Turner out of the top arenas. Turner's response was to start his own pay-per-view shows, cluttering the already crowded PPV schedule and diluting the impact of *WrestleMania*.

Wrestle Mania

The WWF currently includes these wrestlers: Albert, Kurt Angle, Steve Austin, Paul Bearer (manager), Chris Benoit, Big Boss Man, Big Show, Steve Blackman, Blue Meanie, Bradshaw, Gerald Brisco, British Bulldog, Brooklyn Brawler, D'Lo Brown, Bull Buchanan, Christian, Chyna, Buh Buh Ray Dudley, D-Von Dudley, Edge, Faarooq, Funaki, Gangrel, Godfather, Eddie Guerrero, Billy Gunn, Matt Hardy, Jeff Hardy, Headbanger Mosh, Headbanger Thrasher, Hunter Hearst Helmsley, Mark Henry, Crash Holly, Hardcore Holly, Scotty 2 Hotty, Ivory, Jacqueline, Chris Jericho, Kane, The Kat, Jerry Lawler, Lita, Dean Malenko, Shane McMahon, Stephanie McMahon, Vince McMahon, Mean Street Posse, Taka Michinoku, Mideon, Fabulous Moolah, Pat Patterson, Rikishi Phatu, Stevie Richards, Essa Rios, Road Dogg, Rock, Jim Ross (announcer), Terri Runnels, Perry Saturn, Grandmaster Sexay, Ken Shamrock, Al Snow, Trish Stratus, Tazz, Test, Tori, Undertaker, Val Venis, Viscera, X-Pac, and Mae Young.

Wrestle Mania

WCW wrestlers currently include: Tank Abbott, Arn Anderson, Brad Armstrong, The Artist, Asya, Buff Bagwell, Bam Bam Bigelow, Eric Bischoff, Booker T, Crowbar, Shane Douglas, Hacksaw Jim Duggan, David Flair, Ric Flair, Demon, Disco Inferno, Elizabeth, Los Fabulosos, Fit Finlay, Jerry Flynn, Terry Funk, Goldberg, Juventud Guerrera, Chavo Guerrero Jr., Miss Hancock, Ron Harris, Don Harris, Bret Hart, Jimmy Hart, Kaz Hayashi, Bobby Heenan, Shane Helms, Curt Hennig, Hulk Hogan, Idol, Jeff Jarrett, Johnny The Bull, Jung Dragons, Chris Kanyon, Evan Karagias, Billy Kidman, Kimberly, Brian Knobs, Konnan, Kronic, Lane, Lash LeRoux, Lex Luger, Madusa, Maestro, Meng, Ernest "Cat" Miller, Mona, Shannon Moore, Hugh Morrus, Rey Mysterio Jr., Kevin Nash, Gene Okerlund, Diamond Dallas Page, Paisley, La Parka, Roddy Piper, Psychosis, Dustin Rhodes, Kid Romeo, Mike Rotunda, Vince Russo, Tony Schiavone, Norman Smiley, Rick Steiner, Scott Steiner, Stevie Ray, Sting, Big T, Mike Tenay, Daffney Unger, Vampiro, Sid Vicious, Big Vito, The Wall, Torrie Wilson, and Larry Zbyszko.

The two soon began a game of "anything you can do, I can do better." Take the WWF's *RAW is WAR* program, for instance. It had always been a huge success— a showcase of sorts for the WWF and a major promotional vehicle for its PPV events. Turner countered by moving his own show to Monday nights, calling it *Monday Nitro.* The resulting ratings war between the two promotions, more than anything, popularized wrestling to today's frenzied heights. The direct competition increased the quality of both shows. Plot lines, which used to take months to resolve themselves, now came and went in two weeks. Matches between superstars, formerly reserved for pay-per-view events, now occurred every week. Before the ratings war, both wrestling programs could get away with what were called "squash matches," which pitted a name star against a "jobber," a gimmickless fellow who always lost. Now they could no longer get away with this, and every match featured two superstars squaring off. That's hood news for the fans, but bad news for the jobbers who no longer get to work on TV.

Eastern Championship Wrestling (ECW)

You'd think that with the WWF and the WCW so dominant, there'd be no room for any other organizations. But you'd think wrong. During the 1990s, as the two major organizations changed their story lines from a focus on blood and simulated injuries to more convoluted plots and juvenile raunchiness, more busty valets and managers, and more human action-figure acrobatics, they left a void. Hardcore wrestling—the way it used to be, with lots of blood, gore, weapons, and over-the-top violence—was missing. And missed. The organization that best filled the void left by the WWF and WCW was Eastern Championship Wrestling (ECW). The ECW presented alternatives to the fare offered by the WWF and WCW: harder story lines, lots of blood, and plenty of weapons and violence.

ECW began its life in a bingo hall in South Philly in the early 1990s, the creation of Tod Gordon and the wrestler Eddie Gilbert. When Gilbert left, he was succeeded by wrestling visionary Paul Heyman. In an earlier WCW life, Heyman had been known as Paul E. Dangerously. Heyman changed the "E" in the ECW from "Eastern" to "Extreme," bought infomercials on major TV stations in major markets in the wee hours of the morning, and brought the newly named Extreme Championship Wrestling organization to the attention of millions of fans who were hungry for old-time violence.

Characters such as The Sandman and Sabu, along with strippers working as ring valets, brought ECW a big following—big enough for ECW to graduate to prime-time TV and pay-per-view. Ironically, with its success, ECW's hardcore style was adopted by WCW and the WWF.

Wrestle Mania

ECW wrestlers currently include: Bill Alfonso, Angel, Chris Chetti, Steve Corino, Justin Credible, Cyrus the Virus, Dangerous Alliance, Lou E. Dangerously, DeVito, Simon Diamond, Danny Doring, Tommy Dreamer, Spike Dudley, Elektra Francine, Joel Gertner, Sal E. Graziano, Vic Grimes, Jason, Jazz, Little Guido, Kid Kash, Jerry Lynn, Balls Mahoney, Dawn Marie, New Jack, Nova, Raven, Rhino, Dusty Rhodes, Roadkill, Sandman, Sinister Minister, Lance Storm, Joey Styles, Super Crazy, Yoshihiro Tajiri, Masato Tanaka, Rob Van Dam, Jack Victory, and Mikey Whipwreck.

ECW has become a semimajor organization, although not quite in the same league as the WWF and WCW. It has two weekly TV shows, which appear on the MSG and the Nashville networks, and has proven that there is still plenty of room for others.

The Least You Need to Know

➤ Wrestling promoters are lineal descendants of old-time carney promoters.

➤ The NWA was wrestling's first major organization.

➤ The McMahons—Jess, Vince Sr., and Vince Jr.—are wrestling's first family of promoters.

➤ Vince Jr.'s ground-breaking promotion, *WrestleMania*, and his intelligent use of cable TV have combined to make the WWF the premier wrestling organization in the world.

➤ Ted Turner used his superstation, TBS, and WCW to challenge the WWF in an all-out, head-to-head war for wrestling supremacy.

➤ In the United States, besides the two major wrestling organizations there are dozens of other affiliations on the wrestling landscape today, such as ECW.

Chapter 4

Smoke and Mirrors

In This Chapter

➤ Creating reality in the wrestling ring

➤ Tricks of the trade

➤ Staging the sound effects

➤ Real pain

So how do wrestlers perform their magic, such as flying off the top rope and landing on an opponent's chest or throat without smashing him into smaller, tidier pieces? Or what about hitting an opponent with an iron folding chair without rendering the hit-tee senseless? Or smiting the opponent with a jarring punch that sounds like it should have felled six or seven bystanders? In this chapter, you find out.

Reality Is in the Eye of the Beholder

As you know, what you see in wrestling is not always what you get. It *looks* real. But there's a secret, one I'll let you in on. After all, a real hammerlock could break a guy's arm; a real step-over toehold could destroy his ankle. As we've learned, professional wrestling was born out of the carnival, where a scam a day kept the creditors away.

When the carneys teamed up with hustlers and barnstormers, it's no wonder that wrestling lost any resemblance to the scientific style of the old days and became a performance sport. These men traveled from town to town, touting "champions" with phony, that is *kayfabe*, biographies who offered to take on anyone in the audience—or each other—all in the name of money. And if these early promoters were in danger of losing money, they would stop at very little—even hitting a local yokel over the head with a bat—to avert any kind of payoff.

All right, pro wrestling has less than noble ancestry. Now we know we can take many of the things that happen in the ring with the proverbial grain of salt—and others with an entire barrelful.

Spikeless Punches and Other Sleights of Hand

How, you may ask, can a person take repetitive blows to the head from a huge, strong opponent and keep coming back for more? The answer can be found in some basic laws of physics and in an audience's ability to suspend disbelief. Put the two together, and you have spectacular theater in the squared circle.

The most well-known law of physics, almost the first rule in Physics 101, involves the collision of parallel flat surfaces—the rule describing "dispersing the force of impact across the plain of contact." Every time a wrestler whacks another with a folded chair, he hits something flat, like the back, with the flat part of the chair. (If the blow is to the head, it's usually to the front of the skull, where the bone is thickest.) And guys leaping off the top strand of ropes always aim at a man either standing up (so that he can be caught) or lying completely prone; so that they can collide chest to chest—flat body part to flat body part.

Flat to flat is the first rule. The clothesline is a fine example of the second rule: Attackers never put their full weight behind a blow. Rather, a wrestler will soften it by going off to the side when possible so that, rather than frescoing his opponent, he is merely lacing him gingerly.

Fighting Words

Professional wrestling's roots are so intertwined with old carnival operators—or "carneys"—that the language of wrestlers today is called **kayfabe,** a derivation of the carnival dialect in which the con men could discuss the con right in front of the mark without the mark knowing it.

Captain Lou's Corner

Whenever possible, wrestlers work together. And while nothing guarantees that one will not hurt another, wrestlers take precautions. Pain is no problem for these gifted athletes, but missing the next show—now *that's* a problem.

So while the fans may see contact, hear contact, and believe that there was contact, what contact there was actually was incidental—and the effect was illusory. Punches actually land, but they have very little impact and are rarely as forceful or as lethal as they look and sound. They are not delivered with the fist—at least not a closed fist—as much as with the forearm. The fist, after all, is bony and hard, while the forearm softens the blow for both wrestlers while, at the same time, making a loud, slapping sound. And even on those rare occasions when the closed fist is employed, the punch is "pulled"—although contact is made, there is very little power behind it.

Then there are the slaps, as opposed to the closed-fist hits. An open-handed slap makes lots of noise and stings only a little, reddening the recipient's skin. Little damage is done, but the echoing sound carries throughout the arena and adds to the illusion of reality—visually as well as audibly.

"Chops," those punches in which the arm comes down in an axelike move, work in a similar manner. Keep your eye fixed on a wrestler throwing a chop, or a chopping punch, and you may see the edge of his hand being turned at the very last second—turning it into a slap instead of a hard chop.

Bert's Corner

Oh, sure, some wrestlers in mom-and-pop circuits are so bad that you can see their moves, which might appear almost burlesque-y. It can be instructive to watch them. Then you'll know just how good "good" can be.

Only the Ring Is Square

A wrestling ring—with its ropes, turnbuckles, and aprons—offers great opportunities for moves and maneuvers. First there are the turnbuckles. Those are the four corner posts that hold the ropes. The padding on the turnbuckles is thick and is one of the softest, most flexible places in the ring. It not only cushions blows extremely well, but it also is as safe a place as a wrestler can find—outside of the dressing room, that is. However, on those rare occasions when the padding slips and the metal part of the turnbuckle shows through, it can become extremely dangerous.

Then there are the ropes themselves. There was a time when their sole purpose was to define the sphere of action, to keep wrestlers inside the ring. Now, however, they have become part and parcel of most wrestlers' repertoires, either as a platform from which to jump or as a springboard from which to propel themselves. And wrestlers with derring-do have used ropes for gravity-defying aerial gymnastics worthy of Douglas Fairbanks Sr.—who, not incidentally, attended wrestling bouts in the old days to pick up pointers for his stuntman antics in silent movies.

Jimmy "Superfly" Snuka was arguably the best at flying off the ropes. This human cannonball could manage almost three complete rotations of his balled-up body between the time he left the top rope and the time he landed atop his opponent—the guy lying flat on the canvas at the time. But how can a man jump from somewhere up in the stratosphere and land on another without crushing him into a virtual pancake? Sorta the same way porcupines make love, that's how: very carefully.

In Your Face

The recently retired Mick Foley likes to tell the story of going to Madison Square Garden in New York City to see wrestling as a teenager. "When I saw Superfly Jimmy Snuka jump off the top of the steel cage, I knew what I wanted to be when I grew up," says Foley.

Bert's Corner

The modern wrestling ring, with its springs, makes the moves and falls look more acrobatic and even more devastating. Seeing a wrestler bounce off the canvas almost doubles the effect of the blow—and the ring is designed to make a big thumping noise every time the mat is struck.

One way to do it is the near-miss. This is a jump executed to look like a direct hit when, in fact, the flying wrestler has landed close to—but *not on*—his opponent. Another is to make the landings flesh-to-flesh—knees, elbows, and other hard, bony parts are kept out of the way and don't make the impact. But a flying maneuver can be injurious to your health if you do not execute it correctly. If you get it wrong, there's a strong chance that someone will be hurt, and a potentially great stunt will have gone awry.

Then there's the mat itself. Mats in the old days were toted around from place to place, from smoky beer halls to church basements. Dirty and bacteria-laden, in those pre-penicillin days they were dangerous to the wrestlers, especially to their eyes. After years of having his face rubbed into the canvas, Strangler Lewis went partially blind. Things are better today, but staph infections still occur. Fortunately, now they are treatable. In the old days, promoters used the same ring for boxing and wrestling, and the ring floor was rock hard. Today, wrestling rings have some give and there are springs underneath—and the canvas is changed after every show.

Slamming and Jamming

There's a whole lot of slamming and jamming going on in a professional wrestling bout. If you've watched many televised wrestling events, you've seen wrestlers lift other, often heavier, wrestlers over their heads and then, as the laws of gravity would dictate, slam them into the mat. What you may not see is that the wrestler being lifted is assisting in what seems to be his own destruction. He's helping the lifter—either by pushing off the mat or by holding onto his opponent's trunks or some other handy spot to help both of them keep their balance.

And, when slammed to the surface, the trained professional knows how to tuck his chin, roll his shoulders, and prepare his body for as soft a landing as possible. Don't think that the fall doesn't sting—but don't buy into all the pain and suffering either. Learning how to fall and how to roll with a punch is essential for successful pro wrestlers, many of whom turn the moves into an art form. Knowing how to fall is even more important in this day and age, when wrestlers are increasingly expected to fall from the top rope to the sometimes un-padded arena floor outside the ring.

Pulling Your Leg—and Other Holds

Legs have meant different things to different people. I always thought that without two pretty good ones, you couldn't get to first base. In the world of wrestling, legs mean two things: They are good weapons and they are good targets. Of all the action in the ring, legwork is most likely to be the closest to the real McCoy—the most real-real.

Body Slam

If a 300-pound wrestler lands on another wrestler's stomach or arm with an extended knee, the effect could be devastating. Still, it's a frequently used move—the key to executing it properly is to manage a near-miss to soften the impact.

When legs are used as weapons, there is room for some magic. For example, a wrestler who does a leg drop has options as to how the contact will be made. After all, the human thigh has a lot of meat surrounding the bone. This makes the thigh a good contact point for the leg drop, with the flesh acting as padding to protect both wrestlers. Or, a wrestler might land with the back of his knee on a contact spot. The knee can be bent split seconds before impact to lessen the effect of the blow.

Then there is the knee drop. This uses the extended knee as a striking force. If not ex-ecuted properly, this move could be very painful—for both wrestlers. The leg also makes an especially inviting—and extremely vulnerable—target. Many submission holds involve an attack on a wrestler's leg or legs. And as I've said, most times action involving leg holds, twists, and the like is real. When you see a wrestler with his leg or legs bent backward, you can assume that it's no act.

And while we're dealing with the lower half of the anatomy, let's not forget kicks. Some wrestlers in modern pro wrestling get their kicks out of kicks. Everyone can surely agree that a full-powered kick can be, as they say, detrimental to one's health. But a truly professional wrestler can control it, ending the move with a near-miss, which is all but impossible to see. (On TV, directors switch cameras at the moment of impact to further the deception.)

Another way of minimizing the damage done by a powerful-looking kick is to use the inside or arch portion of the boot, not the toe. This reduces the risk and the in-evitable pain. Kicking with the inside of the foot takes the power out of the kick at the last second (remember the flat to flat rule). It looks real because it *is* real—except that the sound of the impact is exaggerated. Experienced wrestlers know where to accurately place their kicks to avoid real damage to the opponent. For example, kicking someone in the kneecap could easily result in a painful and crippling career-ending injury. But kicking at a fleshy part of the body won't do much damage when the kicker and his opponent are working together.

Lucha Libre

Wrestling is every bit as popular "south of the border" as it is in the U.S., but things are a little different down there.

Lucha libre—or, in literal translation, freestyle fighting—is Mexican pro wrestling. Although it greatly resembles the American version, there are cultural differences. The bad guys, known as *rudos*, represent characters who are apt to make life more difficult for solid Mexican citizens. Some *rudos* have even played the role of corrupt policemen. The good guys, known as *technicos*, of course represent solid citizens and fight evil. Although the good guy versus bad guy format has remained more intact there than in the United States (where antiheroes are in vogue), the tradition of rooting for the bad guys and booing the good guys actually began in Mexico long before American audiences—or, a portion thereof—started thinking that babyfaces were lame and villains were cool.

Mexican wrestlers, or *luchadors*, are far more likely to wear masks. The characters represent classic symbols in Mexican culture such as animals, body parts, death, and religious entities. The masks come from the Mayan and Aztec traditions of ancient Mexico, and it is the mask that makes the wrestler a superhero. A masked wrestler who loses his mask during a match is humiliated. As one old-time *luchador* put it, "Losing your mask is like being raped." The loss of the mask takes the *luchador* off Mount Olympus and places him once again among the mortals. In today's financial climate, in which many *luchadors* work in the United States at mid-card level rather than in Mexico as superstars because there is more money to be made, *luchadors* are unmasking for the WWF and WCW. American bookers find the men more marketable with their faces showing, and American fans don't care. But, back in Mexico, scandals erupt each time a mask comes off.

Gimmicks and Tricks

There are literally bagsful of gimmicks and misdirections—all of which are part of wrestling magic. Let me tell you about the first time I became aware of gimmickry in wrestling—and it wasn't in a "real" wrestling bout. Back in 1952, as a young Captain Lou, I had just started out in wrestling. It seems that one of Jackie Gleason's advisers had called Vince McMahon Sr. in search of four wrestlers to put on a skit for "The Great One's" variety show (this even predated the *Honeymooners*).

Vince Sr. called me up to the old WWF office and said, "The pay is $750." That was for all four of us; after the office took a third of the fee, there was $500 for us to divvy up. Vince laid out the plot: We were going to wrestle Jackie Gleason—or, more specifically, Jackie's character, Reginald van Gleason III. And so the four of us—Tony Altimore, Skull Murphy, Arnold Skaaland, and me—showed up at the Ed Sullivan Theater in Manhattan. And all Gleason told us was, "Gentlemen, if I get hurt, the skit's off." Then and there, we made up our minds to make sure that nothing happened to him.

The skit called for Skull and me to face Arnold and Jackie, with Tony acting as the referee. After the introductions, which had me as "The Monk" and Jackie as "the legendary wrestler, Reginald van Gleason the Third," Gleason came onstage in a Turkish sedan chair carried by four beautiful girls and surrounded by midgets. He was clothed in a leopard loincloth. Truth be told, although he was dressed like Tarzan, he looked more like Jane to me.

Now the bout started. Gleason pulled out a can opener that he had stashed in his trunks and used it to unscrew the turnbuckle—out of which he pulled a bottle of vodka. He took a swig, then walked over and hit me. Following the script, I flew out of the ring. He then took a shot at my partner, who also flew out of the ring. He looked at his partner, Arnold, who went over to shake hands with him for a job well done. Boom! He hit Arnold, too, sending *him* flying out of the ring. And when I say we flew, I mean it: We were all attached to harnesses that had us flying around like Peter Pan. (Now I don't mean to say that in regular wrestling bouts we use harnesses, but we've used just about everything else, especially hidden gimmicks. In the four decades that I've been in wrestling, I've seen hundreds of them.)

The Best Stuntmen in Modern Wrestling History

Terry Funk: Still wrestling at 50-something, he still does what's called a "moonsault"—a backward somersault off the top turnbuckle for the pinfall.

Rey Mysterio Jr.: This Mexican wrestler invents new acrobatic maneuvers every match and often appears to defy gravity.

Shawn "The Heartbreak Kid" Michaels: His athleticism is first-class. In big matches—cage matches, ladder matches, and so on—he always delivers.

Superfly Jimmy Snuka: The father of modern wrestling in many ways. He dove off things (ropes, turnbuckles, and so on) in Madison Square Garden in the 1970s and upped the athleticism ante for everybody.

Mick Foley: The wrestler most apt to jump off the Empire State Building into a slightly damp sponge—and live.

Gimmicks Galore

Dr. X used to hide a piece of metal in his mask to make his head butts more effective. Harry Finkelstein brought a piece of soap into the ring for rubbing into his opponent's eyes. Chief Chewchki secreted sheets of sandpaper studded with carpet tacks in his trunks, and Count Dracula carried a hidden bottle labeled chloroform. Killer Tim Brooks wore heavy objects in his elbow pad, and Professor Toru Tanaka snuck salt into the ring. And the gimmicks never, ever maimed or crippled an opponent. That was part of the magic!

Stunts Gone Wrong

Sometimes, however, things go wrong—like the time during the spring of 2000 when Eddy Guerrero dove off the top rope onto an opponent during an episode of *Smackdown*. Guerrero landed on his elbow wrong and grotesquely dislocated it. Although he had been scheduled to win the match, he was in so much pain that he rolled onto his back and asked his opponent to pin him so that they could get down to the important business of calling an ambulance.

Fighting Words

Blading means using a piece of razor to open a cut and get the blood flowing. The usual place to cut was the forehead because the blood flows freely over the face, creating the "crimson mask" effect.

Speaking of blood, throughout the years many fans have asked if we use blood capsules, like they use in movies. The answer is, sometimes. When a wrestler is seen bleeding from the mouth it usually means that he has bitten on a blood capsule. But most of the blood in wrestling comes from a practice called *blading*. A small sliver of a razor is hidden in the wrestler's trunks or bandages and is used to slice open his forehead. There isn't as much blading as there used to be. The practice leaves scars and isn't healthy—especially in these days when diseases can be transmitted through blood.

The Sounds of Pain

Wrestlers, their managers, and especially promoters are well aware of the importance that sound effects have in a match. Wrestling has a language all its own, one that dates back to ancient times, when the participants would grunt, yell, or scream as they made their moves or took their hits. I'm not talking here about the verbal abuse heaped on villains and nonfavorites by the fans. I'm talking about the sounds made by the wrestlers to "hype" or excite the audience. The more a hit sounds like it hurts, the more the fans believe that it *must* have hurt.

Wrestle Mania

Gestures are another way that the wrestler communicates with the audience. Nothing subtle, mind you—the wrestlers are playing to the whole crowd, not just the front rows. One of the best at using gestures is Hulk Hogan: He can command the entire arena with a single movement. Hogan nudges the audience with his gestures, connecting with the crowd with an extended arm, a pumped fist, or a toss of his golden mane until the noise of the fans reaches a decibel level that could beat a 747 taking off. Other virtuosos of the gesture are Chris Jericho and The Undertaker.

Grunting is also part and parcel of every wrestler's repertoire. It not only adds to the overall effect of the impact, but it underscores it for the audience. And the screaming and hollering of mock pain adds to the overall effect of theater.

Injuries and Accidents

No matter how choreographed or how practiced, sometimes things go wrong. And when they do, when a near-miss becomes a non-miss, or when a safe fall falls short, you get injuries—and sometimes even fatal consequences.

I have had almost every bone in my body broken, and most wrestlers can't get through a career without a serious injury. The most famous one happened in Montreal during the early 1950s, when Walter "Killer" Kowalski took on Yukon Eric. On a missed attempt at a knee drop near Yukon Eric's head, Killer caught and knocked off Eric's *cauliflower ear*!

More recently, Mick Foley (also known as Cactus Jack, Mankind, and Dude Love) lost part of his right ear when, during a match in Germany, his head got caught between the ropes. So, make no mistake about it: Not all you see is just smoke and mirrors. Some of it, unfortunately, is all too real.

Fighting Words

A **cauliflower ear** is a condition common to wrestlers and boxers—anyone who takes a lot of hits to the ear. When the ear has been damaged enough to bleed internally, it calcifies, like bone. Yukon Eric's ear was pretty much *all* cauliflower by the time he wrestled Kowalski and lost it.

45

Wrestle Mania

One of the scariest injuries of recent times happened in front of millions of fans on pay-per-view. It was a championship match between Stone Cold Steve Austin and the late Owen Hart. Austin was scripted to win—but not before a Hart piledriver planted Austin smack-dab on his head, causing Austin to fall heavily and hurt his neck. Austin lay there, unable to feel anything from the neck down; Hart, sensing Austin's inability to move, had to think fast. Handling the unmoving Austin ever so gingerly, Hart began maneuvering, as much to stall for time as to try to set up a satisfactory ending to the match.

Finally, after what seemed an eternity, Hart managed to wrestle the almost inert Austin so that he was actually on top. The ref quickly counted Hart out, and a couple WWF officials jumped into the ring to help Austin to his feet, drape the intercontinental belt across his shoulder and lift his limp arm in victory. Austin was then taken to a hospital, still complaining that he couldn't feel anything. The injury was originally diagnosed as a "stinger," but it turned out to be more serious. Austin has since had the vertebrae in his neck fused, and it remains to be seen if he ever returns to a full wrestling schedule.

Stone Cold Steve Austin's neck injury has kept him out of action for a long time.

The Least You Need to Know

➤ Wrestlers learn to take hits and falls similar to how movie stuntmen work.

➤ The bounce of wrestlers in the ring is due partly to springs under the canvas.

➤ Leg holds are usually the most realistic moves in wrestling.

➤ Sound effects are extremely important because they involve the fan and bring excitement to a professional wrestling match.

➤ No matter how practiced and rehearsed a match, the chances of injury are still great.

Chapter 5

Rules? What Rules?

> **In This Chapter**
>
> ➤ The concept of rules
>
> ➤ Referee rules
>
> ➤ Group rules
>
> ➤ On the spot rules

There's the Golden Rule, rules of thumb, and wrestling rules. And all three are honored more in the breach than in the observance. So, as you can probably guess, this chapter on the rules of pro wrestling is a short one. Since wrestling is a contest for fan appreciation rather than for athletic superiority—except, of course, in the sense that athletic superiority leads to fan appreciation—the wrestling rules that have survived the test of time are those that heighten the drama of the event rather than those that most fairly determine a winner.

If You Think the Rules of Dating Are Tough—Try These

In other words, textbook rules for sports are supposed to be the very mortar that hold a contest together, that control its action, and that determine the winner and loser. Wrestling's rules, however, are like quicksand—they shift constantly to satisfy the demands of the moment. The plain truth of the matter is that few of the rules in wrestling today are observed. But there are still a few—a very few—and in these pages you'll learn what they are.

Rules Are Made to Be Broken

In fact, the extremes of the moment seem to call for their own rules. Take the case of George Zaharias, for example. George was a member of the infamous Zaharias Brothers, major wrestlers of the 1930s. When asked about his conversion from a *babyface* to a *villain*, George explained it this way: "One night in Memphis in 1930, I said to this promoter, 'Look at my eyes, they're all cut. Nobody wrestles by the rules.' And this old promoter told me, 'Hit him first!' So I became a villain and saw to it that there were always fireworks when I wrestled."

Fighting Words

A **babyface** (or, often, just **face**) is a good-guy wrestler for whom fans usually cheer. A **heel** is the **villain** wrestler who tries to bring down the face in a match. Getting **heel heat** means making the fans boo.

True, there are few stages for true anarchy like that of pro wrestling, but, once upon a time, there were rules for wrestling just as for any sport. The New York State Athletic Commission's first set of rules covering wrestling read, in part, as follows:

> "Matches to be decided by falls, two out of three or three out of five, as may be agreed upon in making the match. All matches shall be limited in time to two hours. Should there be only one fall in the two hours, the winner of that fall will be declared the winner of the contest ...

> "The referee will be instructed by the Commission to disqualify any wrestler who indulges in the following unfair and foul methods: striking, scratching, gouging, any display of bad temper, strangle-holds, so-called head-holds, toe-locks, and scissors holds, which are held specially for the purpose of punishing an opponent, are declared to be foul methods and, if indulged in, the offender will be at once disqualified and the match given to the opponent. He will further be punished by having his license revoked."

It all sounds so quaint, doesn't it? After wrestling was designated as entertainment rather than a sport, the control of the state athletic commissions was gone. But even as late as 1954, the New York State Athletic Commission was attempting to impose strict rules. It was fighting a losing battle. Today there is no controlling body, outside the promoters themselves, to impose or enforce rules. Because the promoters choose the rules, those rules can change at any time and can be selectively enforced.

To win a pinfall, a wrestler must pin his opponent's shoulders to the mat for a count of three.

Ways to Win a Match

Of course, there have to be *some* rules—after all, without any, there would be no way of telling when a match was over. According to the rules, there are five traditional ways to win a wrestling match. Sometimes they're honored; more often, they're not.

1. **The pinfall.** Pin your opponent's shoulders to the mat for a three-count.

2. **Submission.** Similar to making an opponent say "uncle"—making him (or her) "tap out." Wrestlers give up rather than risk serious injury. After a wrestler has submitted, he is supposed to be released from the hold that brought him down—but that doesn't always happen. Other wrestlers frequently break into the ring to free their trapped colleagues.

3. **Disqualification.** When an opponent breaks the rules (or the stipulations of the match— whatever they may be), or when his allies interfere with the match in progress, the of- fending wrestler is disqualified (DQ'd). Punching with a closed fist is supposed to be grounds for disqualification, but no one has been DQ'd for it since time imme- morial. The same is true about foreign objects—wrestling's term for weapons— they're not allowed in the ring, but they turn up all the time. Somehow, the referee is always otherwise occupied.

Body Slam

Referees are supposed to break the hold when one wrestler has submitted—but most referees are no match for the bruisers in the ring, so the hold is often held long after the wrestler has cried "uncle."

4. **Count out.** When a wrestler leaves the ring, whether voluntarily or involuntarily, his opponent must wait in a neutral corner. If the fallen wrestler does not make it back into the ring in 20 seconds, the bout is awarded to the wrestler in the corner. But should that wrestler leave the neutral corner, the count begins again from the start—unlike boxing, where the count is just suspended until the boxer returns to his corner. You'd be surprised at the number of wrestlers who do not know, or ignore, this rule—so the referee rarely, if ever, gets to 20. (And many times a stunned wrestler gets an opportunity to clear the cobwebs before re-entering the fray.)

5. **Render your opponent unable to continue.** The sleeper hold, for example, can earn a victory for the wrestler applying it, even if his opponent never submits and is never pinned.

Captain Lou's Corner

The ring-rope rule has been exploited by smart wrestlers—they grab the ring ropes when in trouble. And if they can't do that, they will lay an ankle on the ropes, which is all that is required for the referee to break the hold. This is one of the few rules that is religiously observed.

The Ring-Rope Rule

If a wrestler has a hold on his opponent and the opponent manages to get part of his body under—or on—the ring ropes, the hold must be broken before the count of five. This rule also applies for illegal holds, such as chokeholds.

But there are ways around this. If the hold is broken and then reapplied, the count starts all over again—a loophole in the rules that allows a villain to choke his opponent for somewhat more than the union scale, provided that he never chokes his opponent for more than 10 consecutive seconds (that is, in a single application of the hold).

True veterans of the wrestling wars have been known to use the ring ropes for leverage to help them attain a pin. They know that the referee will be paying close attention to their opponent's shoulders and will not take notice of the infraction.

Don't Touch That Man in the Middle

Outside of a bank guard in Alaska who must distinguish between regular customers wearing ski masks and the bank robbers wearing the same thing, the wrestling referee has one of the most arduous jobs in the world. Not only must he be fast enough to get out of the way of projectiles weighing upwards of 300 pounds flying around the ring at warp speed, but he also must stay out of their way when they rumble in his direction. And he's got to avoid getting rolled upon when the two behemoths are on the mat and he's beside them trying to tick away three seconds by pounding the canvas to signify a fall. As you might expect, every once in a while—actually, all the time—this is a *ref bump* and the ref gets knocked into la-la land. In fact, injuries to the referee have become a staple of the modern match, to the point where it has become a wrestling cliché.

Modern referees wear earpieces and can hear the show's director who times the matches. When the allotted time for the match is almost up, the ref is alerted and he instructs the wrestlers to begin the match's prearranged finish.

Tag-Team Rules

It's double your pleasure, double your fun—and double trouble for the referee when tag teams get together. The rules themselves are simple: Two wrestlers go up against two others, but *only* two wrestlers (one for each side) are supposed to be in the ring at any one time. The match starts with one man—called the *legal* man—from each team in the ring. For a wrestler to get his partner into the act, the legal man must touch, or *tag* his partner's hand—hence the name, *tag team*. When the tag has been made, the new man then becomes the legal man, and the first wrestler—the one who made the tag—has 10 seconds to vacate the premises.

Those are the rules. In most tag-team matches, however, the wrestlers seem to have misplaced the rulebook. We've seen wrestlers play the tag-team hokey pokey—you know, "you put your left foot in, you pull your left foot out"— to get closer to the tag. We've seen double-teaming during the 10-second changeover interval. And we've even seen teammates dress alike so that the referee, having trouble figuring out which wrestler is which, will award pinfalls mistakenly.

As is true of most wrestling rules, tag-team rules were obeyed far more often in the past than they are today. Now it's quite common to have all four wrestlers surge into the ring at once, while the referee is reduced to clinging to the back of one of them like a shell on a turtle, futilely trying to restore order.

Bert's Corner

One of the earliest rules in wrestling was "Thou shalt not touch the referee." One wrestler who did was Everett Marshall. He was suspended by the Pennsylvania State Athletic Commission in 1934 after attacking referee Ben Paul in a match against Jim Londos. Today's referees are fair game. They take as much abuse as everyone else, but wrestlers are rarely—if ever—penalized for touching them.

Fighting Words

When a referee takes a hit and is knocked out of commission, allowing the heels to go nuts, that's called a **ref bump.**

Wrestle Mania

In the U.S. it is customary for tag matches to be two on two, or four-man matches. Six- and eight-man matches are held, too, but they are novelties. In Mexico, six-man matches, or trios, are the norm.

Refs still make at least some attempt to enforce tag-team rules. But their problems are compounded because, while they're trying to keep track of four wrestlers, they're also trying to deal with the wrestlers' managers or valets. Just about everybody usually ends up attempting to insinuate themselves into the fray—either by actively joining in the melee or by causing distractions so that their wrestler can gain the upper hand.

So. Rules for tag-team matches? As they say in New York—fuhgeddaboudit!

In Your Face

Butch of the Bushwhackers says, "The second Luke and I saw each other we knew we'd make a bloody good tag team. Refs couldn't tell us apart. They had no idea who was the legal man in."

By the Seat of Their Trunks

Some rules are written in stone. Others are made up to suit the moment. Those on-the-spot rules can vary greatly and are known as stipulations. If both wrestlers agree ahead of time to wrestle under certain conditions that differ from the usual conventions, those conditions—or stipulations—become the rules of the match. For example, a Falls Count Anywhere match obviously bends, if not breaks, the rule that the wrestling is supposed to happen only in the ring. In such a match, the action can spill out onto the arena floor. It can be carried into the crowd and can even spread to the concession stand. Or, a match can have a weapons stipulation, as in a Brass Knux match, which allows—actually, requires—that the wrestlers use brass knuckles. And then there are Cage matches, fought in an enclosed ring, where the rules are very different from a regular ring match.

Dress Code? What Dress Code?

It has been said that men wear clothes for warmth, women for spite, and children 'cause they have to. But in wrestling, none of this counts. Wrestlers can wear trunks, tights, blue jeans—even stretch pants. Me, I always dressed as if the Goodwill box just threw up on me. And most of the women wrestlers look like they're wearing something that they just threw on and damned near missed!

If there's anything similar to a dress code restriction, it has to do with the show itself. For instance, if the wrestler is dressed in full cowboy regalia—with hat, boots, and the whole magilla—that's all right. But if there are heels on those boots, they're there for one reason only—to smash the opponent's face in. That is definitely *not* all right (unless, of course, the heels are there as a gimmick). Other than that, anything goes. After all, this is *wrestling!*

The Real Rules

Ah, but these are the rules to a *sport* that doesn't actually exist—and it's a good thing because there would probably be about three fatalities a day if it did. Wrestling as "sports entertainment" does exist, and it has its own rules that are followed to the letter by all true professionals:

1. Protect your opponent.
2. Remain in character, at least while in the building.
3. Know your lines.
4. Respect the fans.
5. Play to the back row.
6. The show must go on.

Captain Lou's Corner

As a manager I've resorted to jumping up and down, shouting, and screaming. I've done just about anything that I could think of to exhort my wrestlers and distract the referee or the opposing team. I've even taken to shouting "three ... three ..." when the referee seems to forget how to count that high before one of the opposing team jumps up off the canvas.

Bert's Corner

It's bad enough that refs have to worry about all four tag-team wrestlers ending up in the ring at once. It's even worse when the managers and valets get into the act, too. But when visiting wrestlers—or other wrestlers appearing later on the bill—join in the fun, well ... you might say that things get a little out of hand.

As you can see, the real-deal rules to pro wrestling borrow from the world of show business more than from the world of sport. The trick is to keep the audience's disbelief suspended. And the audience helps, because fans want to believe.

The Least You Need to Know

➤ What rules there are in wrestling are made to be broken.

➤ The referee has one of the hardest jobs in the world.

➤ Foreign objects aren't allowed in the ring—unless stipulated before the bout.

➤ Tag-team partners are *supposed* to tag each other before entering the ring.

Part 2

The Founding Fathers: Wrestling's Colorful History

Who was responsible for transforming wrestling from a sport enjoyed in ancient Greece to the spectacle and excitement we enjoy today? The vision of a few founding fathers started the movement. As momentum grew, pro wrestling took on more power than almost anyone could imagine.

Wrestling transformed into today's modern extravaganza in a series of jumps— quantum leaps, if you will. And those responsible are the Founding Fathers of Wrestling. They should have their faces chiseled into the face of Mount Suplex.

In this part of the book, we will introduce you to wrestling's most influential people.

Chapter 6

Wrestling's Warriors Extraordinaire

In This Chapter

➤ Gotch and Hackenschmidt

➤ The Strangler—greatest wrestler of all time

➤ Lou Thesz claims the crown

➤ How Jim Londos got his name

➤ The Glorious Gorgeous George

Only a few graybeards who have not collapsed under the weight of their collective memories may remember the founding fathers of wrestling, but these are the colossi who bestrode the ranks of wrestling in times past. Their legends date all the way back to the early days and are part and parcel of pro wrestling's glory days. In this chapter, you learn about some of the greats.

The Peerless One

Frank Gotch was to professional wrestling what John L. Sullivan was to boxing: its first universally recognized major attraction, and the founding member of the long line of professional wrestling champions that extends to this day. Gotch was born in Iowa in 1878. He stood 5 feet, 11 inches tall, weighed 210 pounds, and was known for his strength and cleverness in the ring.

Early Career

From the time of his debut in Humboldt, Iowa, against Marshall Green, in 1899, until his retirement almost 14 years later in 1913, Gotch was professional wrestling's most popular attraction with his catch-as-catch-can style. He first won the championship in Bellingham, Washington, in 1904, beating Tom Jenkins to win the heavyweight title; then he lost it back to Jenkins the following year in Madison Square Garden. Gotch lost to Jenkins again two months later at the Garden. The first fall of that match went to Jenkins in an hour and 27 minutes; the second went to Gotch in 36 minutes; and the third and deciding fall went to Jenkins again, this time in just 11 minutes.

Gotch finally won back the title in 1906, only to lose it later in the year when challenger Fred Beall won the third and deciding fall by throwing Gotch out of the ring, rendering Gotch *hors de combat* when he struck his head on the floor. But 16 days later, Gotch would reverse that loss in two one-sided falls to become the American heavyweight champion for the third time.

World Class

But Gotch earned everlasting fame in his two matches against George "The Russian Lion" Hackenschmidt, the European champion. Their first match, to decide the world's heavyweight championship, was three years in the making—and finally took place on April 3, 1908, at Chicago's Dexter Park Pavilion.

The bout was highly controversial. *The New York Times* reported that Gotch "side-stepped, roughed his man's features with his knuckles, butted him under the chin, and generally worsted Hackenschmidt until the foreigner was at a loss how to proceed." Hackenschmidt continually complained to the referee about such infractions, but the ref turned the proverbial deaf ear to his plaints. Finally, after two hours and three minutes, The Russian Lion threw up his hands in resignation and quit the match. The referee promptly awarded the match—and the championship—to Gotch.

Hackenschmidt later charged that Gotch "dug his nails into my face, tried to pull my ear off, and poked his thumb into my eye." Moreover, the Russian claimed that Gotch's body was "literally soaked in oil," making the American all but impossible to grasp.

In Your Face

In his book *Hooker*, wrestling great Lou Thesz wrote, "The picture that emerged of Gotch was that of a man who succeeded primarily because he was, for lack of a kinder description, a dirty wrestler. Gotch would gouge, pull hair, and even break a bone to get an advantage in a contest, and he was always careful to have the referee in his pocket, too, if you follow my meaning."

Gotch was famous for his toe hold, demonstrated here.

(Source: Norman Kietzer)

The controversy that arose after the match dictated a return bout, which took another three years to arrange. This time, determined to get what former champion Lou Thesz described in his book *Hooker* as "an illegal edge," Gotch employed Ad Santel, a known hooker—someone willing to hurt, even cripple, an opponent—to insinuate himself into Hackenschmidt's training camp as a training partner to purposely injure The Russian Lion. The hooker, who was paid $5,000 for the mugging, did so—all but ruining Hackenschmidt's knee.

Now Hackenschmidt, unable to participate fully in the big return match, pleaded with the promoters to postpone it. But the promoters, who had spent most, if not all, of the advance money (some $87,000 in Taft dollars), declined. The bout went on as scheduled, in front of an estimated 35,000 at Chicago's spanking-new Comiskey Park. The bout itself was anticlimactic, with Gotch prevailing over the injured Hackenschmidt in two straight—and quick—falls.

The press, having caught wind of Gotch's dirty deed, became disillusioned with the sport of wrestling, which up to that time had been front-page sports news. Now wrestling coverage found itself buried under the shipping notices in the back of most newspapers. This was the beginning of the end for wrestling's first glory years.

Body Slam

The end of wrestling's first Golden Era was hastened by Gotch's retirement the year after he defeated Hackenschmidt. Gotch didn't get too far away from the grappling game, however. He toured with the Sells-Floto Circus wrestling exhibitions.

Gotch injured his leg in an exhibition match at a Sells-Floto performance in Kenosha, Wisconsin, in 1916, and never wrestled again. Within a year he was dead—according to Thesz, of either syphilis or uremic poisoning.

The Strangler

The greatest name in the long and storied history of professional wrestling wasn't even the real name of the man who carried it. Ed "Strangler" Lewis, who replaced Gotch in the affections of professional wrestling fans, performed epic feats for more than three decades. In the process, he entered his name in the pages of wrestling as its greatest wrestler of all time. His record, in a time when record keeping was only a sometime thing, was estimated at more than 6,000 bouts with only 33 losses.

Captain Lou's Corner

All claimants to world championship honors trace their lineage back to Frank Gotch, the first universally recognized catch-as-catch-can champion who made his mark in the first decade of the twentieth century.

Born Robert Friedrich in Madison, Wisconsin, in 1890, young Friedrich adopted the name Ed Lewis at the age of 14 to keep his parents from discovering his activities. The "Strangler" nickname came later, as much a tribute to his deadly use of the headlock as to the original holder of the name, Evan "Strangler" Lewis, who had wrestled back in the 1880s.

Young Friedrich-Lewis was working his way through college in Lexington, Kentucky, as the school's athletic director when he was discovered by manager Billy Sandow. At that time, he looked nothing like a wrestler—he weighed all of 175 pounds and had what might delicately be called a spavined back. But he showed potential, having already met such outstanding wrestlers as Charley Cutler, Fred Beall, and Americus, so Sandow took him under his wing.

The Birth of the Strangler's Trademark Hold

Sandow and Lewis studied and practiced day after day, perfecting the hold that would become Lewis's signature: the headlock. Finally, after months of intensive training, Sandow decided that his charge was ready for competition. He entered Lewis in the International Wrestling Tournament, held at the Metropolitan Opera House in New York. The tournament, a three-month competition (November 1915 to January 1916) featured more than 50 of the world's best wrestlers, with big-name wrestlers such as Alex Aberg, Waldek Zbyszko, Charles Cutler, and B. F. Roller. In the end, it was Lewis, and his headlock, who emerged victorious.

Wrestle Mania

Lewis's headlock became so famous—and so deadly—that it was all but impossible to get wrestlers to train with him. And so, with no human targets willing to accept his embrace, Sandow devised a substitute—a wooden dummy with several sets of springs inside to provide high resistance. Lewis practiced with that dummy day in and day out, squeezing the two halves together until he had all but squeezed the sawdust out of it.

In addition to his unbeatable, unbreakable headlock, Lewis also possessed enormous defensive skills. With the extra weight he had gained under Sandow's watchful eye, Lewis looked like a dancing bear as he maneuvered around the ring.

Championship Material

This defensive maneuvering nearly derailed Lewis's storied career before it began. Challenging heavyweight champion Joe Stecher in a bout in Omaha in 1916, Lewis put on his offensive nonoffensive tactics for the entirety of the match. The fans, disgruntled with Lewis's defense, showered the ring with seat cushions. Finally, after five hours, the match was declared a draw. Four years later, Lewis beat Stecher in a match lasting one hour and 41 minutes.

In all, Lewis won the heavyweight title five times during the next 12 years. Fans were more than bored with Lewis, who was winning bout after bout with startling frequency and alarming monotony. But Lewis and Sandow knew that wrestling was, bottom line, a business. Something had to be done; the belt was going to have to be put out on loan.

In the fall of 1924, Sandow attended a University of Nebraska football game and came away with the idea that he could make a wrestling attraction out of one of the Cornhusker stars, a 6-foot, 6-inch giant of a player named "Big" Wayne Munn. Persuading Munn to try his hand, and the rest of his anatomy, at wrestling, Sandow took him under his wing, just as he had done for Lewis years before. Sandow trained him and got him matches with wrestlers that he could control.

Munn captivated sports fans throughout the Midwest and, on January 8, 1925, captured the heavyweight title by "beating" Strangler Lewis. It was pure performance, which heralded the beginning of wrestling as a performance art rather than a sport.

Lewis's last competitive match was against Lee Wycoff at Madison Square Garden in 1938, but throughout this Indian summer of his career, he was all but invincible. Those few times he lost, he lost for the sake of the show. And he was rewarded handsomely: Over his long career, he earned an estimated $4 million. He was, simply stated, the greatest there ever was.

Upon retiring, Lewis set up a training camp in New Jersey, and crowds came come to watch him train at $1 a head. A lot of the town residents challenged him, feeling that if they beat—or even looked good—against the World's Champion, they'd gain instant immortality. Lewis declined each and every offer, saying, "You want to wrestle me? Before you do, there's a little guy over there. Beat him, and you can wrestle me."

That little guy was Frank Jensen, one of the great "shooters" of his day. Jensen, of course, proceeded to hand the challenger his head on a silver platter, leaving the local fellow scratching his head in wonder: "If *he* did that to me, imagine what the Strangler would do."

Jim Londos, The Golden Greek

Jim Londos, known in the wrestling world as "The Golden Greek," was the most popular wrestler of the 1930s. Londos was born Christopher Theophelos, and he used that name throughout his early years in the sport. His favorite writer was Jack London, so he went with the phonetically similar Jim Londos as his ring name.

Londos is credited with executing wrestling's first "sleeper hold" in the main event of a card at New York's Yankee Stadium in June 1931. The controversial hold, which enabled Londos to defeat Ray Steele in one hour and nine minutes, was, in the wrestler's own words, "simply a new hold I've perfected which shuts off the jugular vein."

Lou Thesz

An athlete's greatness is measured by many things: consistent performance, accomplishments transcending time, overall excellence, and dominance. With the exception of Strangler Lewis, no wrestler ever accomplished so much over so long a period of time and dominated the sport more than the great Lou Thesz.

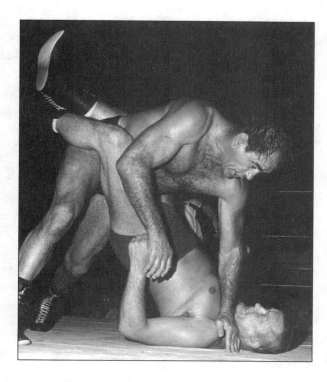

Lou Thesz is on his way to the mat, caught in a body scissors by Gene Kiniski.

(Source: Norman Kietzer)

Thesz was introduced to wrestling at the age of 8 by his father, once a Greco-Roman wrestler in his native Hungary. The city of St. Louis—where Thesz's family lived and after which Lou was named—was a hotbed of wrestling. Each and every ethnic neighborhood in the southern part of the city sported an amateur club where children were taught the sport and competitions were staged as entertainment.

With support from his father, the young Thesz soon became extremely adept at Greco-Roman wrestling, winning many of the citywide club competitions. And, upon seeing his first professional wrestling match, the young Thesz fell in love with the sport—in *all* its forms.

Under his father's tutelage, young Lou practiced for hours, weaving, swerving, straining, and shoving in the Greco-Roman style that had by now gone the way of the horse and buggy. He became so good at his craft that George Tragos, a former Olympic champion from Greece then living in St. Louis, came to see him. After one look, Tragos was moved to say, "This is a future champion."

Strangler Takes Over Thesz's Career

With that, Tragos took over Lou's training. As legend has it, one day after a particularly heavy workout in the gym, Tragos told his protégé, "Lou, take a rest for a few days. I'm setting up an appointment for you to wrestle a friend of mine. He's pretty good, so I want you to be in top shape." The youngster, confident of his abilities, answered, "Sure. Who d'ya want me to wrestle? Strangler Lewis?" Trago eyed the youngster, now a strapping 210-pound, six-foot-tall athlete, and answered slowly, "That's exactly who you're going to wrestle."

Strangler Lewis recalled the meeting this way: "I could see right away that if he had nothing else, this Thesz squirt had the *look* of a real wrestler. I had a feeling I was about to have my hands full, unless he fainted first. Poor Lou kept staring at me as though I was a god or something. And for a few minutes after we squared off it looked as though I'd have to stick a hot coal in his pants to get him moving. Then we started to wrestle, and this 17-year-old hunky pinned me in 22 seconds with a combination arm-bar and half-nelson."

Lewis decided then and there that Thesz was to be the next champion, his successor to the unofficial title of "greatest wrestler in the world." And he promptly took control of Thesz's training and management.

Lewis' judgment wasn't far off—Thesz *did* become world champion, although it took him four years to get there. Everett Marshall, a powerful wrestler out of Colorado, had beaten Thesz to the crown—having beaten Ali Baba, who had beaten the last of the long string of wrestlers who had held the title after Lewis.

Thesz Becomes Champion

To get a shot at Marshall, Thesz first had to learn the ropes, literally—he took on all comers as part of his apprenticeship. One of those early opponents was former amateur champion Ray Steele who, in Thesz's words, "was even tougher than his name sounds." Steele knocked Thesz on his keister in the opening seconds of the bout, but Thesz escaped from a combination toehold and hammerlock to turn the tables, gaining a win over Steele and, in the process, earning a crack at Marshall's title.

The match against Marshall, held in St. Louis at Kiel Auditorium on the night of December 29, 1937, was one of the toughest matches in Thesz's career—maybe the toughest in the annals of pro wrestling. It lasted three full hours, with Thesz winning the last two falls. Both men were exhausted after the bout—Marshall needed three months to recuperate. But when the bout ended, Marshall took the time to shake Thesz's hand and tell the new champ, "Congratulations ... now your troubles are just beginning."

And so they were. Now every shooter in the business was out gunning for the 21-year-old champion, looking to take the title from him. Like Lewis before him, Thesz would lose and win back the title five more times, facing such greats as Bronko Nagurski, Steve Casey, Whipper Billy Watson, Dick Hutton, Baron Michele Leone, and Gene Kiniski in epic battles.

After World War II, Thesz cemented his claim to the championship by taking on—and beating—anyone who deserved a shot at the title. The newly formed National

Wrestling Alliance recognized him as its champion in 1949. From that point on, he defended the title not only for himself, but also for the NWA as he battled against wrestlers from other organizations who challenged his supremacy. Two such bouts were against Gorgeous George and Baron Michele Leone, two West Coast claimants to the title.

Thesz would retire and make more comebacks than Frank Sinatra, making his final exit from the ring in 1973 when he was in his 70s. Even then, the still perfectly proportioned Thesz said, "I feel like I'm 22 years old." And for many who watched him take his leave, not only did Thesz still *look* young, but his memories as heavyweight champion for 18 years kept every one of his fans feeling young at heart.

Captain Lou's Corner

Lou Thesz was such a tough man to handle in the ring that at a recent roast honoring this wrestling legend, one roaster, Gene LeBell, elicited guffaws when he suddenly leaped up and stood behind Thesz. "There!" LeBell shouted, "I finally got behind you!"

The Gorgeous One

Many people think that modern professional wrestling began with Gorgeous George. And, in a way, they're right. The wrestler who became known as "The Human Orchid" began life as plain ol' George Wagner, born in Seard, Nebraska, and raised in Houston, Texas. As a wrestler, he was more than adequate—he was even, in the estimation of no less an authority than the immortal Lou Thesz, "a good wrestler." But it was not his wrestling that would ultimately make him a legend. It was his showmanship.

The Human Orchid, Gorgeous George (Wagner), in a publicity pose.

(Source: Norman Kietzer)

The Metamorphosis Begins

The development of the character who would become known the world over as "Gorgeous George" was a slow process involving several steps. One of the first was his 1939 wedding, performed midring in Eugene, Oregon, to a local cashier. The wedding drew so many fans that George and his new bride, Betty Hanson, took the act on tour, repeating it several times in arenas around the country.

The next step in the metamorphosis from George Wagner to Gorgeous George happened soon after, when Betty made her new bridegroom a special robe, which he took to ostentatiously folding and carefully placing in his corner before each bout. The audience began riding him for his fastidiousness until, finally, Betty got into a shouting match with some ringside fans and ended up slapping one. That brought double the crowd to the next match—and quadruple the noise as the fans booed George mercilessly while he went through his robe-folding routine. In retaliation, George took even *more* care with the offending garment, and one of the greatest drawing cards of wrestling in the Pacific Northwest came into being. George became an unequivocal "baddie," a wrestling villain—what we call today a heel. From there, the next stop was L.A.

In Los Angeles, the evolution of Gorgeous George continued. By the mid-1940s, his once brown hair had become auburn, and he was wearing it longer and wavier. Concerned about it, George went to two hairstylists, Frank and Joseph of Hollywood, who recommended that he let it grow long and dye it blond—if, that is, he "had the guts." Of course he did!

Then George heard from an old wrestling friend of his, Sterling Davis, who had traveled to Mexico and had made a name for himself by throwing gardenias to the crowd, becoming known as Gardenia Davis. Taking a page from Davis's book, George decided to make something of his new coiffure. He wouldn't throw out flowers, he'd throw bobby pins. And not just any old bobby pins—these would be golden "Georgie Pins," costing $85 per half-pound.

The Glorious Gorgeous One Goes Big-Time

By now George was calling himself "Gorgeous George," and his fame was spreading, courtesy of the national radio broadcasts of the top comedians of the era: Bob Hope, Jack Benny, and Red Skelton. They'd work his name and act into their routines and jokes: "George wants to join the Navy and have the world see *him*." Or, "Gorgeous George always walks into a room voice first." Or, "Gorgeous George would go broke if he had to pay taxes on what he *thinks* he's worth."

With the advent of television, George's name and fame spread ever farther. Postwar America was hungry for celebrities who mirrored their new, carefree attitude, and Gorgeous George fit the bill. He even appeared on TV so often that he was called "Mr. Television."

Next came George's triumphal entrance. To the scratchy strains of a record playing "Pomp and Circumstance," (wrestling's *first* entrance music, today used by Randy Savage) he would walk slowly down the aisle, stopping every now and then to tell a fan that he or she was "beneath contempt." Then he would haughtily enter the ring, the valet holding the ropes just far enough apart so that George wouldn't have to bend too far, and he'd wipe his dainty white shoes on the red carpet that the valet had ever-so-respectfully laid out for him in the corner. After the valet had removed the spun-gold hairnet that held his locks in place, George would walk around so that the crowd could gaze upon his locks and looks, which brought on a round of booing.

Bert's Corner

Gorgeous George not only changed the face of wrestling, but he changed its casting as well—he was the first to switch to using female valets in 1958, changing the look of wrestling forever.

Next, he removed his fur-trimmed robe—one worthy of Liberace—and handed it to his valet for the ostentatious folding ritual, inspiring further antagonism from the crowd. After a few more spritzes of disinfectant by the valet, George would finally, reluctantly, submit to the referee's obligatory hands-on inspection for gimmicks or grease. But he would pull back midway through the inspection, shouting, "Take your filthy hands off me!" At that point the valet would rush forward and spray disinfectant on the referee's hands.

The ring announcer's introduction came next: "The Human Orchid, the Toast of the Coast, Gorgeous George!" And then the bell sounded, sending Gorgeous George into his bout mode: a gouging, biting, kidney-punching villain. His favorite hold was the "flying side headlock," in which he grabbed his opponent in a traditional headlock and then fell back to the mat, flipping his opponent. He became a phenomenon: part celebrity and part wrestling's version of "the man you love to hate." With kinescopes of his matches at L.A.'s Olympic Auditorium being televised across America, requests for his services poured in. Gorgeous George was in such demand that he was able to dictate terms to the promoters: a guaranteed $100,000 or a third of the gate. And, finally, he came East to strut his primping and preening act in Madison Square Garden.

Fighting Words

When a promoter tells a wrestler that one thing is going to happen in the ring but then orchestrates events so that something completely different occurs, that's called a **doublecross.**

A Star Is Born

Red Smith, writing in the 1940s for the *New York Herald-Tribune,* attended a bout between George and Ernie Dusek. Afterward Smith wrote, "It is difficult to do justice to Gorgeous George's act, this side of the libel laws. Groucho Marx is prettier than he, Sonny Tufts a more gifted actor, Connie Mack a better rassler, Happy Chandler funnier, and the Princeton Triangle Club has far superior female impersonators." But, whatever the media thought, Gorgeous George was all the rage for a while, and he brought the cult of personality into the wrestling game.

The Least You Need to Know

➤ Frank Gotch was the first great champion, wrestling's version of John L. Sullivan.

➤ Ed "Strangler" Lewis was arguably the greatest wrestler of all time.

➤ Lou Thesz held the championship title for 18 years.

➤ Gorgeous George brought wrestling fully into the world of show biz.

Chapter 7

Post-War Wrestlers and the New Pro Wrestling

In This Chapter

➤ Antonino Rocca: wrestling's king of exaggeration

➤ Killer Kowalski: the biggest and baddest of the bunch

➤ Verne Gagne: science and athleticism return to wrestling

➤ Bruno Sammartino: Style and substance

It cannot be ignored: When George Wagner finally finished his metamorphosis into Gorgeous George, pro wrestling, as we know it today, was born. With the post-war crop of wrestlers, whole new dimensions of excitement and action were introduced. These, then, are the men who brought wrestling into the television age—and this chapter tells you all about them.

Antonino Rocca

Wrestlers are given to exaggerations: Everything is "the best," "the biggest," or "the worst." But no one ever engaged in exaggerations like Antonino Rocco, the self-described "greatest wrestler in the world." Take the time he told an interviewer, with a straight face, that he had once wrestled 17 Chavante Indians, giving each a broken arm with his fearsome wristlock. Any ethnologist could tell you that no more than one or two of these natives of the Amazonian rainforest have ever been close enough to civilization to see a Coca-Cola bottle. But this was Rocca's story—and he stuck to it.

Beginnings: Far from Amazonia

What few facts can be pieced together about Rocca indicate that he was born in Treviso, Italy, sometime around 1923, was christened Antonino Biasetton, and emigrated with his parents to Buenos Aires in 1938 at age 15. What happened between then and 1947 we can only guess at, but to hear Rocca tell it, he was, by turns, a track star, a fencing great, a master rugby player—you name it, he claimed to have done it. In 1947, while wrestling in Buenos Aires, he was spotted by a tourist named Nick Elitch—himself an ex-wrestler—who knew that he had stumbled onto something potentially big. Elitch called Dr. Karl Sarpolis, a wrestling promoter in Texas, and described Rocca's barefooted antics—leaps, flying moves, drop-kicks. After listening to 10 minutes of ravings, Sarpolis told Elitch to put Rocca on a plane, pronto.

Wrestle Mania

The flying drop-kick, in which a wrestler leaps up and kicks his opponent in the face or chest before falling back down to the canvas, has been around since the 1930s, when it was introduced by Gus Sonnenberg. Antonino Rocca repopularized the move in the 1950s. But both had to play second fiddle to Marvin Mercer. He could deliver what he called his "Atomic Dropkick" and land back on his feet!

Rocco planted his size-13 feet on American soil in June 1947 with a thump that would be heard around the wrestling world. For the next 13-plus years, he would remake the sport.

Rocca's Aerial Athleticism

All of Rocca's moves were soon on display: his midair splits, his leaps from the top rope onto the shoulders of his opponents (he'd ride them around like a jockey at the local race track), and his Argentine back-breaker. He actually made two debuts. The first was in Houston, against Lord Blears. The second came after he listened to the blandishments of New York promoter Toots Mondt, who brought him to Brooklyn's Ridgewood Grove in 1948 to face Benito Gardini.

An up-in-the-air Rocca brought a whole new dimension to wrestling.

(Source: Norman Kietzer)

Gardini recalled the experience this way:

"When he started flying at me out of nowhere, I was shocked. First thing I knew, he's running toward me—then he disappears and wham! I got those big bare feet in my face. Then, when I get up, he gets me in the chest, wham! It's like running into a battering ram. He jumps onto the ring post. I think he's running away, but no, he comes sailing toward me like a big bird and the next thing I know, I'm carrying him around the ring on my shoulders, with his legs locked around my head so I can hardly breathe."

Bert's Corner

The 247-pound and well-proportioned Rocca wowed the crowds with his pre-bout antics, sometimes going into the ring, dropping to the mat, and doing 200 to 300 push-ups before the bout started.

Rocca's gravity-defying acrobatics and his challenge that no human could get out of his "Argentine Back-Breaker" stirred the imagination of wrestling fans everywhere and brought them out in record numbers, revitalizing the once-moribund New York wrestling scene—especially energizing the city's large Latino population.

Captain Lou's Corner

Another acrobatic star of the 1950s was Ricki Starr, who had studied ballet and put his training to use in the wrestling ring. Dancing around on ballet slippers, he delivered shots with Bolshoi Ballet moves. His combination of skills in both dance and wrestling made him a very colorful attraction.

Killer Kowalski crashes down on opponent Ed Carpentier.

(Source: Norman Kietzer)

Killer Kowalski

If only one legend represents pro wrestling, it could be that of Wldadek "Killer" Kowalski. No wrestler has ever been more intimidating than Killer. He was feared, reviled, and despised. Adjectives used to describe him include vicious, tough, mean, ruthless, rough, and destructive.

Tall and lean compared to the huge wrestlers of his day, the homicidal-looking Kowalski more than made up for his lack of wrestling heft by using whatever methods were at hand—or foot—to win, regardless of the rules. His arsenal included biting, kicking, gouging, and clawing—in short, anything it took to disable an opponent. His most famous maneuver was his notorious "throat stomp," delivered by landing on an opponent's Adam's apple (one foot landed on the throat, the other simultaneously thumped onto the floor with equal force to heighten the effect but lessen the impact).

Even considering the special effects, the impact of the stomp was horrific. Ask Verne Gagne, who explained what it felt like: "I was on the floor, and he just jumped up in the air and landed feet-first on my windpipe." Gagne tried to explain to author Joe Jares in a strained voice, "It knocked the breath out of me. It's a pretty rough hold if his aim isn't just right." And one night it wasn't—which is where the legend of Killer Kowalski began. That was the night in Montreal, in 1954, when the Killer ripped off Yukon Eric's ear in a bout at the Forum.

Kowalski's Cauliflower Incident

Yukon Eric's ear wasn't just any ear—it was a cauliflower ear so large and calcified by the many blows that it had received that it was barely attached to Eric's head, looking like it could use a ton of hollandaise. It was an inviting target for Kowalski as he mounted the top rope and leaped onto his prostrate opponent in his famous throat stomp. This time, however, he missed his landing, his heel grazed Eric's head, and he pinned the ear to the mat. Eric tried to twist free, but by twisting he merely severed his calcified ear in the process.

Kowalski fought his way back to the dressing room through a hostile crowd, their chorus of boos blending with the wail of an ambulance siren outside. When he returned to the Forum the next week, a record crowd of 14,657 incensed fans greeted him with jeers, chanting "*Le Killer.*"

Body Slam

Kowalski visited Yukon Eric in the hospital the day after the accident and the press followed. Eric's head was heavily bandaged so that his head looked like a big egg and when Kowalski first saw him they both laughed. The press made Kowalski's laugh out to be sadistic and their ensuing stories enhanced his "killer" image.

The Toughest Man of All

Killer's name soon became legendary, and he was in demand throughout the world. Everyone wanted to see the man who, decked out in his unique purple tights, with lightning bolts on both sides, and his glittering gold boots, had severed a man's ear from his head. In life outside the wrestling ring, Killer Kowalski was a winner, too. He was a soft man who read, painted, took photographs, and went on religious retreats. Outside, he could be a perfect gentleman. Inside the ring, Killer Kowalski was anything but.

In Your Face

Of Yukon Eric's ill-fated ear, Kowalski later said: "It was so cauliflowered it was going to come off sooner or later anyway!"

Verne Gagne

Just when it seemed that all wrestling's technicians had disappeared entirely, there came Verne Gagne. Gagne knew the intricacies of wrestling, having been the four-time Big Ten wrestling champion, twice the NCAA champion, and a member of the 1948 Olympic squad. Added to this were his impressive credentials as a football player at the University of Minnesota, where he starred as a halfback and played in the 1949 College All-Star game. All together, you had the makings of a helluva athlete—and wrestler.

From College to the Canvas Mat

Gagne considered a career in pro football first, saying that the world of professional wrestling was "too rough and show-offish" for him: "I was the typical college type then … you know, fast and purely scientific. All the extra frills and gaudiness of pro wrestling gave me the wrong impression at first." But he turned his back on a promising career in football to become a pro wrestler. Some didn't think he'd make it at first. One was Minneapolis promoter Tony Stecher, brother of the great Joe Stecher. Stecher wasn't impressed, thinking that the-then 195-pound Gagne was "too light for a good wrestler." Still, he put Gagne in against Abe Kashey in April 1949 in his pro wrestling debut.

Verne Gagne with an arm bar hold on Nick Bockwinkel.

(Source: Norman Kietzer)

Gagne won the match but failed to win over Stecher, who still harbored doubts about the ability of this great college wrestler to make it in the professional ranks. So Gagne headed out for Texas, where he struck proverbial oil, selling out every arena in the area. The combination of good wrestling and showmanship made him a crowd favorite—and a winning one, at that. He took the NWA junior heavyweight title just a year and a half after his debut against Kashey. Then Gagne moved up to the heavyweight ranks; by the end of 1951, he was wrestling the top names in the field, including the legendary Lou Thesz.

The Quest for the Title

Gagne eventually won the U.S. heavyweight title in September 1953 and kept it for 31 months, until he was toppled by Wilbur Snyder in April 1956. He won the title a second time, in April 1958, beating Dick the Bruiser in Chicago. But it was the world title that Gagne thirsted for. This was the title that Lou Thesz seemed to be constantly winning and losing in alternate bouts.

In 1959, Gagne finally beat Edouard Carpentier, who had beaten Thesz to gain the NWA title. However, several members of the NWA chose to ignore Carpentier's—and, therefore, Gagne's—claim to the title, instead continuing to recognize Thesz. Fed up, Gagne tucked his title belt under his arm and walked, forming the American Wrestling Alliance (AWA) in 1960. The AWA's territory extended from Indianapolis on the east through Chicago, Milwaukee, and Minneapolis, all the way to Omaha and Denver in the west. For the next two decades, the American Wrestling Alliance rode on Verne Gagne's broad back and on the title belt he held.

Bert's Corner

Today's wrestlers who employ the scientific wrestling style include Chris Benoit, Dean Malenko, and Kurt Angle—all of whom have amateur wrestling experience.

Fighting Words

Wrestlers who use a scientific style are called **mat wrestlers** because they spend so much time down on the mat rather than on their feet.

By the time he retired in the early 1980s, Gagne had built a legacy. He also had brought in a group of new wrestlers and taught them the ropes, including Bob Backlund, Ric Flair, Hulk Hogan, Jesse Ventura, Shawn Michaels, Ken Patera, and Ricky Steamboat, among countless others—many of whom became the biggest wrestling stars of the 1990s.

"The Living Legend"—Bruno Sammartino

It has long been something of a bar argument over who was the "greatest" in wrestling history. Some graybeards will inevitably bring up the names of Gotch or Hackenschmidt, while others will pull out yellowing newspaper clippings to invoke the names of Strangler Lewis, Jim Londos, or Lou Thesz. But for the wrestling fan of the 1960s, there is only one name: Bruno Sammartino—called by promoter Vince McMahon Sr., "The greatest athlete as well as the greatest wrestler of all time."

Bruno Sammartino takes down Stan Stasiak.

(Source: Norman Kietzer)

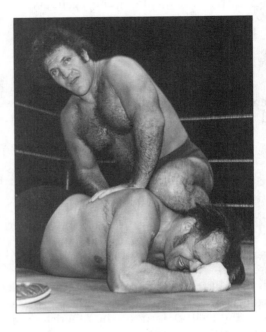

Born and raised in the Abruzzi and Molise regions of Northern Italy, up in the Apennine mountains, young Bruno and his family endured the hardships of World War II and the Nazi occupation of the area. His father had gone to America before the war; communication was nonexistent, other members of the family were killed, and the rest subsisted on whatever they could find, foraging for grass under deep snows and once living off the carcass of a dead horse for two months.

Coming to America

After the war, Bruno's father was finally able to make contact with the family back in Italy. He had settled in Pittsburgh, and wrote, "You're coming to America, the land of opportunity." Bruno, then age 13, packed up and headed for America with the rest of his family. Shortly after his arrival, the 67-pound youngster was introduced to weight training. By the time he was 18, he weighed 257 pounds, could bench-press 565 pounds 38 times consecutively, and had won the title of Mr. Pennsylvania.

While working out, Sammartino caught the eye of Vince McMahon Sr. McMahon was then planning to establish his own wrestling circuit, independent of the then-dominant NWA. He decided that Bruno would be the perfect man to head the new organization's assault on both the NWA and the East Coast establishment.

Moving on up with the McMahon Machine

By 1963, Bruno was headlining in New York and the fans were celebrating his strength and brawling. Bruno, The Tower of Power, rewarded their support with win after win. Then McMahon decided to make his move on the NWA. When Lou Thesz beat NWA World Champion Buddy Rogers in one fall in January 1963, McMahon broke away from the NWA to form the WWWF, continuing to recognize Rogers as the champion. But Rogers's title was only temporary. On May 17 of that year, Sammartino pinned an injured Rogers in less than a minute in a bout at Madison Square Garden.

Bruno's reign as champion lasted eight long years. He defended the title against Gene Kiniski, Killer Kowalski, Lou Thesz, Ray Stevens, John Tolas, Johnny Valentine, Freddie Blassie, Dr. Bill Miller, Professor Tanaka, and Waldo von Erich, among others. Finally, on January 18, 1971, Bruno lost his title to Ivan Koloff—The Russian Bear—in a controversial match and afterward went into semiretirement. After 10 months out of the ring, he was back, and he retook the title from Stan Stasiak by the end of the year.

Honor and Integrity: The Sammartino Hallmark

Captain Lou's Corner

The first time I laid eyes on Bruno, at a gym right off Eighth Avenue in New York where wrestlers went, I was impressed by his brute strength as he lifted weights. I was also impressed by his size, his brawny arms, his massive chest, and his shoulders, which always looked like you could use them to serve a sit-down dinner for six. The source of his then 6-foot, 270-pound body was his exercise regimen, his diet, and his refusal to take any sort of drugs—especially steroids.

Bert's Corner

Bruno lost the crown a second time in a controversial bout with Superstar Billy Graham at Baltimore's Civic Center in 1977.

During his second go-round as champion, Bruno suffered a serious injury—a broken neck—in a title bout against Big Stan Hansen. Many feared that Bruno was permanently injured, but the man who had always gone from strength to strength overcame his injury. In a rematch against Hanson—a wild, brawl-filled bout at Shea

Stadium—he evened the score by thoroughly thrashing the man that, he believed, had intentionally injured him.

Gorilla Monsoon

Gino Marella was born on June 5, 1939, in Rochester, New York. By the time he wrestled in high school, he stood 6 feet, 7 inches tall and weighed 401 pounds. With that kind of size, it seemed only natural that he would not only become a wrestler, but also that he'd take on the guise of a vicious villain. Wild Red Berry managed Marella, by this time renamed Gorilla Monsoon, and the 1960s saw him rise to the top of the WWWF Tag-Team championship with Killer Kowalski. By the early 1970s, he had become a fan favorite.

Wrestle Mania

Everybody's favorite, Gorilla Monsoon's moment came in 1976 when he had his famous encounter with Muhammad Ali. Ali was at ringside jawing at Monsoon, and Monsoon invited him to come on up into the ring to give wrestling a try. Ali did! Monsoon circled Ali for a few moments and then put the boxing champ into his trademark airplane spin. Ali, perhaps concerned about avoiding injury before his scheduled bout with Antonio Inoki that was just weeks away, scampered away at the first opportunity.

Gorilla Monsoon mauls El Mongol.

After Monsoon retired from active wrestling, he stayed on with the WWF as an announcer. He paired up with former manager Bobby Heenan to become one of wrestling's great TV announcing teams. He is known for his long-winded wordiness, particularly when describing the body parts of the wrestlers in the ring. Monsoon served as WWF president during the late 1990s and sadly passed away after a long bout with heart disease in 1999.

The Least You Need to Know

➤ Gorgeous George revolutionized wrestling in the modern era, but other performers soon followed his lead and helped carry wrestling into the TV age.

➤ Antonino Rocca's spectacular leaps in the ring added an airborne element to wrestling's magic.

➤ Killer Kowalski brought new meaning to the term "villain" when he tore off Yukon Eric's cauliflower ear.

➤ Verne Gagne was a pure athlete, but his showmanship was second to none.

➤ Bruno Sammartino returned class, style, and substance to pro wrestling.

Chapter 8

Sexy, Serious, and Supreme in Their Roles

In This Chapter

➤ A history of women in wrestling

➤ Taking on all male challengers and then wrestling other women

➤ The Fabulous Moolah reigns supreme

➤ Managers and valets: Women's new role in wrestling

I once uttered the immortal words on the *David Letterman Show*, "Women are good only for having babies and cleaning house." Little did I realize at the time that I was in a spot you wouldn't give a leopard. Thousands of angry women called the CBS network switchboard to protest. And hundreds more picketed the studio demanding that I take back my words. And I won't even *begin* to tell you how mad my wife, Geri, was.

While I can't promise that I learned my lesson, I will say this: Women wrestlers have been in the sport for a long time now. They helped keep it alive during the lean years of the Depression, and without them today, it would be a lot uglier to watch. In this chapter, you learn about the pulchritudinous pro women wrestlers.

Girls Just Want to Have Fun

Women have been a part of wrestling since "back in the Greek era of super sports," according to the February 1953 issue of *Ring* magazine. Of course, that was just a little bit before my time.

Captain Lou's Corner

Women were always a part of the old carney At Shows that traveled the landscape in the early twentieth century. And some, like Cora Livingstone, also wrestled on the vaudeville circuit. Most of the time, these early women of the ring wrestled against men who challenged them from the audience.

Wrestle Mania

Vince McMahon Sr. once said, "Most girls will tell you they'll keep going as long as the body holds out, but as soon as they meet the right fella, they get out." Lots of the time, however, Mr. Right is a fellow wrestler—marriages made in center ring include Penny Banner and Johnny Weaver, Joyce Fowler and George Becker, and June Byers and Sammy Menacker. More recently Randy Savage and Elizabeth, Goldust and Marlena, Tammy Lynn Sytch and Chris Candido, Diamond Dallas Page and Kimberly, and Marc Mero and Sable have been partners both in the ring and out.

Bertha Rapp

The first woman who challenged males was Bertha Rapp, a teacher of calisthenics at a Cincinnati school. She made history, of sorts, by challenging her fellow passengers aboard the White Star liner Adriatic in 1911.

Although she was not small in size, Ms. Rapp—at 5 feet, 9 inches and 150 pounds—was no Big Bertha either. Her two male challengers weighed in at 149 and 185 pounds, respectively (if not respectfully). The first one she pinned in eight minutes. The second she battled to a 30-minute draw, proving that the so-called weaker sex could more than hold its own in a wrestling bout.

Mildred Burke

Jump ahead two decades, to the mid-1930s and Mildred Burke, the first great woman wrestler. She started in much the same way as Bertha: by challenging any and all males to wrestle her. After pinning 199 out of 200 men, Burke (and her manager, Billy Wolfe) sought to display her talents against other women. Woman versus woman wrestling actually sold tickets, surprising promoters. Soon women wrestlers were making up to $100 a match, and promoters were putting out calls for any and all to wrestle.

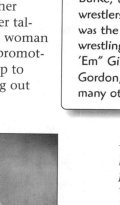

Captain Lou's Corner

With the popularity of Mildred Burke, the ranks of women wrestlers soon began to fill. This was the era of such female wrestling greats as Gladys "Kill 'Em" Gillam, Rose Evans, Wilma Gordon, Mae Weston, and many, many others.

Mildred Burke—the first female pro wrestler—in a publicity pose. This is where today's headbangers got the idea for their outfits.

(Source: Norman Kietzer)

Body Slam

Hatpin Mary, the famous New York wrestling fan of the 1940s, thought that women wrestlers had clear superiority over their male counterparts: "They're as dirty as the men, and they never stall. They pull hair, bite, kick, punch, and squeeze each other's heads between the ropes. And when one of them gets heaved out of the ring, she don't waste time crying for sympathy like some of them men pleaders do. No sir, she climbs right back in there, punching and clawing."

Gladys "Kill 'Em" Gillam was probably the most colorful of them all. She was, by turns, a wrestler, a circus lion tamer, and an alligator wrestler. Called a hellcat in the wrestling ring and a daredevil in the circus ring, Gladys had a habit of landing on her head. She did it so often that Mildred Burke remembers, "Her head was just mushy back there—you could just push in on it."

In one bout, Burke had sent Gillam through the ropes and onto the concrete floor, head first. "My God, I've killed her!" thought Burke. But Gladys got right back up and charged into the ring, swinging.

The Opposition Gets Organized

Although some believed that putting women in the ring was a crime against nature, several women still traded in their rolling pins for mat pins. Those wonderwomen who filled the ranks of women's wrestling to overflowing included June Byers, who succeeded Mildred Burke as women's champion; Nell Stewart; Elvira Snodgrass; Mars Bennett; Cot Cotson; Lilly Bitter; and one who would dominate women's wrestling for the next three decades, Fabulous Moolah.

The Fabulous Career of Fabulous Moolah

Fabulous Moolah started life as Lillian Ellison, the 12th of 13 children—and the only girl in the carload. As a young girl of 9, she fell in love with the sport of professional wrestling after watching a match in her native Columbia, South Carolina. From that time on, wrestling was her calling.

Ellison began her professional career in 1949 as a wrestler for Mildred Burke's manager and husband, Billy Wolfe. In her first bout, she pinned a wrestler named Cecilia Blevens in 15 minutes flat. Looking for bigger and better conquests, she came east to seek out wrestling promoter Jack Pfefer. "Vhy do you vant to wrestle?" he asked her. "For the moolah," she replied with all the straightforwardness of youth. And so, Moolah she became.

Before her wrestling career truly took off, she served as Slave Girl Moolah, valeting first for Buddy Rogers and later for the Elephant Boy, a bushy-haired warrior who posed as an Indian *mahatma* of tremendous wealth. But Lillian needed action, so in 1954, Slave Girl Moolah became the Fabulous Moolah. Within two years she had taken the title Women's Champion, defeating 13 other women in a Baltimore tournament—among whose number was the then-reigning champion, June Byers. Moolah remained champion, off and on, for the next 40 years.

Bert's Corner

For the longest time, the Fabulous Moolah dominated women's wrestling, both as its champion and as its foremost villain. Amazingly, she remains active today as a performer. Along with her fellow veteran of the ring, Mae Young, the Fabulous Moolah still appears each week on WWF TV programs.

The Fabulous Moolah.

(Source: Norman Kietzer)

A Temporary Lapse—Women's Wrestling Fades in the 1970s

The Fabulous Moolah's success in the ring inspired others to try their hands at wrestling. Some of the comely newcomers included Penny Banner, Maria Laverne, and Viviane Vachone. But sometime during the 30 years that Moolah ruled the women's roost, the bloom came off the women's wrestling rose. Once a fan favorite, women's participation in the sport became first an afterthought, then a nonthought.

Madame Manager

It wasn't that women had left wrestling shows; it was just that their roles were changing. Fewer women were shown as combatants and more became lady managers—sometimes called valets (actually more like girlfriends) to the male wrestlers. The valets, always attractive, performed the function of a manager outside the ring, shouting encouragement and distracting the referee. It wasn't a new idea—Gorgeous George had traded in his male valet for a shapely beauty 25 years before.

Miss Elizabeth: First Lady of Professional Wrestling

The first female valet to reach superstar status was Miss Elizabeth, who became a key figure in many of the early *WrestleMania* shows. At the time, she was the real-life wife of Macho Man Randy Savage, but as a valet, she alternated between managing Savage and his sometimes-friend/sometimes-enemy Hulk Hogan. (Elizabeth and Randy were "married" in Madison Square Garden at a *SummerSlam* pay-per-view, but it was just an act because the two were already wed. Now legitimately divorced from Savage, Elizabeth works for WCW, where she valets for Lex Luger.)

Sensational Sherri

Although no woman in wrestling was more popular than Miss Elizabeth during the early 1990s, Liz did have her limitations. If trouble broke out, she was too ladylike to throw a punch. Sherri Martel didn't have that problem. Sherri, who became Savage's valet after he turned evil—and after Liz switched to the Hulkster—had been a former women's wrestling champ and knew how to handle herself in and around the ring. During one key portion of a show, Sherri proved her worth. Liz was to hit Sherri at a climactic moment. Trouble was, Liz slaps like a, well, like a girl. So, when Sherri received the slap, she *sold* it for all it was worth, flying backward across the ring, over the top rope and to the floor below. "What a right hand!" Vince McMahon screamed into the microphone.

Sunny: First of the Down-Loadables

In the late 1990s, the biggest star among the wrestling valets was the beautiful blonde Tammy Lynn Sytch, better known at the time as Sunny. For several months, Sunny was wrestling's golden girl—the most downloaded girl on the Internet, which I'm told means she was pretty doggone popular.

Tammy Lynn is the real-life wife of wrestler Chris Candito. The couple are currently working in WCW after several years in Philadelphia working for Paul Heyman's Extreme Championship Wrestling.

Fighting Words

To **sell** a move means to make your opponents' offense look legitimate by reacting to his blows. Even if the punch missed by six inches, you sell it by doing a backward flip and then holding your jaw.

Sable's Turn

Just as Sunny's star was shining at its brightest, in 1997, another blonde bombshell made her debut in the World Wrestling Federation. Her name was Sable, and she first appeared as the valet of "Mean" Marc Mero. Sable, in real life, was Mero's wife, Rena. It wasn't long before the ultra-buxom blonde surpassed her hubby in star power. She replaced Sunny as the woman most downloaded on the Internet. In July of 1998 Sable won a WWF bikini contest by appearing in an imaginative bathing suit, the top of which was comprised only of two painted black hands in strategic spots. Only after establishing Sable as a superstar, did she actually begin to wrestle. And even then, because she was not a trained wrestler, she only wrestled on big shows in tightly choreographed matches.

A match between champion Jacqueline and challenger Sable for the World Wrestling Federation's women's title was held during the *Survivor Series: Deadly Game* pay-per-view on November 15, 1998 in St. Louis. Special referee for this match was Shane McMahon. Sable delivered a powerbomb to Jackie to get the pin and win the championship. "I would like to take this time to thank all my fans that have supported me throughout my career at the WWF," Sable said. "This is the highlight so far! I will be taking the women's belt all over the world, promoting our sport and defending it when I have to."

Sable's fame peaked with the appearance on the newsstands of the April 1999 issue of Playboy, which featured her on the cover and in a revealing pictorial inside. But Sable did not last much longer in the WWF. She was getting acting jobs because of her fame and decided to switch to show business. She was prohibited from using the name Sable—her WWF name—after she left the organization. Although the acting roles did not pour in as she had hoped, Rena Mero, now working under her real name, still makes occasional appearances on talk shows.

Women's Wrestling Today

During the past few years, women's wrestling has become more about the women than the wrestling. With the exception of the female phenomenon known as Chyna—who will be dealt with extensively later in the book. There is less emphasis today on technical maneuvers than on the loser ending up in her underwear. This is demonstrated most blatantly through the stipulation matches that dominate women's wrestling today. The most often used stipulation is the Evening Gown match. The rules for an Evening Gown match read: Two women face off against each other in evening gowns instead of normal wrestling tights; the first to rip the gown off her opponent wins the match.

That is not to say that there are no talented women wrestlers today. The best of the women's division now wrestle with the men. Chyna usually acts as a valet, first with Triple H and currently with Eddie Guerrero, but she is always involved in the action. At *WrestleMania 2000,* she was involved in a six-man (or is that six-person?) tag-team match between the Radicals and her team, Too Cool. Lita, Essa Rios' valet, usually gets involved by pulling *lucha libre* moves on Rios' opponents. Madusa, in WCW, had a feud with Oklahoma—a parody of the WWF's Jim Ross by Ed Ferrara—and most recently faced off briefly against Diamond Dallas Page after defeating Kimberly. With the exception of the few female stars, the women's division in wrestling has become virtually nonexistent. The WWF Women's champion is currently Stephanie McMahon-Helmsley, who has never *really* wrestled a match in her life, and WCW's Women's division has been dissolved.

The women of today's pro wrestling are magnificent and numerous: Kimberly, Trish Stratus, Stephanie McMahon, Terri Runnels, Torrie Wilson, and so on. Many of them wrestle if the story line calls for it. They must be willing to take a bump, just like anyone else on the wrestling show. But the reason they are there is never because they're tough. It is their attachment, and sometimes fickle loyalty, to the male wrestler that gives them their importance. This is an important distinction, even down to a subconscious level, when it comes to wrestling's young, and predominantly male, audience.

And oh, how they can act up! Many have the temper of a belligerent hornet, and they've been known to use that temper to get what they want. It's not unheard of for one of them to grab the referee and try to intimidate him—or go the other route and try distracting him with their feminine wiles.

Miss Hancock

One of the most beautiful valets working today—and certainly the one with the longest legs—is Miss Hancock, who first appeared around the ring at WCW matches in February 2000. A gorgeous blonde in a short minidress, a business hairdo, and a clipboard, she would appear conspicuously when a wrestler she found attractive was in the ring. After scouting all the hunks of WCW, Miss Hancock decided whom she wanted to represent: Los Fabulosos, comprised of *luchadors* El Dandy and Silver King, who were hardly hunks. It turned out that Miss Hancock liked "fixer-uppers."

Miss Hancock is a long-legged valet in WCW.

Bert's Corner

There is an argument for using women announcers when women are wrestling in the ring. On a recent WWF broadcast, Luna was wrestling with Jacqueline when announcers Michael Cole and Jerry "The King" Lawler had the following exchange:

Cole: "Luna hit Jacqueline right in the Adam's apple!"

Lawler: "I don't think she has an Adam's apple."

Cole: "It was to the sternum!"

Lawler: "Uh, I don't think she has a sternum either."

Mae Young

Wrestling is generally a sport for young men, most of whom are athletes. The intense physical nature of the sport-entertainment takes its toll on even the most well-conditioned athlete, much less on a near-80-year-old woman. But Mae Young is possibly the toughest elderly woman on the face of the planet. Since entering the WWF in 1999 as a sidekick for the Fabulous Moolah, Mae Young has developed a sort of cult following of her own. She has put her body on the line, and out in the open, every night that she has appeared on a WWF broadcast. For a 78-year-old woman, Mae has performed some amazing stunts. One of the most incredible of these involved Buh Buh Ray Dudley and his penchant for power-bombing women through tables. Buh Buh Ray had decided that Mae was to be his next victim and set out to put her through a table. Mae was in a wheelchair and could not get away when he finally got his hands on her, and he power-bombed her through a table set up on the arena floor near the entrance ramp—a 10-foot drop.

In Your Face

Buh Buh Ray Dudley, backstage, did not want to slam 78-year-old Mae Young through a table. He asked her if she was sure she wanted to do it. "Honey, I not only want to be put through the table, I want to be put through the table hard."

Lately, Mae and Moolah's relationship has become strained. Although they were once best friends, Moolah has grown jealous of Mae's growing popularity. With her notoriety surrounding the Miss Royal Rumble 2000 contest and her willingness to put her body on the line, Mae "She Stay Forever" Young has grown into a WWF Superstar.

Terri Runnels

The lovely Terry Runnels has possessed a number of personae during her creative stint in wrestling. She started her career as a computer-toting, glasses-wearing egghead and valet for Michael Wallstreet (Mike Rotundo) in WCW. She became the real-life wife of Dustin Rhodes, and together they have a daughter named Dakota. In the WWF, Terri debuted as Marlena, the cigar-smoking sexually ambiguous "Director" for the flamboyant Goldust, played by her real-life husband. But none of those incarnations was as evil as her current incarnation as "Devil Woman" Terri Runnels. Though diminutive and va-va-voom, she is one of the most hated women anywhere on TV. Wagging her fingers over her head, emulating horns, and inevitably wearing an outfit that's barely legal, Terri recently ruined several consecutive matches for the tag team of Edge and Christian, the poor saps who found themselves in her crosshairs. Finally, they decided that they'd had enough and power-slammed her in the center of the ring. Then they left her there—and no one felt sorry for her.

The Least You Need to Know

➤ Women have been part of professional wrestling almost as long as men, first appearing in the carnival shows.

➤ The first woman wrestler was Mildred Burke, who pioneered women's wrestling in the mid-1930s by taking on any male who dared challenge her.

➤ Women wrestling women, which was introduced as a novelty in the 1930s to fill empty houses, became a standard part of wrestling during the 1940s and 1950s.

➤ By the 1950s, women's role in wrestling had changed, and the once-popular women's circuit had slowly begun to disappear.

➤ Today's pro wrestling features women in the ring, but now they participate mostly as valets and managers.

Chapter 9

Wacky '70s and '80s

In This Chapter

➤ Andre the Giant was the most extraordinary wrestler of the era—and maybe of all time

➤ If Bruiser Brody had lived, he would probably still be one of wrestling's biggest stars

➤ The Von Erichs were wrestling's number-one family until tragedy took its toll

➤ Blue collar Americans chasing a dream

Although pro wrestling struggled as a TV sport during the 1970s and early 1980s, it was more popular than ever during this era as an arena sport. There were more shows with greater attendance than during any other era, including today. The stars of that era are as beloved as any who ever performed. And all too many of them died young and tragically. The top star of the time was the most extraordinary wrestler ever to step over the top rope into the squared circle: Andre the Giant.

Andre the Giant: The Eighth Wonder of the World

It's no wonder that Andre the Giant was called "The Eighth Wonder of the World." At 500-plus pounds, he was so big that you could have printed "Goodyear" on his back and floated him over arenas. During his heyday, he was one of the most recognized people in the world. One thing was for sure: You couldn't lose him in a crowd.

The man known as Andre the Giant was born Rene Rousimoff on a farm in Grenoble, France. His father, Boris Rousimoff, was 6-foot-2, his mother was of normal size, and so were his brothers and sisters. Andre once told me that he'd gotten his height from a grandfather who stood more than 7 feet. But who knows if that was true.

Andre was 6-foot-7 by the time he graduated from high school. It's said French-Canadian wrestler Edouard Carpentier discovered Andre in France, where he was wrestling as Monster Eiffel Tower, and brought him over to North America, where he wrestled for a time as Jean Ferre. By this time he was billed as being 7-foot-4 and 400 pounds. His first North American matches were for Grand Prix Promotions, a Canadian outfit, and it was while working for this company that Andre was first known as "The Eighth Wonder of the World," a line taken from the movie *King Kong*. This was in the early 1970s, and the biggest villains at the time were Don Leo Jonathan and Killer Kowalski. But Andre made these monsters look like Munchkins, so small were they in comparison. And he beat them both easily. Before he made his debut in the United States, the Giant had already drawn more than 20,000 paying customers in Montreal.

Captain Lou's Corner

Sadly, Andre knew that he wasn't going to live to be old, and he lived each day as if it were his last. He could be cranky in and out of the ring when he wasn't feeling well, and he could drink a case of beer before you could finish pouring your first.

Then, in 1972, Vince McMahon Sr. signed him. He changed the wrestler's name forever to Andre the Giant and put him in the ring in Madison Square Garden against Buddy Wolfe, whom Andre destroyed with a mere flick of his wrist. (Well, not quite, but he sure didn't break a sweat.) Those who remember Andre only during his last years would be surprised at how athletic he was in his youth. And because he was notoriously moody, the other wrestlers respected him greatly. He was not the sort of fellow that you got angry.

Andre was a babyface during his prime. He didn't turn evil in wrestling's story lines until the 1980s, when he was already past his prime and his condition had taken its toll. You see, Andre was really a giant. He suffered from a disease called acromegaly. His body secreted too much human growth hormone—ironically, the same drug that some wrestlers foolishly pump into their bodies to make their muscles grow freakishly large. Andre never stopped growing, and eventually his own size became too much for his heart.

Andre's fame stretched from the wrestling ring to the silver screen. His 1987 role in Rob Reiner's fantasy film *The Princess Bride* not only delighted children of all ages but also earned him critical acclaim.

Bert's Corner

Andre loved his beer, and it has been said that one night, when Andre had had a bit too much to drink, he decided to take a snooze right in the middle of the hotel lobby where he was staying. The management tried everything to move him, but he couldn't be budged. So they did the next best thing. They threw the piano cover over him and put up a sign that read: "Please walk around."

Andre the Giant versus Black Jack Mulligan.

(Source: Norman Kietzer)

Body Slam

Bruiser Brody made brawls appear so spontaneous that even the most jaded fans couldn't believe he was following a script.

Andre was well past his peak athletically by the time he had his famous *WrestleMania* match versus Hulk Hogan in front of more than 90,000 fans in the Pontiac Silverdome. He had grown to 525 pounds, and he spent as much time as he could holding onto the ropes, trying to take some of he pressure off of his aching knees. But he still had a way of putting a crowd in awe. He had a charisma, almost a magic about him, that transcended his size. Andre died on January 27, 1993, from a heart attack. He was in France at the time, having two weeks earlier attended his dad's funeral.

Bruiser Brody: Wild Life, Mysterious Death

Bruiser Brody, a controversial wrestler throughout his career, ended his life in a death, by stabbing at the age of 42, that was just as controversial. Born Frank Donald Goodish on July 14, 1946, in Albuquerque, New Mexico, Brody joined the pro wrestling world in 1973. A tremendously popular, hardcore brawler, the Bruiser stood 6 feet, 4 inches and weighed 284 pounds.

Bruiser Brody gives Gino Hernandez a headache.

(Source: Norman Kietzer)

Bruiser was willing to give the crowds what they wanted in the blood and gore line—he bled so much so that by the end of his career, his forehead was so scarred that it looked like tripe. For 16 years, Brody wrestled—first as one of the WWWF's monsters, where he tried and failed to take the title from Bruno Sammartino; and then in World Class, where in the late 1970s, he feuded with Fritz Von Erich. A decade later, he finished as a tag-team partner for Fritz's son, Kerry.

The Bruiser's running feuds against the Spoiler, Ox Baker, and Dick the Bruiser were legendary. He was hugely popular with the fans and would probably still be wrestling today had he not had a run-in with a local promoter and wrestler by the name of Jose Gonzalez in Bayamon, Puerto Rico. In circumstances that remain unclear, Gonzalez fatally stabbed Brody but claimed that the injury was inflicted in self-defense. Gonzales was tried for murder and was acquitted. Showing perhaps the worst taste in the history of a sport never known for tastefulness, Gonzales parlayed his notoriety and, in the process, became his promotion's number-one heel.

Ric "Nature Boy" Flair: Simply the Greatest Ever

Ric Flair was born in Minnesota on February 25, 1949. A big man (6 feet, 1 inch, and 245 pounds), it's not surprising that he played offensive guard on the football team at his college, the University of Minnesota. But after he joined the pro wrestling fold, it was clear that he belonged.

Flair is called "The Nature Boy," a nickname originally belonging to 1950s wrestler Buddy Rogers—he even entered the ring with the same strut that the original Nature Boy had perfected. With a definite flair for the ladies, Flair is known to be cocky and arrogant—but then, he's a 13-time NWA/WCW world champion and a 2-time WWF champ, so he's got something to be cocky about. He has held a world title every year from 1981 to 1997. His matches rank among the best ever, and most experts agree that, in terms of combined charisma and wrestling skill, Flair is one of the best wrestler/performers ever. The most famous practitioner ever of the *figure-four leglock*, Flair remains active in WCW to this day as a tag-team partner of Lex Luger.

Captain Lou's Corner

Among his many contributions to modern pro wrestling, Flair formed one of the very first of the "outlaw" groups that have become so popular. His group was The Four Horsemen, with Arn Anderson, Ole Anderson, Tully Blanchard, and Flair, managed by J. J. Dillon. After a popular run, the group broke up in 1997—although various incarnations came and went until 1999.

Fighting Words

The **figure-four leglock** is called that because when you are administering it, your legs form the numeral 4.

Ric Flair in one of his many battles with the legendary Dusty Rhodes.

(Source: Norman Kietzer)

Bert's Corner

Hogan took a brief detour from wrestling to appear in the third installment of the *Rocky* films, playing a wrestler named Thunderlips, a role that made him a household name. He's since starred in more than a dozen films.

Hulk Hogan: Taking Wrestling into the Mainstream

Probably the best-known figure to ever wrestle, the 6-foot-8-inch, 275-pound Hulkster was born Terry Bollea on August 11, 1953, in Venice Beach, California. Hogan was a bass player in a rock band and a yo-dude surfer when he switched from tubes to rings in 1978 under the management of Jimmy Hart. In 1979 Hulk moved to the WWF as a heel with Freddie Blassie for his manager. He couldn't manage to defeat the then-champion, Bob Backlund, so he moved on to spend several years in the now-defunct AWA, where he began to develop the great fan following that he's had ever since.

In 1983, Hogan returned to the WWF, this time playing a good guy defending all things American against the Iron Sheik. He defeated the Sheik for the WWF title on January 23, 1984, and the fan phenomenon known as "Hulk-A-Mania" was born.

The first *WrestleMania* shows were largely Hulk Hogan affairs: He was featured in the main event matches in all but one of those early years. Perhaps the most famous one was his battle with Andre the Giant in *WrestleMania III*—he pinned the till-then all-but-invincible Andre to the roar of thousands of cheering fans. Hogan lost the belt to Andre in 1988, but he won it back a year later, defeating Randy Savage for the title.

At *WrestleMania VI,* Hulk Hogan lost the belt again—this time to the Ultimate Warrior in a "straight" match (no cheating, no interfering)—a rare occurrence indeed. Hogan almost always won his matches in the WWF. WCW lured Hogan to its fold in 1994, where he won the title in his first match by defeating Ric Flair.

In Your Face

"When I beat Andre at *Wrestle-Mania III,* it was like the passing of the torch," says Hulk Hogan. But the truth is that Hulk was already a bigger star than the aging Andre when it happened.

Hulk Hogan's most famous WWF feud was with Andre the Giant, against whom he had some of his most memorable matches.

In the WCW, Hogan's good-guy character did not go over well—fans booed him no matter what he did. It was a new crowd of youngsters, and they'd seen this act before. So Hulk took a little time off to make a film. When he returned, his orange-and-yellow bandana had turned black (along with his blond beard) and his name had also been changed to "Hollywood" Hogan. He was now the leader of the New World Order, an outlaw group within WCW that included former WWF'ers Scott Hall (Razor Ramon) and Kevin Nash (Diesel). With the nWo, Hogan helped bring WCW a hugely successful few years, from 1996 through 1998. Today he's back to Hulk and he feuds with the New Blood, younger wrestlers who want him out of the way so that they can rise to the next level.

Jimmy "Superfly" Snuka: High-Flyin' Innovator

Born James Reiher in the Fiji Islands on May 18, 1943, Snuka began wrestling professionally in 1969 in Hawaii. During his earliest years as a pro wrestler, he wrestled under the name Jimmy Kealoha. After five years of wrestling in matches in the Pacific Northwest, Snuka moved to Texas, where he became the WCCW champion in 1977. He finished out the decade of the 1970s working for the NWA, where he was managed by Buddy Rogers and was frequently teamed with Paul Orndorff and Ray Stevens.

Snuka became a superstar in the 1980s with the WWF, where he waged a long and furious feud against Rowdy Roddy Piper. He was one of the earliest of the high-flying wrestlers, and because of his aerial acrobatics—derived from the *lucha libre* moves used in Mexico—he became one of the most influential wrestlers in history.

Wrestle Mania

Jimmy Snuka's airborne antics earned him his nickname of Superfly. Snuka was the first wrestler of his size (6 feet, 250 pounds) to sail through the air the way he did. He is most famous for being the first wrestler ever to jump off the top of a cage during a cage match. Snuka disappeared from the scene for a time, but he re-emerged in the ECW, where he won its version of the World Championship in 1992.

Bob Backlund: He Looked Like Howdy Doody, but He Could Tie You in Knots

The 6-foot-1, 234-pound Bob Backlund was much, much smaller when born in Princeton, Minnesota, on August 14, 1950. Red-headed and freckled, his open-faced charm has led to comparisons with Andy Griffith's TV boy, Opie, and (less flatteringly) Howdy Doody. He started out in amateur wrestling, winning the championship, but it wasn't long before he was knocking on pro wrestling's door. He joined Verne Gagne's AWA lineup in 1974, where he built a reputation for his gimmick-free, purely scientific style. During the next couple years, he wrestled for the NWA and then joined the WWWF in 1977, where he was to finally reach his destiny as a star.

Bob Backlund takes his punishment from Jimmy Snuka.

(Source: Norman Kietzer)

Backlund reached wrestling's pinnacle early in his career on February 20, 1978, when he bested Superstar Billy Graham and took the championship belt. The belt stayed in his possession for nearly six years, until he lost it to the Iron Sheik in 1983.

After losing the belt, Backlund wasn't seen much for the rest of the 1980s. He had a few matches here and there, but without any real visibility. In 1992, however, he was back in action for the WWF with a vengeance. He'd made the transformation from a clean-cut, clean wrestler to a bow-tied heel, basing his character on everybody's worst memory of the high-school teacher from hell. Today, Backlund appears occasionally on WWF telecasts, still in his bow tie. And lately, inspired by Jesse Ventura's success, Backlund has been threatening to go into politics. I think he's serious.

"Superstar" Billy Graham: Modern Muscle Man

The original balding, blond, muscular WWF champion, Graham is the prototype upon which Hulk Hogan was fashioned. Born September 10, 1943, in Paradise Valley, Arizona, Graham was a teenaged body-building phenomenon. The physique that ultimately won him the Mr. Teenage America contest was, by his own admission, created with steroids.

Captain Lou's Corner

During recent years, Superstar Billy Graham has dropped from public view. Since leaving wrestling, Graham has had several operations on his damaged joints and now lives quietly, devoting his time to his newfound hobby, painting.

Graham entered the world of professional wrestling in 1969, first for a variety of NWA promotions as a tag-team partner with such stars as Dr. Jerry Graham (billed as his brother), Pat Patterson, and Ox Baker. But it was not until he made the move to the WWF in the 1970s that he earned his nickname: Superstar.

After he lost the belt to Bob Backlund in 1978, Graham left the WWF to work the independent circuits, but physical problems—particularly arthritis—curtailed his schedule. Graham later learned that his physical problems were the result of his early steroid abuse. Graham attempted a comeback in the WWF in 1987, but that was cut short. He carried on with his schedule of public appearances into the 1990s, but his active days were by then definitively over.

"Terrible" Terry Funk: Straight from the Double-Cross Ranch to You

Terry Funk was born on June 30, 1944, in Amarillo, Texas. His father, Dory, and his older brother, Dory Jr., were both champion wrestlers before he got into the act. (Dory Jr. and Terry are the only brothers to each be NWA world champs.)

Terry Funk in full regalia.

Like his brother and dad, Funk was a respected scientific wrestler early in his career. The 6-foot-1-inch, 247-pound Funk soon developed into a hardcore pro wrestling legend, featured in some of the most violent matches of all time, both in Japan and in the United States. His trademark finishing move is the spinning toehold.

Funk amazed his critics in 1997 when, at the age of 53, he won the ECW championship on the *Barely Legal* pay-per-view event. He put on an astonishing performance that included a moonsault—a backward somersault off the top turnbuckle to land with a thud on his prone opponent.

In addition to wrestling, Funk has appeared in several movies, including *Over the Top*, and has made guest appearances on several TV shows, including "Thunder in Paradise." He is now trying to break Frank Sinatra's record for most retirements and comebacks. Well, he hasn't stopped working yet and remains a regular on WCW telecasts, where he is still a challenger for its Hardcore Championship.

The Von Erich Saga

The biography of Fritz Von Erich in the Fall 1959 issue of *Wrestling Revue* began:

> Nazi Germany was on its last legs. Before long, Russian and American flags would fly over Berlin and a guy named Hitler would make an ash of himself. Meanwhile, however, discipline for both soldiers and civilians was hard. One day, between air raids, a battalion of infantry passed an almost deserted playground. Several boys were lifting weights, oblivious to the carnage going on about them. One of the lads caught the Prussian officer's eye. He halted his unit. 'You—the big one—come here!' he shouted. The big one walked over slowly. The officer sneered. 'Here I have to put up with rabble like this,' he pointed to his men, 'while specimens like you are wandering around. You're big enough to be in the army. Why aren't you?' But the tall blond boy never flinched. 'I am only 14 years old,' he said.

The bio went on to recount how the Prussian officer took a swipe at the boy with his swagger stick and how the 14-year-old tore the stick away and threw the officer to the ground. It told of how one observer, a corporal, looked up the youngster after the war and pleaded with him "to recapture our physical prestige" by becoming a wrestler. To this the boy is said to have answered, "I am going to America to wrestle. I am going to cripple every *schwienhunt* of an American wrestler I meet. Single-handed, I will continue the war against the Yankees!"

And Now for the Real Story

There's only one problem with this story: Fritz Von Erich was, in reality, Jack Adkisson, a tough 6-foot-4, 260-pounder who had played football for Southern Methodist University back in 1948 and 1949 and had probably never been closer to Germany than Paris, Texas.

But in the immediate post-World War II era, being a German was visual shorthand for being a villain, and Adkisson entered the wrestling arena as the quintessential villain. His long-time partner, Cowboy Bill Watts, said, "The German gimmick was a natural. With that scowl of his, he was an easy guy to hate." Equally easy was his selection of a German moniker: He borrowed the name Fritz from a member of his family, and Erich was his mother's maiden name. (When Fritz was a Nazi, von Erich was spelled with a small v. When he became a hero during the 1960s, the V went uppercase and stayed that way.)

As he traveled the state of Texas and beyond, he developed yet another gimmick: his deadly "Iron Claw" grip. And Adkisson/Von Erich soon converted his Iron Claw into an iron grip on wrestling in and around Dallas, developing World Class Championship Wrestling (WCCW), which soon became a family enterprise as he brought in five of his six sons to become part of a family show. The Von Erichs—David, Kerry, Kevin, Mike, and Chris—soon became the hottest thing to hit Texas since salsa. And the WCCW caught fire along with them. They played to full houses at the Sportatorium, with occasional superstar extravaganzas at the Cotton Bowl and Texas Stadium. The weekly WCCW TV shows were syndicated in 66 U.S. television markets, Japan, Argentina, and the Middle East.

Tragedy in the Second Generation

But, in the 1980s, the Von Erich success story suddenly turned tragic. David, probably the best wrestler of the bunch, died during a 1984 tour of Japan. The rumored cause was a drug overdose, but the official word was that he had suffered an intestinal hemorrhage. In his honor, a gigantic David Von Erich Memorial Show was staged at Texas Stadium.

A couple of years later, a second Von Erich brother, Mike, had a close brush with death involving drugs, but Fritz told anyone who would listen that Mike suffered from toxic shock syndrome. It was impossible to mask his condition, and the Von Erichs had to resort to having him score one-punch or single drop-kick wins to cover up his inability to perform for long in the ring. In 1987, Mike committed suicide, and again a memorial show was staged, this time honoring both David and Mike at the Texas Stadium. As with the earlier memorial show, the stadium was jammed with fans.

With Mike's death, it fell to Kerry to carry the Von Erich banner. By this time, ESPN had begun broadcasting Texas wrestling, and Kerry quickly became a favorite on the show. Kerry battled Ric Flair, winning and then losing the WCCW and NWA championships. But tragedy stalked Kerry, too; soon after losing the title to Flair, Kerry was involved in a motorcycle accident in which he severely dislocated his right ankle.

Recovery and Return to Glory

Nobody wanted to see Kevin and Chris wrestle: The fans wanted Kerry, of the Greek godlike features and flowing blond hair. Without a wrestling son to pump up attendance, promoter Fritz had to resort to trickery to punch up his weekly TV show ratings—including a faked heart attack, with ambulance and all.

Meanwhile, Kerry's rehabilitation had to be rushed. It consisted of putting a walking cast on the ankle and shooting his leg full of novocaine. All it took was one match. Kerry was in agony as soon as the painkiller wore off, and he ripped up his ankle during that bout. In the end, the injured foot had to be amputated.

Recovery took another year, but Kerry came back sporting an artificial foot. The TV announcers, unaware that he had lost a limb, said, "Kerry hasn't lost a step." Although fans noticed that Kerry didn't come off the top rope anymore, few suspected the extent of his problem. Having become so adept at wrestling on one foot, and having learned to spend as much time as possible hanging onto the ropes, Kerry made it all but impossible for the fans to detect his missing foot.

Rumors circulated that something was wrong, very wrong, with his foot, fueled in part by his refusal to remove his wrestling boots in dressing rooms. But Kerry was so adroit at hiding his injury that Vince McMahon hired him away from the WCCW and introduced him into the WWF as The Texas Tornado. With his departure from the WCCW, there were no remaining big attractions, and the crowds at the Sportatorium began to dry up. With that, ESPN dropped its weekly WCCW show.

Death, Drugs, and Disaster

Tragedy continued to stalk the Von Erich clan. In 1991, 21-year-old Chris committed suicide. Then Kerry ran afoul of the law and was caught forging prescriptions for drugs to ease his constant pain. Facing jail time, Kerry followed his brothers Mike and Chris, taking his own life in 1993. Finally, the patriarch of the family, Fritz, succumbed to brain cancer in August 1998. The first family of professional wrestling, save for Kevin, was all gone.

Sergeant Slaughter

Born with a chin and a jaw that resembled Popeye's, Robert Remus was never going to win beauty contests. This son of Paris Island, South Carolina, joined the pro wrestling business in 1977 in the Pacific Northwest. At 6 feet, 3 inches, and 310 pounds, and with a face only his mother could love (maybe), he started out as the facetiously named Beautiful Bobby Remus. That didn't last. Soon he became Sergeant Slaughter.

Sgt. Slaughter takes flight with the help of his opponent, Bob Backlund.

(Source: Norman Kietzer)

Slaughter was an NWA wrestler until the mid-1980s, when he switched to the WWF. There he not only became a wrestling superstar, but was immortalized by a best-selling action figure as well.

Slaughter left the WWF for a time to wrestle on the independent circuit, but he returned to McMahon's fold in 1990 as a villain on the side of the Iraqis during the Gulf War. That year he battled the good guy Hulk Hogan in the main event of *WrestleMania*. He briefly held the WWF World Heavyweight Championship title in 1991, defeating the Ultimate Warrior for the belt, but he ultimately lost it to Hulk Hogan two months later.

Slaughter is now retired from active wrestling, but he still can be seen working in the WWF as one of the security personnel who come out to break up fights after the bell.

What's Under the Kilt: Rowdy Roddy Piper

Roderick Toombs was born on April 17, 1951, in Glasgow, Scotland, and grew up to become one of the biggest stars of the early *WrestleMania* era: Rowdy Roddy Piper. Piper wrestled with the NWA during the late 1970s, but his real rise to fame came only after he began starring in "Piper's Pit," an interview and commentary segment of the WWF television shows of the early 1980s. This was no ordinary talk show: Piper's interviews with wrestling's heroes and villains during these segments inevitably ended in a fight.

Being from Scotland, Piper wore a kilt much of the time (except for when he was actually wrestling) and occasionally played the bagpipe. He won his matches with The Sleeper hold. He teamed with Paul Orndorff to face Hulk Hogan and Mr. T at

WrestleMania I. His most famous feud was with Superfly Jimmy Snuka, which began when Piper hit Snuka with a coconut.

In 1996, he served as interim president of the WWF, filling in for Gorilla Monsoon during a time when Monsoon was too ill to fulfill his duties. Piper still wrestles occasionally for WCW and remains one of wrestling's top movie stars, having played the lead in many features.

Rowdy Roddy Piper: Even the trunks are Scottish tartan.

Dusty Rhodes: The American Dream

Dusty Rhodes was wrestling's embodiment of the American Dream, a colorful wrestler beloved by all. Rhodes was known as a man of the people. He often described himself as the "son of a plumber"—which, in fact, was the case. He was born Virgil Riley Runnels Jr. in 1945 and made his debut as a professional wrestler in Toronto Canada in November 1969. At 6-foot-1 and 300-plus pounds, he never was a svelte man. "The American Dream" was known as the king of the bull-rope match. And his finishing move was the elbow drop, much like The Rock's finishing move today.

Rhodes has worked for every major wrestling organization. Today he is still in the wrestling biz, sometimes dropping an elbow or two in an ECW match and other times booking matches for WCW. He is the father of Dustin Rhodes.

Kevin Sullivan humiliates
Dusty Rhodes.

(Source: Norman Kietzer)

Harley Race

One of the NWA's all-time greatest wrestlers, Harley is a seven-time holder of the NWA world heavyweight championship. His winning streak set a record that was broken only with the explosive arrival of Ric Flair on the wrestling scene. Born on April 11, 1943, in Kansas City, Missouri, the 6-foot-1, 268-pound Race was burly even in youth. He became the personal protégé of wrestling promoter Gus Karras, who trained Race in the ways of pro wrestling in St. Jose, Missouri.

Race began wrestling in 1959 in the AWA, a Midwest promotion. His move to superstardom came in 1965 when he teamed up with Larry "The Ax" Hennig. Together they defeated Crusher and Dick the Bruiser to win the AWA tag-team titles. As a solo, Race was the NWA World Heavyweight champ throughout the 1970s, surrendering the title in 1983 when Ric Flair became the promotion's top man. In the mid-1980s, Race worked in the WWF and won the "King of the Ring" tournament in 1986. Forced into retirement by injuries in 1988, Race worked in the WCW as a manager. On January 25, 1995, he was seriously injured in a car accident that cut short his managerial career.

The Least You Need to Know

➤ Wrestling during the 1970s and early 1980s was not as popular on TV but was more popular than ever in arenas around the country, with several superstars of the era contributing to its popularity.

➤ Andre the Giant was called "The Eighth Wonder of the World."

➤ Bruiser Brody, one of the biggest stars of the era, was stabbed to death in a locker room in Puerto Rico.

➤ Ric Flair was the greatest combination wrestler/entertainer in history.

➤ Fritz Von Erich tried to build a wrestling dynasty in Texas, and he almost pulled it off before personal tragedies destroyed his family.

Stars of the '90s

Wrestling during the 1990s had its ups and downs. It struggled during the first half of the decade with steroid scandals and half-empty arenas. But by the second half of the decade, stars such as Stone Cold Steve Austin (more about him later), Mick Foley, Shawn Michaels, and Bret Hart led wrestling out of its blue funk—not to be confused with its Terry Funk—and into the previously unimaginable levels of popularity that it enjoys today.

Mick Foley

Perhaps the biggest wrestling story of 1999 was that of Mick Foley, a professional wrestler who wrote a book that went to number one on the *New York Times'* bestseller list. And I don't say that with a wink, wink. Most celebrity books, of course, are written by professionals called ghostwriters who stay behind the scenes. But that is not how Foley's book was written. It started out that way, but Foley quickly fired his ghostwriter and went to work himself. Writing in a notebook, Foley submitted a 500-page manuscript, twice the length that the publisher was expecting. The book turned out to be a poetic and poignant look at the emotional and physical wear and tear that a pro wrestler endures.

Born Mick Foley on June 7, 1965, in Bloomington, Indiana, and raised on Long Island, in New York, Foley grew up dreaming of nothing but becoming a pro wrestler. His hero was Jimmy "Superfly" Snuka, who had shocked the world by jumping off the top of a steel cage onto an opponent. In what is now a famous videotape, Foley is seen as a teenager jumping off the roof of his suburban house onto a mattress in the yard below.

Wrestle Mania

Some may think that a teenage Mick Foley executing an elbow drop off the roof of his suburban home onto a mattress below was the very first example of what has become a genre of activity known as "Backyard Wrestling," but I see it more as clear evidence that Foley was nuts right from the git-go.

Bert's Corner

Mick Foley has an encyclopedic knowledge of every "all-you-can-eat" restaurant in the United States—and probably in the Free World.

To get closer to the wrestlers, the college-aged Foley got a job on the team that assembled and disassembled the ring before and after wrestling shows. These were local shows, mostly in high school gymnasiums, promoted by a man named Tommy Dee.

The irony was that there was no pay. In return for his labor, Foley did not receive money. What he got instead was an opportunity to workout (that is, get the daylights beaten out of him by the pro wrestlers on the card).

"Usually, however, Mick didn't have anyone to practice with but himself," says *Wrestling All Stars* editor George Napolitano. "But this didn't deter him from getting into the ring and taking those ridiculous bumps off the ropes. Eventually Dominic DeNucci befriended him and began to work with him whenever he was booked on a Tommy Dee card in New York. This was

Mick's introduction to the sport, and it laid the groundwork for his future rise to fame and fortune."

During the late 1980s, and for most of the 1990s, Foley wrestled as Cactus Jack, claiming to be from Truth or Consequences, New Mexico (the only town in the United States that allegedly agreed to change its name when bribed by a game show). Cactus Jack made his pro debut in June 1983 in Clarksburg, Texas, as Cactus Jack Manson. He gained fame during the late 1980s working for World Class Championship Wrestling in Texas as part of General Skandor Akbar's organization.

The 6-foot-4, 277-pound Foley had a memorable stint in ECW from 1995 to 1996. Then Cactus Jack moved to the WWF, where, wrestling as any one of his other three personae—Cactus Jack, Mankind, and Dude Love—he became a superstar. His 1998 cage match against the Undertaker was as wild as wrestling gets. During the match, he was tossed from the top of the cage straight through a ringside table, dislocating his jaw and knocking out three teeth. That bout stands as one of the most memorable in WWF history. And yet, even after incurring all that damage, he still insisted on finishing the match.

Foley's awesome match at the *Royal Rumble* was a highlight of wrestling in the year 2000. Just as it had appeared in his dream, the match was held in front of a sold-out crowd in New York's Madison Square Garden, in the very ring where he had seen Superfly Jimmy Snuka leap from 15 feet onto a fallen Bob Backlund. Foley walked away from that match a battered man. Both knees needed operations. He had been hit in the head so many times that he admitted that he was having trouble finding his way home some nights. He told his family and the world that he would wrestle only one more time, and that if he lost he would retire. He would walk away from the squared circle and never come back. The match was to be held against Hunter Hearst Helmsley, and this one was to be in a steel cage—a "Hell in a Cell" match, much like the one several years before versus the Undertaker in which he had lost so many brain cells.

Fighting Words

A **"Loser-Must-Retire" match** means just that; the wrestler who loses must never wrestle again. There's only one problem with the stipulation: In the history of pro wrestling, it has never been upheld. No wrestler has ever actually retired after losing a "Loser-Must-Retire" match.

Once again, just as he had during the famous "Hell in a Cell" encounter, Foley fell from the top of the cage to the ring below, this time falling so hard that he crashed through the ring, making a big hole in the center. Paramedics rushed into the ring with a stretcher. But Mick Foley, wrestling under his toughest persona, that of Cactus Jack from Truth or Consequences, New Mexico, refused to get on the stretcher. He had lost the match, and he would never wrestle again. With dried blood caked upon his face, Mick Foley looked out over the

Hartford, Connecticut, arena and, seeing that his long, strange, 15-year journey through pro wrestling was at an end, was determined to exit the arena under his own power—and that was just what he did.

Lex Luger: The Total Package

Born Lawrence Pfohl on June 2, 1958, in Chicago, Illinois, Luger played a stint in the Canadian Football League. He moved on to play for the Orlando Bulls of the now defunct United States Football League in 1985 and began wrestling in local Florida promotions soon thereafter.

With his 6-foot-5, 265-pound bodybuilder's physique, Luger quickly moved up to join the NWA/WCW, where he became known as The Total Package. Luger left the NWA/WCW in 1992 to join Vince McMahon's short-lived World Bodybuilding Federation. In June 1992, Luger was injured in a motorcycle accident in Atlanta and had to have a metal plate inserted in his arm. He still has that plate—which he has been known to use to great effect as a weapon when he's working as a villain.

In Your Face

Sometimes you really can't tell the players without a program—wrestlers switch federations or change persona with increasing frequency. If you want to follow one or more current wrestlers, track them on the Internet. Most of the big ones have their own Web pages, not to mention the numerous ones maintained by their fans. Use your favorite search engine.

Lex Luger overpowering an opponent.

Luger wrestled as The Narcissist in the WWF until 1995, after which he took on the persona Lex "Made in the USA" Luger. He was at one time the WWF's number one hero, feuding with then-WWF champ Yokozuna. From 1995 to the present, Luger has worked for WCW, where he remains one of wrestling's top stars. Luger's favorite finishing move is the "Torture Rack," which involves draping his opponent across the back of his neck and pulling down on both halves of the body with his arms.

Kevin Nash: From Diesel to Big Sexy

Kevin Nash was born on July 9, 1960, in Las Vegas, Nevada, and was raised in Southgate, Michigan. Standing 7 feet tall and weighing 356 pounds, he played basketball for the University of Tennessee. After college, he worked as a nightclub bouncer for a time before beginning his wrestling career with WCW.

With little experience but lots of size going for him, Nash originally experimented with a few gimmicks, but they were mostly unsuccessful. Using the name Steel, he started out as half of the tag team The Master Blasters, partnered with Blade. Then, as a solo wrestler, he took on the persona of Oz, wearing a mask and a green cape in the ring. After that he became Vinnie Vegas, an oversized lounge lizard.

Captain Lou's Corner

Today Luger continues to do battle in WCW. His valet is the former "First Lady of Professional Wrestling," Miss Elizabeth, and his partner is Ric Flair. Together they fight as Team Package against Eric Bischoff's New Blood.

Captain Lou's Corner

Sometimes a gimmick or partnership is all it takes to blast a wrestler's career into the stratosphere. It's all a matter of finding what works for you and gets the fans' attention at the same time.

Nash's career finally took off when he moved to the WWF in 1993 as Diesel, Shawn Michael's bodyguard. As Diesel he went on to become the WWF World Heavyweight champion by defeating Bob Backlund on November 26, 1994. The title match lasted only six seconds—but sometimes that's all it takes. Nash returned to WCW in 1996; teaming up with Scott Hall, he remains a top star as a founding member of the New World Order. Although his time in the ring has been hampered by injuries, he remains one of WCW's top stars.

Scott Hall: As Sharp as a Razor

Scott Hall was born in Miami, Florida, on October 20, 1959. His early athletic involvement was as a basketball player for St. Mary's University in Maryland. The 6-foot-8,

287-pound Hall began to wrestle professionally only in 1984 and didn't become a big star until eight years later. Hall wrestled as Starship Coyote and as the Diamond Studd during his early years.

In May 1992, after stints in the AWA and NWA, Hall joined the WWF and became famous as Razor Ramon, a "Cuban" wrestler who chewed a toothpick and tossed it into the face of his enemies. Razor Ramon's finishing move was called the "Razor's Edge."

Hall will always be remembered for his Ladder matches with Shawn Michaels during his last days as Razor Ramon. He left the WWF in the spring of 1996 to join WCW and has returned to wrestling under his real name. He was one of the founders of the outlaw group the New World Order.

Macho Man Randy Savage: "Ooooooh, yeah!"

Born Randy Poffo on November 15, 1952, Randy spent five years in the St. Louis Cardinals Cincinnati Reds and Chicago White Sox minor league systems before becoming a wrestler. Starting out as a masked man, "The Spider," he joined the WWF in the 1970s for a few years, moved on, and then returned to the McMahon fold in 1984 along with his manager and wife, Miss Elizabeth. (The marriage of their wrestling personas outlasted their real-life union—they divorced in the early 1990s.)

In 1994, Savage moved over to WCW and re-started his long-running feud with Hollywood Hogan. One of only four men to win both the WWF and WCW world championship titles, Savage is best known for his "Snap into a Slim Jim" commercials on TV.

Need a little excitement? Check out a Randy Savage match!

The Ultimate Warrior: Cosmic Visitor

One of the most wildly popular, yet mysterious, figures in wrestling history, the Ultimate Warrior, was known for his face paint and incredible bulging muscles. He was one of wrestling's top stars until one day he vanished without a trace. No one in the past 20 years has generated more false death rumors than the Warrior.

The 6-foot, 5-inch, 275-pound wrestler was born June 16, 1957, in Queens, New York, as Jim Hellwig. Because the WWF owns rights to the wrestling name Ultimate Warrior, Hellwig recently had his own name legally changed to The Warrior. He began his wrestling career in the early 1980s as Rock (no, not The Rock), and formed the tag team Blade Runners with the wrestler Flash (who went on to become Sting).

The Warrior first gained national recognition as the Dingo Warrior, working for Fritz von Erich's World Class Championship Wrestling in Texas during the late 1980s. The highlight of his career came during *Wrestlemania VI* in Toronto, when he pinned the previously invincible Hulk Hogan to win the WWF World Heavyweight Championship. In the late 1990s, the Warrior starred in his own comic book and briefly returned to active wrestling, coming out of retirement to rekindle his feud with Hulk Hogan.

Ron Simmons: a.k.a. Faarooq

This native of Warner Robins, Georgia, was born on May 15, 1962, and grew to be a strapping 6-foot-2, 260-pound Florida State football star. After his spectacular collegiate career in the late 1970s, for which he received consideration for the Heisman Trophy, he eventually migrated into a solo professional wrestling career in Florida. From his beginnings in 1986, he built a solid reputation, but he achieved national fame only in 1990 after he teamed up with Butch Reed as the tag team Doom in WCW. Doom, managed by the notorious Woman, started out as masked wrestlers but quickly lost their face coverings when they defeated the Steiner Brothers on May 19. This victory earned them the WCW World Tag Team title, which they held until February 1991, when the Freebirds defeated them.

In 1992, Simmons once again worked solo. In that year, he became the first African-American wrestler to win a world championship by winning the WCW crown. Since the mid-1990s, Simmons has wrestled for the WWF as Faarooq, one-time leader of a racially mixed gang known as the Nation of Domination. Today Faarooq wrestles as one of the security-for-hire Acolytes, along with Justin Bradshaw.

"Ravishing" Rick Rude: Stop the Music

Born Richard Rood on December 7, 1957, in Robbinsdale, Minnesota, the 6-foot, 4-inch, 246-pound Rude began his pro wrestling career in 1984 in the mid-South region. Back then he was managed by Jim "The Anvil" Neidhart and was accompanied by his beautiful valet, Angel.

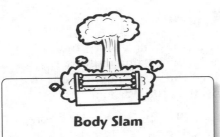

Body Slam

Sadly, Rude became another wrestling star who died young of a heart attack in 1998.

From his successes in the mid-South, he moved on to wrestle for World Class Championship Wrestling in Texas, where he was managed by Percival Pringle (the manager and wrestler now known as Paul Bearer). He moved on to NWA/WCW in 1986, but he then made the switch to the WWF during the spring of the following year.

Rude returned to WCW in 1991, where he remained until a 1994 back injury forced him to retire from active wrestling. For his entire career, Rude's gimmick never changed. He came on as God's gift to women. When he kissed them, they fainted. When he wiggled his hips, they squealed. And he can't wrestle without addressing the crowd over the public-address system: "Stop the music! Why don't you fat, stupid people from (insert town here) shut up and let your women see what a real man looks like!"

Bam Bam Bigelow: Tattoo Artists' Wrestler of Choice

When Momma Bigelow first laid eyes on her baby boy Scott on September 1, 1961, she had no idea that he would turn into the 6-foot, 3-inch, 368-pound behemoth that we know today as Bam Bam. Bigelow began his wrestling career as Crusher Yircov in 1985, but the Bam Bam moniker came soon after—specifically, Bam Bam Bigelow, the Beast from the East.

Bam Bam Bigelow.

Bigelow's most famous match was in the main event at *WrestleMania XI* in 1995, where he went up against New York Giants linebacker (and wrestling neophyte) Lawrence Taylor. Bam Bam lost. His response to fans who chided him for losing? "You should see the check I got!"

Today Bigelow wrestles with WCW, where he is a contender for that promotion's Hardcore Championship. Oh, and his most striking physical feature? The tattooed flames that cover his bald head.

Many wrestlers are not heroes—they just play them on TV. This is not true of Bigelow, however. Bigelow became a real-life hero in 2000 when he risked his life to save several children from a fire.

Shawn Michaels: The Heartbreak Kid

Born Michael Hickenbottom on July 22, 1965, in San Antonio, Texas, the 6-foot, 230-pound Michaels was one of the most spectacular wrestlers of the 1990s. A good-looking blond kid who had a thing with the ladies, Michaels affected a wise guy persona that brought heel heat worthy of Freddie Blassie.

Michaels was not only an athletic performer, he was also willing, like few others, to sacrifice his body to please his fans. Time and again, bump after bump, he would take falls that left fans wondering how he was going to get up from that one—often being thrown into the guardrail face first. But he always did get up. Unfortunately, after being involved in many of the greatest wrestling matches ever, he had to quit wrestling in the late 1990s because of an injured back.

Bret Hart: The Best There Was, The Best There Is, and The Best There Ever Will Be

Bret Hart was born on July 2, 1957, in Calgary, Canada. He was no shrinking violet—Hart's favorite self-description is "The best there was, the best there is, and the best there ever will be."

Hart joined the WWF roster in 1985 and stayed with the federation until 1997. His first manager was Jimmy Hart, who teamed him up with Jim "The Anvil" Neidhart as the original Hart Foundation, one of the most successful tag teams of the 1980s.

In the 1990s, Hart achieved great success as a singles wrestler. During the first seven years of the decade, he carried on memorable feuds with Shawn Michaels, Yokozuna, Jerry Lawler, Steve Austin, and his own brother, Owen. A contract dispute brought an end to his WWF affiliation in 1997, and he went over to the WCW to join Hollywood Hogan's New World Order.

Bret Hart was known as the "Excellence of Execution."

The Tragic Death Of Owen Hart

The saddest day in wrestling history came on May 23, 1999, when 33-year-old Owen Hart, husband, father of two, and the youngest of the wrestling Hart family, died in a freak ring accident. Hart had been performing during the previous weeks as The Blue Blazer, a send-up of a masked superhero who "flies" into the ring. On this night, Hart was about to enter the ring from the ceiling on a wire when something happened and his security harness gave way, dropping him 50 feet into the ringpost at the Kemper Arena in Kansas City.

He was given CPR while still in the ring and was rushed to Truman Medical Center where he was pronounced dead on arrival. The horrifying scene was witnessed live by more than 16,000 fans. There was little reaction from the live crowd, who at first thought that it was just a wild WWF stunt. Soon it became apparent that it was not an angle, but a genuine tragedy. Owen's fatal fall did not appear on TV, despite the fact that it occurred during a live Sunday night pay-per-view broadcast of a show called *Over the Edge*.

Owen "The Rocket" Hart was born May 7, 1965, the youngest of the wrestling Hart boys, sons of Stu Hart, who had trained many a wrestler in the downstairs room at the Calgary, Alberta, Hart home known, appropriately enough, as "The Dungeon."

Hart felt drawn into the wrestling business, even though becoming a pro wrestler was not his first inclination. "I wanted to be a phys. ed. teacher," he said in a 1993 interview. "I wrestled only to appease my father. I was compelled to get into the ring. Once I started, there was the pressure of having the Hart name. I was expected to be good."

Hart's first pro matches were for his dad's Stampede Wrestling in Canada and the American Northwest. From there, he went to Japan, where he achieved great success. Although he was not huge (227 pounds), Hart was a remarkable wrestler, as fast, imaginative, and athletic as any who have ever entered the squared circle. Then he came to the WWF in the early 1990s, where his big brother, Bret "Hitman" Hart, was already a veteran superstar. But Vince McMahon didn't see Hart in a starring role. He was a small heavyweight, and size meant everything, especially back in those days. Vince made Hart work under a mask, calling him The Blue Blazer.

It took a while, but McMahon finally figured out the potential of having brothers Owen and Bret feud against one another. The advantages of feuding brothers were multiple. For one thing, they were together a lot anyway, so they would have plenty of time to talk about their matches and work out bits; for another, they were both trained by Stu, and their styles were compatible. Not to mention the fact that wrestling fans, even the ones who consider themselves oh-so-sophisticated, get all heated up over familial problems. (The McMahons did the same thing building up to *WrestleMania 2000*, playing Stephanie off her mother and Shane off his father to sell pay-per-views. It works!)

As the baby brother who always felt that he wasn't quite as good as his big brothers, Owen Hart was magnificent. The whinier he got, the more fans loved him. Bret, who was playing the wiser and more stable older brother who tried to be patient but inevitably lost his temper, started to hear scattered boos. The pattern of heels getting cheered and babyfaces getting booed was already in full force by this time. It has long been the tradition in Mexico to cheer the "rudos," but only in the last five to eight years have U.S. fans reacted contrary to a wrestler's good guy/bad guy status.

Owen and Bret staged one of the greatest matches ever at *WrestleMania X*, with Owen winning. He earned the nickname "The King of Harts" in 1994 when he won the *King of the Ring* tournament on a WWF pay-per-view. Owen followed up that victory with the WWF Tag Team Championship, which he won with his brother-in-law, "The British Bulldog" Davey Boy Smith. On April 28, 1997, he won the Intercontinental title from Rocky Maivia—the wrestler who is better known today as The Rock. Then, in November 1997, Bret Hart left the WWF after losing his WWF championship to Shawn Michaels under a cloak of deception.

Owen Hart's tragic death was the saddest day ever for pro wrestling.

Bret had been told that he was going to win the match and was shocked when the bell rang, indicating that he had submitted. Shawn Michaels, referee Earl Hebner, and Vince McMahon had conspired to get the belt off Bret because they knew that he was about to bolt to WCW. In protest of the screw job, Owen's brothers-in-law, Davey Boy Smith and Jim Neidhart, also left the WWF. For Owen Hart, working at the WWF had been a family affair. Now he was alone.

Owen Hart worked as a loner after that and feuded against the original D-Generation X members Hunter Hearst Helmsley and Shawn Michaels. He won the WWF's European title and occasionally was working as the tag-team partner of "Double J" Jeff Jarrett. In 1999, the Blue Blazer reappeared as a satire of the old-fashioned wrestling hero. The Blue Blazer would even poke fun at Hulk Hogan by telling the kiddies to take their vitamins and say their prayers.

Following the accident, the Hart family sued the WWF and Kemper Arena. The WWF, in turn, sued Owens' widow for breech of contract, and everybody had the sue-me-sue-you blues. And the fans just cried.

The Least You Need to Know

➤ Mick Foley, who retired in 2000, was willing to hurt himself to put on a great match, and his fans rewarded him by making him a legend.

➤ Shawn Michaels, like Foley, took hard bumps to please fans—but a back injury brought his career to a premature end.

➤ Everybody in wrestling needs a gimmick: Bam Bam Bigelow has flames tattooed on his bald head.

➤ Bret Hart left the WWF under the worst of all possible conditions, having been publicly cheated out of his championship belt.

➤ Owen Hart's tragic plunge to his death in Kansas City put the spotlight on the dangers of wrestling.

Part 3
Today's Superstars

As you learned in Part 2, Gorgeous George was one of the first and best showmen in professional wrestling. The gimmicks, the looks, and the flair used in modern wrestling to whip a wrestling audience into a frenzy—this is his legacy. What George started, the stars of today carry on—only bigger and better than ever.

The truth is, today's wrestling superstars are more famous and make more money than the wrestling superstars of yesterday. In other words, the stars of today are the biggest wrestling stars of all time.

In this part, you'll be reading detailed biographies of today's four biggest stars—The Rock, Stone Cold Steve Austin, Goldberg, and Triple H—plus shorter bios of many of the other talented athletes and performers who make up today's wrestling phenomenon.

Years from today, when young wrestling fans talk about the Golden Age of Wrestling, there's a good chance that they will be talking about these wild wrestling days at the start of the twenty-first century!

Chapter 11

The Rock

In This Chapter

➤ The Rock is a third-generation wrestler

➤ Dwayne becomes Rocky

➤ The Rock becomes popular

➤ The Rock becomes a multimedia phenomenon

As we go to press, The Rock is not only a three-time and current WWF Heavyweight champion, but he is also the biggest star in wrestling today. Most impressive of all, he is only 27 years old. He has never suffered a serious wrestling injury, so there is no reason to think that he can't stay at the top of his game for many, many years to come.

His Name's Dwayne?

The Rock was born Dwayne Johnson in 1973. He was a natural athlete, which shouldn't surprise anyone who has seen his physique. He was a star football player in high school and received a football scholarship to attend the University of Miami. While attending school, Dwayne became a star for the Hurricanes. For a time he considered making pro football his career, but he couldn't do it—wrestling was in his blood.

Rocky Maivia: Third-Generation Wrestler

Although there are many pro wrestlers today whose dads were wrestlers, Dwayne Johnson can take his wrestling heritage a step further than that. He is third-generation, the son of the legendary Rocky Johnson and the grandson of High Chief Peter Maivia. In 1996, with suitcase in hand, young Dwayne headed for Stamford, Connecticut to the WWF offices to show Vince McMahon his stuff.

It didn't take McMahon long to realize that he was witnessing wrestling's future. To draw attention to Johnson's family heritage, the first thing McMahon did was to change Dwayne's name to Rocky Maivia—the first name of his dad and the last name of his grandfather. Rocky made his professional debut at the WWF pay-per-view event known as the *Survivor Series* on November 16, 1996. In an eight-man tag match, Rocky defeated both Crush and Goldust to win for his team.

When the brouhaha was over, young Rocky Maivia stood alone in the ring, a sure sign that he was a superstar in the making. Normally, a wrestler doesn't command the spotlight shone on him in his pro debut unless his superstardom has been pre-ordained. Nine hundred ninety-nine wrestlers out of 1,000 have to toil away for years in high school gyms and firemen's carnivals for $20 a shot. But not Rocky Maivia.

Teaming up with Salvatore Sincere (Tom Brandi), Rocky won a series of matches in late 1996 and early 1997. At the *Royal Rumble,* a WWF pay-per-view that features the year's top battle royal, Rocky performed very well and was one of the last eight in the ring.

An Intercontinental Type of Guy

Rocky earned his first shot at the Intercontinental title against Hunter Hearst Helmsley on a special Thursday edition of *RAW* held on February 13, 1997. Triple H dominated most of the match, but Rocky used his, as they say, "superior wrestling skills" to reverse Triple H's finishing move, The Pedigree, to come away with a surprise pin and the Intercontinental belt.

There was one problem: The fans weren't digging him. His super-face attitude, with a big grin and greenhorn overzealousness, caused the fans to boo him. They chanted vulgarities. Slowly but surely, Rocky's personality changed from the tenderfoot that was Rocky Maivia to the ultracool character that we know today as The Rock. The more egotistical and antisocial Rocky behaved, the more the fans loved him, until soon he became The Rock, The Chosen One, The People's Champion.

The Rock will always be "The People's Champion."

From Super-Face to Supercool

The incident that more than any other caused WWF fans to cheer Rocky came at *WrestleMania* in 1997, when he defeated a masked wrestler called The Sultan (today we know him as Rikishi Phatu.) The Sultan had two managers, The Iron Sheik and Bob Backlund, so Rocky's dad, Rocky Johnson, came out to watch his son's back. Young Rocky became irritated by this and in no uncertain terms told his dad that he could take care of himself and didn't appreciate being treated like a kid. Rocky's rebellion earned him many points with the fans. Rocky's next pay-per-view match came against Savio Vega of the Nation of Domination. Rocky lost this match by count out, but because a WWF championship cannot change hands on a disqualification or a count-out finish, he kept the title. He eventually lost the belt to Owen Hart on April 28, 1997, on an episode of *RAW is WAR*. At the next pay-per-view, Rocky lost to Mankind.

He took a couple of months off after that. When he returned, he had changed completely into The Rock, a take-charge kind of guy. Making his return on *RAW is WAR*, he appeared unexpectedly at ringside during a match between Chainz and Kama (today known as The Godfather). "Nice to have the ol' Rock back with us," WWF announcer Jim Ross said. The words were barely out of J.R.'s mouth when Rocky Maivia spike-slammed Chainz and helped Kama win the match.

Bert's Corner

The Rock's guest-host appearance on *Saturday Night Live* became a major TV happening. The March 18, 2000, show became the highest-rated *SNL* of the season. Other WWF superstars who appeared on the show were Mick Foley, Triple H, and the Big Show.

Captain Lou's Corner

A lot of wrestlers today have catch phrases that have become popular, such as, "If you can smell what The Rock is cookin'?" and "'Cause Stone Cold says so!" But my favorite is one by Chris "Y2J" Jericho, who says, "I am the Ayatollah of Rock 'n' Rolla!" The man is a poet!

Getting Stone Cold's Attention

Along with his new name and new attitude, The Rock now gained a new stature and success. His next feud was a biggie. It was with Stone Cold Steve Austin who, at the time, held the Intercontinental Championship title. To get Stone Cold's attention, The Rock stole his belt. Week after week on WWF TV shows, Stone Cold tried to get his golden strap back, but he never quite succeeded—The Rock always got away with the belt.

The Rock finally got his title shot on December 7, 1997, at the *In Your House: D-Generation X* pay-per-view event. The match was a bizarre one, fought inside and outside the ring, and it included weapons and motor vehicles. Austin worked part of the match behind the wheel of a 4x4 pickup truck. He ended up winning the match to retain his belt. The Rock had been impressive, but he was denied.

Fighting Words

When the Rock asks his opponent if he has ever had pie, he is calling his foe a virgin.

The next night, on *RAW*, Vince McMahon ordered a rematch, saying that Austin should have been disqualified the previous night for using a truck, which certainly qualifies as a foreign object—even if this one happened to have been built in Detroit. Despite the ruling, Austin refused to give The Rock a rematch, instead handing him the belt. And thus began The Rock's second reign as Intercontinental Champion. In the following weeks, Austin stole the belt back, just as The Rock had stolen the belt from him, only this time Austin didn't stick around to taunt The Rock with it. Instead, Austin took the belt to a nearby river and threw it in! It took four weeks for the WWF to get The Rock a new belt.

In Your Face

A typical Rock tirade would go something like this: "The Rock does not care about your championship belt. The Rock is going to take your championship belt, turn it sideways, and shove it right up your rootie-poo candy-ass!"

A Not-So-Lucky Shamrock

The Rock began his feud with "The World's Most Dangerous Man," Ken Shamrock, in December 1997. The Rock offered Shamrock a title match at the Royal Rumble in January 1998. During that match, The Rock cold-cocked Shamrock with a pair of brass knuckles. He then put the brass knuckles in Shamrock's shorts. Later, when Shamrock pinned The Rock for the apparent victory, the referee discovered the brass knuckles in Shamrock's shorts and disqualified him, ruling that The Rock was the winner and still Intercontinental champion.

Body Slam

One of the sharpest things about The Rock are his sideburns, which come to an extremely sharp point well below his earlobes. Photographic research reveals that his surge in popularity and those sideburns were simultaneous phenomena. So, was it The Rock's hard work that got him over—or was it the sideburns? Hmmmm.

The Nation of Domination

The Rock was encountering trouble on a couple of fronts in 1998. Faarooq, the leader of the Nation of Domination, thought that The Rock wasn't displaying the appropriate humility. The Rock was also getting heat from Ken Shamrock, who was foaming like a rabid dog over the thought of a rematch with his cheating and conniving rival.

Shamrock's shot came at the 1998 *WrestleMania*. Shamrock out-grappled Rock, administering an ankle lock that caused Rock to say "uncle." The submission meant that Shamrock was the new Intercontinental champ. But no! Shamrock refused to release the hold and was disqualified. And The Rock remained the titleholder.

During 1998, The Rock controlled the Nation of Domination before the group disbanded. He then joined The Corporation, the wrestlers who represented the suits at the top of Titan Towers. This affiliation set up a feud with Stone Cold that led to their classic 1999 *WrestleMania* match.

Great Sayings of The Rock

Most wrestlers are lucky if they have just one catch phrase that actually catches on, but The Rock has turned the coining of catch phrases into an art form. The following are some of my favorites:

1. "If you can smell what The Rock is cookin'!"

2. "Finally, The Rock has returned to (your town here)."

3. "The Rock is the most electrifying man in sports entertainment today."

4. "The Rock says this ...."

5. "You rootie-poo candy-ass jabronis are no match for The People's Champion."

6. "You can suck a monkey's nipple."

7. "Know your role."

8. "It doesn't matter what your name is!"

From Corporate Champ to People's Champ

The Rock had started out in the WWF as a babyface who got booed, but in a startling turnaround, he turned into a heel who got cheered. One final adjustment was needed. So, when Stone Cold Steve Austin went down with a neck injury and had to take time off in 1999, The Rock switched from the Corporate Champion into the People's Champion, for the first time in his career becoming a face who gets cheered. He also became, in short order, the no. 1 wrestler in the promotion and perhaps the biggest star ever to work inside the squared circle.

Wrestle Mania

Examining the story line biographies of veteran wrestlers is an exercise in the absurd. It is like analyzing the story line bio of a long-term character in a soap opera who has been married 23 times and tried and acquitted of murder on five separate occasions—which are both way above the national average. Wrestlers turn evil, then good, and then evil again. They make new friends and alliances and then betray them in the most ghastly fashion. Luckily, none of the characters in wrestling have really good long-term memories. The distant past is usually irrelevant—except, of course, in the memories of the fans.

The Rock Layeth the Smacketh Down

The Rock earned the WWF World Heavyweight Championship for the third time on April 30, 2000, when he defeated Triple H at the *Backlash* pay-per-view. When Triple H tried to stack the deck against The Rock by putting Vince McMahon in his corner to watch his back, The Rock one-upped his rival by putting none other than Stone Cold Steve Austin in his corner. And it became Austin's interference that led to The Rock recapturing the title. The Rock, as we go to press, has the WWF belt—but he also owes Austin a big favor. And, considering the egos of the two, you can't help but wonder how long The Rock and Austin will stay on the same side.

Bert's Corner

Today The Rock is all over the place: He has his own postage stamp, compliments of the Liberian government; he was the host of *Saturday Night Live*; he starred in an episode of *Star Trek: Voyager*; and he is starring in *The Mummy II*. His autobiography, *The Rock Says This*, also went to number one on *The New York Times* bestseller list.

The Least You Need to Know

➤ The Rock, whose real name is Dwayne Johnson, is a rare third-generation professional wrestler.

➤ Starting his professional career as Rocky Maivia, The Rock was "too nice" for modern wrestling fans and was booed, despite the fact that he was supposed to be a good guy.

➤ The Rock played second fiddle to Stone Cold Steve Austin in the WWF until Austin's neck injury forced him to take time off and gave The Rock the opportunity to take the spotlight.

➤ The Rock is now a three-time WWF World champ.

➤ The Rock's stardom has transcended wrestling, taking him into many other fields—TV, books, and movies.

Chapter 12

Stone Cold Steve Austin

In This Chapter

➤ Austin gets his start in Texas

➤ Partnership with Brian Pillman brings out Austin's greatness

➤ A working class hero is something to be

➤ Injuries take their toll

During the peak of his popularity, Stone Cold Steve Austin sold more merchandise—souvenirs, that is—than any other wrestler, ever! His "Austin 3:16" T-shirt is one of the biggest-selling shirts in the history of licensing.

But Austin did not start out as a superstar. He was hardly the wrestler born with a silver spoon in his mouth. Austin paid his dues, working long and hard as a mid-card performer for years before blasting off into the big-time during the late 1990s.

Sorry, There Already Is a Steve Williams

Steve Austin's real name is Steve Williams—but he wouldn't have been allowed to wrestle under his real name even if he'd wanted to. That's because Steve "Dr. Death" Williams was already an established wrestling star and no doubt would have objected to a newcomer sharing his moniker.

Instead, Steve Williams changed his name to Steve Austin after the name of the hero in the old television show *The Six-Million Dollar Man,* played by Lee Majors.

Originally from Victoria, Texas—at 6-foot-2 and 252 pounds—Austin in 1989 became the first graduate of Gentleman Chris Adams's wrestling school in Texas. He made his professional debut for World Class Championship Wrestling in Dallas that same year, defeating Frogman Lablanc. All Austin's match-ups were easy victories until February 23, 1990, when student met teacher as Austin stepped into the ring against Gentleman Chris Adams himself.

Austin won the match by disqualification, and it was now clear to everyone that he was a star in the making. The student-teacher angle was used again later in the year when Austin, now teamed up with Jeff Gaylord, took on the team of Adams and Matt Borne. (Borne is best known for his stint, a few years later, as the WWF's evil Doink the Clown.)

Airing Out Dirty Laundry

Wrestling is never ashamed to take real-life intrigues and turn them into angles that might put butts in the seats, so much was made of the fact that Adams's wife, Jeanne, had left him and married Austin. In wrestling, the athletes not only air their dirty laundry in public, but they often act it out with microphone in hand, making the ring a stage. The feud was made complete when Adams's new wife, Toni, was brought into the fray to feud with Jeanne. This mixed-doubles action turned into the hottest feud of 1990.

The ensuing matches soon got out of hand. On July 4, a no-contest was declared after Austin pile-drove Adams outside the ring while Toni choked out Jeannie inside. The feud was hot enough to earn Austin the Best Rookie award for the year, as voted by the readers of *Pro Wrestling Illustrated* magazine.

"Stunning" Steve Hits WCW

From World Class, Austin moved to WCW, where he was known as "Stunning" Steve Austin. In his first WCW match, on May 31, 1991, he defeated Sam Houston (the real-life brother of Jake "The Snake" Roberts). Austin's wife, Jeanne, made the trip to Atlanta with him and worked as his valet. A blond, buxom lass, she was known as Lady Blossom. Together they rose quickly up the ranks in WCW.

In only his fourth day with WCW, Austin defeated the much-respected Beautiful Bobby Eaton to win the WCW Television Championship. Austin wore the belt for 429 of the next 455 days. On August 25, 1991, Austin competed in a tournament to determine the new WCW United States champion, a title only recently vacated by Lex "The Total Package" Luger. Austin made it to the finals, eventually losing to former world champ Sting.

Steve and Jeanne parted ways—first in the ring and then in real life. Austin lost his TV title to Barry Windham on April 27, 1992.

The Hollywood Blonds

Austin's new manager was Paul E. Dangerously (Paul Heyman, who later changed wrestling history as the creative force behind ECW). Dangerously's troupe of wrestlers was known as the Dangerous Alliance. They were the losing team at that year's *War Games* pay-per-view. Austin's tough streak continued six days later, when he lost the TV title for the final time to Ricky "The Dragon" Steamboat at *Clash of the Champions XX*, a live prime-time special broadcast by TBS.

About a month later, Austin parted ways with Paul E. and became half of one of the greatest tag teams of all time, forming the Hollywood Blonds with the late Flyin' Brian Pillman. (They have the honor, or the notoriety, of being Jesse "The Body" Ventura's all-time favorite tag team.)

The pair quickly climbed up the tag-team ladder and, on March 2, 1993, defeated Ricky Steamboat and Shane Douglas to win the WCW World Tag-Team Championship. The Blonds defeated team after team, including Arn Anderson and Paul Roma (representing the Four Horsemen) at *BeachBlast '93*. Then the world, for the Blonds, came a-tumblin' down. Brian Pillman was in an all-terrain vehicle accident and crushed his ankle, an injury that would cause the painkiller addiction that later contributed to his death.

A Who-You-Know World

Stunning Steve returned to singles wrestling with Colonel Robert Parker as Austin's new manager. Pillman returned from his injury prematurely, refused to be on a team managed by the very southern Parker, and parted ways for good with Austin.

Captain Lou's Corner

After Brian Pillman left the Hollywood Blonds, Lord Steven Regal took his place. But the magic was gone and the "new" Blonds lost the tag-team titles to Anderson and Roma.

Bert's Corner

My favorite Austin quote was a poetic one: "I've traveled the world these past few years. Sometimes I think of home, and even Stone Cold has to fight the tears. Another car, bus, or plane takes me to faraway places. What I remember most is all the smiling faces. Short people, tall people, people with glasses. The bottom line is, I'll whoop all your asses!"

Austin turned on Pillman, leading to a memorable feud that culminated in their classic match-up at *Clash of the Champions XXV*. Austin pinned Pillman to win the match, but he had more than a little help from the interfering Colonel Parker. Stunning Steve went on to defeat Dustin Rhodes for the WCW United States title at *Starrcade '93* in a controversial, best two-of-three falls title match. Austin won the match in two straight falls: the first by disqualification and the second by pinfall. According to the bylaws of the organization, WCW championships are not supposed to change hands on a count-out or a disqualification. However, the decision stood.

Austin then canned Colonel Parker and went out on his own. After eight months as U.S. champion, Austin dropped the belt at *Clash of the Champions XXVII* to Ricky Steamboat. Less than a month later, an injured Steamboat forfeited the title back to Austin at *FallBrawl '94* when he could not defend it, thus beginning Austin's second reign as United States champ. It didn't last long.

Stunning Steve promptly lost an impromptu match against Hacksaw Jim Duggan. In the match, Commissioner Nick Bockwinkle shoved Austin into a waiting Jim Duggan, who power-slammed and pinned Austin to take away the U.S. title in just 27 seconds. Because Duggan was not the number-one contender at the time, there was speculation about why he had received the title shot instead of other wrestlers who were more deserving of the opportunity. Well, it's a who-you-know world. Rumor had it that Duggan's friendship with Hulk Hogan had helped his career greatly. Hogan was new in WCW at the time, having only recently left the WWF, and WCW officials were doing everything they could to keep the Hulkster happy.

The Knee Injury

In a rematch against Duggan in November 1994, Austin tore ligaments in his left knee. (He still wears a brace on that knee.) He was supposed to be out of action for up to one year. But, just like his old tag-team partner Pillman, Austin was impatient to get back into action, so he didn't bother to wait for his knee to completely heal. Instead, he returned after only three months. (All too often, wrestlers return too early from injuries, afraid that if they are sidelined for too long they will lose their spots in the pecking order to superstardom.) Rumors began to circulate about a possible Hollywood Blonds reunion, but it never happened.

Austin then bolted WCW and wrestled in Japan over the summer. WCW's head honcho, Eric Bischoff, fired him over the telephone. In retrospect, of course, this was not Bischoff's finest moment. As one might expect, Austin did not stay unemployed for long.

ECW Days

Paul Heyman (Paul E. Dangerously), the head honcho for ECW who had managed Austin in WCW, could see what every other wrestling promoter in the world could see: Austin had the look. He was huge, had a great physique, and was handsome. But Heyman saw something else—or, to be more precise, he heard something else. Austin could talk. Austin not only continued putting on fine wrestling matches with a wide variety of opponents, but he also gained a reputation as a wrestler who could do interviews with the best of them.

Bert's Corner

Austin made his debut in ECW on September 23, 1995, where he was known as "Superstar" Steve Austin. It was during this time that the character that would eventually become known as Stone Cold developed. Austin's interviews became increasingly noteworthy as he verbally attacked sacred cows such as Hulk Hogan and Eric Bischoff.

Birth of Stone Cold

Vince McMahon has always been impressed by two things in wrestlers: size and articulation. Austin was huge, and, as he was proving in ECW, he had the gift of gab.

Austin was brought into the WWF as "The Ringmaster" in 1996 with "The Million Dollar Man" Ted DiBiase as his manager. That gimmick didn't last long, and soon "Stone Cold" Steve Austin was born.

In its early days, the Stone Cold persona was that of a sociopathic serial killer, a heartless so-and-so who took matters of life and death very lightly. Despite this, the character quickly became the most popular one in the WWF.

In Your Face

Austin loves beer. Next to Andre the Giant, he might be the thirstiest wrestler ever. His brewskies are usually Budweisers, which Austin referred to as "Steve-weisers."

A Budweiser and a Belt

During his first years with the WWF, Austin feuded with the late Owen Hart, former tag-team partner Brian Pillman, Rocky Maivia, and Bret Hart. After taking the WWF championship title in March 1998 (at *WrestleMania XIV*) from Shawn Michaels, his character made an attitude adjustment, and Austin became a nonconforming, working man's hero.

The Great Sayings of Stone Cold

During his tenure in the WWF, Austin has developed a gaggle of defiant slogans, all designed to communicate to the audience that this was a fellow who took no guff.

Following are some of the classics:

1. "'Cause Stone Cold says so!"

2. "And that's the bottom line!"

3. "I'm gonna open up a can of whoop ass!"

4. "What a bunch of crap!"

5. "Because it ain't a race thing, it ain't a color thing, it's a me-kicking-your-ass thing, and can't nobody stop me!"

6. "I will strike down upon your ass with great vengeance and furious anger."

Fighting Words

The most popular T-shirt in wrestling history is black with big, white letters that read "Austin 3:16." Other than elevating Stone Cold to religious proportions, what does it mean? Stone Cold says, "Austin 3:16 means I just kicked your ass!"

Never ask Austin why because the answer is always the same: "'Cause Stone Cold says so! "

The Neck Injury: Austin's Prospects for Return

During a match in 1998 with the late Owen Hart, Austin took a bump wrong and was temporarily paralyzed. A slightly panicked Hart managed to conclude the match and alert medical help for the seriously injured Austin. The injury was so severe that Austin needed several months to recuperate, finally returning despite a doctor's warning that he couldn't take any more bumps on his head or he would risk permanent injury. That is why you will never see Austin getting pile-driven or hit in the head with a chair.

Problems with Austin's neck persisted into 1999, and he finally decided to have the vertebrae in his neck fused. He has not wrestled since the operation, but he returned to the WWF fold in the spring of 2000, appearing in The Rock's corner at the *Backlash* pay-per-view and helping The Rock get the WWF championship back. And he did drive a big crane into the parking lot behind one arena so that he could blow up the bus that Vince McMahon had given to his daughter, Stephanie. But judging from the way Austin is moving, he is still far from being in wrestling shape.

Body Slam

Stone Cold has been associated since his birth in 1996 with heavy equipment. He can frequently be seen driving monster trucks, bulldozers and other humongous construction vehicles. The point is clear: Whatever Stone Cold is driving, it can crush the puny thing you drive.

Captain Lou's Corner

No one knows how well Austin's neck injury will heal, but as long as he can still move his mouth, he'll always have a job in the wrestling biz if he wants one. After all, Austin has options these days. He is much in demand in Hollywood and has landed a regular role on the TV series *Nash Bridges*.

The Least You Need to Know

➤ Steve Austin got his name from the hero in *The Six-Million Dollar Man*.

➤ Steve Austin, with Flyin' Brian Pillman, formed a tag team called Hollywood Blonds, one of the best tag teams ever.

➤ Stone Cold Steve Austin learned the true art of the wrestling interview while working for ECW.

➤ Stone Cold turned into a megastar when he acquired a "take-this-job-and-shove-it" attitude.

➤ Stone Cold remains a major star, but ring injuries have compromised his career.

Chapter 13

Goldberg

> ### In This Chapter
>
> ➤ Goldberg's gimmick is himself
>
> ➤ As a kid, Goldberg's dream was to play football
>
> ➤ Goldberg played for the University of Georgia and the Atlanta Falcons before an abdominal injury ended his pro football career
>
> ➤ Goldberg began his pro wrestling career with an impressive winning streak
>
> ➤ A serious arm injury has curtailed Goldberg's career

Bill Goldberg is the strangest of all ducks in wrestling. His real name is Bill Goldberg. Wearing just a black pair of shorts, the 6-foot-3, 285-pound Goldberg is as gimmick-free as professional wrestlers come. His gimmick is his own intensity, and it has been enough to make him one of the truly astounding success stories of the late 1990s. He is a man whose neck is thicker than his head and whose finishing moves, the Spear and the Jackhammer, are as primal as anything in wrestling and yet are devastatingly convincing.

Obake

He has what the Japanese call *obake*, the spirit of the monster. (Today, he owns a gym and calls it the Obake Gym.) When Goldberg enters the arena, he stands in the middle of the ramp that leads to the ring and becomes the silhouetted centerpiece of a fountain of fireworks. When the light show is over, Goldberg steps out of the circle of sparks and exhales smoke. Then he shakes the last sparks off his body and begins to smack his own arms, getting himself ready for hand-to-hand combat. The crowd loves it.

Goldberg is *the* star of World Championship Wrestling now—and he has been around for only a couple years, a blink of an eye in the grunt-and-groan circuit. He is a former football player who entered the big-time like any other rookie and captured audiences so quickly that it caught even his own promoters by surprise. How did he get there? Well ....

Along with just a touch of wasabe, Goldberg has Japanese obake—and plenty of it!

A Sooner Says "Later"

Bill Goldberg, the son of a doctor and a concert violinist, was born on December 27, 1966, in Tulsa, Oklahoma, where he attended Thomas Edison High School. He enjoyed flying gliders and acrobatic planes with his brothers, but his first true love was football. He was a star football player from the start. As a kid, Goldberg was an Oakland Raiders fan, especially of the wild man, the late John Matuszak. He was first team All-State in high school and had his pick of colleges willing to foot the bill for his education in exchange for a few Saturday afternoons of his talent on the gridiron.

Captain Lou's Corner

During his senior year at Georgia, Goldberg had 12 sacks. Wearing number 95, Goldberg had 348 career tackles, 121 of them in his senior year alone. His career–high for a game was an animalistic 19 tackles versus the Florida Gators.

Bulldog Brilliance

Goldberg chose the University of Georgia. He red-shirted for the 1985 season; he went to class and practiced, but didn't play, saving a year of his amateur eligibility. Then he was the Bulldogs' starting noseguard from 1986-1989. Goldberg is most fondly remembered by his Georgia alumni for his game-saving interception against South Carolina during the 1987 season. That was the year that Goldberg won Georgia's coveted "Most Promising Defensive Sophomore" award. As a senior, he was selected for the Associated Press All-SEC team and received All-American honors by *Football News*.

Captain Lou's Corner

Like many other wrestling stars, Goldberg is taking advantage of show business opportunities that wrestling has opened up for him. In 1999, he starred with Jean-Claude Van Damme in the movie *Universal Soldier II*.

The Pro Gridiron

Chosen in the 11th round by the then Los Angeles Rams, Goldberg was cut by the Rams and signed by the Atlanta Falcons, where he played 14 games in three seasons before he severely tore a muscle in his lower abdomen. The injury ended his career.

Goldberg was minding his own business working out in an Atlanta, Georgia, gym when he met a few wrestlers who worked for WCW, including Diamond Dallas Page. Page and the others convinced Goldberg to attend a wrestling school called The Power Plant. Needless to say, he graduated as the star of his class.

Bert's Corner

Television shows that Goldberg has appeared on include: *The Love Boat*, *Live with Regis & Kathie Lee*, *The Tonight Show with Jay Leno*, *The Dennis Miller Show*, and the *Kids' Choice Awards*, where he was a presenter.

Who's Next?

Goldberg never wrestled a match in the minor leagues. He made his professional debut on September 22, 1997, on WCW's *Monday Nitro*. His opponent was Hugh Morrus. Much was made during Goldberg's first months with WCW of his undefeated status.

In a business where one never discusses the win-loss records of the performers, Goldberg's record—or, as I suspect, a slightly exaggerated version of it—was mentioned every week. Nitro announcer Tony Schiavone would say, "Goldberg is now 135-0. Who's next?" "Who's next?" became Goldberg's slogan.

The Raven Is Champ—Nevermore!

Goldberg first won a WCW title on April 20, 1998, when he defeated Raven in Colorado Springs, Colorado, to win the United States Championship. Many TV viewers fondly remember this match as the moment that they became incurable fans of Goldberg.

The match had the stipulation that it was to be fought under "Raven's Rules." That meant no rules at all. At the time, Raven was a hotshot in WCW and came with his own posse of wrestling followers who called themselves Raven's Flock. At one time or another, every member of the Flock—which included grapplers who later became better known as Billy Kidman and Lodi—hit the ring.

Fighting Words

A **suplex** is a leverage flip move whereby, at the top of the arc of the flip, the suplexee's body is straight and his feet are pointing straight up. Suplexes, which come in many varieties, resemble jiu jitsu but in reality cannot be accomplished without the cooperation of the victim.

Stop Signs Can't Stop Him

The Flock brought weapons so that the match began to resemble what has become known today as a hardcore match. Garbage cans, frying pans, everything that they could think of, were used atop Goldberg's practically bald head—and absolutely none of it had an effect. One of the Flock ran in carrying a real stop sign and slammed it down on Goldberg's rock-hard head. But even that failed to stop him.

It was obvious to the rabid fans both in the electrified arena and at home that Bill Goldberg had been blessed with the hardest head on TV since Stooge "Curly" Howard!

A Suplexer of Giants

At the time, WCW featured a giant of a man named Ron Reis, or "Reese," a 7-footer who had been trained by Killer Kowalski and who was wrestling as a member of Raven's Flock. When Reese ran into the ring to attack Goldberg, he didn't bring a weapon. He didn't need one. He just grabbed Goldberg around his formidable neck with both hands and lifted him up into the air. Goldberg broke the hold with a savage head butt that must have had Reese seeing stars for days. Goldberg then *suplexed* the 400-pound giant into oblivion, turned to the handheld camera, and screamed. Raven attacked Goldberg with the customary chair, but he could do nothing to avoid the Spear and the Jackhammer that secured Goldberg's victory—and his first professional championship.

Selling Out the Georgia Dome

Goldberg eventually had to give up the U.S. belt, but not because he lost it. In fact, he had to give it up because he won. Goldberg defeated Hollywood Hogan to win the WCW World Heavyweight Championship on July 6, 1998, in Atlanta, at which time he was forced to vacate the U.S. title. When Goldberg matched up against the legendary Hulk Hogan at the Georgia Dome, the home of the Atlanta Falcons, the joint was sold out. The details of this match itself will be discussed in Chapter 24, "Greatest Matches of Today," but for WCW it was the peak of popularity as a promotion. WCW had a TV ratings advantage over the WWF, had the hottest star in the world, and was selling out football stadiums.

Bert's Corner

Goldberg held the world championship until December 27, 1998, when he lost to "Big Sexy" Kevin Nash. Goldberg won the U.S. title a second time on October 24, 1999, when he defeated Sid Vicious in Las Vegas, Nevada.

The Arm Injury

Just when WCW fans were starting to think of Goldberg as superhuman, as invulnerable as Superman himself, it became all too clear that he was made of flesh and blood after all. On December 23, 1999, during a taping of *Thunder*, Goldberg was supposed to smash in a limousine window. The plan called for him to use a hammer, but when it came time to do the scene, the hammer was missing. Goldberg, without thinking, did what he thought was the next best thing. He punched the window out with his fist. Unfortunately, in extracting his arms from the broken glass, he severely cut himself, shredding a tendon in his arm in the process. WCW trainer Danny Young was on the scene and immediately treated Goldberg, who was bleeding profusely. Goldberg was then rushed to a nearby hospital, where he underwent emergency surgery. Following his surgery, Goldberg's arm had to be placed in a protective brace, and he was warned by doctors that any training whatsoever would jeopardize his arm.

In Your Face

During the summer of 2000, Goldberg—having made a successful return from a horrible arm injury—was accused by WCW of refusing to go along with the script. After committing several despicable acts designed to transform himself into a heel, Goldberg undid all the work by grabbing a microphone and saying on live TV: "I never wanted to become a heel, but management is making me." Either Goldberg is acting unprofessionally, or this is the opening move in a ploy to transform Goldberg into the ultimate heel.

WCW fans thought Goldberg was invulnerable until an altercation with a limo window almost ended his career.

Prognosis for Return

During the months following his injury, Goldberg worked as a sort of goodwill ambassador for WCW. He advanced the cause of animal rights and even testified before Congress on the subject. He made several appearances on WCW programs, always promising to return to active duty in the ring. He rang the bell to open the New York Stock Exchange in February 2000. After a long rehab, Goldberg returned to action during the summer of 2000 and promptly "turned heel."

The Least You Need to Know

➤ Bill Goldberg plays a Neanderthal on TV, but his dad is a doctor and his mom a concert pianist.

➤ Goldberg was a star noseguard at the University of Georgia whose pro football career with the Atlanta Falcons was cut short because of injuries.

➤ Goldberg got into wrestling because he met Diamond Dallas Page, who suggested that he give wrestling a try.

➤ Goldberg's gimmick is his own intensity. He is WCW's most popular wrestler and sold out the Georgia Dome for his match with Hulk Hogan.

➤ Goldberg recently recovered from a serious arm injury.

Triple H

Paul Michael Levesque, the wrestler who later became Hunter Hearst Helmsley—Triple H—learned his craft at Killer Kowalski's wrestling school in Boston. After school, his first job as a pro wrestler came with the independent IWF, where he performed as Terra Ryzing. He eventually became IWF champion.

Terra Ryzing

Triple H made his major-league pro debut with WCW in 1994, at first using his Terra Ryzing gimmick. His first match for WCW was against Brian Armstrong—the wrestler who would later be known as Road Dogg in the WWF and who would join Triple H in that promotion's rebellious D-Generation X posse.

Wrestle Mania

Bad things happen to wrestlers who do not follow the script, and Triple H learned his lesson the hard way. In the WWF story line, Helmsley and Shawn Michaels were supposed to be feuding with Razor Ramon and Diesel (Scott Hall and Kevin Nash), and the latter pair quit the WWF and signed up to work for WCW. On Hall and Nash's last show, Shawn defeated Diesel and Hunter defeated Razor. (Wrestlers always have to lose their last match with an organization, especially if they are moving to the competition.) In real life, however, Michaels, Helmsley, Hall and Nash were good friends, a group known both in and outside of wrestling as "The Clique." After Hall and Nash lost their final matches with the WWF, they stood in the ring with Helmsley and Michaels and celebrated—not part of the script. Vince McMahon became very upset. Helmsley had been scheduled to win that year's King of the Ring tournament but instead the victory went to Stone Cold Steve Austin.

French-Canadian Aristocrat

After a few matches using the old gimmick—including a loss to Larry Zbyszko for the WCW Television Championship—Triple H then performed under the name Jean-Paul Levesque. This was very similar to his real name, Paul Michael Levesque, but he changed it a little to make him sound more French-Canadian. The Levesque character was snobby and aristocratic, apparently derived from the in-ring persona of Lord Steven Regal. He was never happy with WCW, however, because his character was not pushed by the promoters, and he was losing more than he was winning.

Captain Lou's Corner

Many wrestlers don't strike gold with their first gimmick. Like The Rock, Hunter Hearst Helmsley had to try out a few personas before he hit upon the one that clicked with the fans.

The Greenwich Snob

When he joined the WWF in 1995, Triple H was immediately given the name he retains, Hunter Hearst Helmsley, but his gimmick was completely different. He was known as "The Greenwich Snob," a rich kid from Connecticut who looked down his nose at every-

one. There may have been an element of truth
in that original gimmick, as Levesque really was
born and raised in Greenwich. Following a break-
ing-in period—during which he feuded with
Duke "The Dumpster" Droese and Marvelous
Marc Mero (over Sable)—he was given a push by
Vince McMahon, which included a stint as the
WWF Intercontinental Champion. He was assigned Sable to escort him to the ring. Fans
quickly wearied of the snob, so Triple H's persona
got an overhaul in 1997 with the formation of D-
Generation X.

D-Generation X

D-Generation X (DX) was the WWF's response to
WCW's New World Order (nWo), a story-line
group within the organization that was rebelling
against the powers that be. The rebels in WCW—
Scott Hall and Kevin Nash, among others—were
turned into megasuperstars by the formation of
the nWo, and Vince McMahon hoped that the
formation of DX would also make its members
stars.

Fighting Words

It has been years since Triple H
has been known as "The
Greenwich Blue Blood." The
snobbiness of the original Triple
H was quickly written out of his
character. The only residue from
that characterization is the name
of Triple H's finishing move, **The
Pedigree,** which refers to the
pureness of his bloodline. The
move resembles a piledriver, except Helmsley drops to his knees
from a standing position to ram
his opponent's head into the
canvas.

*Triple H's persona was
tinkered with a few times
before it was perfected.*

Captain Lou's Corner

The original lineup for D-Generation X was Triple-H, Shawn Michaels (the leader), and Chyna—who became Triple H's real-life girlfriend for a time. During this period, Michaels, known as The Heartbreak Kid, was the WWF World Heavyweight Champion. Triple H was a top contender for that belt, and Chyna functioned as their "bodyguard." Soon X-Pac and the "New-Age Outlaws"—The Road Dogg, and "Bad Ass" Billy Gunn—joined DX.

Bert's Corner

Replacing Shawn Michaels as leader of D-Generation X didn't immediately help Triple H's career. Michaels was extremely popular, and at first Triple H was thought of as a lesser character. The longer Michaels was gone, however, the more Triple H's popularity grew.

A Leadership Role

In 1998, Triple H earned some serious heel heat when he defeated the late Owen Hart to win the WWF's European Championship. That year at *WrestleMania*, Shawn Michaels injured his back and has not wrestled for the WWF since. Triple H moved into Michaels' spot as the leader of DX, a position that he retains to this day.

Feuding with The Rock

Triple H lost his European title to D-Lo Brown, which enabled him to start a feud with The Rock. It was a feud that raised Triple H to main-event level in the minds of WWF fans. The feud peaked in intensity at the 1998 *SummerSlam* pay-per-view event in which Triple H took on The Rock in a ladder match with the Intercontinental title on the line. Triple H won the match but ended up relinquishing the title when a knee injury prevented him from defending it.

A Corporate Minister

Triple H made his big comeback at *WrestleMania XV* in 1999. At that event, he turned on his D-Generation X colleagues and joined the Corporate Ministry. Now, instead of rebelling *against* the powers that be, Triple H would work as an enforcer for those very same powers. His next serious feud was against The Undertaker. Later that year, Triple H battled The Rock with the stipulation that the winner would become the number-one contender for Stone Cold Steve Austin's WWF World Heavyweight Championship.

Triple H was to win the match to become the number-one contender. But by the time the match took place, the WWF story line had gone through its usual curves and swerves, so the match, at *SummerSlam 1999*, ended up being a three-way dance—Triple H versus Stone Cold Steve Austin versus Mankind (Mick Foley) for the WWF belt. To add even more interest in the match, the special referee was Minnesota Governor Jesse Ventura. Mankind won the *SummerSlam* main event to win the title, but he didn't keep it for long: Triple H defeated him to win the championship the very next night on *RAW is WAR*.

Doing a Job for the Boss

Triple H once again was an enemy of the state, so to speak, feuding with Vince McMahon, who was injecting himself into WWF story lines with greater fervor each week. Triple H even lost his title briefly to Vince on an episode of *Smackdown*—not that Vince won the belt fair and square. Far from it. Triple H got his belt back at the subsequent *No Mercy* pay-per-view event. D-Generation X was re-formed at that point, with Triple H once again its leader. The New-Age Outlaws and X-Pac were once again part of the group. Triple H's new posse didn't do him much good, however, in a match against The Big Show, in which he lost his belt.

Seducing Stephanie

Triple H's next role in the WWF was a pleasant enough one to play. In December 1999, he became the story-line husband of Vince McMahon's daughter, Stephanie, who up until that time had been portrayed as a naive lass. Stephanie was madly in love, or so we were led to believe, with WWF wrestler Test (now half of T&A). But, on the eve of Test and Stephanie's wedding, Triple H revealed he had taken Stephanie to Las Vegas and married her himself. Triple H took great delight at the time in informing his boss McMahon that he and Stephanie had "consummated the marriage many, many times." Stephanie's personality (along with her eye makeup) changed immediately. She was now a woman of experience and took a leadership role in DX and, eventually, in the entire WWF. When Vince McMahon and his son, Shane, learned of Triple H and Stephanie's marriage, they walked away from the whole business, leaving Triple H and Stephanie in charge of the WWF until the days before *WrestleMania 2000*.

Triple H and Stephanie are not really a married couple—but they play one on TV.

The Spritz!

Triple H's entrances today are very popular with WWF fans. His primary gimmick involves entering the arena with a bottle of water. When he gets to the ring, he spits the water up into the air in a fine spray. Turning oneself into a human lawn sprinkler is not only an impressive shtick, but it's one that male fans find analogous to other bodily functions as well.

He is still "married" to Stephanie McMahon (although there are harbingers of trouble in paradise), but now all the McMahons (except Mom) are on the same side, and their crew is known as The McMahon-Helmsley Regime.

The Least You Need to Know

➤ Hunter Hearst Helmsley learned to wrestle at Killer Kowalski's school in Boston.

➤ Triple H did not become a superstar until he had gone through several unpopular gimmicks.

➤ When Shawn Michaels was injured, Triple H took his place as leader of D-Generation X.

➤ Triple H is one of the WWF's most popular wrestlers.

➤ In the WWF story line, Triple H is now the husband of Vince McMahon's daughter, Stephanie.

Other Superstars

With the dawning of the twenty-first century, professional wrestling is more popular than ever, and its stars are once again household names. Casual fans who 10 years ago could name only one professional wrestler (probably Hulk Hogan) can now name a handful—maybe even two.

So, here are a few brief biographies of those stars who have made professional wrestling the most popular programming on cable TV today.

Chyna—The Ninth Wonder of the World

Chyna is called the Ninth Wonder of the World. (For those of you who are asking, "Hey, what happened to the Eighth Wonder of the World?" we suggest that you turn back to the section about Andre the Giant in Chapter 9, "Wacky '70s and '80s.") The billing may seem like an exaggeration, but Chyna is indeed one of the most unique women in the annals of pro wrestling.

Chyna: A unique woman and wrestler.

She's huge, and she has muscles that most men would give their eyeteeth—and more—for. She has arms like pythons yet still retains the curvy-curves of a woman. In short, she is an Amazonian dream. Always dressed in a sexy leather outfit that shows off her multiple assets, Chyna wrestles with the men these days—not with the women—just like a modern-day Mildred Burke. And, like Mildred, she kicks butt!

Captain Lou's Corner

A lot of folks have noticed that Chyna has changed since she originally appeared in the WWF. I did my homework and found this list of her cosmetic surgeries: breast augmentation, December 1997; second breast augmentation, March 1998; facial reconstruction, November 1998.

Joanie Laurer, the woman that we know today as Chyna, was born in Rochester, New York, and raised by her older sister. She has had no contact with her parents for many years. "My sister is my mother ... my sister and my best friend," she says. At age 16, Joanie got her first taste of world travel when she went to Spain on a United Nations scholarship. So, if every once in a while Chyna says something intelligent or twinkles like she might have a clue, now you know that she started out as an egghead.

After school, Laurer joined the Peace Corps in Costa Rica, where she taught the natives to read. Then she entered fitness competitions and even tried night-club singing for a time. Deciding that professional wrestling was her calling, she signed up at Killer Kowalski's wrestling school in Boston. She didn't even finish the course before she started getting jobs as a pro wrestler, using the name Joanie Lee. After a few matches with Special Events Promotions, Joanie came to the attention of Vince McMahon. Soon thereafter, Joanie became Chyna—and her life will never be the same.

Chyna was not in the WWF long before she became a real-life romantic item with the wrestler known as Hunter Hearst Helmsley (Triple H) whom she'd met in wrestling school. The pair even announced their engagement at one point, but they have since broken up. The reason given: Triple H was determined to enjoy his new home in New Hampshire, and Chyna was determined to get into movies and needed to spend as much time as possible in Hollywood. (Chyna has already achieved some success, landing a recurring role on the hit TV sitcom, *Third Rock from the Sun*.) Her first WWF appearance was on the February 1997 edition of *RAW is WAR*, in which she worked as Triple H's bodyguard and roughed up Terri Runnels, who was then known as Marlena. Since then Chyna has worked as a valet, has wrestled men and women, has worked comedy bits between TV matches and, in general, has done everything that Vince McMahon has asked her to do.

Wrestle Mania

The Chyna who arrived in the WWF was considered somewhat of a freak of nature, a woman with huge muscles. Some thought that perhaps she had been a man and had had a sex change operation. But perceptions of Chyna have changed. Her feminine personality, as well as the re-shaping of her body to make her more curvaceous, has turned her into a sex symbol. Now she has her own comic book and, in the November 2000 issue of Playboy, she showed off all of her assets and a couple of her attributes as well.

The Big Show

The 7-foot-4, 450-pound wrestler known today as the Big Show—who no doubt would have been Ed Sullivan's favorite wrestler if Ed were still with us—was born Paul Wight, a native of South Carolina. His physical resemblance to Andre the Giant is so strong that when he first came to WCW in 1995, it was said that he was from France and was Andre's son. He was called simply, The Giant. Resemblances notwithstanding, The Giant was in many ways a physically unprecedented wrestler: He was every bit as big and tall as Andre, but he's about 20 times more agile. The Giant even climbed to the top of the ropes to dive down onto his opponent. What's more, he was the heaviest man in wrestling history to deliver a flying drop-kick.

The Big Show (The Giant) is as big and tall as Andre the Giant, but 20 times more agile.

The Giant drifted in and out of the nWo and its various factions, never keeping with one alliance for very long during his time with WCW. For a little while, part of his shtick was to enter the ring smoking a cigarette while the announcers frantically warned the kids in the audience not to smoke because it would stunt their growth. He's media-friendly, too, just in case he decides to contemplate a show biz career after his wrestling days are over. In fact, he appeared as a game show celebrity panelist on the Nickelodeon program *Figure It Out*.

Wight, who became known as the Big Show when he entered the WWF, is one of the few wrestlers in history to win both the WCW and WWF versions of the World Heavyweight Championship. He continues to be a celebrity outside the ring—he has performed memorable comedy bits on NBC's *Saturday Night Live* and was the latest spokesman for Chef Boy-R-Dee canned foods. His ability to laugh at his size—a quality that Andre never had—may make Wight less awesome than Andre, but a hundred times more likable.

Undertaker

The Undertaker is actually a large wrestler named Mark Calloway who started his career in the big leagues of wrestling in WCW as Mark Callas, King of the Heart Punch. For a man his size, he was very agile, able to walk the top rope like a tight rope so that he could leap down on opponents even when they weren't near a turnbuckle. But Callas was doomed to remain forever a midcarder until Vince McMahon and his genius for wrestling gimmicks took hold of him.

After making the switch to the WWF, Calloway re-emerged as the Undertaker, a man who represented death itself, who hailed from the Dark Side, and who couldn't be killed because (cue spooky music) he was already dead! His character enabled the

WWF to book graveyard matches, close-the-lid-on-the-coffin matches. The Undertaker appeared in the first "Hell in a Cell" match with Mick Foley (see Chapter 24, "Greatest Matches of Today"). The Undertaker was a main-event wrestler—or close to it—for most of the 1990s, longer than just about anyone in the modern era.

The Undertaker has always been popular with the lady fans, who find his combination of size and morbidity oddly sexy.

The Undertaker was on hiatus during the spring of 2000, rehabbing a knee, and he returned in May with his gimmick slightly altered. Now he is a biker—the kind who rides a motorcycle—from beyond death, a true Hell's Angel of the squared circle.

Chris Jericho: Y2J

Chris Jericho has been a name wrestler for almost a decade now, but only in the spring of 2000 has he finally reached main-event status. And he did it for Vince McMahon's WWF. Jericho is a good-looking blond kid that the babes love—yet he's an obnoxious bad boy and can wrestle an exciting match, so he appeals to males in the audience, too. With Shawn Michaels, another of the same type, out of commission because of injuries, McMahon saw Jericho as the perfect wrestler to take his spot in WWF story lines.

Jericho these days is enemies with the McMahon-Helmsley Regime. He has been particularly harsh on Stephanie, calling her suggestive names and questioning her virtue right in front of her father. Naturally, Jericho always gets stomped (stomped real good!) by the Regime in revenge for his insults. But somehow, come the next episode, he's back to being as mouthy as ever. Jericho is the real-life son of former NHL star Ted Irvine.

Chris Jericho: He's good-looking and obnoxious—and he can wrestle!

Jeff Jarrett

Jeff Jarrett has been around wrestling his entire life. His father is promoter Jerry Jarrett, and Jeff acted as a referee in Memphis before making his ring debut in April 1986. Since then, Jarrett's career has gone skyward. He teamed with the late great Owen Hart in the WWF before moving to WCW with Vince Russo, who immediately pushed Double J to the top of the organization. He has since been a four-time WCW champion, last losing the title to Booker T at *Bash At The Beach* after the bizarre scenario where Vince Russo made him lay down for Hulk Hogan and then told the crowd that Hogan didn't get the real belt. Jarrett is the perennial contender, working hard to make both his opponent and himself look good in the ring, and will continue to be a big part of the WCW title picture for quite a while.

Bert's Corner

My favorite story regarding The Dog was when Finley and Knobs lost him temporarily and they looked in the bathroom to make sure that he wasn't "drinking out of the toilet again."

The Dog

The Dog is completely out of control. He may be rabid. He's growling and snarling and foaming at the mouth and looking for someone to bite. Leading The Dog to the WCW ring with his collar and leash are his "masters," Fit Finley and Brian Knobs. The only way to calm The Dog is to throw a bag over his head. That makes him kneel quietly with his hands folded and his head bowed.

The Dog does bite his opponents on occasion, but he also uses state-of-the-art wrestling moves. His finishing move is called "The Dog Pound," an upside-down body slam off the top rope that's doggone effective.

Buff Bagwell

Buff Bagwell is unusual. Since the early 1990s, he has had only one employer, WCW. After making his pro debut as The Handsome Stranger for the Global Wrestling Federation in Dallas, he started out in WCW as Marcus Alexander Bagwell (his real name), a rich and frightfully good-looking babyface. Gradually he has evolved into Buff Bagwell, a conceited heel whose motto is: "Buff's got the stuff."

At 6 feet, 1 inch, and 245 pounds, Bagwell isn't going to win any size contests but he does have one of the best physiques in the business. Before joining the grunt-and-groan circuit, Bagwell worked as a male dancer.

Buff Bagwell has the size and charisma to wrestle beyond his size.

Born on January 10, 1970, Bagwell is originally from Marietta, Georgia. He possesses the charisma and the athleticism to, what I call, "wrestle beyond his size." (Ric Flair is a perfect example of this. The Nature Boy always wrestles bigger than he really is because his aura is so big.) His finishing move is called the Buff Blockbuster.

Val Venis

The WWF character most affected by the recent parental and sponsor protests against wrestling has been Val Venis. Along with The Godfather, Venis has had to have his character revamped.

When he first entered the WWF in 1998, it was clear that Val Venis was a veteran star of many adult movies. Even his finishing move, the Money Shot, derived its name from the adult entertainment industry. Venis had an entourage of scantily clad cuties with him at all times (Val's Gals) and entered the arena with a towel over his bikini-style wrestling trunks. Venis's arrogant ladies' man style was reminiscent of that used by the late "Ravishing" Rick Rude.

Val Venis: "Helloooooo, ladies!"

When the protests first started, claiming that the WWF's ratings-boosting strategy was really that of marketing adult themes for kids, Val Venis's character became vaguer: The entourage was gone; the towel was gone; the adult film background was never mentioned again. However, some things remained unchanged, not the least of which was the suspicious spelling of Venis's last name. The finishing move remained "The Money Shot," and Val's signature line, "Helloooooo, ladies," remained.

Mikey Whipwreck and The Sinister Minister

The creepiest duo in ECW these days is composed of the diminutive Mikey Whip-wreck and his new "manager," The Sinister Minister, who would appear to actually be Satan. As seen through a first-person POV camera in the filmed segments that ECW uses to promote this devilish duo, we first are waiting for an elevator. Next to the button for the basement is written the word *Hell*. We press the button. The elevator arrives, and we go down. When the elevator doors open, we are in a small room.

Sitting behind a desk is The Sinister Minister with his pointy beard; long, pointy fingernails; and evil grin. Mikey Whipwreck, who was once an ECW hero, now has circles around his eyes. He is unkempt and has developed the laugh of a hyena. He lives under his master's desk. Still using the first-person POV camera, we sit, and The

Minister gives us a fortuneteller's card reading. As the tarot cards are turned over and the portents become gloomier, we slowly figure out which ECW character we are by the Minister's prognostications.

In other segments, the Sinister Minister has been seen sitting in the stands at ECW shows. With him is Whipwreck, who has strings attached to him like a marionette. Naturally, the Evil One is at Whipwreck's controls.

Taka Michinoku

Michinoku is one of the more popular Japanese wrestlers ever to work the United States. Although Japanese wrestlers have historically been portrayed as heels, Michinoku has always worked as a babyface—and made it work. He has size—or lack thereof—that makes him easy to root for. And he also has the charisma to carry that off.

Recently, Michinoku missed several months because of a serious shoulder injury. He went over the top rope and landed on his right shoulder on the floor, completely dislocating the shoulder at the *Royal Rumble* and was unable to wrestle again until one week before *WrestleMania*.

These days Taka wrestles as half of the tag team Kaientai, with teammate Funaki.

K-Dogg

Originally known as Conan the Barbarian when wrestling in the AAA promotion in Mexico, this wrestler had to change the spelling to Konnan to avoid conflict with the Marvel Comics trademark.

The 6-foot-2, 250-pounder was a major star in Mexico working under a mask, but he unmasked and settled for a comfortable midcard position with WCW. Such are the economic times in Mexico that a wrestler would rather be midcard—even an opener—in America instead of a super-duper star in Mexico.

K-Dogg was a serious competitive athlete before becoming a wrestler, and he boxed on the U.S. Navy team. His favorite quote is "*Viva la raza!*" ("Long live the 'hood!") He is best known for his outrageous inner-city videos in which he is riding in a bouncing car playing his hot hip-hop theme song, in which he does the lead vocal himself.

Berlyn

Berlyn's real name is Alex Wright, and it was under that name that he first appeared in the major leagues of pro wrestling, WCW, as a teenager in the late 1990s. A cruiserweight from Berlin, Germany (he speaks English with a German accent), Wright was only 18 when he began wrestling the big boys of WCW.

A good-looking kid, Wright danced a strange boogie on his way to the ring. He tried to be a good guy. He smiled. He fought by the rules. But he tried a little too hard, and the fans booed him mercilessly. Going with the flow, Wright, now known as "Das Wunderkind"—that's pronounced *Vunderkind*—began to brag about how great he was.

Worse, at least as far as American audiences were concerned, even though everyone knew that he knew how to speak English, he refused to use the Queen's language in public. When "Mean" Gene Okerlund would ask Wright questions, the answers would come back sounding like a Hitlerean speech from a crackly old newsreel. The fans booed even louder.

Wright continued to go with the flow and made his character even more despicable. He shaved his head into a mohawk and wore sunglasses to the ring.

Wright changed his name to Berlyn, and because he was smaller than many of the superstars of WCW, he always kept a huge bodyguard named The Wall at his side. Berlyn's rhetoric became increasingly fascistic. The Wall has since gone off on his own, and now Berlyn is on his own. Still only in his early 20s, Berlyn has many more years of ruthless goose-stepping ahead of him.

Crash Holly

Crash Holly is a man on the run. During the spring of 2000, Crash, perhaps the smallest male wrestler in the WWF, was the WWF Hardcore Champion. Holly had won that belt under the stipulation that he must defend it seven days a week, 24 hours a day. All an opponent had to do was pin him (with a qualified WWF referee present) anywhere, anytime. The referee of choice was Theodore H. Long—a wrestling veteran who had worked as a manager during the early 1990s for WCW.

The Mean Street Posse, with Teddy Long in tow, attacked Holly in a hotel room. They would have won the belt except for the fact that they couldn't agree on who would do the pinning; they all wanted to be the Hardcore champ, so they pulled each other off Holly until their prey had an opportunity to flee.

The female wrestler Ivory used her sex appeal in an attempt to catch Crash unaware. Pretending that she liked him, she gave him a massage. While he was relaxed, she pulled referee Teddy Long into the room and then hit Crash over the head with a glass jar.

These days Crash can never relax. He has even been attacked by his cousin and tag-team partner, Hardcore Holly.

Chris Benoit: The Crippler

Chris Benoit (pronounced ben-WA) is a Canadian wrestler who first gained fame in Japan. Although he's a gifted athlete, it was commonly thought by U.S. promoters that Benoit lacked the size and the verbal skills to make it in the big-time. Benoit has been proving them wrong ever since.

An innovator in both on-the-mat scientific wrestling and the aerial variety, his first steady gig in the United States was with ECW. While working for Paul Heyman, Benoit managed to shuck the "can't talk" rap by giving long and compelling monologues. And he earned his nickname, "Crippler," when he legitimately broke Sabu's neck during an ECW match in Philadelphia. (Not that Sabu was actually crippled, but it was close.)

Chris Benoit is one of the hardest-working wrestlers around.

From there, Benoit moved to WCW, where he got rid of his "too small" rap, taking on the big boys and holding his own. Benoit is another one who wrestles bigger than he is. But, with WCW struggling, and feeling that he was stuck at the midcard level, Benoit—along with Dean Malenko, Eddy Guerrero, and Perry Saturn—bolted en masse for the WWF. The four deserters, known as The Radicalz, entered the WWF together and have been getting steady work ever since.

Ernest "The Cat" Miller

Ernest "The Cat" Miller, a former real-life karate champ, is working on being the smoothest, yet most obnoxious, character since the original "Big Cat," Ernie Ladd. Miller says that he's been hanging around with the "Godfather of Soul" James

Captain Lou's Corner

"What are you planning to do tonight?" a reporter asked Miller before a match.

"I'm gonna do what I gotta do and then get the hell out of this town," Miller replied.

Brown—and it shows. Miller says he needs someone to pick up his shoes and someone to put his cape on, and for this he has Mr. Jones (who was known as Virgil in the WWF).

The Cat always dresses in leopard skin and usually has the psychological advantage over his opponent—except, of course, when he is wrestling The Dog.

These days, there are a lot of dancers in World Championship Wrestling—3 Count, Disco Inferno, and Norman Smiley—but Miller is the best, getting on the "good foot," as James Brown would say.

The Demon

The Demon is the first character in the United States to be licensed from an outside source. The Demon—portrayed by Dale Torborg, son of ex-major league baseball player and former New York Mets manager Jeff Torborg—wears makeup that is a precise duplicate of that worn by Gene Simmons of Kiss. The Demon lives inside a coffin and drinks a goblet of blood before he wrestles, always smearing the last of the blood on his chest.

He does wag his tongue a bit, but it isn't nearly as impressive as when the real Gene Simmons does it; the Demon's tongue is inches shorter than that of the original. WCW reportedly paid Simmon's mucho moolah to use the gimmick.

So far, The Demon's popularity has been disappointing, and he has not made an impressive showing in the ring. His tag-team partner is the flamboyant Norman Smiley.

The devilish duo known as Team XS (Lane and Rave) decided to play a trick on The Demon and glued his coffin shut, but luckily for The Demon, he was out having a goblet of cappuccino at the time.

Dustin Rhodes

Dustin Rhodes is in what will be considered his post-Goldust period of his career, a time when it is important to be as macho as possible. When Rhodes first entered pro wrestling, he was known almost exclusively as the son of wrestling legend Dusty "The American Dream" Rhodes. He had the size to be a superstar, but there was a charisma gap between him and his flamboyant dad. He became known as "The Natural," a name that implied that Dustin, unlike many of his contemporaries, was naturally huge rather than pumped up on steroids. But Dusty was still around and as popular than ever. Dustin seemed doomed to remain in his father's shadow forever. Then Vince McMahon came to the rescue—sort of. McMahon could see that Rhodes was not going to be a main-event wrestler until he became disassociated from his father in the fans' minds. So the character of Goldust was created.

Unrecognizable in his gold makeup, blond wig, and tight gold costume, Goldust was an effeminate character of ambiguous sexual preference. Accompanying him to the ring was Marlena, a cigar-smoking babe who was obviously in charge. Marlena was played by Rhodes' real-life wife, Terri Boatwright, who is currently "Devil Woman" Terri Runnels in the WWF. Goldust became a big hit.

When Dustin left the WWF to rejoin WCW in 1999, he was no longer the son of Dusty. He was the guy who used to be Goldust, so he still has a cross to bear. But at least it's a different one. And he did get his stint as a main eventer in the WWF, even if the role called for him to do humiliating things every now and again.

Today Dustin is a supermacho cowboy, hardcore wrestler, a specialist in the "Cowbell Bull Rope" match in which the wrestlers are tied together by a bullrope with a cowbell on it. Sounds like the American Dream to me.

Booker T

Booker T debuted in WCW in 1993 along with his brother Stevie Ray. Together the two formed the tag team Harlem Heat. Harlem Heat quickly became one of the premiere tag teams in WCW, winning the tag team title on numerous occasions. In late 1999, however, the team split up and Booker T entered singles competition. Booker quickly rose to the top of the ranks as the fans warmed to his undeniable in-ring talent and no-nonsense attitude. However, Booker's momentum faltered somewhat with an ill-advised gimmick change that involved him going by the name GI Bro and wearing military fatigues. Thankfully the new gimmick was soon shelved, and Booker T returned to pick up where he left off. Then, at the *Bash at the Beach* pay-per-view, he finally got his title shot. Booker T made the most of the opportunity and defeated Jeff Jarrett to win the WCW World title, becoming only the second man of African descent to do so.

Vampiro

Although his name may imply it, Vampiro is not one of wrestling's blood drinkers. (You'll have to look at the sections on Gangrel and The Demon to read about the true vampires of the sport.) Not that Vampiro can't be doggone ghoulish when he wants to be, such as the time he fought Sting in a cemetery.

What Vampiro has going for him is truly frightening makeup. His defleshed countenance would have made Lon Chaney proud! Vampiro is actually Canadian, but he comes to WCW through Mexico and the world of *lucha libre*.

Vampiro is very sensual in his interviews, projecting a certain Gothic sex appeal when he says things like, "I have been selfish. It is time for someone else to taste the pain!" His finishing move is called "Nail in the Coffin."

Vampiro's most famous match was the one in which he battled Sting in a cemetery.

Team Package

Three legends of the sport—Lex "The Total Package" Luger, "The Nature Boy" Ric Flair, and "The First Lady of Professional Wrestling," Miss Elizabeth—have grouped together to wipe out those New Blood whipper snappers.

Miss Elizabeth carries a baseball bat around with her these days, although she has been inconsistent in effectiveness when it comes to actually swinging it. Like Elvis's guitar, it's for holding only.

Billy Kidman

Kidman is a WCW light heavyweight and a babe magnet. His valet is super-blond Torrie Wilson, who might be the most beautiful woman in wrestling. As of spring 2000, the two are in love, and every time he enters the arena for a match, she is hanging on him, kissing him on the lips and generally distracting him from the business at hand. (Or maybe it's wrestling that's distracting him from the business at hand—and lips.)

Anyway, Torrie is doing nothing for Billy's in-the-ring performance, and his out-of-the-ring performance isn't public knowledge. Torrie appears to have done more draining than training for her man. It's hard to get a three-count on a man when life has been like a perpetual honeymoon.

The Godfather

The Godfather is one of the WWF's most controversial characters, the one that always gets mentioned when parental groups complain about the subject matter of WWF story lines. He is, shudder, a pimp—a good-natured pimp, to boot. His favorite slogan is "Pimpin' ain't easy," and the crowd chants along. He wears the big hat and the whole bit.

He's so much a caricature of a stereotype that anyone who is actually watching the show can't possibly take him seriously. Yet parental groups are complaining while ratings are skyrocketing.

The Godfather's favorite saying is, "Pimpin' ain't easy!"

The Godfather brings several lovely ladies (usually from a local strip joint), referred to as The Godfather's "Hos," to the ring with him. Fans are invited to climb aboard The Godfather's Ho Train. Before the complaints started and the WWF lost a few TV sponsors, The Godfather would offer his Hos to his opponent. If the opponent refused, there was a fight. The opponent always refused.

Sid Vicious

At 6 feet, 8 inches, and 318 pounds, Sid Vicious is one of the most fearsome-looking individuals ever to enter the ring. He was born on July 4, year unknown, in West Memphis, Arkansas. His real name is Sid Eudy. Today the former two-time WWF champ is a WCW superstar, but it wasn't that long ago that most wrestling insiders thought Sid would never work for WCW again.

In 1993, during Sid Vicious's notorious first stint with World Championship Wrestling, Sid got into a real-life brawl with Arn Anderson while on tour in London, England. Anyway, the fight got out of hand. Somebody grabbed a table leg, somebody grabbed a pair of scissors, and Arn ended up with a stab wound in the leg. It was considered unlikely that Sid would ever work at the major-league level again. When he became so popular during his occasional appearances with ECW in the late 1990s, some thought that this was as high as he could go, considering the glass ceiling that he had created for himself.

But the Monday night ratings war had created desperate times, especially at WCW, where *Monday Nitro* is chronically running a poor second in 2000. Sid was brought back and is now the champ.

On March 22, 2000, in Orlando, Florida, Sid Vicious turned on Hulk Hogan. Although Hogan was convinced that Vicious was his friend and ally, Vicious did something dramatic to get the Hulkster's attention. He grabbed ring announcer (and Hogan's friend) "Mean" Gene Okerlund by the necktie and pulled until the announcing legend's face started to turn purple. Okerlund, although a normally sized man, looked like a midget beside the humongous Vicious.

Sid Vicious is one of the most fearsome-looking individuals to ever enter the ring.

Hulk took the bait. He came running to save Okerlund. Vicious released his grip on the announcer as Hogan attacked. The two huge men brawled around the arena, and it took every security guard in the joint to separate them. Sid got the Hulkster's attention—and his enmity.

Disco Inferno

Disco Inferno may be a stereotype, but he's a funny one, so we'll let him slide. He is one of those Italians from Brooklyn who went to see the movie *Saturday Night Fever* in the 1970s and has been under the delusion that he is John Travolta ever since.

Today, Disco, as his closest friends call him, hangs out with Johnny the Bull and Big Vito LoGrosso—and together they are known as the Mamalukes. His catch phrase, which usually brings a lot of derisive oral noises from the crowd, is, "Disco is in the house!" Fans chant back, quoting from one of the 1970's most popular bumper stickers: "Disco s(tink)s!"

Disco's creativity has led him to a position on the WCW *booking committee*.

Gangrel

Gangrel is the WWF's version of a vampire. He wears the fangs of a vampire and otherworldly contact lenses that give him the eyes of a cat, and he rises up out of the top of the ramp standing inside a circle of fire.

He wears a tuxedo shirt with the tails hanging out and carries a golden goblet of red fluid (supposedly blood) to the ring with him. Just before he gets into the ring, he drinks from the goblet and blows a spray of red fluid up and over the crowd. Gangrel always allows the last of the "blood" to drip down his face and down onto his white shirt.

Fighting Words

The booker or **booking committee** is in charge of writing the scripts for the wrestling shows. For TV, they write the skits between matches, as well as what the wrestlers will say during their interviews. In the old days, the booker had considerably less to do. His job was to hand out the finishes to the wrestlers before the matches so they would know who was supposed to win. Now a complex story line must be maintained with a certain level of continuity, and it all has to fit between the sponsors' commercials.

X-Pac

X-Pac—real name Sean Waltman—has had more names than any of the FBI's most wanted during his 10-year pro career. When Sean first showed up as a blip on the wrestling radar screen in the early 1990s, he was wrestling as The Lightning Kid for the Global Wrestling Federation out of The Sportatorium in Dallas, Texas.

His first shot at the majors came with the WWF, wrestling as The 1-2-3 Kid, where, on one of the very first episodes of *RAW is WAR*, he unexpectedly pinned Razor Ramon (who now wrestles for WCW under his real name, Scott Hall).

Sean then moved back to World Championship Wrestling where he was called Syxx, a member of the original New World Order. Then it was back to the WWF as X-Pac, a member of D-Generation X.

X-Pac's daredevil, high-flying style has made him a major star.

Back in Dallas, the word on Sean was that he lacked the size to make it in the big-time. How he has proven those experts wrong. Sean's daredevil, high-flying style and savvy psychological approach to wrestling have made him a crowd favorite wherever he has wrestled—at whatever level and under whatever name he wore at the time.

Rey Mysterio Jr.

At 5 feet, 3 inches, and 140 pounds, Rey Mysterio Jr. does not appear big enough to wrestle the monsters of WCW, but the phenomenal Mysterio has been proving that he belongs for years. Rey—whose name in English means King Mystery Junior—is another import from Mexico's *lucha libre* wrestling, another masked *luchador* who was talked out of his mask by WCW. As it turned out, losing his mask did nothing to diminish Rey's popularity.

Rey began wrestling professionally at the tender age of 15, and before a recent series of leg injuries slowed him down, he was the most athletically gifted wrestler in the world. His mid-air maneuvers defy gravity and appear physically impossible. People look for the wires, but there are none. He is always a crowd favorite because he inevitably takes on wrestlers bigger than him. The only wrestlers smaller than him wrestle in the minidivision—what we used to call back in my day "midgets." But Rey is a fully grown man and takes on only other fully grown men. He has yet to go into a match as a clear favorite, yet his finishing move, the Huracanrana, has been known to take down opponents who outweighed him by half or more.

Tank Abbott

Tank Abbott first came to public attention on pay-per-view telecasts during the 1990s as the most entertaining—if not the best—of the Ultimate Fighters, those wrestlers who battled it out to the finish. With a flat-top brush cut and a beard that a Fuller Brush Man couldn't unload, Tank was a notorious discipline problem at the Ultimate Fight Championships that he participated in. He fought hard in the octagon (the eight-sided caged ring used for UFC bouts), but the trouble was that he fought hard everywhere else, too: backstage, in the restaurant, and at the hotel. Because he won only about as often as he lost, and because the lawsuits were mounting, the UFC powers-that-be eventually banned him from future competitions—so the Tankster turned to pro wrestling, and WCW hired him.

Abbott's ability to knock out a man with a single bare-knuckle punch remains his forte as he feuds with other WCW Hardcore specialists such as Meng, Fit Finley, and Brian Knobs. (Abbott was recruited as an opponent for Goldberg, so don't expect his potential to be realized until Goldberg returns from his arm injury.)

Chris Candido

Chris Candido is the real-life husband of Tammy Lynn Sytch, best known for her stint in WWF as the manipulative valet Sunny, the most downloaded woman in the history of the Internet. Candido first achieved fame as Skip of the fitness-minded Body Donnas (with Tom Pritchard and Sunny as their valet). From there he went to ECW, taking his wife with him, where they both worked under their real names.

Chris Candido first gained fame as Skip of the tag team known as The Body Donnas.

The pair has recently returned to the big leagues, this time WCW. Candido is known for his nervous and fast-talking interviews. His finishing move is a head butt off the top rope, very similar to that used by Chris Benoit.

The Acolytes

Faarooq (Ron Simmons) and Justin Bradshaw make up the Acolytes. The Acolytes are seen on WWF programs just as frequently outside the ring as inside it. That's because at every show, while other matches are going on, Faarooq and Bradshaw can be found backstage smoking a few cigars and having a couple beers while playing poker. Many of the Acolytes' matches are directly or indirectly caused by their poker games. When the Acolytes win a lot of money from those who sit in on their games, they often make powerful enemies; when they lose a lot of money, they often pay off their debts by offering a little help in an upcoming match.

Rikishi

Rikishi Phatu, whose real name is Solofa Fatu Jr. from American Samoa, has been a pro wrestler for 15 years. He is the son of Sika and the nephew of Afa, who comprised the original Wild Samoans. Rikishi wrestled with his cousin as the Samoan Swat Team in WCW and as the Headhunters in the WWF, but it wasn't until he dyed his hair blond and put on a thong bottom that left his massive and puckered buttocks exposed that he became a main eventer. Naturally, Rikishi uses that butt as a weapon—both to administer concussive blows and, perhaps more frighteningly, as an instrument of asphyxiation. That move is called the "Stinky Face."

Rikishi: 400 pounds of dance fever!

Ah, but Rikishi is more than a 400-pound destroyer in there. He flies like a light heavyweight jumping off the top of steel cages onto hapless foes. And he is also quite a dancer. Rikishi is affiliated with a rather silly team of light heavyweights known as Too Cool, consisting of Grand Master Sexay (portrayed by Jerry "The King" Lawler's real-life son, Brian Christopher) and Scotty 2 Hotty. After Rikishi's victories, Too Cool gets in the ring. They put a pair of yellow-rimmed sunglasses on Rikishi, transforming the Samoan into a dancing machine. The three of them then line up in the ring and get down, get in the groove, and boogie the night away. Crowds go crazy with delight when the Samoan shakes his formidable body and booty.

Raven

One of ECW's all-time favorite wrestlers is Raven—a character portrayed by Scott Levy, who had previously wrestled as Scotty the Body and Johnny Polo. Raven is the guy you least want your sister to date. Ah, but he's got that certain *je ne sais quoi*, and she might see something in him anyway. He's the kid who always got kicked out of high school, a juvenile delinquent, a troubled lad. But with appeal. And did we mention he's a chick magnet?

Raven: a juvenile delinquent with appeal.

As Raven, Levy started in ECW, moved to WCW for a stint, and then returned to the land of extreme in Philadelphia. In his monologues, Raven rarely touches upon the subject of wrestling. His intent is to tell of his dysfunctional upbringing and how it has warped his utopian dreams into a back-alley reality. A consistent trademark of Raven's gimmick, right from the inception of his character, was his ending every interview with the word "Nevermore"—so you can never forget that his character is based on an Edgar Allan Poe poem. Raven recently earned an enemy for life in ECW when he stole away the lovely Francine (with a lipstick kiss mark tattooed elegantly upon her left buttock) from Tommy Dreamer.

The Wall

Bringing mayhem to WCW is The Wall, a really, really big guy. If The Wall doesn't want you to get past, you are not going to get past. These days The Wall is feuding with Bam Bam Bigelow. After giving Bigelow—the man with the tattooed head, called the "Beast from the East"—a severe beating, The Wall decided to hurt Bigelow even more by hurting his friends.

In separate incidents, The Wall first attacked Crowbar and then David Flair, seriously injuring both. To execute his dangerous finishing move, The Wall stands at the edge of the ring while his foe stands on the apron, the ring ropes between them. He then grabs his opponent by the throat and throws him down as hard as he can. It's a simple but effective move, and, of course, you have to be a behemoth to use it. The Wall threw Crowbar through the announcer's table, rendering him *hors de combat* and necessitating his removal on a stretcher.

The following week, he stacked two tables on top of each other and threw David Flair down through both of them, all the way to the concrete floor. Flair also had to have his head taped to a stretcher so that he could be taken to a hospital in an ambulance. (In a moment that amazed viewers, Flair's father, Ric Flair, was asked what he thought of his son's serious injury. The elder Flair seemed only mildly distracted by the incident, saying, "Ahhh, he's 21, he'll bounce back." Sounds like the man had read the next week's script!)

The Wall received his name when he first started with WCW and was working as the bodyguard for a wrestler named Berlyn (the genuinely German Alex Wright, with his head shaved into a mohawk). The Wall, Berlyn—get it?

Essa Rios

After being dormant for years, the WWF's Light Heavyweight Championship was claimed on March 6, 2000, by Essa Rios (a Mexican wrestler formerly known as Papi Chulo), who is always accompanied into the ring by his redheaded and amazingly athletic valet, Lita. Rios got to hold on to the belt for only one week, however. On the March 13, 2000, edition of *RAW is WAR*, Rios faced, and lost to, Dean "The Man of 1,000 Holds" Malenko. Rios was robbed of the belt when Malenko's partner in crime with The Radicals, Eddy Guerrero—his arm in a sling because of a dislocated elbow suffered several weeks before—power-bombed Lita at ringside. This, understandably enough, distracted Rios long enough for Malenko to sneak up behind him and roll him up for the pin.

Essa Rios and Lita were joined in March 2000 by Stevie Richards, a wiseguy, conman type of wrestler recently imported from ECW. Rios and Richards wrestled as a tag team with Lita as their valet. Richards always tried to "fix" matches before they happened so that a victory would be guaranteed. The trouble is that something always goes wrong—instead of guaranteeing victory, Richards's actions always manage to get Rios and Richards stomped in the ring by the very team that he had just tried to bribe. Essa Rio and his butt-kicking valet, Lita, are going to put up with this only for so long, and then you'd better believe that the two recent imports from south of the border are going to kick Richards out of their lives so hard that the footprint on his butt will linger for weeks.

Kurt Angle

One of the most obnoxious of the new superstars in the WWF is Kurt Angle, who was launched into fame when he won a gold medal at the 1996 Atlanta Summer Olympics. Angle was a great amateur wrestler and quickly turned pro, signing with the WWF. But would he make a great pro? The two did not necessarily go together. Many an amateur great has crashed and burned when he tried to hack it in the rough-and-tumble world of the pro game. His first few matches in the WWF were nothing to write home about, but he steadily improved.

He loved to brag about his gold medals to the crowds, telling them just how wonderful he was, and—to Vince McMahon's delight—WWF fans booed their lungs out in response. Angle quickly captured the European and Intercontinental Championships, becoming the first WWF wrestler in many years to hold two championship belts at the same time. Angle's archenemy is Chris "Y2J" Jericho.

In Your Face

Jericho once entered the arena while Angle was battling Rikishi Phatu, the Samoan known for his massive derriere and said, "Angle, looks can be deceiving. The biggest ass in the ring is you."

The Least You Need to Know

➤ Chyna is a woman—but what a woman! She wrestles men.

➤ The Big Show is the same size as Andre—but 20 times more agile.

➤ The Undertaker cannot be killed because—get this!—he's already dead.

➤ Chris Jericho is a veteran who is wrestling main events for the first time.

Part 4

History of *WrestleMania*

Until 1985, pro wrestling lacked a focal point. Because of the territories that split the country, there was rarely a situation in which the whole world was watching. That ended when Vince McMahon Jr.'s WWF presented the first WrestleMania.

WrestleMania, which is always held on the Sunday closest to April Fool's Day, has become that focal point. The annual event became wrestling's Super Bowl—and you'll find that WrestleManias are even numbered with Roman numerals the way Super Bowls are.

For younger fans today, the history of WrestleMania is the history of wrestling. In this section, you'll be reading in detail about the lead-up to and the execution of WrestleMania 2000. In addition, we'll be looking at all the WrestleManias, going all the way back to that seemingly ancient night in 1985 when Hulk Hogan and Mr. T defeated Paul Orndorff and Rowdy Roddy Piper in New York's Madison Square Garden—and the whole world changed.

Chapter 16

2000: Setting Up the Main Event

In This Chapter

➤ Events leading up to *WrestleMania 2000*

➤ How the McMahons have turned wrestling into a family affair

➤ Mick Foley's soon-to-retire status becomes a major plot point

➤ Buy rates for pay-per-views are determined by pre-event hype

WrestleMania 2000, the most successful pay-per-view event in history that didn't feature Mike Tyson, did not happen overnight. Hype for *WrestleMania 2000* began two months before the event. It is WWF tradition that the winner of the main event at the pay-per-view called the *Royal Rumble* becomes the number-one contender and mandatory opponent for the champion at *WrestleMania.* But, at the *Royal Rumble 2000,* nine weeks before *WrestleMania,* there had been a controversial finish: Though The Rock had been declared the official winner, the Big Show believed (and he had a case) that he had, in fact, won the *Royal Rumble* and deserved to be the opponent in *WrestleMania's* main event.

Foley's Gone

A month before *WrestleMania,* fans knew that the WWF promoters had their work cut out for them—simply stated, they were running short of stars. Stone Cold Steve Austin had been unable to perform for months because of a serious neck injury. And Mick Foley, the WWF's biggest star during the first months of 2000, was a battle-scarred warrior who had had just announced his retirement.

Vince McMahon, head honcho of the WWF, decided to replace his stars with replacements who wouldn't put much of a stress on his payroll. He decided to use his entire family as onscreen talent: his wife, Linda; son, Shane; and daughter, Stephanie.

During the days leading up to *WrestleMania 2000,* Hunter Hearst Helmsley and his (story-line) wife Stephanie McMahon-Helmsley—he the WWF champ, she a spoiled brat from Connecticut who was running the WWF in place of her absent father, Vince—had joined up with the Big Show (now teamed up with Stephanie's big brother, Shane McMahon) to put the hurt on The Rock to prevent him from winning the WWF championship.

Because Stephanie and Triple H had the power to determine who was going to wrestle whom on WWF shows, they saw to it that The Rock had to wrestle sometimes three times a night against some of the WWF's top competition. If The Rock had allowed things to go the way they were going, he might not even have survived long enough to get to *WrestleMania 2000.*

The Rock's Retirement Match

Tiring of The Big Show's belly-aching, The Rock made a fateful decision. On the March 13, 2000, edition of *RAW is WAR,* addressing his gathered enemies, The Rock said, "The Rock says this—The Rock will wrestle the Big Show tonight, one-on-one. If The Rock beats the Big Show, The Rock wrestles Triple H at *Wrestlemania 2000* with the WWF World Heavyweight Championship on the line. And, if the Big Show beats The Rock, The Rock will never wrestle again." The Rock, who always refers to himself in the third person, stunned his fans. He was only 27 years old and presumably had a long and successful wrestling career ahead of him. Did he have something up his sleeve?

Later in the show, when The Rock entered the arena to battle the Big Show, he was shocked to discover that there was a surprise referee: Shane McMahon, who was representing the Big Show. Nobody ever said that life, or pro wrestling, was fair. So The Rock went on with the battle anyway. His career was on the line, and he knew he was in for the tussle of his life.

The men battled all over the Meadowlands Arena in East Rutherford, New Jersey. At times, the two scattered the screaming crowd as they took turns ramming each other's head into hard objects. While the pair was beating the tar out of one another, Triple H and Stephanie were backstage, cuddling on a couch, smugly watching the action, which eventually returned to the ring.

Bert's Corner

Whenever The Rock is out-manned in a match and someone asks him if he wants a second in his corner, The Rock always replies: "The Rock has 'The People' in The Rock's corner, and that's good enough for The Rock."

The Rock tried to hit the Big Show over the head with a folding chair, but Shane managed to pull the chair out of The Rock's hands before the blow landed. The Big Show then lifted The Rock high over his head and dropped him face first onto the broadcaster's table.

As expected, Shane did not referee the match fairly. He fast-counted whenever the Big Show had the Rock's shoulders pinned to the mat, and sl-o-o-o-w counted when the positions were reversed. Despite Shane's obvious attempt at chicanery, The Rock always somehow managed to get one shoulder up before Shane could complete the three-count and end The Rock's career. Then Shane got a little bit too close to the action and was knocked over the top rope to the floor below. Knocked groggy, Shane lost track of what was happening in the ring. The Rock hit the Big Show with his patented finishing move, The People's Elbow, and proceeded to pin the Big Show, but Shane was not there to make the three-count. He was still rolling around on the floor outside the ring trying to shake off the cobwebs. Then veteran WWF referee Earl Hebner ran into the ring, and The Rock again pinned the Big Show. But Hebner managed to count to only two when Shane McMahon pulled him off.

Captain Lou's Corner

Both WWF and WCW TV shows allow us to see "behind-the-scenes" candid moments between wrestlers backstage who are always blurting out things and getting themselves in trouble because, somehow, they've failed to notice there's a guy with a handheld TV camera in the room. In reality, these vignettes are carefully planned-out sketches designed to move the plot along.

The two referees were now battling outside the ring; Shane, by far the younger and stronger of the two, was getting the best of it. Shane finished off Hebner, grabbed a chair, and climbed into the ring. With one swing, Shane knocked The Rock cold. The Big Show pinned The Rock, Shane McMahon counted to three, and for a moment it looked as if The Rock's career was over. Then came the surprise finish. The TV screen in the building showed a long stretch limo pulling up to the arena.

Vince Returns

To the roar of the crowd, WWF president Vince McMahon exited the limo. After a long absence, the elder McMahon had finally returned, determined to see that justice was done. Triple H went out to meet Vince before Vince could make it inside the arena, but Helmsley's father-in-law greeted him with a single right hand to the jaw. The next thing he knew, Triple H was laying on the floor in la-la land.

Bert's Corner

Although the experienced athletes did by far the more difficult stunts, the crowd always reacted most strongly to those moments when a McMahon was whomping the tar out of a McMahon. The family affair was always the *thing.*

Captain Lou's Corner

Vince McMahon says that six months is like forever in the mind of a wrestling fan. That's why, in the days leading up to *Wrestlemania,* McMahon was able to effortlessly turn himself into a babyface, even though he had been "Mr. McMahon," the evil owner who, only six months before, had been one of the most hated men in wrestling—the boss who, spelled backward, could be called a double S.O.B.

Vince proceeded up the aisle and into the ring. Using the same chair that Shane had used to knock out The Rock moments before, Vince cold-cocked his son. Vince then tore the referee's striped shirt off Shane and put it on himself. The Rock, alert to the way the chips were falling, quickly pinned the Big Show, and Vince counted one-two-three.

The roof practically came off the Meadowlands, and the main event at *WrestleMania 2000* had been determined: Triple H would take on The Rock, with the belt on the line. Or so we thought. However, things are never quite that easy in the World Wrestling Federation. If Vince McMahon had written the Beatles song, it would have been called "The Long and Swervy Road."

Triple Threat

On the March 16, 2000, edition of *Smackdown,* Shane McMahon, assuming the power that belongs to all McMahons in the WWF, and determined to push the Big Show, proclaimed that the *WrestleMania* main event would be a "Triple Threat" match—sometimes referred to as a "Three-Way Dance." That is, all three men would be in the ring at once: Triple H versus The Rock versus the Big Show. The first one to pin one of the others would get the belt.

The Rock did not take kindly to Shane's proclamation. He pointed out that if the Big Show pinned Triple H, he would become the champion, and if Triple H pinned the Big Show, he would retain the title. And in neither case did anyone actually have to pin The Rock to win. Still, The Rock said that he would be a good sport and take the match. What else could he do? When the McMahon kids start barking orders, all anyone could do was, as the old saying goes, grin and bear it.

The McMahons weren't through, though. Now Shane made it clear that he would be in the Big Show's corner at *WrestleMania.* And Stephanie took the hand mic and told everyone that she would be in the corner of her husband, Triple H. Then came the surprise. Vince McMahon's theme music was heard, and he entered the arena to tremendous applause.

Vince McMahon can be a hero one minute and a villain the next. And he was one of the best wrestling announcers for years.

Now the crowd was screaming and going nuts because Shane and Stephanie's daddy was back—and it was going to be great to see them spanked. But Vince did no spanking. He simply announced that, at *WrestleMania,* he was going to make this a family affair. He was going to be in The Rock's corner. For the rest of *Smackdown,* the three *WrestleMania* main-eventers took turns sabotaging each other's matches. And they worked up a good, healthy hatred toward one another.

Three Warriors, Three McMahons

At the March 20 edition of *RAW* in Chicago, Vince announced that he knew what was "good for business." It was Monday night, which meant that he knew how to pump up the ratings to defeat WCW's competing *Nitro.* The Rock, Triple H, and the Big Show would have their "Triple Threat" match as the main event *that* night. Triple H accepted the challenge with the stipulation that he would not have to defend his title with a three-way match at *WrestleMania.* So, with 15 minutes left in the show, the "Triple Threat" match got underway.

Three warriors were in the ring, and three McMahons were on the outside. When The Rock threw Hunter Hearst Helmsley out of the ring, Vince was there, waiting for him with another knuckle sandwich. At one point, The Rock threw Triple H into the Big Show, thus putting the hurt on both with a single move. Stephanie was practically drooling with power lust as she watched the match from ringside. For a good portion of the match, the Big Show and Triple H teamed up on The Rock. Triple H took time out from stomping The Rock to kiss his "wife" while Vince watched, looking as if he were about to become violently ill.

Body Slam

The Rock has a nifty move that he uses when he is punching out an opponent. In perfect rhythm, he hits his foe with a right hand, another right, another right, then he spits in his right hand and hits him a fourth time.

Triple H's Revenge

But cooperation between the Big Show and Triple H would not last for long. Within minutes, the Big Show had turned on Triple H, and The Rock got an opportunity to catch his breath while those two went at it. The best bump of the match was taken by Triple H, who was choke-slammed by the Big Show from a standing position on top of the broadcasters' table to the concrete floor below. The Rock had the Big Show out of it and looked as if he were about to win the match with his famous finishing move, The People's Elbow, when Shane McMahon interfered, tripping The Rock as he bounced off the ropes.

The Rock tried to attack Shane, but instead Shane whacked him with a chair. Vince then knocked Shane out with a big right. The elder McMahon was about to follow up with a familial chair shot when Triple H saw his opportunity for revenge. Triple H KO'd Vince with a single punch and then entered the ring to pin the still-prone Big Show to win the match—the match originally scheduled as the *WrestleMania* main event—and successfully defend his title.

"M" Is for the Many Things—Or, Four McMahons, Four Warriors

Enter Linda McMahon—Stephanie and Shane's mom and Vince's wife. "So what will be the main event at *WrestleMania* now that it can't be a 'Triple Threat' match?" she asked. "I'll tell you what it is going to be—it will be a 'Fatal Four-Way Elimination' match. Triple H, you will defend the WWF championship against the Big Show, The Rock, and this man, Mick Foley!" (This was a surprise but not a shock. Foley had made it clear in interviews that being in a *WrestleMania* main event remained an unfulfilled dream. That was why he participated in the "Loser-Must-Retire" match in the first place.) With Linda's introduction, Foley entered the arena to a standing ovation. His "retirement" had lasted less than a month. Foley, still hobbled by his knee injuries, moved crablike into the ring and was in the process of kicking everybody's butt when the show ended.

Stephanie Gets Heel Heat: The Slap

In Cincinnati on March 23, Stephanie further heated up the McMahon family feud. Standing in the ring with the hand mic, Stephanie called for her mother to join her. Linda came—at which point Stephanie gave her a piece of her mind, scolding her for giving her *only* a $100 a week allowance when she was growing up, for making her make her own bed despite the fact that there were two maids in the house, and for telling her she could *just* have a sports car and not the Turbo sports car.

"It was all for your own good," Linda replied.

Then Stephanie called her "a cold-hearted, manipulating (w)itch." To make matters worse, she slapped her mother so hard that Linda fell to the canvas and began to cry. One sure thing, if you wanted to see Stephanie get her comeuppance—and who wouldn't?—you were going to have to pay to see it.

Fighting Words

Remember, getting **heel heat** means getting booed. It means getting the crowd to hate you and maybe even throw stuff at you—and, in wrestling, that's a good thing.

On the same show, Triple H played a little psychological warfare of his own on Linda McMahon. He told her that he was going to cripple Mick Foley at *WrestleMania*, and because it was she who had talked Foley into ending his four-week retirement, she would forever have the weight of his crippling on her conscience. Later, Foley himself came out and said that, yes, Linda McMahon had talked him into coming out of retirement, but it was for one match only.

Wrestle Mania

Whether Vince McMahon wants to admit it or not, Stephanie has turned into a sex symbol. First of all, she's cute, but her strong appeal has to do with the fact that she is the only woman in the WWF who never, ever dresses provocatively. She is hidden, a mysterious woman compared to the scantily clad others.

Blistering Butts and Festering Guts

If possible, tensions between the McMahons grew even more heated at the March 27 edition of *RAW* in Houston, Texas. The show opened with Linda McMahon in the ring, asking Stephanie to come out and apologize. Instead, Vince entered the ring to tell Linda that he was concerned that she would get hurt if she continued to get involved in the athletic arena rather than the corporate arena, where she belonged.

"You've known me for a long time, Vince. I can take care of myself," Linda said.

Then Vince turned the subject back to Stephanie, calling on her to apologize and to "do it without your degenerate husband at your side." He urged her, "Come on, Stephanie, do you have the guts or not?"

Surprisingly, she did, saying, "I'm sorry, Mom. It was a mistake for me to slap you." At this point, her "true" personality once again emerged. "I should have slapped Daddy—I should have slapped him as hard as I could!"

Vince replied like a typical father: "I'm gonna blister your fanny until it turns blue!"

That brought Triple H out to protect his wife and make an attempt to take charge of the situation.

"What kind of family did I marry into?" Triple H wondered of the soap opera mess the McMahons had gotten themselves into. "This has got to be the most dysfunctional family of all time! I think it is time for the ancient era to resign and to let the new era take command."

Shane McMahon entered the scene at that point, grabbed a microphone, and started running down his sister, saying that he hoped her "guts will rot and fester" for what she did to their mother. Then, out of the blue, Shane attacked his father from behind, hitting Vince over the head with the mic. Triple H ran into the ring and started to stomp the fallen McMahon. Stephanie climbed through the ropes and grabbed a handful of Shane's hair, but Linda came to her son's aid. Then all four of the main-event wrestlers ran into the ring as chaos reigned.

By the time the dust had settled, Triple H and the Big Show had left Vince, Mick Foley, and The Rock lying in the ring. Triple H stood with his foot on Vince's chest, one arm around Stephanie, the other holding the WWF World Heavyweight Championship belt high over his head.

The main event for *RAW* shaped up as The Rock and Vince against the Big Show and Shane, with Mick Foley and Triple H as the two guest referees. Of course, the match featured the usual chaos, with everyone betraying everyone. The best segment came when Vince beat up Shane to get revenge for the mugging that he had suffered earlier in the show. Vince even wrapped a headphone cord around Shane and choked him before the Big Show arrived to rescue Shane. In the end, The Rock pinned Shane to win the match—a match that the people of Houston, Texas, are not going to forget for a long time.

Stephanie Goes Gold

On the March 27 edition of *Smackdown*, Linda McMahon accused husband Vince of being the catalyst in her family's bigger-than-life problems. Vince said he'd fix it, all right, saying, "Stephanie, since you like to slap people so much, it's time you had your first real match here in the WWF—against WWF ladies' champion, Jackie."

Stephanie appeared nervous at first, but by the time she came into the ring, appearing for the first time ever in a T-shirt and shorts, she had a foolproof plan. Accompanying her to the ring were X-Pac and Tori, two friends from her husband's D-Generation X organization.

Naturally, Stephanie's friends interfered with the match and ambushed Jackie at every turn, preventing Jackie from actually getting her hands on Triple H's wife. They eventually knocked the WWF ladies' champ cold in the center of the ring. Stephanie almost reluctantly climbed aboard for the three-count and then smiled with embarrassment as they handed her the gold belt.

WrestleMania 2000 was only days away. The scene was set.

The Least You Need to Know

➤ Big event pay-per-views don't just happen—they take careful planning.

➤ The key to making people buy a show is getting them emotional about it.

➤ The one way to heat up an audience's emotions is to involve them—especially in the problems of wrestling's leading family.

➤ All four members of the McMahon family sided with a competing wrestler going into *WrestleMania.*

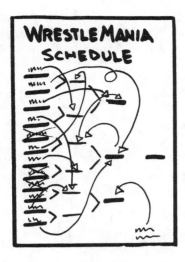

Chapter 17

How We Got Here

In This Chapter

➤ With days left, the WWF turns into a publicity machine

➤ Backgrounds of the main event stars

➤ Although the least experienced of the main eventers, the Big Show is a trusted performer

➤ According to fans, the stars of *WrestleMania* are worth the money

As the big event grew closer, WWF crews were already in Anaheim preparing the arena for the mayhem that would occur on Sunday night. WWF wrestlers were plugging the event wherever they could—on TV, on the radio, and on street corners. Up to the moment the show started, the WWF became an efficient publicity machine.

Secrets Revealed

On March 31, 2000, only two days before the big event, ECW's TV show was broadcast on TNN. During the show, the ECW announced that Stone Cold Steve Austin and "The Heartbreak Kid" Shawn Michaels were both going to return to the WWF at *WrestleMania*. (As it turned out, both stars appeared at a fan festival associated with *WrestleMania*, but neither appeared on the pay-per-view itself.)

The bulk of the public appearances were being made by the show's eight main stars, the four McMahons and the wrestlers in the main event, The Rock, Triple H, the Big Show, and Mick Foley. All four wrestlers were veterans of *WrestleMania* and knew the drill.

In Your Face

I can't imagine that McMahon was too upset about the slightly exaggerated press leak because the news no doubt increased the number of buys for his pay-per-view event. Indeed, the more cynical fans might say that Vince McMahon planted the news leak himself just to stir up further interest in the event, only 48 hours away. That means that 8.7 percent of those watching TV were watching wrestling, and, of those, three quarters of them were watching *RAW*.

Wrestle Mania

How was WCW doing during the build-up to *WrestleMania 2000*, with the McMahon family falling apart before America's eyes? Not too well. On one typical Monday night, the WWF's *RAW* averaged a 6.2 rating, while WCW's *Nitro* drew a 2.5.

The Rock's *WrestleMania* Record

For The Rock, the 2000 event was his fourth *WrestleMania*, but the first in which he was the star attraction. In fact, in 2000, The Rock's star was burning about as brightly as any wrestler's ever had. In past appearances, The Rock either had been a rookie—remember the mega-babyface Rocky Maivia?—or had been overshadowed by Stone Cold Steve Austin. In 2000, he was the main dude.

In 1997, the Rock made his first *WrestleMania* debut, defeating the Sultan, who was accompanied to the ring by both Mr. Bob Backlund and The Iron Sheik.

After the young Rocky Maivia defeated the Sultan, his father, former wrestler Rocky Johnson, ran to the ring to help his son battle Backlund and the Sheik. Although young Rocky appreciated his father's help, friction developed between the two afterward. The son let the father know, in no uncertain terms, that he was big enough and tough enough to fight his own battles. This was the first sign of the "edge" that The Rock would slowly acquire, the razor-sharp edge that has propelled him to the upper galaxies of superstardom.

DQ Victories Are Like Kissing Your Sister

On March 30, 1998, at *WrestleMania XIV* in Boston's Fleet Center, The Rock defended his Intercontinental title against Ken Shamrock. During the match, Shamrock looked to be getting the best of it, but The Rock was not about to surrender. Finally, Shamrock had The Rock just where he wanted him: in an ankle submission hold—a hold designed to make The Rock say "uncle." After withstanding as much pain as possible, The Rock signaled for the referee to stop the bout. But as the bell sounded, Shamrock refused to release his grasp. Only after a swarm of WWF officials descended on the ring did Shamrock release the agonizing ankle hold. By that time, the referee had reversed his decision and awarded The Rock the victory via disqualification. The Rock had his first *WrestleMania* victory, but it wasn't the kind he wanted.

Mick Foley: Never Before a Main-Eventer

Mick Foley, wrestling as Cactus Jack, first appeared at *WrestleMania* on March 30, 1988, teaming up with a man named Chainsaw Charley with a stocking pulled over his head—who always sounded to me a heckuva lot like Terry Funk. The pair of hardcore legends took on the New Age

Fighting Words

When a wrestler **pops** a crowd, it means that the audience exploded with the noise of spontaneous joy. A crowd will pop for an underdog's unexpected victory, for example.

Bert's Corner

Here's a behind-the-scenes tidbit: The Sultan, who wrestled in a mask in 1997, is the man known today as Rikishi Phatu.

Captain Lou's Corner

In 1999, The Rock lost his belt to Stone Cold Steve Austin in a wild match in which three referees were knocked out.

Outlaws (Road Dogg and Billy Gunn) in a "Dumpster Match"—the winners had to push the losers into a designated dumpster in the arena. The brawl between the foursome went all over the arena. Cactus and Funk—er, Chainsaw—appeared to win when Chainsaw, now driving a forklift, pushed the Outlaws into a dumpster. The following day, however, on *RAW,* it was revealed that the Outlaws had been pushed into the wrong dumpster and therefore were allowed to keep their belts.

On March 28, 1999 in Philadelphia, this time wrestling as Mankind, Foley took on the Big Show, Paul Wight. Mankind was injured in the match and had to be carried off on a stretcher. The injury was of the story-line variety only; he was actually fine. With Foley, you can never be sure. Usually, though, if the injury is real, he continues wrestling. Foley made a solemn horizontal exit from the arena, but he re-emerged during the main event between Stone Cold Steve Austin and The Rock. Several refs had been knocked out during the match, when Foley (as Mankind) donned the striped shirt and entered the ring just in time for Austin to nail The Rock with his Stone Cold Stunner. Mankind counted to three, and Austin was once again champ.

Wrestle Mania

Mick Foley had refereed a main event at *WrestleMania,* but he had never wrestled in one—and the distinction was important enough for him to be brought out of retirement for one last match at *WrestleMania 2000.*

Triple H Changes Squeezes

Like Foley, Hunter Hearst Helmsley had never been in a *WrestleMania* main event before 2000. But for Triple H, there was a bigger difference. *WrestleMania 2000* represented the first time that Triple H (who is referring to himself more frequently as The Game) has appeared in wrestling's biggest event without Chyna. Chyna, the muscular woman who is big enough to take on the men and win, had always watched Triple H's back. Now it would be Stephanie McMahon's job, a chink in The Game's armor, one would have to believe.

Helmsley first appeared on *WrestleMania* in 1997, losing to Goldust. The following year, at Boston's Fleet Center, Triple H took on the late Owen Hart for the Intercontinental championship. Helmsley's victory came after Chyna took the fight out of Owen with a low blow. On March 28, 1999, in Philly, Triple H defeated Kane, but once again the key was Chyna, who rendered Kane nice and unconscious, courtesy of a steel chair.

But Triple H and Chyna have gone their separate ways since then—don't feel sorry for Chyna, she's doing okay—and now it is the spoiled brat Stephanie who is expected to come to Triple H's rescue when he gets in trouble. Hmmm, *he* could be in trouble.

The Big Show's Big Show History

The Big Show had made only one previous *WrestleMania* appearance, in Philadelphia the previous year. But it was a doozy. (Before that, Paul Wight was known as The Giant and worked for WCW.) In 1999, the Big Show's role was as enforcer for Vince (Mr.) McMahon, the "evil" owner of the WWF.

McMahon's archenemy was Stone Cold Steve Austin, who was wrestling in that year's main event against The Rock. As insurance, McMahon set up a match between the Big Show and Mankind (Mick Foley) to determine who would be the special referee in the Rock/Austin match. the Big Show proceeded to send Mankind to the hospital—temporarily, anyway—with a series of chair shots to the head and back that qualified as Excedrin headache Number One! Trouble was, the Big Show didn't know when to stop. He became so violent that he got himself disqualified by the referee and technically lost the match.

McMahon became mad at the Big Show's lack of control and called him "stupid." The Big Show acted like he was going to choke-slam the Boss.
McMahon managed to talk the big guy out of it, and then it was the Boss' turn to lose control: He slapped the Big Show across the face! That pushed the big guy even farther over the edge. The Big Show slapped Mr. McMahon back with a paw the size of a catcher's mitt. McMahon, as was his wont in those days, called the cops and had the Big Show thrown in jail.

Body Slam

Wrestling plot lines are not set in stone. Injuries can cause a plot line to swerve, of course, but sometimes the reasons are more subtle. If crowd reactions are not what they are supposed to be or if the plot is simply "not working," story lines are changed and tweaked as they go along.

Bert's Corner

Getting disqualified in the WWF these days is as hard as getting kicked out of the world's most animalistic frat house. You've really got to get out of hand!

Captain Lou's Corner

Vince McMahon still has the same concept of *WrestleMania* that he had back when I was involved. Put on great matches that fans care about, mix in some glitz and a few celebrities, and, as they say at MGM, "That's entertainment!"

And so, all the wrestling stars in the main event were experienced wrestlers who could be depended on to deliver a product that was worth paying for. In the other key positions, Vince McMahon had cast his family, who, with the exception of Linda had wrestling in their blood.

The Least You Need to Know

➤ Enticing rumors and tidbits about the pay-per-view performers usually help the buy rate, even when they are not true.

➤ The Rock was a much bigger star in 2000 than he had been at any of his previous *WrestleMania* appearances.

➤ The Big Show had the least *WrestleMania* experience of the bunch.

➤ Fans thought that Mick Foley's final-final match had to be a doozy.

➤ This would be Triple H's first *WrestleMania* without Chyna watching his back.

➤ Vince McMahon stacked his *WrestleMania* deck with wrestlers that he knew he could count on.

All the WrestleManias

WrestleMania I: Captain Lou's Memories

If any one moment defined the success of the WWF, cementing its position at the top of the wrestling ladder, it was *WrestleMania*. Truth to tell, Vince Jr. had actually been thinking about it for a long time as a new way to put the WWF over the top. The idea had its roots in McMahon's perception of wrestling: He knew that the WWF was in the entertainment business, much as Broadway and Hollywood were. And so, borrowing from their example, he began planning attractive main events and bringing in celebrities who were, in his word, "hip"—who could add to the event and help make it into an entertainment spectacular. In time, it became the Super Bowl and the World Series of wrestling all in one.

Soon Vince Jr. began pulling together all the elements for *WrestleMania I,* bringing in the likes of Hulk Hogan, Sergeant Slaughter, the Iron Sheik, and celebrities such as Muhammad Ali, Mr. T, Liberace, and Billy Martin. But Vince Jr. has always been open to new ideas—he encourages his staff to give him creative input. It was in that atmosphere that I, ol' Captain Lou, went to Vince with an idea: Wendi Richter versus Lelani Kai. In reality, however, it became me, Captain Lou, versus Cyndi Lauper. Maybe I should explain how that came about. It started a few years before, on a plane from

Captain Lou's Corner

The idea came to McMahon, he said, while he was on vacation with his wife, Linda. According to McMahon, he turned to her and said, "We're going to do a big promotion and we're going to close-circuit it all over the country (there was no pay-per-view back then) and we're going to call it *WrestleMania*."

Captain Lou's Corner

There's no truth to the rumor that Cyndi Lauper is my daughter. Yes, I played her father in all those videos—"She Bop," "Girls Just Want to Have Fun," "Time After Time," and "Goonies"—and her real mother played the mom. But I was just acting—you know, artistic license, or something like that.

Puerto Rico. There I was, just sitting there, when a young lady came over. "Cripes," I said—or something that sounded like it—"it's Cyndi Lauper." She introduced herself and said that she'd been a wrestling fan all her life, and then she asked if I would like to be in a video she was making of her big hit "Girls Just Want to Have Fun."

While we were filming the videos—a sort of merging of the worlds of wrestling and rock—Rowdy Roddy Piper saw an opportunity to create some mischief. He asked me to appear on his TV show, *Piper's Pit*, for what I thought was going to be a straight interview. He started egging me on about male supremacy; being a bit chauvinistic anyway, I took the bait and made some rather rash remarks, like, "Women are garbage and only good for having babies and cleaning the house."

Well, that tore it. To make it worse, one night down at Madison Square Garden, I ran into Cyndi, and we started in. Again, I said some intemperate things, like, "You were just a dirty little broad before you met me." Cyndi wasn't going to take that, so she fired back: "Tell you what, fat man—I'm going to put a woman wrestler up against one of your choice. And if my woman wins, you're going to have to apologize and admit women are at least as good as men—maybe even better!"

Cyndi picked Wendi Richter to carry her banner—a young lady out of Texas who was then rising in the WWF ranks. My choice was a natural: Lelani Kai, protégé of the Fabulous Moolah, the women's champion.

When I persuaded Vince to include the Kai-Richter match on the first *WrestleMania*, I had to go out and publicize it to make it pay off. I went on the Letterman show, and wouldn't you know it, a whole bunch of women's lib advocates started picketing me and booing me from the audience. I told Letterman that they were really calling out, "Lou, Lou," and added, "I have the body women love and men envy." Needless to say, it went over like stale pizza.

To top it off, Wendi Richter won, and I had to eat my words. But all in all, it was a successful promotion, and it added to the success of *WrestleMania I*. So, although Vince Jr. was the man behind the promotion, I feel that I had a large part in turning it into the major promotion that it became. *WrestleMania* became the standard for wrestling—its Super Bowl—and made the World Wrestling Federation number-one in the world of wrestling.

WrestleMania I

March 31, 1985

Madison Square Garden, New York

Tito Santana defeated the Executioner via the figure-four leg lock submission.

Bert's Corner

The formal challenge of Kai versus Richter was issued on Roddy Piper's show because he had stirred up the trouble to begin with. And although Lou was somewhat worried about Leilani having to face Wendi, he had to accept the challenge to save face—or whatever he calls what's above his neck.

King Kong Bundy pinned S.D. Jones with a five-count running "avalanche" pin.

Ricky Steamboat pinned Maniac Matt Borne.

Brutus Beefcake, managed by Luscious Johnny Valiant, and David Sammartino, seconded by his father, former WWF Champion Bruno Sammartino, battled to a double DQ.

The Junkyard Dog defeated Greg "The Hammer" Valentine via count-out in an Intercontinental Title match.

The Iron Sheik and Nikolai Volkoff, with "Ayatollah" Fred Blassie as their manager, defeated Barry Windham and Mike Rotundo, managed by Captain Lou Albano, to win the WWF Tag Team title.

Andre the Giant body-slammed Big John Studd in a special $15,000 challenge match. If Studd had body-slammed Andre first, the Giant would have had to retire. But the Giant won and began tossing the money into the audience before Bobby Heenan snatched the moneybag!

Wendi Richter pinned Lelani Kai to win the WWF Women's World title.

Mr. T. and Hulk Hogan, with Superfly Snuka in their corner, defeated Roddy Piper and "Mr. Wonderful" Paul Orndoff, with "Ace" Orton in their corner. Wrestling great Pat Patterson was the official referee inside the ring. Boxing legend Muhammad Ali patrolled outside. Pianist Liberace was the guest timekeeper, and baseball star Billy Martin served as the ring announcer. The winners were Hogan and Mr. T, when the Hulk pinned Orndorff after Ace Orton accidentally hit him in the back of the head with his plaster cast.

Mr. T versus Rowdy Roddy Piper in the first WrestleMania, held at Madison Square Garden.

(Source: Associated Press)

WrestleMania 2: **Triple Main Event**

Always looking for ways to make his events bigger and better, Vince McMahon decided to spread his second *WrestleMania* across the country. The event would take place simultaneously in three locations: Los Angeles, Chicago, and New York. Fans in each of the three arenas were able to watch the matches at the other venues through closed-circuit TV. In the three separate main events, Andre the Giant won a Battle Royal—no surprise there because he won every battle royal he was ever in—Hulk Hogan defeated King Kong Bundy in a cage match and Mr. T beat Rowdy Roddy Piper by disqualification in a boxing match when Piper resorted to wrestling.

Bert's Corner

George "The Animal" Steele wrestled only in the summer. That was because he was a high school gym teacher the rest of the year. "Hey Ma, my teacher eats turnbuckles!"

WrestleMania 2

April 7, 1986

Held simultaneously in three locations: Los Angeles Sports Arena, Los Angeles; Nassau Coliseum, Uniondale, New York; and Rosemont Horizon, Chicago. Triple main event!

From Los Angeles: Ricky "The Dragon" Steamboat defeated Hercules with his patented Dragon Leap from the corner post.

Adrian Adonis, managed by Jimmy Hart, pinned Uncle Elmer.

Terry and Dory Funk defeated Tito Santana and the Junk Yard Dog, with an assist from their manager, Jimmy Hart, and his trusty megaphone. Terry pinned Junk Yard Dog in 13:00.

Hulk Hogan defeated King Kong Bundy in a WWF title match that took place inside a steel cage.

From Nassau Coliseum: Macho Man Randy Savage, with Miss Elizabeth in his corner, pinned George "The Animal" Steele in an Intercontinental title match in 5:10.

Paul "Mr. Wonderful" Orndorff and the Magnificent Muraco battled to a double-count out in 4:10.

Jake "The Snake" Roberts pinned George Wells with his DDT in 3:15. Then Roberts unleashed his pet Python, Damian, on Wells.

Mr. T defeated Rowdy Roddy Piper via disqualification at 1:15 of Round Four of their special challenge boxing match.

From Rosemont Horizon: Andre the Giant won a special 20-man Invitational Battle Royal by eliminating Bret Hart. Also in the Battle Royal were: Jim Neidhart, John Studd, Hillbilly Jim, Bruno Sammartino, the Tonga Kid, Jim Brunzell, Pedro Morales, Tony Atlas, Ted Arcidi, Dan Spivey, Brian Blair, and the Iron Sheik, as well as pro football stars William Perry, Bill Fralic, Russ Francis, Harvey Martin, Jim Covert, and Ernie Holmes.

In other matches: Corporal Kirchner pinned Nikolai Volkoff in 2:05. The Fabulous Moolah pinned Velvet McIntyre in 1:25 in a WWF Women's World title match.

The British Bulldogs (Davey Boy Smith and the Dynamite Kid) defeated Greg Valentine and Brutus "the Barber" Beefcake in 13:03 to win the WWF Tag Team title.

WrestleMania III: Hogan Versus Andre, 'Nuff Said!

The third *WrestleMania,* held before a record crowd in the Pontiac Silverdome, is best known for its match between Hulk Hogan and Andre the Giant. Hogan managed to pick up the Giant and body slam him, a feat that had never before been accomplished, in defense of his WWF championship.

Historical revisionists, including Hogan himself, have tried to portray this match as a "passing of the torch," in which the role of wrestling's number-one star shifted from Andre to the Hulkster, but this is not actually the case. The truth of the matter was that Hogan was *already* the biggest star in the game at the time, and Andre was at the tail end of his legendary career.

What many fans don't remember is that the Hogan-Giant match-up was not the only classic match on the show. The Ricky Steamboat versus Randy Savage match on the same card has also been called one of the greatest matches ever.

WrestleMania III

March 29, 1987

Pontiac Silverdome, Pontiac, Michigan

The Can-Am Connection (Rick Martel and Tom Zenk) defeated Magnificent Muraco and Cowboy Bob Orton, managed by Mr. Fuji, in 5:37.

Hillbilly Jim along with midgets, the Haiti Kid and Little Beaver, won by disqualification over King Kong Bundy and his mini teammates Little Tokyo, and Lord Littlebrook in a mixed six-man tag team match. Bundy was DQ'd for splashing Little Beaver in 3:25!

Billy Jack Haynes and Hercules battled to a double count-out in 7:44.

Nikolai Volkoff and the Iron Sheik defeated the Killer Bees by disqualification in 5:44 when Hacksaw Jim Duggan interfered on the Bees' behalf.

Honky Tonk Man pinned Jake Roberts in 7:04.

Butch Reed pinned Koko B. Ware in 3:30.

The Dream Team (Brutus Beefcake and Greg Valentine) beat Jacques and Ramon Rougeau in 4:03 when Valentine pinned Ramon.

King Harley Race pinned the Junk Yard Dog in 4:22.

The Hart Foundation (Bret Hart and Jim Neidhart) and Dangerous Danny Davis defeated the British Bulldogs (Davey Boy Smith and the Dynamite Kid) and Tito Santana in 8:52 when Davis pinned Davey Boy Smith.

Roddy Piper defeated Adrian Adonis in 6:20 in a "Retirement match."

Ricky Steamboat defeated Macho Man Randy Savage in 14:53 to capture the WWF Intercontinental title.

Hulk Hogan pinned Andre the Giant in 12:01 to retain his WWF Heavyweight title.

WrestleMania IV: I Wanna Be a Macho Man

The WWF championship was vacant during the spring of 1988, so a tournament was set up at *WrestleMania IV* in Atlantic City, New Jersey, to fill the spot. After making its way through the brackets, the final match was between Randy "Macho Man" Savage, with Miss Elizabeth in his corner, and the evil Ted "The Million Dollar Man" DiBiase, who had Andre the Giant in his corner. Andre did his job, tripping up Savage several times during the early stages of the match. Elizabeth left the arena at this point and returned with Hulk Hogan to help even out the sides. DiBiase had Savage in a sleeper, and Savage was trying to make his way to the ropes to break the hold. But every time he got close, Andre smacked him. Then the Hulkster swung into action. Grabbing a chair, Hulk climbed into the ring, smacked DiBiase, and left. The Macho Man pinned The Million Dollar Man and won the belt.

WrestleMania IV

March 27, 1988

Trump Plaza, Atlantic City, New Jersey

WWF Title Tournament: Round 1—"The Million Dollar Man" Ted DiBiase defeated Hacksaw Jim Duggan in 4:54.

Macho Man Randy Savage pinned Butch Reed in 5:07.

Magnificent Muraco won via disqualification over Dino Bravo in 4:53.

Greg "The Hammer" Valentine pinned Ricky Steamboat in 9:12.

One Man Gang won via count-out over Bam Bam Bigelow in 2:56.

Ravishing Rick Rude and Jake Roberts battled to a draw.

Round 2—One Man Gang received a bye and proceeded to the semifinals.

Hulk Hogan and Andre the Giant were both disqualified and thereby eliminated from the tournament in 5:22.

Ted DiBiase pinned the Magnificent Muraco in 5:44.

Macho Man Randy Savage defeated Greg Valentine in 6:06.

Semifinal—Ted DiBiase proceeded to the final round with a bye.

Randy Savage defeated the One Man Gang by disqualification in 4:05.

Finals—Macho Man Randy Savage, with help from Hulk Hogan, pinned Ted DiBiase to win the WWF Heavyweight title in 9:27.

In other matches: The Islanders (Tama and Haku) and Bobby Heenan defeated the British Bulldogs (Davey Boy Smith and the Dynamite Kid) and Koko B. Ware in 7:30. Heenan pinned Koko.

Demolition (Ax and Smash) defeated "Strike Force" Tito Santana and Rick Martel to win the WWF Tag Team titles in 12:53. Ax pinned Martel.

The Ultimate Warrior pinned Hercules in 4:29.

In an Intercontinental title match, Brutus Beefcake defeated the Honky Tonk Man via DQ when Jimmy Hart clobbered the referee with his trusty megaphone in 6:30.

Bad News Brown eliminated Bret Hart in a 20-man Battle Royal. Other participants in the Battle Royal included: Sika, Jim Neidhart, Raymond Rougeau, B. Brian Blair, Jim Brunzell, Ron Bass, Ken Patera, Hillbilly Jim, Danny Davis, Jimmy Powers, Nikolai Volkoff, Boris Zhukov, Jacques Rougeau, Harley Race, The Junk Yard Dog, and Paul Roma.

WrestleMania V: Hulkster's Revenge

The fifth *WrestleMania*, the second to be held at the Trump Plaza in Atlantic City, New Jersey, was built around a classic love triangle. Miss Elizabeth, the former valet for Macho Man Randy Savage, had taken up with Hulk Hogan. For more than 17 minutes, the two went at it as if their lives—and love lives—depended on it. Then Hogan caught Savage charging toward him and caught him with a big boot to the face. That put Savage on his back, ready for Hogan's patented leg drop and the referee's three-count. In the story line, the Hulkster got both the belt and the girl—but in real life, Savage got to go home with Miss Elizabeth. After all, they were husband and wife at the time.

WrestleMania V

April 2, 1989

Trump Plaza, Atlantic City, New Jersey

Hercules defeated King Haku in 6:37.

The Twin Towers (Akeem and the Big Boss Man) defeated The Rockers (Shawn Michaels and Marty Jannetty) when Akeem pinned Shawn Michaels in 8:22.

Mr. Perfect defeated the Blue Blazer (Owen Hart) with his perfect-plex in 5:38.

The Bushwhackers (Luke and Butch) defeated Jacques and Raymond Rougeau when Luke pinned Raymond in 5:10.

The Brain Busters (Arn Anderson and Tully Blanchard) defeated Strike Force (Rick Martel and Tito Santana) in 9:17 when Arn pinned Santana.

Dino Bravo pinned Ronnie Garvin in 3:48.

Hacksaw Jim Duggan and Bad News Brown battled to a double DQ in 3:49.

The Red Rooster (Terry Taylor) pinned Bobby Heenan in 32 seconds.

The Hart Foundation defeated Honky Tonk Man and Greg Valentine in 7:40 when Bret pinned the Honky Tonk Man.

Bad News Brown and Hacksaw Jim Duggan battled to a double disqualification.

Demolition (Ax and Smash) defeated the Powers of Pain (The Barbarian, Haku, and Mr. Fuji) when Ax pinned Fuji.

Jake Roberts defeated Andre the Giant by disqualification in 9:44.

Ravishing Rick Rude (with help from Bobby Heenan) pinned the Ultimate Warrior in 9:36 to win the Intercontinental title.

Hulk Hogan, with Miss Elizabeth in his corner, defeated Macho Man Randy Savage to win the WWF Heavyweight title in 17:54.

WrestleMania VI: Ultimate Challenge

More than 65,000 fans showed up at the Skydome in Toronto, Canada, in 1990 for the match between the WWF's intercontinental champion, The Ultimate Warrior, and the world champ, Hulk Hogan. The Ultimate Warrior ended up doing something to Hogan that had not been done since the early days of the Hulkster's career: He pinned him in the center of the ring. The Ultimate Warrior ended up leaving the arena with both belts—although the Intercontinental belt was soon taken away from him because of a WWF rule that said a wrestler could not possess both belts at the same time.

WrestleMania VI

April 1, 1990

The Skydome, Toronto, Canada

Rick Martel made Koko B. Ware submit with his Boston Crab hold in 5:31.

The Barbarian pinned Tito Santana in 4:33.

Ravishing Rick Rude pinned Superfly Jimmy Snuka with his Rude Awakening in 3:51.

Hacksaw Jim Duggan pinned Dino Bravo with the help of his trusty 2x4 in 4:15.

Brutus Beefcake, with help from The Genius, pinned Mr. Perfect in 7:48.

Earthquake pinned Hercules with his Avalanche Splash in 4:52.

Rowdy Roddy Piper and Bad News Brown were both counted out of the ring in 6:48.

The Orient Express (Sato and Tanaka) defeated The Rockers (Marty Jannetty and Shawn Michaels) when Jannetty was counted out of the ring.

The Big Boss Man defeated Akeem in 1:49.

The Hart Foundation (Bret Hart and Jim Neidhart) defeated Nikolai Volkoff and Boris Zhukov when Bret pinned Zhukov in 19 seconds.

Ted DiBiase defeated Jake Roberts by count-out in 11:56.

In a mixed tag team match, Dusty "The American Dream" Rhodes and Sapphire defeated Macho King Randy Savage and Queen Sherri when Sapphire pinned Sherri in 7:52.

Demolition (Ax and Smash) defeated the Colossal Connection (Andre the Giant and Haku) to win the WWF tag-team championship when Ax pinned Haku in 9:15. After the loss, Andre beat up Haku and then manager Bobby Heenan.

The Ultimate Warrior pinned Hulk Hogan to win the WWF Heavyweight title in 22:51.

WrestleMania VII: Sergeant Slaughter Brings the War Home

This turned out to be one of the most controversial *WrestleMania* events because of the story line. The Gulf War had just occurred, and the villain of the main event, Sergeant Slaughter, was siding with the Iraqis. Slaughter had defeated the Ultimate Warrior to become the WWF champ, and now it was up to All-American hero Hulk Hogan to get the belt back—which, of course, he did. Slaughter quietly turned back into an American patriot, and Hogan began his third reign as WWF champ. Celebrities in the L.A. crowd included Alex Trebek (of *Jeopardy* fame), Marla Maples (then Mrs. Donald Trump), Regis Philbin, and Willie Nelson.

WrestleMania VII

March 24, 1991

Los Angeles Sports Arena

The British Bulldog Davey Boy Smith pinned the Warlord in 8:51.

The Rockers (Marty Jannetty and Shawn Michaels) defeated the Barbarian and Haku. Michaels pinned Haku in 10:41.

Tenryu and Kitao defeated Demolition (Ax and Smash). Tenryu pinned Smash in 4:44.

The Texas Tornado (Kerry Von Erich) pinned Dino Bravo in 3:11.

The Earthquake pinned Greg Valentine in 3:14.

The Mountie (Jacques Rougeau) pinned Tito Santana.

The Undertaker pinned Superfly Snuka with his Tombstone pile driver in 4:20.

In a match in which both wrestlers had to wear blindfolds, Jake "The Snake" Roberts pinned Rick Martel with his DDT.

The Legion of Doom (Animal and Hawk) defeated Power and Glory (Hercules and Paul Roma) in 59 seconds when Animal pinned Roma.

The Big Boss Man defeated Mr. Perfect by disqualification in an Intercontinental title bout in 10:47.

Virgil (with Roddy Piper in his corner) defeated "The Million Dollar Man" Ted DiBiase by count-out in 1:21.

The Nasty Boys (Brian Knobbs and Jerry Saggs) defeated the Hart Foundation (Bret Hart and Jim Neidhart) to win the WWF tag-team title in 12:10.

The Ultimate Warrior pinned Macho Man Randy Savage in a "Retirement Match" in 20:48.

Hulk Hogan defeated Sergeant Slaughter in 20:26 to regain the WWF Heavyweight title for the third time.

WrestleMania VIII: Hoosier Brouhaha

Hulk Hogan doesn't often take on opponents who are larger than him, but he did at *WrestleMania VII*, where he wrestled Sid Vicious. Hogan won the match, but only because Vicious's manager, Harvey Whippleman, interfered and got caught by referee Earl Hebner, who DQ'd Vicious. Bret Hart defeated Roddy Piper to win the Intercontinental title, and, in a fine show of sportsmanship, Piper even buckled his belt onto Hart after the match. In the main event, Randy Savage defeated Ric Flair to win the WWF championship for a second time, despite constant interference from Flair's second, Curt "Mr. Perfect" Hennig. Reba McEntire led the lineup of celebrities.

WrestleMania VIII

April 5, 1992

Hoosier Dome, Indianapolis, Indiana

"The Rocket" Owen Hart pinned Skinner in 1:11.

Tatanka pinned Rick Martel in 4:32.

Shawn Michaels pinned Tito Santana in 10:39.

Big Boss Man, Sergeant Slaughter, Hacksaw Duggan, and Virgil defeated the Nasty Boys (Saggs and Knobbs), The Mountie and Repo Man, in 5:22 when Virgil pinned Knobbs.

The Undertaker pinned Jake Roberts in 6:41.

The Natural Disasters (Typhoon and Earthquake) defeated Money Inc. ("The Million Dollar Man" Ted DiBiase and Irwin R. Schyster) by disqualification in 8:39.

Bret "The Hitman" Hart pinned Rowdy Roddy Piper in 13:56 to win the WWF Intercontinental title.

Hulk Hogan defeated Sid Justice by disqualification in 12:44 due to the interference of manager Harvey Wippleman.

Randy Savage pinned Ric Flair in 18:05 to win the WWF Heavyweight title.

WrestleMania IX: Under the Vegas Sun

The long history of Bret Hart getting a raw deal in the WWF started at this event. Hart came into *WrestleMania,* held in an outdoor arena in Las Vegas, as the WWF champion. In the main event, Hart was matched up against the 600-pound Yokozuna. Hart looked like he had the match won when Yokozuna's manager, Mr. Fuji, threw salt into Hart's eyes, allowing Yokozuna to roll him up for the pin. Yokozuna was champion—but only for about 5 minutes. Hulk Hogan challenged Yokozuna right then and there, beat him in about a minute, and became the champion. So, the belt moved from Hart to Hogan without Hart having to "do a job" for the Hulkster, something that he apparently didn't want to do.

WrestleMania IX

April 4, 1993

Caesars Palace, Las Vegas, Nevada

Rick and Scott Steiner defeated the Head Shrinkers (Fatu and Samu) when Scott pinned Samu.

Razor Ramon pinned Bob Backlund.

Lex Luger pinned "Mr. Perfect" Curt Hennig.

Doink pinned Crush when a second Doink interfered.

The Undertaker won by disqualification over Giant Gonzales.

In an Intercontinental title match, Tatanka won by count-out over the champion, Shawn Michaels.

Money Inc. ("The Million Dollar Man" Ted DiBiase and Irwin R. Schyster) won by disqualification over the Mega Maniacs (Hulk Hogan and Brutus Beefcake).

In the WWF Heavyweight title match, Yokozuna pinned Bret Hart when Mr. Fuji threw salt into Bret Hart's eyes.

In a special challenge match, Hulk Hogan defeated Yokozuna to win the WWF title.

WrestleMania X: The Hitman's Garden Party

In 1994, wrestling's number-one event returned to wrestling's number-one arena, Madison Square Garden. Bret Hart defeated Yokozuna to win the WWF title in the main event. The special referee for the main event was *WrestleMania* veteran Rowdy Roddy Piper. What made the match unusual was that it was the second match on the card for both Bret Hart and Yokozuna. Earlier in the show, Bret had wrestled—and lost—to his kid brother, the late Owen Hart. Yokozuna had already defended his belt once on the card, successfully, against Lex Luger. Celebrities in the crowd included Burt Reynolds and Jennie Garth.

WrestleMania X

March 20, 1994

Madison Square Garden, New York

Heavenly Bodies (Jimmy Del Ray and Tom Prichard) defeated the Bushwhackers. Del Ray pinned Luke.

"The Rocket" Owen Hart pinned Bret Hart in 20 minutes.

Bam Bam Bigelow and Luna defeated Doink and Dink.

In a match where falls counted anywhere, Randy Savage pinned Crush.

Alundra Blaze (Madusa) pinned Lelani Kai in a WWF Women's World title match.

Men on a Mission (Mo and Mabel) defeated the Quebecers (Jacques and Pierre).

Yokozuna defeated Lex Luger by disqualification in 14:41.

Earthquake pinned Atom Bomb in 36 seconds.

Razor Ramon (Scott Hall) defeated Shawn Michaels in 18:47.

Bret "The Hitman" Hart pinned Yokozuna to win the WWF title in 10:36.

WrestleMania XI: L.T. Steals the Show

The main event was between former New York Giants linebacker and NFL Hall-of-Famer Lawrence Taylor and wrestling veteran Bam Bam Bigelow. L.T. and Bigelow put on a better show than anyone had a right to anticipate. Despite never having worked a match before, L.T. ended up winning the match with a series of flying clotheslines. He won the match but was so exhausted afterward that he had to be helped from the arena. The L.T. theme song was sung by recording stars Salt-n-Peppa. The biggest star in attendance was Pamela Anderson (now known as Pamela Lee) who was then appearing on *Baywatch*.

WrestleMania XI

April 2, 1995

Hartford Civic Center, Hartford, Connecticut

Lex Luger and "The British Bulldog" Davey Boy Smith defeated the Blue Brothers when Luger pinned Jacob Blue.

Yokozuna and Owen Hart defeated the Smoking Gunns (Billy and Bart Gunn) to win the WWF Tag Team titles when Yokozuna pinned Billy Gunn.

Razor Ramon defeated Jeff Jarrett via disqualification.

In an "I Quit Match"—winner must make loser say "I quit"— Bret Hart defeated Bob Backlund with the Sharpshooter.

The Undertaker pinned King Kong Bundy.

Lawrence Taylor pinned Bam Bam Bigelow.

Diesel retained the WWF Heavyweight belt when he pinned "The Heartbreak Kid" Shawn Michaels.

WrestleMania XII: A Couple of 60-Minute Men

Shawn Michaels pinned Bret "The Hitman" Hart during the sudden-death overtime portion of their 60-minute "Ironman Match" at *WrestleMania XII* on April 1, 1996, to win the WWF World Heavyweight Championship. The stipulations of the match—held before a sold-out crowd in the Arrowhead Pond in Anaheim, California—stated that the man who scored the most decisions (pinfalls, count-outs, disqualifications, and submissions) in 60 minutes would win the match. But, after a full hour of back-and-forth action, neither man had scored a decision.

Thinking that the match was a draw and that he had retained his title, an exhausted Bret Hart left the ring with his belt slung over his shoulder. Then Gorilla Monsoon, who was officially reinstated as the WWF president before the match, announced that there would be a sudden-death overtime and that the match would continue until there was a clear-cut winner. Less than 2 minutes into overtime, Shawn Michaels—who was accompanied to the ring by his longtime teacher and former mat superstar, Jose Lothario—summoned up his last bit of strength and "played a little chin music" on the Hitman in the form of a perfectly executed superkick. Michaels fell on the champ for the three-count, and his arm was raised by referee Earl Hebner in victory.

Bert's Corner

Typical of California crowds, the *WrestleMania XII* audience became more interested in beating the traffic home than in seeing the outcome of the main event. Only two thirds of the live audience was still in the house when the match finished.

Judged by old-time standards, this match was a classic, but the truth is, in an age when wrestling can no longer put itself over as a real sport, many fans found this boring. When they realized, after 25 minutes or so, that there weren't going to be any pinfalls, they began to leave.

WrestleMania XII

April 1, 1996

The Coliseum, Anaheim, California

The Body Donnas (Skip and Zip) captured the WWF Tag Team titles when Skip (Chris Candito) pinned Phineas I. Godwinn.

Stone Cold Steve Austin pinned Savio Vega in 10:29.

The Ultimate Warrior pinned Hunter Hearst Helmsley in 1:39.

In a six-man tag team match, Vader, Davey Boy Smith, and Owen Hart defeated Jake Roberts, Ahmed Johnson, and Yokozuna. Vader pinned Roberts.

Roddy Piper defeated Goldust in a "Back Lot Match."

The Undertaker pinned Diesel in 16:44.

"The Heartbreak Kid" Shawn Michaels pinned Bret Hart in an "Ironman Match" to win the WWF Heavyweight title in 61:53.

WrestleMania XIII: Visitor from the Dark Side

The Undertaker won the WWF World Heavyweight Championship at this *Wrestle-Mania,* held in Chicago, but not without a whole lot of help from Bret Hart. The Undertaker's opponent was "Sycho" Sid—Sid Eudy, that is—the wrestler who has been known at other times in his career as Sid Vicious and Sid Justice. Hart helped The Undertaker by hitting Sid across the back with a chair. This allowed The Undertaker to choke-slam Sid, but Sid still managed to lift a shoulder before the referee could finish the three-count. Bret wasn't through. He distracted Sid again, and this allowed The Undertaker to give Sid a tombstone pile driver, get the pin, and win the belt.

WrestleMania XIII

March 23, 1997

Rosemont Horizon in Chicago

Billy Gunn defeated Flash Funk by pinfall following a perfectly executed DDT in a "dark" match. (That means that the match was held in the arena before the pay-per-view telecast began.)

The Headbangers (Mosh and Thrasher) won a four-way tag-team battle featuring Phineus I. and Henry O. Godwinn (with Hillbilly Jim), the New Blackjacks (Barry Windham and Justin Bradshaw), and Phil Lafon and Doug Furnas.

Rocky Maivia defeated The Sultan—who was accompanied to the ring by both of his managers, Mr. Bob Backlund and the Iron Sheik—to retain the Intercontinental title.

Hunter Hearst Helmsley, with Chyna, defeated Goldust, with Marlena.

Owen Hart and "The British Bulldog" Davey Boy Smith fought Vader and Mankind to a double-DQ.

Bret "The Hitman" Hart beat Stone Cold Steve Austin in a "Submission Match" when the bout was stopped by referee Ken Shamrock due to loss of blood.

Ahmed Johnson and the Legion of Doom (Animal and Hawk) defeated the Nation of Domination (Faarooq, Crush, and Savio, with Clarence Mason) in a six-man Chicago Street Fight.

The Undertaker defeated "Sycho" Sid to win the WWF Heavyweight title with more than a little help from Bret Hart.

WrestleMania XIV: Stone Cold and Tyson

Shawn Michaels, "The Heartbreak Kid," got a figure-four leg lock on Stone Cold Steve Austin. When Austin broke the hold, Michaels followed up with a sleeper hold. Meanwhile, referee Mike Kiona was driven into a corner—"bumped," if you will. Michaels now looked as if he was going to give his famous foot-to-the-chin superkick, but he missed his move and Austin stunned him instead. With the ref out of action, guest referee Mike Tyson stepped into the ring. He was supposed to be in league with Michaels, but he counted his purported cohort out with the obligatory one-two-three. Austin took the WWF Heavyweight title that night, and when Michaels confronted Tyson for his duplicity, he got clocked for his efforts with a well-aimed punch.

WrestleMania XIV

March 30, 1998

From the Fleet Center, Boston, Massachusetts

Titled: "DX-raided"

The evening opened with the first ever Tag-Team Elimination Battle Royal, when LOD2000 (Hawk and Animal), along manager Sunny (Tammy Lynn Sytch), beat Jim Cornette's "New" Midnight Express.

Taka Michinoku defeated the "teen sensation," Aguilar, to retain the WWF Light Heavyweight title.

Ken Shamrock defeated The Rock for the Intercontinental title with his ankle submission lock. However, the ref rescinded the decision and took away Shamrock's victory and title after he refused to release the hold.

Sable and Marc Mero defeated Luna Vachon and Goldust when Sable pinned Luna.

"Triple H" Hunter Hearst Helmsley defeated Owen Hart for the WWF European title after Chyna interfered with a low blow. Chyna was handcuffed to Sergeant Slaughter but was able to distract him by throwing baby powder in his eyes.

The Undertaker defeated Kane after delivering four Tombstone pile drivers.

Cactus Jack and Chainsaw Charlie (Terry Funk) defeated the New Age Outlaws (Road Dogg and Bad Ass Billy Gunn) to win the tag-team belts in a "Dumpster Match"—in which one team must put its opponents in a dumpster to win. (The decision was reversed on *RAW* the next night when it was brought to light that the dumpster used was the wrong one.)

In the main event, Stone Cold Steve Austin defeated "The Heartbreak Kid" Shawn Michaels to win the WWF championship.

WrestleMania XV: For Austin, a Belt and a Brew

The Rock entered the arena as the WWF Champion in 1999 and was defending his strap in his first *WrestleMania* main event against the number-one man in the Federation: Stone Cold Steve Austin. The match between the two most popular wrestlers in the WWF was pure chaos. Not one, not two, but three referees were knocked cold during the melee. Austin caught The Rock in his "Stone Cold Stunner," and it was Mick Foley, in his Mankind persona, who put on the striped shirt and counted to three, enabling Austin to become the WWF champ. Pete Rose was on hand, disguised as the San Diego Chicken, and the WWF caught flack when the wrestler known as Big Boss Man was hanged by a noose from a steel cage during a match against the Undertaker.

WrestleMania XV

March 28, 1999

First Union Center, Philadelphia, Pennsylvania

A three-way dance for the Hardcore title saw Hardcore Holly defeat Al Snow (with Head) and Badd Ass Billy Gunn.

Owen Hart and Jeff Jarrett (with Debra) defeated D'Lo Brown and Test (with Ivory) to retain the tag-team titles.

In a "Brawl for It All" match, with Vinny "The Pazmanian Devil" as the special referee, Butterbean destroyed Bart Gunn with a pair of hard rights.

Road Dogg defended his Intercontinental title in a "Four-corners Match," defeating Val Venis, Goldust, and Ken Shamrock, after Ryan Shamrock accidentally tripped Goldust.

Triple H beat Kane when Chyna interfered and hit Kane over the head with a steel chair.

Sable beat Tori when Nicole Bass, serving as Sable's bodyguard, slammed Tori, giving Sable the win.

Shane McMahon defeated X-Pac when Triple H and Chyna interfered, beating up X-Pac and showing the world that they had left DX for the Corporation.

The Undertaker beat the Big Boss Man in a "Hell in a Cell" match.

Mankind defeated the Big Show by disqualification in a match to determine the referee for the main event. Mankind was taken out on a stretcher with a broken arm, and Mr. McMahon declared himself the referee. The Commissioner, Shawn Michaels, overturned McMahon's self-appointment and assigned a regular WWF ref to the match.

In the main event, Stone Cold Steve Austin defeated The Rock to regain the WWF title in a no-disqualification match.

The Least You Need to Know

➤ *WrestleMania* has become the Super Bowl of wrestling.

➤ Hulk Hogan dominated the early *WrestleMania* events.

➤ Throughout the history of *WrestleMania*, celebrities have added glamour to the event.

➤ Wrestlers tend to save their best matches for *WrestleMania*.

Chapter 19

WrestleMania 2000

In This Chapter

➤ A battle royal—hardcore style

➤ Angle loses two belts without being pinned

➤ A "Ladders and Tables Match"

➤ A "Fatal Four-Way Elimination Match"

At last the big day, April 2, 2000, arrived. The Arrowhead Pond in Anaheim, California, was packed to the rafters with rabid wrestling fans. Hours before the matches began, the lines at the souvenir stands were long—and growing even longer.

These days *WrestleMania* is more than just a high-quality house show that is televised on pay-per-view with a few celebrities thrown in. It is now a weekend-long celebration of wrestling, featuring a fan festival and parties. The 2000 pay-per-view lasted all day and featured highlights from all the previous *WrestleManias* before the live event.

Pimpin' Ain't Easy

The opening match featured the Godfather and D'Lo Brown, who were accompanied to the ring by their lovely "hos." Also joining the pair was Ice-T, the superstar rapper, who debuted his new rap number named after Godfather's favorite saying, "Pimpin' Ain't Easy." Facing this team were Big Bossman and Bull Buchanan, who share a back-

Bert's Corner

If you have G-rated sensibilities, today's wrestling is decidedly PG-13. Proceed at your own risk.

ground in law enforcement at correctional facilities in Georgia. Announcer Jim Ross, in a classic understatement, called the match-up "a contrast in lifestyles."

Godfather and D'Lo made excellent use of teamwork to dominate the early action. Buchanan then reversed the tide by dropping D'Lo with a leaping clothesline off the top rope. D'Lo turned the momentum around, felling Buchanan with a huracanrana, but Bossman turned the match around for good when he destroyed D'Lo with the sidewalk slam. Bull followed that up with a big leg drop off the top, and D'Lo was toast.

Chester McCheeserton?

If the previous match featured toast, this one surely featured toasted cheese. Al Snow and Steve Blackman, known unofficially as Head Cheese, took on T&A—that's Test (T) and Prince Albert (A), who were with their new valet, the delectable Trish Stratus. Snow and Blackman were accompanied to the ring by a midget in a wedge-of-cheese costume, whom Snow referred to as Chester McCheeserton. Blackman, of course, hated the gimmick. Al Snow may be lousy at coming up with gimmicks, but he has fantastic aerial moves, as he proved when he moonsaulted from the top rope onto Test, who was outside the ring at the time.

Chester, in the meantime, had a good time chasing Trish at ringside. Blackman was having less luck. He got himself pinned by Test. Afterward, Snow said he understood Blackman's frustration, and to prove it, helped Blackman beat the snot out of Chester McCheeserton, a bullying act that never fails to please the crowd.

Hardcore Battle Royal

Crash Holly defended his Hardcore title in a special 15-minute battle royal in which weapons were allowed. The stipulations were that the belt could change hands through pinfalls and submissions only, and the title could change hands multiple times during the match. The wrestler who held the belt when the 15 minutes were up would be champ. The challengers were Tazz, Viscera, the Mean-Street Posse, Kaientai, the Headbangers, the Acolytes, and Hardcore Holly.

Crash Holly lost his Hardcore title to his cousin Hardcore with just 1 second remaining in the 15-minute limit. (At least, that is what we were supposed to have seen. By mistake, Tazz rolled into the referee during the final three-count, which, in reality, had reached only two.) During the match, just about every competitor held the title at one point or another. Several wrestlers were busted open during the melee—most notably, Shane McMahon's buddy Pete Gas. There were a lot of guys bashing each other over the head with various kitchen appliances, with cookie sheets being a favorite.

Captain Lou's Corner

Like many of the previous *WrestleMania* events, *WrestleMania 2000* was preceded by a fan's convention called WWF Axxess, in which fans had access to the WWF superstars. There were play-by-play booths where fans could announce hold-by-hold action over a video projected on a screen. They then received a videotape of the match, featuring their dubbed-in announcing. Several booths were set up, and all the stars were available for autographs. Our favorite was the Andre the Giant exhibit, where kids could put their own hand over Andre the Giant's handprint. Awe-inspiring!

A Three-Way for Angle

During the hour before *WrestleMania*, on the WWF program *Sunday Night Heat*, former WWF champ-turned-aging-supernerd Bob Backlund revealed that he had arranged for Angle to defend both of his belts in a pair of three-way dances against Chris "The Canadian Crippler" Benoit and Chris "Y2J" Jericho. This ticked Angle off so much that he put Backlund's own signature hold, the cross-face chicken wing, on Backlund to dispose of him. At least now Angle didn't have to worry about Backlund interfering during the matches themselves. The first fall, it was determined, would be for the Intercontinental title, while the European title would be up for grabs in the second fall. In the first fall, Benoit knocked Jericho off the top rope so hard that he landed on the broadcaster's table.

Angle, a Pittsburgh native, looked like he was about to retain his Intercontinental title when he got the cross-face chicken wing on Jericho—but Benoit, a native of Edmonton, Canada, landed a flying drop-kick to Angle's head to break it up. With Jericho stretched out in the center of the ring, Benoit climbed to the top rope and delivered a flying head butt. This enabled Benoit to get the pin and win the Intercontinental belt.

The second fall commenced immediately. Angle almost took himself out of commission for good early when he missed a moonsault. Then, in a separate incident, the referee was knocked out. Angle hit Y2J with the belt, but it was Jericho who finished off the action with a springboard moonsault and subsequent pin on Benoit, winning the European title. So, thanks to his "buddy" Bob Backlund, Kurt Angle came into *WrestleMania* with two belts and left with none. And not once had he submitted—not once had his shoulders touched the mat.

Not Chutes and Ladders—But Close

It made sense to put The Dudleys, The Hardys, and Christian and Edge together in a "Ladders and Tables Match" with the tag-team belts dangling 20 feet above the ring. The Dudleys were known for their table matches—although they had lost once to The Hardys. Christian, Edge, and The Hardys were the participants in the very first Tag-Team Ladder match in WWF history. And what a match it was! The ladder in that match was a seesaw-catapult, with one wrestler jumping on one end of the ladder, which was balanced across a table, while those in the way of the other went flying.

Bert's Corner

Buh Buh Ray Dudley had his name spelled "Buh Buh" when his character was first developed in ECW. When someone would ask him his name, he'd reply, "Buh ... Buh ... Buh ..." You get the idea.

In the *WrestleMania* match for the title, although it was a tag-team match, there would be no tagging. All six would be in the ring at the same time. There were 13 ladders and 13 tables under the ring. As expected, the match was pure anarchy. The men took turns slamming each other into ladders and then hitting each other in the face with chairs. Buh Buh Ray Dudley stuck his head between the wrungs of the ladder, stood up, and spun around, turning the ladder into a helicopter blade. When his foes foolishly attempted to attack, they were swatted away like flies. He didn't stop until Edge and Christian managed to get under the ladder and double drop-kick Buh Buh off his feet. Christian set up a ladder in the ring and leaped from the top out of the ring and onto both Dudleys, who were standing outside the ring. Jeff Hardy then climbed the ladder and was about to pull down the belts when Christian climbed to the top rope and leaped, spearing Jeff and knocking him off the top. Buh Buh DDT'd Christian off the top of the ladder, head first to the canvas. Then Edge and Christian suplexed D-Von Dudley off the top of the ladder.

Two ladders were set up in the ring, side by side. A table was placed across their tops to form a platform, and another table was set up between the ladders on the ring floor. Christian and Matt Hardy made it to the platform atop the ladders, and both were going for the belts. Christian threw Matt off, sending him crashing through the table below. Edge joined Christian at the top, and together Christian and Edge pulled down the WWF World Tag Team Championship belts to win the match.

A 5-minute break was needed before the next match because of the debris, some of it human, that had to be cleaned up.

Kat Fight

The female action on the card featured The Kat (formerly known as Miss Kitty), who was accompanied to the ring by Mae Young, versus the "Devil Woman" Terri

Runnels, who entered the arena wearing cute little red horns on her head and accompanied by the Fabulous Moolah. The first woman to throw her opponent out of the ring would win the match. The special referee for the match was Val Venis. Both The Kat and Terri had bribed Venis, using their bodies, but it was unknown whether their favors were going to do them any good. (Mae Young had also attempted to bribe Venis in a similar fashion, but her advances were also rebuked and it was unclear whether Mae's actions had helped or hindered The Kat's cause.)

The Kat wore a fishnet body stocking with a thong underneath. Terri was fully covered in tights. The Kat had dyed her hair blonde for the occasion. The women took turns kissing the referee just to make sure that he remembered their bribes. Then, Mae Young tried to kiss him, to remind him that … uh, well, just because she wanted to kiss him. The Kat threw Terri out of the ring and should have won the match then and there, but Val didn't call it. He was still busy trying to keep Mae Young's tongue out of his mouth. Then Moolah threw The Kat out of the ring while Val still had his back turned. When Venis's attention at last returned to the wrestling action, he saw The Kat out of the ring and proclaimed Terri Runnels the winner. That, understandably, ticked off The Kat. She attacked Terri, and to the delight of many in the crowd, pulled down Terri's tights so that her G-string—they call them thongs these days—could be seen as well.

Eddy's Latino Heat

Next up was a six-person tag match featuring Chyna and Too Cool (Scotty Too Hotty and Grand Master Sexay) versus The Radicalz (Eddy Guerrero, Perry Saturn, and Dean Malenko). Before the match, Eddy was full of himself, telling his teammates that he was going to render Chyna useless in the ring with his sex appeal, which he referred to as his "Latino Heat." In the match itself, Eddy drew more heat than he gave. First Grand Master Sexay suplexed him over the top rope to the floor below. Then Chyna, oblivious to his charms, body-pressed him and slammed him down. Chyna then pinned Guerrero for the win.

Captain Lou's Corner

Some readers may already know that Chyna did not stay oblivious to Eddy's Latino Heat for long. Within two weeks of *Wrestle-Mania 2000* Chyna was Eddy's *mamacita*.

Pete Rose

For the past two years, Pete Rose, the baseball great who is being kept out of the baseball Hall of Fame because of allegations that he bet on baseball, has made appearances at *WrestleMania*. During that time, "Charlie Hustle," as he was called, has become a big-time enemy of Kane. Each year Rose gets himself pile-driven or choke-slammed or otherwise rudely thrown to the canvas, sometimes after doing heel shtick, standup comedian-style to run down the hometown crowd.

In 1999, Rose attacked Kane while dressed as the San Diego Chicken, the mascot of the San Diego Padres baseball team. We knew ahead of time that Pete was in the building. He had been interviewed earlier and was holding a baseball bat as if he intended to use it. But there had still been no attempts by Pete to interfere in the action when Kane came out for his match.

The Butt of the Joke: Rikishi's Two-Cheek Attack

In Your Face

Rikishi, whose popularity is truly amazing considering the performer has been around so long, has a name for his finishing move, whereby he flattens his opponents with his ample derriere. It's called "Back That Ass Up!" The T-shirt is a top seller.

Rikishi and Kane then did battle with X-Pac and Tori—Kane's ex-girlfriend and ex-partner, both of whom betrayed him—along with Road Dogg. Kane was accompanied by his story-line "father," Paul Bearer. It soon became apparent that Rikishi's awesome butt was the most dangerous weapon in the match. First, Road Dogg was obliterated when Rikishi backed up into him. Kane wanted Rikishi to give Tori the butt-in-the-face treatment, but X-Pac repeatedly saved her at the crack of doom. X-Pac tried to quit the match and take Tori to safety, but Rikishi, against all odds, chased him down and caught him.

Back in the ring, X-Pac unexpectedly launched a major offensive, downing Kane and Rikishi with a series of spinning kicks and broncobusters. Road Dogg chipped in by hitting Rikishi with the Shake, Rattle, and Kneedrop. Kane then threw Road Dogg over the top rope, causing him to strike his face hard on the ring apron on the way down. Finally, after several tries, Rikishi had the opportunity to stick his huge, puckered buttocks into Tori's face. Kane destroyed X-Pac with a tombstone pile driver to get the pinfall victory.

Body Slam

Rikishi is in the family business. Though thoroughly house-trained and civilized—Uncle Afa runs a top-notch wrestling school, after all—the Samoans have made a living for years playing savages on TV. Now another cousin has gotten into the act: top heavyweight boxing contender David Tua. When asked what he thought of fighting Mike Tyson, Tua replied, "If he tries to take a bite out of me, I will take a bigger bite out of him. My ancestors were cannibals. Cannibalism is in my blood."

While Kane and Paul Bearer celebrated in the ring, Too Cool (Rikishi's dancing buddies) and the Chicken entered the ring. Naturally, even those mind readers who would charge only half-price assumed that the Chicken was Pete Rose in disguise, just like last year. Ah, but it never pays to assume—especially in the WWF. Rikishi put on the sunglasses and started to dance, showing off some new moves that turned out to be crowd pleasers. The Chicken was busting the moves alongside him.

Kane could take it no longer. He, like the rest of us, was convinced that the Chicken was Pete, so he tried to pull the Chicken's head off. But the head wouldn't come off! It was the *real* Chicken! Just at that moment, Pete Rose, not in disguise but carrying the baseball bat that he had been seen with earlier, came charging into the ring, ready to attack Kane from behind. Kane merely turned around, caught Pete by the throat, and choke-slammed him to the canvas. He then threw Pete into the corner so that Rikishi could finish him off. The last we saw of the famed baseball superstar, Rikishi was sitting on his face!

Psycho Dad: Vince's Evil Turn

Then it was time for the main event. Four men were introduced: first Mick Foley with Linda McMahon; Big Show with Shane; The Rock and Vince; and finally, Triple H with Stephanie. There would be no DQ's. To be eliminated, one either had to be pinned or submit inside the ring. The Big Show's power dominated the early action, so the other three decided to team up on him. It was a three-on-one against the Big Show.

Wrestle Mania

Since WrestleMania 2000, Linda McMahon has gotten back at her scheming family by appointing the recently retired Mick Foley as WWF Commissioner—a figurehead position that, in the plot line, settles disputes, punishes rulebreakers and makes matches. Foley has been using his power to break up the marriage of Triple H and Stephanie.

The first McMahon to become involved in the action was Shane, who was knocked from the ring apron to the arena floor by a right hand from The Rock. Foley thwacked the Big Show over the head with a chair, enabling The Rock to pin him. Not unexpectedly, the Big Show was the first of the four to be eliminated. He and Shane left. Foley and The Rock then double-teamed Triple H. The Rock tried to hit

Triple H with the ring bell, but the WWF champ ducked, and The Rock nailed Foley instead. Foley fetched his famous barbed-wire-covered 2x4 and brought it into the ring. Triple H quickly wrestled the board away from Foley, and Foley was the one who ended up getting hit by it—right in the gut. The Rock then attacked, and the board went flying out of the ring. It would reappear later. Foley DDT'd Triple H and then put a sock on his right hand to make Sock-o the Puppet, a gimmick used by Foley when he was known as Mankind to administer the Mandible Claw. Foley stuck his hand into his opponent's mouth and pressed until he said "uncle." In rapid succession, Foley put the Mandible Claw on Triple H, The Rock grabbed Triple H's championship belt, and hit him with it; Foley then put the Mandible Claw on The Rock. Triple H broke this up by smacking Foley and The Rock simultaneously with low blows.

Foley looked like he came close to caving in The Rock's skull when he cracked him over the head with the steel ring steps. The Rock was stretched out on the broadcaster's table while Foley climbed atop the ropes. He leaped across the arena floor toward the broadcaster's table, trying to take out The Rock with a flying elbow. Ah, but Foley looked like a wrestler who needed to retire immediately as he came up short, missing The Rock completely and crushing his own ribs against the edge of the table. Triple H hit Foley with the Pedigree and tried for the pin, but Foley kicked out after a two-count. Triple H then fetched a chair and hit Foley in the side of the head with it. Another Pedigree, and this time Foley's shoulders stayed down for referee Earl Hebner's three-count. As Agatha Christie might say, "Then there were two." But Foley didn't want to leave. He had a piece of unfinished business. Finding his barbed-wire 2x4, he smacked Triple H in the face with it once and then left.

Fighting Words

Just like all other forms of theater, wrestling makes maximum use of what's known in show biz as the **ol' switcheroo**—that is, a surprise ending.

The Rock and Helmsley brawled around the arena, with The Rock suplexing Triple H onto the announcer's table, shattering it. Vince attacked his hated son-in-law, Triple H, just before Shane ran back into the arena and ambushed his dad. Shane hit Vince with a TV monitor and busted him open. Vince was knocked groggy for a moment, but he made a superhuman comeback and took care of Shane with a series of right hands. While Pat Patterson and Gerald Brisco helped Vince out of the arena, Shane remained at ringside with a chair in his hand. Triple H hit The Rock with the barbed-wire board, but The Rock retaliated with a Rock Bottom.

Rock went for the pin, but Helmsley kicked out. Then Vince returned to the ring and punched Shane, sending his son over the top rope to the floor. Vince grabbed Shane's chair and appeared about to hit Triple H when—surprise! the *ol' switcheroo*—he hit The Rock instead. Helmsley covered The Rock, but he kicked out—so Vince hit the People's Champion with the chair a second time, just for those of us who couldn't believe our eyes the first time. This time The Rock was knocked unconscious; when Helmsley pinned him, referee Earl Hebner could have taken a full hour to make the three-count, and The Rock still would not have escaped. Vince betrayed The Rock. Triple H was still champion. Inside the ring, Vince and Stephanie hugged.

"I said I would fix it," Vince said, suddenly sounding like Norman Bates in the shower. Oo-weee-oo, psycho dad. What will happen next? Viewers just had to tune in to the following night's episode of *RAW is WAR* to find out.

And the Cycle Starts Again for the Next Pay-Per-View

The whole cycle had started over again, building toward the next pay-per-view one month down the line. Ah, but this show wasn't quite through. It's an old rule of show business that you always send the crowd home happy. And it is a rule that the real-life Vince believes in wholeheartedly. At that moment, with daddy and daughter embracing in the center of the ring, the crowd was less-than-pleased. In fact, they began littering the ring with all sorts of garbage. Stephanie was getting soaked with Coke.

Cut to The Rock. Seeing Vince and Stephanie hugging, The Rock lost control and ran back into the ring. He delivered Rock Bottoms, a modified choke slam, to Shane, then to Vince, and then, finally—but only after she slapped him—to the spoiled brat, Stephanie. The show ended with her unconscious in the ring.

All the hard work everyone put in before the event paid off. *WrestleMania* turned out to be a tremendous financial success for the WWF. Reports say that approximately 875,000 people bought the pay-per-view, which made it one of the best-selling pay-per-views of all time.

The Least You Need to Know

➤ The Ladders and Table match was considered the best match of *WrestleMania 2000.*

➤ *WrestleMania* had a surprise ending: After only days as a good guy, Vince McMahon once again turned evil.

➤ *WrestleMania* matches are often remembered for their silly gimmicks, but I wonder how fondly Chucky McCheeserton will be remembered—if at all.

➤ Fans were disappointed by the limited nature of Mick Foley's role.

➤ The "family affair" build-up translated into a big buy rate for the pay-per-view.

➤ WCW has *a lot* of work to do if it wants to catch up with the WWF in terms of popularity after the *WrestleMania 2000* blockbuster.

Chapter 20

All the Better to See You With: Fans and Arenas

In This Chapter

➤ How wrestling fans have changed during the years

➤ A list of the top wrestling arenas

➤ How to prepare for a trip to the arena

➤ What to expect when you get there

Professional wrestling works on many different levels—as an athletic exhibition, as a multimedia event, as a soap opera—and fans have always been a major part of the equation. Audience participation is a very important aspect of the whole experience, so the fans at a wrestling show are as important as the event itself. The greatest matches all have something in common: The fans in the arena were doing *their* part— screaming their brains out.

It has always been that way, since time immemorial. But as times have changed, the audiences have, too. In this chapter, you learn about the role played by wrestling's fans and how that role has changed during the years.

Wrestling Fan-dom over the Years

Back in the old-old days, sports were once called "leisure activities." And the fans took them in leisurely, content just to be passive attendees at an event. Those were the days when boxing bouts lasted the better part of 20 rounds; when baseball was dominated by pitchers, and single-run games were the rule; when action on a football field meant 3-yard gains, with no such thing as forward passing; and when wrestling matches went on forever, with little or no movement as the combatants strained and pushed against each other in the ring. Those days changed radically in the 1920s, when both society and sports speeded up. Wrestling was no exception to these changes.

After World War II, the wheels of change turned once more as sports became a national obsession. Spectators at sporting events became the nationally obsessed. And wrestling's fans were the most obsessed of all. Much of that fan involvement had to do with the fact that those in attendance believed wholeheartedly in what was taking place in front of them. The harsh violence of a wrestling match was viewed with complete credulity. And the audience quickly became part of the show.

Living in the Land of Creative Reality

In arena after arena—places too big for an insane asylum and too weird for anything else—wrestling's true believers became caught up in the spirit of the moment. At the Montreal Forum, when the loser of the main event refused to unmask as he was supposed to, the fans rioted. They tore up the seats, broke the windows, and stormed the box office. At the Olympic Auditorium in L.A., the crowd exploded when Gorgeous George threw Jim "The Black Panther" Mitchell out of the ring and kept him out by kicking him in the face every time he tried to crawl back in. And at Madison Square Garden, fans intent on seeing justice done erupted in rage after a defeated Dr. Jerry Graham slugged his opponent, Antonino Rocca, as Rocca was acknowledging the cheers of his loyal following.

Bert's Corner

The wildness of wrestling's early fans has toned down some today, but precautions still need to be taken to protect the stars. Entrance aisles for most big shows are purposefully wide enough so that fans cannot obstruct an unpopular wrestler's entrance or exit.

Maniacal Mob Scenes

Wrestlers have had to fight their way back through phalanxes of angry fans intent on righting the wrongs that they thought they'd just viewed in the ring. Reb Russell remembers one night in Bluefield, West Virginia, after he defeated a local in what he himself called "a very unsportsmanlike manner." The crowd came at him "like a wall of human flesh," and he had to "fight like a man possessed" just to reach the safety of the dressing room.

Every wrestler worth his trunks learned the art of survival back in those days—he'd had to learn it under fire, in a riot or two. As one said, "If you don't have the experience, you can get killed."

Vengeful Vigilantes: Captain Lou's Memories

The mob scene, and what one wrestler called "the silent heat"—that devastating quiet before the storm that presages an eruption from a vicious crowd—was only one threat to the safety of the postwar wrestler. Of equal concern were the self-appointed vigilantes acting alone—the obsessed who took it upon themselves to right some perceived wrong out of misguided notions of vengeance. I was there the night in Boston when a crazed fan jumped into the ring and assaulted Black Jack Mulligan with a carpet knife, opening up his leg. It took 187 stitches to put Jack back together again. And I was in the ring with Bruno Sammartino in Washington, doing my usual feet-don't-fail-me-now trick by fleeing up the aisle when some nitwit reached out with a knife and caught me across the arm. I ran back to the locker room, bleeding like a stuck pig, where my friend Pedro Morales put a tourniquet on my arm to stop the bleeding. (Was it any surprise that the towel he used for the tourniquet was filthy, infecting my wound and nearly killing me?)

Captain Lou's Corner

Watching wrestling on TV has the advantages of convenience, but to me it's like eating a ham sandwich with the waxed paper still on—it just doesn't have the taste and flavor of the real thing. Getting caught up in the audience response is a big part of the whole experience.

These are just a few examples of fanatic fans taking justice into their own hands. Freddie Blassie looked down mid-bout to find a knife stuck in his calf. He handled that just fine: He went back to the dressing room and poured iodine on the wound. Art Neilson wasn't so lucky. Stabbed in the side at a Chattanooga arena, he ended up undergoing two hours of surgery. Stabbings were common: Billy Edwards in Waco, Texas; George Lenihan in New Haven, Connecticut; and Pedro Zapata in Florence, Alabama, all found themselves at the pointy end of a knife. And let's not forget Dan Hodge: He was stabbed in the back and the arm while wrestling in Oklahoma City's Municipal Auditorium—his assailant was his own father.

Early Interactive Participation

Not all the assailants used knives. Weapons of choice ranged from whiskey bottles to lit cigarettes, paper clips shot from rubber bands, fingernails, hatpins, and bare fists. And wrestlers weren't always content to stay on the receiving end of their mistreatment.

Writer Joe Jares's father, who wrestled under the name "The Mormon Mauler," was hit by a lit book of matches thrown by an angry female fan as he made his way to the dressing room. He wouldn't hit a lady—but that didn't stop him from making a few pithy observations about her ancestry. Suddenly a belligerent man stepped between them, shouting, "That's my wife!" The Mauler slugged him and offered the advice, "Teach her better manners!"

In Your Face

Tickets for wrestling shows usually sell out faster than those for rock concerts. Gene Okerlund recalls a recent show in Minneapolis in which the 18,000 tickets sold out in less than 90 minutes.

A Sign of the Times?

I don't know what possessed the fans—especially the ladies—to join in the fray so viciously. It could have been the times that bred them. This was, after all, the era of the McCarthy red scare and backyard bomb shelters. Emotions tended to run a little high back then.

Or maybe it was just because the small arenas of the day were so crammed with howling fans that the hysteria of the moment took over. I do know that some of the small towns I wrestled in had arenas so bad that they'd have to have major improvements just to qualify as slums.

Taking Control of the Audience Urge to Participate

By the 1980s and 1990s, wrestling in particular and society in general had changed again. A more "in-your-face" attitude had come into vogue, youth became the obsession of consumers and advertisers, and the worlds of entertainment and sports began to cater to what can best be described as the MTV world of instant gratification.

Wrestling addressed this change in audience makeup by coming up with more confrontational themes, more complex character development, and enough salaciousness to intrigue any dozen special prosecutors. With these changes, wrestling actively encouraged audience identification with the characters, story lines, and, of course, any tie-in merchandise that they could come up with.

In the quiet of their homes, fans no longer "believed" in wrestling, but somehow in the heat of the arena—even the air-conditioned ones—fans believed as strongly as ever. At least they sounded like they did. Maybe, as The Rock likes to say, the fans "know their role." Their job is to play the part of the crowd—and they are very, very good at it.

WrestleMania *Brings the Audiences into the Fold*

It all began at *WrestleMania I* at Madison Square Garden. On March 31, 1985, 23,000 wrestling-crazed fans identified with Hulk Hogan and Mr. T as together they took on Rowdy Roddy Piper and Paul Orndorff. The Hulk played the crowd like a maestro—in wrestling terminology, he was *building heat.* The crowd connected with his every move and inflection—they roared when he pumped his biceps, and when he shouted, they shouted their "amens."

The crowds attending wrestling events were made up of increasingly younger fans. Now the wrestlers weren't seen as sports legends—they were more like real-life action figures. And all the old questions of "real" or "fake" no longer mattered. The performance was everything. With *Star Wars* laser shows, smoke machines, and theme music marking the wrestlers' entrances, you've got an overall event that the new young audiences not only could identify with, but could really get *into.*

Fans on Camera: The Proliferation of Signs

Vocal participation is one thing, but this is the video generation; for lots of younger fans, an event isn't real unless it's on TV—including their own attendance at an event. So, fan-made signs at sporting events have become a major means of participation. It all started on the ECW show when "Sign-Guy Dudley" held up funny signs during matches. Imitative fans started showing up at other arenas; after a period of struggle, overwhelmed promoters dropped their ban on signs and let them in. Today all manner of messages can be found, many in questionable taste.

Fighting Words

Building heat means whipping the crowd into a frenzy, piquing their anticipation of the match to follow.

Wrestle Mania

Wrestling today is a huge audience draw. It's so big that it can command the largest arena in every city—usually the facilities that normally house the local hockey and/or basketball teams. Only a few cities—Dallas, Philadelphia, and Memphis—have arenas that specialize in wrestling alone. These are cities that have a long history of regular wrestling events. Those local wrestling-only facilities unfortunately lack the capacity to adequately house major-league shows. It would be fun to see the WWF put on a show in the Dallas Sportatorium, but four times as many people fit into the nearby Reunion Arena.

Part 4 ➤ History of WrestleMania

In Your Face

For a while, an enterprising fan set up a small stand outside the ECW arena selling weapons for fans to give their favorite wrestlers—much like the stands selling ladies' underwear that are set up outside Vegas casinos when Tom Jones is headlining. After a few weeks of this ECW decided that arming its fans might not be the best idea in the long run and the practice was stopped.

Bert's Corner

Fans often request seats near the entrance and exit aisle, hoping that they'll get a high-five from their favorite heroes. Most of the time, security arrangements are such that they have to settle for just a little eye contact.

Tools, Gimmicks, and GeeGaws

ECW has tried to introduce other elements of audience participation that have achieved less success in crossing over to the more mainstream federations. Working off its "extreme" image, the ECW has attempted to further fan interaction with the wrestlers by encouraging the audience to bring in weapons to pass along to their wrestlers of choice to help them in their struggles when they tumble out of the ring—everything from frying pans to rolling pins.

But Nothing Beats Tradition—Noise Rules

All innovations aside, the main way that audiences get into the act is the good old-fashioned way: vocally. They cheer, they boo, and they shout words that your mama wouldn't approve of at Eric Bischoff and Vince McMahon, the b-a-a-a-d bosses of WCW and the WWF, when they enter the ring. Audiences chant "Gold-berg!" And, if they are bored or believe that the participants are not working as hard as they are capable of working, they'll let the wrestlers know about it—pronto!

Wrestling Venues

Pro wrestling arenas come in all sizes, shapes, and qualities. Sometimes the facilities are bare-bones basic, while other arenas are as luxurious as wrestling's idea of the Taj Mahal. Fans know in their hearts that nothing on TV can come close to seeing a live match, and they'll make the effort to catch the action in the arenas whenever they can. Extreme fans are like Deadheads who followed the Grateful Dead—they'll travel with the wrestling circuit and visit arenas all over the country. But most people can't just drop their jobs or schoolwork to follow their favorite wrestlers around like groupies, so they have to settle for second best: watching wrestling on television.

232

Is It Live or Is It TV?

True enough, no live event can beat television for convenience. You get a guaranteed great view, the best seat in the house, and no parking or traffic problems. Even better, you can tape it so that you can see it whenever you want, as often as you want. But no matter how good the camera work, sound, and editing, television can rarely, if ever, capture the atmosphere of a live match. There's just a thrill that comes with watching the event at ringside that television can't duplicate.

And then there's the rush that comes from being part of the crowd—no telecast has ever found a way to duplicate that. Thousands of screaming, booing, cheering fans all around, bright lights, and the smell of the ring—nope, you won't get that on television.

Watch Out for That Flying Wrestler

You just can't get the flavor of a live match when you're watching from your living room sofa. There's no sense of immediacy. For the true wrestling fan, that just can't be beat. However, keep in mind that sometimes things can, and do, get out of hand. Timid people need not apply to work at the ticket offices of the arenas.

Still, despite the occasional tossed chair or flying wrestler, the risk of injury for a fan during a live match is almost non-existent. Both the performers and the arena owners take safety precautions—after all, who wants to wipe out a hall full of fans?

Great Arenas Make a Difference

Any hardcore wrestling fan will tell you that *every* live match is a good match. But there's good and there's, as Tony the Tiger likes to say, *grrrrrreat*—and the difference has a lot to do with the arena you see it in. If you're stuck sitting for three hours on a metal folding chair, you just aren't going to have as much enjoyment as if the match were held in a fancy stadium with cushioned theater seats. And having to crane your neck to look around the Panama hat of the guy in front of you cuts down your visibility tremendously—it's much better to go to a stadium with raised seating platforms. After all, you want to see the ring, not the back of some fan's neck.

Captain Lou's Corner

The action at wrestling events can get pretty wild, but there's really little to worry about if you're sitting back beyond the first few rows. It's just a case of using your common sense when choosing your seat. And I don't recommend taking kids to see ECW shows, or any of the other "extreme" wrestling cards available out there. ECW shows are designed for mature audiences only. WWF and WCW shows require parental guidance also, but those are more a matter of taste.

Then there's the size factor. Most of the time, big arenas are best—they've usually got more to offer the fans, and they're usually profitable enough to invest in some creature comforts for the fans. But smaller venues have one major plus: They offer fans the chance to come into close contact with their favorite stars.

Our Favorite Arenas

After some serious head scratching, we've come up with a list of our favorite arenas, past and present. The list is not inclusive of all good wrestling venues, but it's a start. They're all sure bets for giving a good live-match experience for the fans, as well as offering up what wrestlers and managers would agree are the best facilities in which to stage a great battle. The following are our favorites, past and present:

➤ The old Boston Garden (Boston, Massachusetts)

➤ Madison Square Garden (New York)

➤ Uline Arena (Washington, D.C.)

➤ Market Street Arena (Philadelphia, Pennsylvania)

➤ The Mosque (Richmond, Virginia)

➤ Pittsburgh Civic Center (Pittsburgh, Pennsylvania)

➤ Sunnyside (San Francisco, California)

➤ Marigold Arena (Pittsburgh, Pennsylvania)

➤ St. Nick's Parkway Arena (San Francisco, California)

➤ Olympic Auditorium (Los Angeles, California)

➤ Mid-South Coliseum (Memphis, Tennessee)

➤ ECW Arena (Philadelphia, Pennsylvania)

➤ Reunion Arena (Dallas, Texas)

How do you find out where the wrestlers are? Most matches are publicized well in advance. If you watch wrestling on television, you'll see promotional spots for upcoming matches. Fans who have access to the Internet can check Web sites for information on live matches in their areas.

A Night to Remember

Getting ready for a night at a live wrestling match doesn't take much planning—you've got the will, the way, and the tickets, so who needs anything more? But like anything else, your experience is what you make of it. And fans have found lots of things to add some extra excitement, enjoyment, and even comfort to their evening.

If you're taking your kids along, you really want to do a little advance work. The events are intense, and kids do sometimes need a little added preparation for the noise, the lights, and all that action. And you'll want to give them a speech about not repeating the language that they hear in front of Grandma—that is, unless Grandma is there, chanting along with you. Remember, in the arena, there are no bleep-outs of foul language as there are on TV. Beyond that, here are a few tips to improve your ringside experience:

➤ **A lot of facilities have restrictions on what attendees may and may not bring into a match.** For example, you may not be allowed to bring a camera or camcorder to a match. Check with the individual facility to find out what you are allowed to bring into the ring area. If you *can* bring a camera, do so. Always bring a few ink pens and some paper on the chance that you might be able to get an autograph or two.

➤ **If the seating in the ring area is not padded, bring a stadium cushion with you.** Hard chairs, metal or wooden, can become uncomfortable during a long event. Most arenas will not prohibit the use of personal cushions, but you should check local regulations on anything that you plan to bring into the seating area.

➤ **If your seats aren't close to ringside, bring along a pair of wide-angle binoculars.** You don't want to miss any of the action if you're stuck way up in the back of the arena.

Body Slam

If you have questions about what you can and cannot bring to a match, call the ticket office and ask. Don't wait until you get to the event to find out that your camera will not be allowed inside.

Body Slam

Some overzealous fans have been known to attack pro wrestlers whom they identify as enemies of their favorite stars. If you are going to approach a pro for an autograph or even just a quick touch, make your intentions known, and keep an eye open for enraged fans.

➤ **Find out whether bringing food is allowed.** Matches can last for hours, so you might think that it's a good idea. But this is often against house rules. They're hoping to make a lot of money at their concession stands, so they don't want you bringing your own. Check the rules before you decide to haul along a beer cooler and picnic basket.

➤ **About those kids ... call ahead and see what facilities, if any, are available for you and your baby.** Fans who bring small children to wrestling events must make arrangements for everything from feeding, to napping, to changing diapers. Don't sit too close to the ring if you have really young children. It's rare that anything goes wrong at a match, but the first few rows of seats are not an ideal place for extremely young children. Parents of infants and even toddlers should respect the needs of other fans. Not everyone is tolerant of crying children. If you have very young children, you might consider arranging for a babysitter for the night. (Hey, you deserve a break now and then anyway!)

Body Slam

Never run up to a pro wrestler before or after a match unless a definite opportunity exists. A lot of action happens outside the ring, and fans can be hurt if they're where they're not supposed to be.

When You're Ready to Rumble

Okay, you've gotten to the arena and found your seat, and you're ready for the show. Let's hope that you're ready for anything—'cause *anything* can happen. But that doesn't mean that you have anything to worry about. Remember, these are pros that you're watching perform. They've trained long and hard to make the violence that you see *look* real, but they're just as concerned about safety as you are.

So get up off your sofa and find a seat around the ring if you really want to experience all the elements of pro wrestling! Until you attend a live house match, you have not seen pro wrestling at its best. Get into the mix, and experience one of the most exciting events that you are likely to ever see.

The Least You Need to Know

➤ Watching wrestling on TV doesn't deliver the same spice as live house matches do.

➤ The risk of personal injury at live events is almost nonexistent.

➤ Several top-notch facilities, including Madison Square Garden and the Reunion Arena, make wrestling all-the-more rewarding.

➤ Call ahead to see what you are and are not allowed to bring to a live match.

➤ Seriously consider leaving very small children with a babysitter when you go to a live match.

➤ Be ready to enjoy yourself!

Part 5

Spelling Wrestling with Six Letters: A-C-T-I-O-N

Okay, this part of the book might as well be called the highlight reel because it focuses on the greatest in-ring professional wrestling action of all time. First we'll look at the greatest rivalries ever, running feuds that have kept wrestling fans coming back again and again to find out the outcome. These are wrestlers who had the uncanny knack of making the public believe truly, deeply that they hated another wrestler's guts.

Next we'll take an in-depth look at the greatest matches ever, both those of long ago and those of today. Some matches were great because of the athletic skill that it took to execute them, some because of the risks the athletes took, and some because of the build-up to the match that had the crowd frothing at the mouth by the time of the opening bell.

So, get ready, because you're about to go down a never-a-dull-moment road called professional wrestling's greatest hits.

Chapter 21

Rowdy Rivalries

In This Chapter

➤ Kerry Von Erich and Ric Flair's battle royal for the championship belt

➤ Dusty Rhodes's quest for The American Dream

➤ The Living Legend tackles the Superstar

➤ Black Jack the Giant Killer—not!

➤ Ric Flair and Harley Race: caged warriors

There have been some famous go-togethers throughout history, as well paired as salt and pepper. These twosomes have sprung up in every field imaginable: In the Bible, there's Cain and Abel; in mythology, there's Romulus and Remus; in music, think of Gilbert and Sullivan; in finance, there's Dow and Jones; in comedy, there's Martin and Lewis; and in politics, there's Franklin and Delano.

Wrestling is no different. Its twosomes are called rivalries, and the pages of wrestling's long history book are filled to repletion with them, going all the way back to the Gotch-Hackenschmidt rivalry in the first decade of the twentieth century.

Some are more memorable than others. What makes one special? Certainly it's the buildup preceding a match, but there's usually something much, much more—the participants, the stakes they're wrestling for, and how it ends. In this chapter, you read about some of the classic match-ups that have excited wrestling fans during the years—many of them real grudge matches in which the grunts and groans of pain were sometimes very, very real.

Bert's Corner

In a recent survey by Lycos of the most frequently used search terms on the World Wide Web, "WWF" came in number 5.

Kerry Von Erich Versus Ric Flair

It was the quest for "10 pounds of gold" (what Ric Flair called his championship belt) that made for a memorable set of matches between Flair and Kerry Von Erich.

Von Erich first challenged Flair for that belt in April 1982. A few minutes before the match, the Great Kabuki had attacked Von Erich, damaging Von Erich's knee and almost rendering him *hors de combat*—almost, but not quite. Von Erich, in the best tradition of "the show must go on," insisted on wrestling Flair even with his injury. The bout ended unsatisfactorily, with Flair being disqualified—and because a belt cannot change waists on a DQ, Flair retained the belt and the title.

Wrestle Mania

When World Championship Wrestling split into two factions, WCW and the nWo, it was merely part of the story line. Feuds between wrestling organizations are almost always fought behind the scenes. But there was a notable exception during the summer of 2000, when wrestlers from XPW, X-treme Professional Wrestling, invaded the audience during a pay-per-view called *Hardcore Heaven* being held by ECW, Extreme Championship Wrestling. The announcers tried ignoring the problems in the crowd until it became to much to ignore. Eventually, all the XPW wrestlers were ejected from the building and the show went on, but by being acknowledged on the air the wrestlers felt they had accomplished their mission.

Von Erich and Flair were to battle three more times that year. The last time was in a cage match, which ended in what might best be described as chaos once Freebird

Michael Hayes, the guest referee, became involved. Hayes got caught up in the action and decided to take on Flair himself, proceeding to punch him out. Then, looking down at the inert form of the champion, Hayes called for Von Erich to fall on top of him for the pin. Von Erich, however, declined the offer. A disgusted Hayes had started to leave the cage with Von Erich in pursuit, earnestly trying to explain himself, when Flair revived and fetched Von Erich a kick in the back for his good sportsmanship. In the melee that followed, Von Erich bled so profusely that officials at ringside had to stop the proceedings, leaving Flair still in possession of his "10 pounds of gold."

In the year and a half that followed, Flair first lost and then regained the belt in bouts with Harley Race. During that same time span, tragedy struck the Von Erich family as Kerry's brother, David, died during his tour of Japan. Now Kerry had a new incentive—to win the belt for his fallen brother.

It happened on May 6, 1984, in front of 44,000 screaming fans at the Texas Stadium. In 22 action-packed minutes, Kerry Von Erich defeated Flair. Finally the "10 pounds of gold" belonged to him—and to the memory of his brother, to whom Von Erich dedicated the belt in an emotional post-fight oration, shouting out: "I gave my all—for David!"

Ric Flair in one of his epic battles with Kerry von Erich.

Dusty Rhodes Versus Kevin Sullivan

Dusty Rhodes was wrestling's own embodiment of the American Dream. A colorful wrestler who was loved by all fans, Rhodes had an opponent who was everything Dusty wasn't: Kevin Sullivan—the quintessential villain who claimed to be a follower of Satan and who said that he dealt with the dark underside of the occult.

Captain Lou's Corner

You can always count on two things in wrestling: First, if some-body is presented with a birthday cake, his face will end up in it. Two, if Santa Claus shows up, he's up to no good.

Both Rhodes and Sullivan were wrestling under the NWA banner in Florida, and that state just wasn't big enough for the both of them. And so on Christmas night, 1983, Rhodes and Sullivan battled it out in a "Loser Leaves Florida" Cage match (the loser would be barred from competing in the state for 60 days). Before the confrontation, the fans and the press alike ballyhooed the grudge match, believing themselves prepared for Sullivan's well-advertised dirty tactics. But they never expected what took place in the ring that night. On the evening of December 25, 1983, someone in a Santa Claus get-up visited Sullivan and presented him with a Christmas present. Those close enough could see through the disguise and recognize Jake "The Snake" Roberts, Sullivan's cohort. The gift turned out to be a weapon, which Sullivan used to pound Rhodes with from the proverbial pillar to post, turning him into a bloody mess and forcing him to leave the state.

The Midnight Rider Makes the Scene

Within days, however, a mysterious masked wrestler known only as the Midnight Rider appeared in Florida arenas. It became an open secret that the Midnight Rider was none other than Rhodes. And it became even clearer when, after the 60 days of banishment from Florida was lifted and Dusty Rhodes re-emerged, the Midnight Rider rode off into the sunset, never to be seen again.

While Rhodes was waiting out his 60-day exile, Sullivan, the man who had sworn allegiance to the Dark Forces, created a new sidekick, known as the Purple Haze. Dusty was introduced to him firsthand during an appearance on the TV show *Championship Wrestling* from Florida when the two mugged him on camera. Leaving Rhodes in a dusty pile wasn't enough for the craven pair. They then tried to set fire to his eyes. After their base act, Sullivan hissed into the cameras: "Never fool with the powers of the occult. That slob Rhodes did, and look what happened to him—he's a beaten man."

Sullivan's next attack was not long in coming. While Rhodes was a guest at the 10-year anniversary celebration with friends, well-wishers, and family—and, not incidentally, in front of hundreds of thousands of TV viewers—Sullivan gate-crashed and hurled a bottle of ink in Rhodes's direction. The missile missed its intended target, striking Rhodes's younger sister, Connie, in the eye instead. Enough was enough for Rhodes, and he vowed to "pay back Sullivan for all his dirty deeds."

Body Slam

One of the most influential feuds of the late 1990s was that between WCW and the New World Order. According to the plot line, a group of rebellious wrestlers had broken away from WCW and had formed their own organization, the nWo. The remaining WCW wrestlers were forced to band together to combat the menace and a huge civil war erupted within the organization, causing attendance and TV ratings to skyrocket. The "group versus group" concept led to several years in which almost all wrestlers were put together into gangs such as Los Boricuas, D–Generation X, and the Nation of Domination.

Rhodes Returns

Now it was Rhodes's turn to use ink as a weapon—signing a contract to avenge the dastardly deeds of Sullivan. The grudge match to end all grudge matches was set for the Lakeland (Florida) Civic Center. On the night of the bout, the arena was filled to overflowing with Dusty Rhodes fans, with 2,000 more turned away at the door. As Rhodes entered to the strains of the Allman Brothers' "Midnight Rider," every man, woman, and child roared in support. In seconds, the cheers turned to jeers as the diabolic Sullivan entered the ring screaming, "The American Dream will die!"

From the moment the bell sounded and before its echo had been stilled, Rhodes was on the attack. His pent-up anger erupted with a fury that had Sullivan on the defensive. Even Sullivan's usual bag of dirty tricks was ineffective in the face of the torrential attack.

Then, just when it seemed that victory was his, Rhodes was surprised by the entry of a new player—a masked man that was, or appeared to be, the Midnight Rider. This, however, wasn't the Midnight Rider that the fans remembered from Rhodes's time in exile—it was an imposter who now leaped into the ring to come to the aid of the fallen Sullivan.

The masked invader set upon The American Dream with a nightmarish fury, driving him into the canvas like a proverbial tenpenny nail and then continued to pound Rhodes until he was senseless. Satisfied that The American Dream would not awaken, the ersatz Midnight Rider gathered up the remains of Sullivan and hauled him off to the dressing room.

Bruno Sammartino Versus Superstar Billy Graham

The ultimate measure of Bruno Sammartino's greatness was his strength. Time and again, in matches against some of the greats of his time, despite having absorbed terrific punishment, The Living Legend would be able to call upon his enormous reserve of strength to turn the event, and his opponent, over on their backs. The tougher the competition, the better he liked it. As one of his admirers cooed, "Bruno threw all his challengers against a brick wall, and those who got up he let wrestle him for the championship."

The Superstar Challenges the Legend

One of those who challenged Bruno was rough, tough Superstar Billy Graham, of the golden locks and bulging muscles. On April 30, 1977, at Baltimore's Civic Center, Graham stepped into the ring to succeed where so many before him had failed.

On that night of nights, Graham entered the ring first and for a full three minutes used the ring as his stage—strutting, posing, and preening. But the uproarious reception that greeted the emergence of The Living Legend from his dressing room put an end to all that. Graham merely pulled in his feathers and retreated to his corner to watch Bruno bathe in his fans' adulation.

As the house lights dimmed, the audience fell into a quiet, almost churchlike hush, anticipating another great Bruno comeback and victory. Then the bell rang and the two warriors came to midring, circling each other warily, each seeking an opening.

The Battle Is Engaged

Within seconds, the two had joined, like rutting bull moose—their arms intertwined and their muscles straining against one another, both looking for the advantage, the edge. Then Graham got in a well-timed kick to the champion's legs, and the action was under way.

For the next 10 minutes, the two warriors fought furiously, but neither was able to break through the other's defenses anymore than you could open a Maryland clam with your bare hands. No one could get an upper hand—or upper leg, for that matter. Bruno, now frustrated in his efforts to get to Graham, grabbed the blond Superstar by his tresses and began banging his head into the turnbuckle. Graham fell to the floor, his face a bloody mess.

Having tasted his own blood, Graham now fought back with a fury, assaulting the champion and catching him up in his dreaded Superstar Bear Hug. As Sammartino flopped around in Graham's arms like a big fish out of water, it looked as if Graham's famous submission hold might carry the day—and carry off the championship belt as well. But even though he applied every ounce of pressure at his command, Graham could not break the strength nor the spirit of the Living Legend, and Sammartino managed somehow, someway, to break free.

Both began showing the strain of the last 15 minutes of pitched battle. But now Sammartino, famed for his feats of arms, began some feats of feet as well. He backed Graham up into his own corner and drove him to his knees with a series of kicks. Suddenly there was Graham, begging for mercy. But Sammartino would have none of that, and he punctuated each and every one of Graham's pleas with yet another kick.

A Title Lost—and Won

Then, just as it seemed that Sammartino had the bout in his grasp, the man called The People's Champion turned to those whose opinion he prized the most, his fans, to ask them for their support in continuing his attack. Bruno's posturing was a tactical error—one that ranks right up there with Jack Dempsey's failure to retreat to a neutral corner after flooring Gene Tunney. And Sammartino's error would cost him the title, much as Dempsey's momentary lapse had cost *him*.

For as soon as Graham saw Sammartino turn away to the audience, he reached out and grabbed Bruno's leg, dragging him down to the mat, where he pinned the soon-to-be ex-champion's shoulders to the canvas. Referee Jack Davis, unaware that Graham was using the ropes for leverage to hold Sammartino down, began the count. "One ... two ... three." It was all over. Unbelievably, The Living Legend had been defeated.

Official protests were lodged by Bruno's camp, but the Maryland State Athletic Commission, ignoring Graham's obvious use of the ropes to secure the final pin, ruled that after a decision had been rendered, it could not be overruled. Graham, hearing of the controversy caused by his victory, now said, "It's finally over. You can talk all you want about controversy, foot on the ropes, blood on my brow, the State Athletic Commission, or anything you want. But no matter what you say, I am still the champion. I don't have anything else to say —this here belt says it all."

Bert's Corner

When Superstar Billy Graham defeated Bruno Sammartino, it was like "the passing of the torch," with one era ending and another beginning.

Andre the Giant Versus Black Jack Mulligan

Andre the Giant—The Eighth Wonder of the World—was so big that few would dare to challenge him. One who did was Black Jack Mulligan. And therein lies the tale of one of wrestling's biggest grudge matches of all time.

Black Jack Mulligan was a man among men himself, standing some 6 feet, 9 inches tall and weighing more than 300 pounds—with cowboy boots and his infamous Claw to use when the going got tough. In addition to being huge, Black Jack was also a skilled practitioner, able to use his strength and speed to bedazzle his opponents and impose his psychological and physical will on them.

Mulligan had only recently joined the WWF with the stated purpose of wresting the belt from its champion, Bob Backlund. Frustrated in his attempts, he announced to all that he would become a giant killer instead, and take on the man who looked like the guy Jack met at the top of the beanstalk: Andre the Giant.

Like the cat that ate cheese and sat in front of the mouse hole with baited breath, Mulligan tried to bait the trap for Andre, calling him "the freak" and even once jumping into the ring to lend his aid to two men battling Andre, battering the Giant into submission.

But the sleeping Giant stirred. He wanted revenge in the worst way and was determined to get it. A match between the two behemoths was quickly arranged.

It was a *big* match, in more ways than one. The second the bell sounded for the classic confrontation, Andre and Black Jack attacked one another, trying mightily to vent their anger on each other. It was less a wrestling bout than a dogfight. It was attack, attack, attack, as first one and then the other took a turn. Soon even the ring proved too small to contain the fury of the combatants, and the action spilled over onto the floor outside the ropes.

Mulligan somehow managed to maneuver the Giant into his deadly Claw hold and held it until he had brought blood from Andre's face. But after he released it, fear gave wings to his feet—Mulligan soon looked like an Olympic 100-meter gold medalist as he fled the premises for the dressing room, leaving a furious Andre behind.

The official decision read "Double DQ by Countout," with both counted out. And while the title of the true giant of the wrestling world had gone undecided, one thing was certain: This had been the biggest grudge match in wrestling history.

Captain Lou's Corner

When Andre worked with another huge guy, workers would be sent under the ring before the match to put in a few more boards of support to make sure that the whole thing didn't come crashing down under the weight.

Ric Flair Versus Harley Race

While the rest of America was sitting down to Thanksgiving dinner on the last Thursday of November in 1983, the eyes of the wrestling world were focused on a bigger feast: the star-studded wrestling extravaganza in Greensboro, North Carolina, called *Starrcade '83*. The battle at the Greensboro Coliseum pitted the Ric Flair and Harley Race in a battle that would go down as one of the greatest grudge matches in the history of professional wrestling.

To set the stage: Flair had lost the prestigious NWA belt to Race during the summer of 1983, and in the months that followed, his sole goal had been to regain the title, *his* title. But despite the fact that he had enticed Race into the ring on several occasions, Flair had come up empty. On the other hand, Race had tired of hearing Flair's constant challenges and now resorted to a "Race-saving" tactic—one worthy of Machiavelli. He offered $25,000 to anyone who could sidetrack his persistent foe.

Ric Flair and Harley Race go at it.

(Source: Norman Kietzer)

No sooner had the bounty been placed on Flair's golden-tressed head than Cowboy Bob Orton and Dirty Dick Slater appeared at a match between Flair and Race and set upon Flair. They left him with an injured neck and injured pride, and the two of them split the check for $25,000. Flair dropped out of sight for a while after that— long enough to heal his wounds and his pride. Then he resurfaced with a new determination: to get back into the race and to get Race. Picking up some markers along

the way, he repaid both Orton and Slater in kind for their earlier courtesies and then set his sights on the one and only thing that mattered—the only thing between him and *his* belt: Harley Race.

In a battle to end all the battles—and one that will be remembered by anyone who saw it—the two now met once again. But this wasn't just some local event. It was telecast wherever a signal would carry it. Waged in a 15-foot steel cage without benefit of rules—with no time limit, no stoppages even for injury, and a definite winner guaranteed to emerge from the cage—the battle was epic. Both men used everything at their disposal, and then some.

The bout combined brutal force and scientific wrestling, cheap shots and extravagant moves, old-time know-how and modern, crowd-pleasing performance. Here Race used the steel cage to cave in Flair's brow. There Flair used his forearm to drive Race back. And everywhere there was a headlock, a body shot, and a back-flip. Finally, Ric, his face etched in blood, his hopes slowly draining away, brought up a forearm and, from somewhere deep down in the inner recesses of his championship well, found the strength to drive Race to the canvas.

It was all over. Flair had done the all-but-impossible and had yanked victory from the brow of defeat. Now the fans in the stands trumpeted his name, and the wrestlers who had been on the *undercard* all rushed to the ring to hail his triumph. Ric Flair had regained *his* belt and once again stood as the King of the NWA hill.

The Least You Need to Know

➤ The rivalries of pro wrestling are a key feature that keeps the fans coming back week after week.

➤ Even the best of the good guys can get trounced by a bad enough baddie, as Kevin Sullivan showed in his bouts with Dusty Rhodes.

➤ The "biggest" grudge match, at least in terms of the size of the opponents, was between Andre the Giant and Black Jack Mulligan.

➤ Ric Flair and Harley Race engaged in one of the most memorable feuds ever.

Chapter 22

Grunt and Groan Grudge Matches

In This Chapter

➤ The Hulkster defends America

➤ Brotherly hate

➤ Andy Kaufman and the act that (almost) fooled everyone

➤ The first hardcore dumpster feud

Ever since World War II, it had been commonplace for wrestling matches to take on international importance. In other words, German wrestlers continued to goosestep and *Sieg Heil* long after Hitler enjoyed his last smoke in the bunker. During the heat of the Cold War, Russian wrestlers became the top heels, and the Free World was defended every time the American hero kicked some Bolshevik butt.

And so, when the oil crisis came and it appeared that our foes were the Arab world, stereotypical Arabs began to replace the Russians. But then again, stereotyping and wrestling are redundant—if you really want to know the truth, all wrestlers are stereotypes.

Hulk Hogan Versus the Iron Sheik

This brings us to the Iron Sheik and Hulk Hogan—the ultimate Arab villain and American hero of their day. Back in those days, promoters would still wince when Hulk and the Iron Sheik were seen, say, on a game show together and it was obvious that they could be in the same room without pulling foreign objects. But fans didn't care. When face and heel wrestlers are seen together on the street today, fans just ask for autographs.

The Evil Foreigner Incarnate

None of the villainous characters so far could hold a candle to the Iron Sheik, wrestling's version of the exorcist who scared the living hell out of his opponents. And when he couldn't scare them, he beat them with his infamous Camel Clutch.

Wrestling in the name of the hated Ayatollah, the Sheik invaded America's wrestling rings to prove that "American's are weaklings" and to "show what pieces of garbage American wrestlers are." Those were *his* words. His campaign against America culminated in his beating Bob Backlund on December 26, 1983, becoming only the ninth champion in WWF history.

Backlund, who had entered the ring that night with an injury, demanded a rematch. But when he was hurt in a subsequent bout, his tag-team partner Hulk Hogan took his place to prevent the Iron Sheik from taking the belt back to Iran.

Hulk Hogan to America's Defense

Announcing that he would take on the Sheik, Hogan said, "It would be a great crime if the Sheik took that belt out of the United States. It's got to stay right here in the good ol' U.S. of A." And even though the Sheik and his manager, Classie Freddie Blassie, protested, saying that they had trained for Backlund, not the Hulkster, they agreed to one match, one time, before the Sheik returned to his native Iran forever.

And so, in January 1984, in front of a jam-packed house at New York's Madison Square Garden, the two went at it to settle more than a territorial war—they fought for national pride as well. The crowd greeted Hogan with a rousing demonstration of "Hulkamania," while the Sheik responded, true to his scummy character, by jumping atop the turnbuckle and giving the audience an "Iranian salute"—middle finger extended.

Captain Lou's Corner

When people say that wrestling is offensive, I like to point out that it is equally offensive to everyone. Val Venis is no more a credit to his race than the Godfather is to his.

Without waiting for the opening bell, Hogan tore out of his corner and began pummeling the Sheik. No preliminaries, no Treaty of Geneva, thank you. Just a good old-fashioned ass-whoopin', American-style. For a brief second, it appeared that the Sheik's reign would be a short one as Hogan rained blow after blow on the Iranian's shaven head. But just as Hogan was about to apply the *coup de grace* by charging into the cornered Sheik, his opponent moved quickly out of the way and Hogan, unable to alter his charge, slammed headlong into the ring post. He fell to the canvas like a stricken King Kong falling from the top of the Empire State Building.

Bert's Corner

Unlike the usual case where wrestlers use made-up bios with all sorts of outrageous claims, the Iron Sheik really *was* an Iranian.

Body Slam

Vince McMahon tried to repeat his success with the Hulk Hogan/Iron Sheik feud, but sometimes it doesn't pay to go back to the same well too often. In 1991, McMahon, once again using Hogan as his American hero feuded with Sgt. Slaughter, who had defected to Iraq and was siding with that nation in the Gulf War. There were several troubles with this feud, which led to the main event match at that year's *WrestleMania*. One was that Sgt. Slaughter worked best as a hero. Another was that the United States versus Iraq was a mismatch and the third problem, and this was the biggie, was that the war was long over by the time *WrestleMania* rolled around, making Sgt. Slaughter's tirades about "the great Saddam Hussein" seem dated.

Dispatching the Dastardly Villain

The Sheik, seeing his chance, seized it. He went to work on the inert body of the Hulk, stepping over Hogan with his pointy yellow shoes to apply the dreaded Camel Clutch. An eerie silence fell over the crowd as Hogan, his face contorted in pain, tried mightily to resist the Sheik's submission hold, all to no avail.

What seemed like an eternity ticked away—10 ticks of the second hand on the big Madison Square Garden clock, then 20, 30, 40 …. The Sheik continued to exert pressure on Hogan. Finally, after an excruciating 52 seconds, Hogan managed to maneuver his arms underneath the Sheik's massive body. By degrees he began to lift himself and his tormentor up off the canvas. With an incredible show of brute strength, his red, white, and blue corpuscles straining to the task, Hogan managed to stand erect, with the Sheik still clinging to his back. Slowly Hogan turned, backing the Sheik into a corner. Finally, with one giant burst of energy, Hogan rammed the Sheik's back into the turnbuckle, and the Iranian fell to the mat with a thud.

As the dazed Sheik unsteadily made it to legs that were now strangers to him, he was met by a Hulk Hogan Ax Bomber—the Hulkster leaped high into the air and crashed his leg into the Sheik's upper torso. The Sheik fell to the canvas as if pole-axed, to be covered by Hogan for a one-two-three pin count.

As the referee intoned "three," the more than 22,500 fans at the Garden erupted with a bellow, hailing their hero—and the new WWF champion. It had taken 5 minutes and 30 seconds, but Hulk Hogan had turned the tables on the Sheik and saved the belt from going back to Iran. Maybe forever ....

Ricky Steamboat Versus Ric Flair

It has been said that a real friend is someone who walks in when everybody else walks out. And so it was with Ricky Steamboat and Ric Flair, although you'd never have expected it to work out that way judging from their first few meetings. Steamboat and Flair had several encounters in the ring, and the intensity of their skills was matched only by the intensity of their dislike for each other.

Ricky Steamboat Versus Ric Flair.

(Source: Norman Kietzer)

However, as the wrestling wheel turned, the two patched up their differences and became fast friends—so much so that after Flair lost his NWA belt to Harley Race, his former adversary was there for him, consoling him and encouraging him to make a comeback. And, when Flair recaptured his belt, it was Steamboat who ran into the ring and placed the "10 pounds of gold" around his friend's waist. It was enough to bring tears to a grown man's eyes.

This could have been the beginning of a beautiful story—something akin to Claude Rains and Humphrey Bogart walking off into the mist at the end of the movie *Casablanca*, with Rains muttering, "This is the beginning of a beautiful friendship ...." But while cinematic endings are one thing, in wrestling, friendships have to stand up to the challenge of competition in the ring.

Steamboat had gone into retirement, devoting his time and energy to his new gym in Charlotte, North Carolina. But his resolve to stay retired was

Bert's Corner

Ric Flair has been threatening for years to make a North Carolina gubernatorial bid, but after discussing the subject with the governor of Minnesota, Jesse "The Body" Ventura, Flair says now that he *is* leaning against politics.

somewhat less than cast in stone, and soon he was being pressured to return to the ring, not only by his fans, but also by promoter Jim Crockett. Crockett approached Steamboat in front of his hometown fans in the Greensboro (North Carolina) Coliseum with an open contract signed by Flair.

At first Steamboat stuck to his (retired) guns. But when was told that the match would be for the NWA World Championship, he relented. Afterward he was to credit Flair with his decision to sign on the dotted line: "It was a very hard decision," he said. "But the man who pushed me into it was none other than Ric Flair. He reminded me of what I had told him when *he* wanted to retire. And he was right! I may not be able to live with myself several years from now if I don't give myself the opportunity to wrestle for the world's belt today. "Before the match, the two greats came to center ring and exchanged handshakes. Then, in front of a packed house, the two put on an exhibition of scientific wrestling, the likes of which hadn't been seen in many a year. The fans were treated to perfectly executed holds, counterholds, submission holds, and takedowns for the full 60 minutes. First one combatant and then the other attempted to get the upper hand. With time running out and neither man having the advantage, Steamboat tried one last-ditch, figure-four leg lock on Flair. It looked like it might be the end of Flair's championship reign as he flopped around like a freshly caught fish. Then the bell rang, signaling the end of the bout—and of Steamboat's hopes for the belt.

Steamboat merely released his hold and went over to shake Flair's hand. Thus ended one of the finest wrestling matches between two straight shooters in recent wrestling history. And the beautiful friendship continued.

The Undertaker Versus Kane

It was one of the most outerworldly match-ups in the history of wrestling. The Undertaker, one of those inhuman beings who sometimes haunt arenas (usually concocted in the fertile imagination of a promoter), had been claiming to hail from the Dark Side for years. Now he was one of the top stars of the WWF. Sometimes known as The Dead Guy, his matches usually carried some morbid stipulations, such as casket matches in which the winner had to put the loser in a casket and slam the lid on him.

Captain Lou's Corner

The guy who plays Kane didn't always work behind a mask. A few years back he wrestled as Dr. Isaac Yankem, Jerry Lawler's dentist!

The Undertaker's manager at the time was Paul Bearer. However, as happens in many wrestling story lines, Bearer had turned on the Undertaker and taken up with a new wrestler named Kane. Kane, not incidental to our story, was the same size and shape as the Undertaker. And he wore a mask.

Bearer told anyone who would listen that his new discovery was, in fact, the Undertaker's younger brother. Moreover, Bearer would continue, when the Undertaker was but a boy, he had set his own house on fire, and in the ensuing inferno, his mother and father had both perished. But little brother Kane, believed to have perished in the same fire, instead had survived, horribly disfigured (hence the mask). Now Kane wanted revenge on the fiend who had ruined his face and his life.

To further roil the potboiler and make an ugly story even uglier, Bearer let it be known that the Undertaker and Kane were only half-brothers and that he, Bearer, was Kane's real father—The Undertaker's mother being, in Bearer's words, "nothing but a two-bit ...."

With a story line like that, the only thing to be done was to match the two to settle this extended family feud—in the most ghastly manner possible. A casket match was stipulated. After the loser was inside the casket, it was to be set on fire. The only thing missing was Jim Morrison singing, "No one here gets out alive."

The Undertaker and Kane got together to settle matters—once and for all—many times, but every time it looked as if the Undertaker was about to triumph, Kane would resort to one of his heinous tricks and get himself disqualified. The feud has never been settled, and for now the two seem to have united in a ghoulish twosome to take on a common enemy—Vince McMahon, the WWF promoter-turned-wrestler known as The Evil Owner.

Eddy Guerrero Versus Chavo Guerrero Jr.

It was the oldest story in the world: An elder takes one of his youngsters out behind the barn to "teach him a lesson." The elder in this case was Eddy, and the youngster was his nephew, Chavo. Just a few months before, Eddy had been seated ringside at a WCW bout when Chavo lost and decided then and there that Chavo was an embarrassment to the family name.

Determined to make Chavo into a "real man," even if it killed him, Eddy began psychologically tormenting his nephew. The taunts that he threw in Chavo's direction were supposedly designed to motivate the younger Guerrero. The uncle forced his nephew to cheat and even made him wear a T-shirt that read "Eddy Guerrero is my favorite wrestler" on one side, and "Cheat to Win" on the other. Uncle Eddy even took to interfering in Chavo's matches to ensure that he lost.

After weeks of humiliation, Chavo finally snapped and challenged his uncle. The match was set for the *Great American Bash* show on pay-per-view. True to his newly evinced mean streak, Eddy now declared that the loser would truly have to be humiliated, and stipulated that their match would be a "Loser Gets a Haircut" bout.

Eddy was to win the match—by cheating, of course—and gleefully prepared to shear his nephew's locks. But as he turned to Chavo, something in the younger man's eyes signaled a change in his character. No longer the docile youth in the Guerrero family, Chavo screamed that he would cut his own hair. Grabbing the clippers from his startled uncle's hand, he shaved a big bald patch on his own head and then turned on Eddy. With that, Eddy turned tail and ran—in fear for both his hair and his life.

Thus climaxed the most dysfunctional family scene since *Mommie Dearest,* and the stage was set for a family reunion that is sure not to be on the friendly side of family relations.

Jerry Lawler Versus Andy Kaufman

He was better known as Latka Gravas on the TV sitcom *Taxi,* but in the early 1980s, Andy Kaufman became known to wrestling fans at the Memphis Mid-South Coliseum as the World InterGender Wrestling Champion—a title as made-up as the championship belt that he fashioned for himself.

But unlike his gibberish-spouting *Taxi* character or his dead-on impersonations of Elvis, this was no act. At least, no one was supposed to think so. He was, as they say, *working the smart marks*. And the only laughter that it generated was nervous laughter, especially among Kaufman's friends.

Kaufman was serious about his wrestling persona and even made a videotape in which he came off, à la his boyhood idol Buddy "Nature Boy" Rogers, as a baddie. He challenged all women to pin him for $1,000, and he even offered to marry the woman who could beat him.

Fighting Words

In this day and age, when 99.9 percent of all wrestling fans are hip to the fact that wrestling is not a sport but rather sports entertainment, there would seem to be little that a wrestling booker could do to actually con his audience into believing something that isn't true. But it still happens. The wrestling business loves to fool its audience every bit as much as it did back in the days when folks still thought the better man would win. When Andy Kaufman and Jerry Lawler set out to fool a crowd that was otherwise hip to wrestling's act, that was called **working the smart marks.**

In Your Face

Some wrestling fans in Tennessee still hate Andy Kaufman's guts and would spit on his grave if they had a chance.

Kaufman sent his tape to several promoters, but only one showed interest—Eddie Marlin of the Memphis Mid-South Coliseum. It was a decision that brought fans to the arena in record numbers—they all wanted to see Kaufman get his. But in the first four matches, no "hers" came close to succeeding.

Then came Foxy, an oversized lady who outweighed Kaufman by at least 100 pounds. As the bell for their match rang, Kaufman could be seen strutting around the ring in his thermal underwear and boasting about his earlier victories. Foxy came roaring out of her corner and was all over the self-proclaimed InterGender Champion. Finally, after she had thrown him to the canvas and nearly pinned him, Kaufman prevailed. But the bout had been close enough to warrant a rematch.

This time around, Foxy had help—Jerry Lawler coached her. Still, Kaufman managed the win and added insult to injury by rubbing her face into the mat. The fans went wild and screamed for Lawler to enter the ring and help Foxy. When Lawler complied, Kaufman jumped off Foxy screaming, "Lawler, don't you touch me! I'm from Hollywood! I'll sue you for everything you've got …."

No one ever knew whether this was all an act, but it was enough to ignite a feud with Lawler, fueled by Kaufman's media appearances, taunting The King and mocking the Memphis fans. Lawler responded by threatening Kaufman, whom he now called "the Wimp," and warning, "I'm gonna end your fantasy, Andy Kaufman. You're gonna get hurt."

The verbal gauntlet having been thrown down, Kaufman picked it up, accepting the challenge. But he never let anybody in on "the deal"—never meeting with Lawler beforehand to discuss the course that the bout should take. As Lawler put it: "I never could understand why … he would agree to that if he didn't think there would be some kind of meeting, something mutually agreed upon where he wouldn't get hurt."

Instead, Kaufman just showed up, and Lawler was left no option but to wrestle. "I can't just let a little

150-pound comedian come in there and have a match with the Southern Heavy-weight champion and walk out unscathed," he said. "People would have thought *we* were a joke."

On April 5, 1982, the two faced each other in the ring. Kaufman began by ducking out of the ring every time Lawler got near enough to touch him, prompting Lawler to commandeer the ring microphone and mock him. Finally, Lawler let Kaufman near enough to try a headlock, but he turned it into a surprise move and pile-drove Kaufman into the mat—not once, but twice. After the second, Kaufman lay unconscious.

The comedian was taken by ambulance to the local hospital, where he spent the next three days in traction. But that was not to be the end of the feud. The media took after Lawler for his "barbarity." And Kaufman spent his time obsessing about the match.

Three months later the two met again, on David Letterman's show, where Kaufman broke into a stream of obscenities. The King swatted the comedian out of his chair, and Kaufman responded by flinging Letterman's coffee into Lawler's face. The brouhaha sparked a deluge of calls from outraged viewers—outraged at Kaufman, that is. The whole to-do made national headlines.

The two continued their rivalry in arenas across the country, with plots, plans, and double-crosses galore. But the confrontation between wrestling and comedy would forever blur the line between reality and pretense.

New Age Outlaws Versus Cactus Jack and Chainsaw Charlie

Feuds these days are wilder than ever, sometimes involving props and machinery. Here's a case in point: Chainsaw Charlie (in reality, Terry Funk) and Cactus Jack were engaged in a "Falls Count Anywhere Match" and had just wrestled themselves up a ramp and into a dumpster when the New Age Outlaws (Bad Ass Billy Gunn and Road Dogg Jesse James) appeared out of nowhere and clamped the dumpster shut. They pushed it off the ramp, and it fell, crashing onto the arena floor 10 feet below. Doctors came running, and the arena fell silent, the only sound to be heard was Sunny, the valet, sobbing.

Fast-forward to post-recuperation for both Chainsaw Charlie and Cactus Jack—they wanted revenge against the New Age Outlaws. So a "Dumpster Match" was arranged, slated to be part of *WrestleMania XIV*.

The bout was more of a brawl, with most of it taking place in the nether regions of the arena (Boston's Fleet Center), far from the eyes of the fans. TV cameras followed the action, however—and what action it was! Ultimately, Chainsaw Charlie commandeered a forklift to pick up the Outlaws and put them in the dumpster. It appeared that the aggrieved pair was victorious.

But victory was only apparent—it turned out that the rules stipulated a specific dumpster be used, not the one that the Outlaws ended up in. So the rival teams ended up settling their issues with a more traditional (but equally brutal) "Steel Cage Match."

Wrestle Mania

Terry Funk has been threatening to retire for years, but he keeps on wrestling. Why? "It's all I've known all my life," Funk says. "I find myself really torn. Believe me, I love my family so much and my wife so dearly, but I also have a real compassion for my business. That makes it tough, because I know I can't go on forever."

The Least You Need to Know

➤ A mixture of ethnic stereotypes usually produces an emotional crowd.

➤ Ricky Steamboat and Ric Flair were very fine wrestlers.

➤ The Kaufman–Lawler feud forever confused the distinction between real and pretense when wrestling confronted comedy.

➤ Today's feuds often escalate until motor vehicles and weapons are involved.

Greatest Matches of Yesteryear

This chapter takes you back in time to some of the best matches of the "old days." If you saw them today, you might not think so, though. Nobody went through a table, and there was no barbed wire, just two warriors who really knew how to wrestle. But fans back then left the arena just as thrilled as the youngsters today.

For starters, we travel south of the border to Mexico, for a glimpse at *lucha libre* on one of its most amazing nights. It was February 21, 1943, in Mexico City. Wrestling—not just in Mexico, but also all over the world—was about to change forever.

El Santo Versus Ciclone Veloz

The most famous of all Mexican wrestling masks is not very fancy at all. It is *de plata*, plain silver, the mask of El Santo. After 10 years of wrestling under different personae—Red Man, Murcielago II—Rudy Guzman put on a silver mask for the first time at the age of 25 and worked as El Santo, The Saint.

In his first match on July 26, 1942, he wrestled in an eight-man battle royal. These contests are every man for himself, with losers eliminated by being tossed out of the ring. The last two men in the ring were El Santo and Ciclone Veloz, who just so happened to be the Mexican Welterweight champion. In a surprise ending, the unknown man in the silver mask beat the champ and won the contest. That set the stage for the match-up, seven months later, of challenger El Santo against Veloz, one on one, two out of three falls—and this time, Veloz's Welterweight title was on the line.

In the title match, Santo and Veloz each won one fall. In the critical third fall, Veloz tried to elude El Santo by escaping out of the ring. Until this time, bad-guy wrestlers could often deprive the good guys of their championships by getting themselves disqualified because a championship cannot change hands on a DQ. Veloz stood on the arena floor, ready to leave the arena. The referee was counting. It was a strategy that every Mexican wrestling fan just hated, and already the crowd was getting ugly.

The Dive

Veloz was being allowed to quit the match and keep his belt—rewarded!—for his cowardice. It had been done before—but it wasn't going to be done much after this.

Fighting Words

The **plancha** is a dive onto an opponent designed to knock him off his feet and perhaps stun him. El Santo was the first ever to execute a plancha from the ring to the floor below, which necessitated leaping, sailor's–dive-style over the top rope.

El Santo was about to render obsolete the coward's way out. Legends are often launched upon the power of such moments. Babe Ruth calls his shot. Michael Jordan cans a last-second shot to win the championship. Bobby Orr slaps in a shot to win the Stanley Cup. Joe Louis knocks out Max Schmeling. And so it was in that hot summer Mexico City arena that El Santo, for the first time in professional wrestling history, executed the over-the-top-rope *plancha*. Naturally, the aerial maneuver knocked Veloz out cold. El Santo dragged his man back into the ring and pinned him, and the Welterweight Championship was his. And a legend was born.

The crowd was astonished by what they saw, and from that point on, Santo was the biggest star of *lucha libre*, the Mexican form of pro wrestling. Now dead for 17 years, he still lives on in legend.

On February 5, 1984, at the age of 68, just two years after his official retirement as a wrestler, El Santo died of a heart attack. At the time of his death, he was working in a nightclub, with his mask on, as an escape artist, a job that his doctor had said was too strenuous for his age-weakened heart. El Santo was buried with his mask on. Today his name is carried on by El Santo's real-life son, El Hijo del Santo, who is also a star of both ring and screen. And he is every bit as good of a wrestler as his dad. (One of his matches appears in Chapter 24, "Greatest Matches of Today.")

Wrestle Mania

Standing just under 6 feet and weighing between 210 and 225 pounds throughout his adult life, El Santo was a championship wrestler well into his 40s, when he moved his career to the movies. He drove a sports car, solved crimes, battled monsters, kissed the pretty girl (with his mask on), and always made it back to the arena for that evening's wrestling match. Santo was still a semiactive wrestler during his movie career, and the film companies always filmed his matches and used them in the movies. During the 1960s and 1970s, he made more than 50 movies. After becoming the biggest wrestling star in Mexican history, he also became the biggest movie star in Mexican history.

We can only imagine what that first reckless (or so it seemed) dive must have looked and felt like to the astonished crowd. But we do know the influence that moment had on the future of professional wrestling—for nothing would be the same after that. Today, aerial moves are a staple of wrestling on all continents—but they still do it best in Mexico.

Today Mexican wrestling is as much acrobatics as it is brawling, a quick style well suited to the small but agile physiques of Mexican wrestlers. And because they do it better than anyone else in the world, the Mexican wrestlers—such as Mil Mascaras, Rey Misterio Jr., and Essa Rios—have become international stars. And they have the "Man in the Silver Mask" to thank.

Captain Lou's Corner

We really don't know what the young Santo looked like. By the time we saw film of him, he was already 40 years old and had been doing Flying Planchas for so long that he could do them in his sleep.

Edouard Carpentier Versus Lou Thesz

Onward in time we go, from Mexico City to the midwestern United States, from World War II to the days of the Cold War. On June 14, 1957, in the Chicago Amphitheatre, the great Lou Thesz, who had been champion for as long as most of his fans could remember, shockingly lost a match. His opponent was the popular Frenchman Edouard Carpentier, who claimed to be a cousin of former light heavyweight boxing champion Georges Carpentier, one of Jack Dempsey's victims. And, for a day or two, at least, it appeared as if he had won a championship as well.

Wrestle Mania

Lou Thesz was in many of the greatest matches of his era. One match that frequently gets mentioned as one of the best ever was Lou Thesz versus Verne Gagne on October 27, 1951 in Milwaukee for the NWA title. It was what old-timers would call "a wrestler's wrestling match." Many called it the greatest bout of modern times, one that reminded many who saw it of the famous Jim Londos-Strangler Lewis match back in Madison Square Garden in 1932. The Gagne-Thesz match was science versus science as each got a quick start out of the blocks. Each took one fall in the best-two-out-of-three championship match. Both pulled out all the stops in the third and deciding fall. Gagne was trying to work Thesz into his special sleeper hold, and Thesz tried mightily to execute his own pet move, the reverse body slam. Neither succeeded—each knew exactly what the other had in mind—so the match ended in one of those rarities of modern wrestling, a draw.

Bert's Corner

Until the 1970s, all championship matches were two-out-of-three falls. With the diminishing attention spans of the "TV generation," however, championship matches in the United States switched to one fall—and have stayed that way.

In front of a packed house of extremely vocal locals, Thesz and Carpentier wrestled a two-out-of-three-falls match with the NWA title on the line. Both fought intensely—too intensely, as it turned out for Thesz—from the starting bell. Thesz won the first fall with a flying body press, a move referred to today as the flying crossbody block, at the 17:22 mark.

Controversial Ending

The match had been exhausting for both wrestlers, but especially for the older Thesz. Carpentier turned on the gas in the second fall and bombarded Thesz with aerial moves. A powerful reverse body press at the 3:39 mark of the second fall pinned Thesz's shoulders to the mat, and the match was even. The third fall was an extension of the second, with Thesz still acting fatigued and Carpentier pouring on the hurt. Unable to defend himself any longer, Thesz took flight, running from corner to corner in the ring, evading any and all of Carpentier's attempts to finish him off. Finally, at the 4:42 mark of the third fall, referee Ed Whalen called for the bell and disqualified Thesz for refusing to wrestle. At midnight that night, the State of Illinois Athletic

Commission officially recognized Edouard Carpentier as the new wrestling champion of the world. But that was not the end of it. The NWA, the sanctioning body for the match, stuck to its already-established rule that no title can change hands on a disqualification victory.

Making New Champions

The disputed "title doesn't change hands" victory by Carpentier over Thesz was used by promoters to justify several non-NWA title changes. After defeating Thesz, Carpentier would come to town as the "real" champion and get beaten by the local hero, and the local promoter would have a plausible excuse to put a belt on his own top money-maker. Killer Kowalski won a championship in Boston in May 1958, Verne Gagne won a belt by beating Carpentier in August 1958 in Omaha, and Freddie Blassie won a title in Los Angeles in June 1961.

Bert's Corner

Thesz and Carpentier wrestled twice more after their famous match, with Thesz defeating Carpentier by DQ in Montreal on July 24, 1957, and wrestling to a draw in Chicago on August 16, 1957.

Dick the Bruiser Versus Alex Karras

Now let's jump ahead in time just a few years and, from our last stop in Chicago, just a hop, skip, and jump away to Detroit, Michigan. During the first months of 1963, Dick "The Bruiser" Afflis was dining in a Detroit restaurant with Alex Karras, All-Pro defensive tackle for the Detroit Lions. Karras had just been suspended for a year by the NFL for gambling and was seeking other forms of income. He began to tell The Bruiser how easy he thought wrestling was. Taking the bait, The Bruiser challenged him to a match. Karras eagerly accepted. It turned out that the pair couldn't wait to get into the ring and decided to have it out right then and there, which brought the cops and front-page headlines. (Some readers who aren't football fans may best remember Karras as Mongo in *Blazing Saddles* or as George, the dad, on the TV show *Webster*.)

Captain Lou's Corner

Dick "The Bruiser" had an ability to work up a crowd that was second to none. On November 19, 1958, he taunted the crowd during a Madison Square Garden show in New York City. A riot resulted in which 300 people, including 2 police officers, were injured, and The Bruiser was banned from wrestling in the Garden ever again. So, when wrestling a football star in his hometown, you can bet that Afflis knew how to maximize crowd response.

Was It a Shoot?

According to legend, Karras called Afflis on the phone and asked how they were going to "work" the match. "I don't know how you're going to work it, but I'm going to beat the s—- out of you," replied The Bruiser.

Come the night of the match, 16,000 rabid fans had packed Detroit's Olympia. I don't know whether the match was really "on the level," but I do know two things: First, every single spectator thought that it was real—a "shoot," as the wrestlers call it. Second, one Karras punch opened up a nasty jagged cut over Dick the Bruiser's right eye that required several stitches.

Bruiser Grows Bored

Eleven minutes into the match, Afflis decided that he'd had enough fun. He switched from brawling to scientific wrestling and quickly rolled Karras up for a three-count. In the locker room afterward, Afflis was overheard saying to the physician, "Hurry up with the suture, doc, I got a broad waiting."

The Least You Need to Know

➤ El Santo is Mexico's most legendary wrestler.

➤ El Santo's introduction of aerial acrobatics into Mexican wrestling ended up revolutionizing wrestling around the world.

➤ Edouard Carpentier beat Lou Thesz by outlasting the aging champion, but the NWA's refusal to change the title on a DQ finish led to many regional champions, all claiming to be "World Champs."

➤ Dick the Bruiser and Alex Karras convinced the world that their match was for real.

Chapter 24

Greatest Matches of Today

In This Chapter

➤ A new generation of *luchadors*

➤ Saving the honor of Mexico

➤ Hell in a cell

➤ Goldberg's magic night

The great matches of the past 10 years were more elaborately choreographed and more violent, with greater risks to the performers than those of yesteryear. Today's wrestler can no longer get by with a psychological understanding of his audience's needs. He must be willing to put his body on the line. Whether it be diving over the top rope to the floor below and landing skull first, or allowing one's self to be heaved off the top of a steel cage, it is the very real notion that wrestlers are "putting their lives on the line" that causes a performer to rise above the pack in the eyes of the fans.

El Hijo del Santo and Octagon Versus Love Machine and Eddy Guerrero

This match, held November 6, 1994, in Los Angeles as part of the Mexican AAA promotion's *When Worlds Collide* pay-per-view telecast, was a two-out-of-three falls match wrestled under *lucha libre* rules. That meant that both members of a team had to be

Bert's Corner

American promoters were forced to change their standard operating procedures when booking *lucha libre* tours. That's because, for reasons unknown, people of Mexican heritage do not like to buy tickets in advance. Several shows on the 1994 tour were almost canceled because of perceived lack of interest. It's a good thing that they weren't, though, because those shows sold out from the large walk-up crowd.

Fighting Words

Matwork means real grappling—applying holds and countering holds, usually in a situation in which neither wrestler is standing up. Instead, both are working down on the mat.

pinned or submit before a fall was counted. Love Machine was an American wrestler played by Art Barr, who has since passed away. Barr had no equal in playing an ugly American who could make Mexicans truly, deeply hate him.

On this night the Love Machine got the predominantly Latino crowd all worked up even before the match began. He wagged his tongue at the women and made swimming motions at the men—a visual slander equivalent to calling them "wetbacks." Together, Love Machine and Eddy Guerrero (the same guy who's in the WWF today) were called Los Gringos Locos (The Crazy Americans). Accompanying Los Gringos Locos to the ring was Louis "Madonna's Boyfriend" Spiccoli, who unfortunately is also no longer with us, a victim of painkiller addiction.

The tag team they were facing was comprised of the AAA Promotion's ultimate heroes: El Hijo del Santo (the real-life son of El Santo, by far the most popular *luchador* in the history of *lucha libre*) and Octagon. Taking a cue from his dad, El Hijo del Santo, along with Octagon as his co-star, had starred in several Mexican movies. Seconding the good guys was the masked *luchador,* Blue Panther.

The match had two strong stipulations: First, if the heroes lost, they had to remove their masks. Second, if the Gringos lost, they had to shave each other's heads. Old-time *lucha libre* fans knew that the teams had a family history: Eddy Guerrero's dad, Gory Guerrero, Gory's son, and the original Santo had once been tag-team partners. Eddy and El Hijodel Santo were the first two in the ring, now on opposite teams, getting the match off to a solid start with brisk *matwork*.

Santo Lands on His Head

Both men tagged out, and Love Machine battled Octagon next. Octagon attacked Love Machine with a series of acrobatic kicks, but Love Machine retaliated by tossing him clear out of the ring. Eddy then put Santo up on his shoulders while Love Machine climbed to the top rope to deliver a *huracanrana*. Santo was driven head first to the canvas, one of those bumps that sounds like it felled six or seven bystanders and makes a crowd go silent for a moment for fear that they've just seen a wrestler killed. Love Machine pinned Santo while Eddy superplexed Octagon. Love Machine again climbed to the top and crashed down with a "frog splash" atop Octagon, enabling him to get the pin and the first fall.

Santo did not look good for the first few minutes of the second fall, and it was clear that his neck was hurting from the bad bump he'd taken following the huracanrana. He recovered after a few minutes. The Gringos were knocked out of the ring, and Santo and Octagon nailed them both with simultaneous *tope suicidas,* leaping from the ring to the arena floor over the top rope. It looked very bad for the good guys. Octagon, being double-teamed, was dragged back into the ring and thrown into the ropes. The Gringos were setting Octagon up for a backdrop into a power bomb that would surely have ended the match. But no! The crowd exploded with almost unbelievable passion as Octagon reversed the move, turned it into a rana, and pinned Eddy for a three-count. Octagon, on a roll, combined a Russian leg sweep with an arm and headlock, forcing Love Machine to submit. The good guys had won the second fall.

El Hijo del Santo is the son of Mexico's all-time most popular wrestler.

Octagon's Suicide Dive

In the third fall, Santo and Octagon were knocked out of the ring while the Gringos did the double suicide dives to try to crush them. Love Machine's dive onto Octagon was executed well, but Guerrero's foot became caught on the top rope, causing him to fall awkwardly on top of Santo. Guerrero and Santo tangled together on the floor, distracting the referee long enough for Love Machine to nail Octagon with a tombstone pile driver, an illegal move in *lucha libre* and cause for an immediate disqualification. Ah, but the ref had his back turned. He turned around just in time to count to three as Love Machine pinned the unconscious Octagon. Santo appeared unconscious as well, and once again it looked very bad for the good guys.

The Gringos rolled Santo into the ring. Love Machine suplexed him and Guerrero frog-splashed him. But when Love Machine went for the pin, Santo kicked out after a two count. Again, the emotion in the building was unbelievable. Double-teaming Santo again, they tried to set him up for a clothesline. But Santo ducked, and Love Machine accidentally knocked his own partner over the top rope and out of the ring. Santo, now rejuvenated, climbed to the top rope and dove down onto Eddy below. This again distracted the ref. While the official had his back turned, Blue Panther, the heroes' second, snuck into the ring and gave Love Machine a pile driver. Santo rolled back into the ring and pinned Love Machine.

Both teams now needed only one more three-count for the victory. Eddy climbed to the top rope and hit Santo with a rana, but Santo kicked out after a two-count. Eddy clobbered Santo with a dragon-plex—again putting dangerous stress on Santo's already injured neck. Eddy, feeling greedy, decided to give Santo a second dragon-plex—and maybe end his career—but Santo reversed the move and rolled Eddy Guerrero up for the pin and the match.

Captain Lou's Corner

I worked as a bad guy often enough in my career to know something about getting heel heat. Getting a crowd to truly hate your guts is an art form, and nobody—not even Freddie Blassie—was better at doing it than Art Barr. He could make a crowd call for his lynching just by flashing a smirk.

Wrestle Mania

To continue wrestling even though you have suffered a terrible injury in the ring is considered the ultimate sign of hardcore. Mick Foley kept wrestling (briefly) after he lost his ear. Hardcore Holly recently wrestled for five minutes with a broken arm. The situation has gotten out of hand. Wrestlers need to think about their lives after wrestling every once in a while. Not long ago a wrestler, whose name I won't mention, broke his pelvis coming off the top rope and landing wrong. His opponent said, "Keep wrestling! It will make you a legend!" The injured wrestler, however, would hear none of it and insisted on being pinned to end the match. Good for him! At some point the show must end and real life set in—and that point comes when the health of the wrestler is in serious jeopardy.

Octagon had to be taken to a hospital in an ambulance, while Love Machine and Eddy Guerrero cut off each other's hair. El Hijo del Santo, in delight, grabbed clumps of the bad guys' hair and threw it into the crowd, where many were still weeping over what they'd just seen. (Fans will note that Eddy Guerrero today calls his car Love Machine as an homage to his late buddy, Art Barr.)

The Undertaker Versus Mankind: Hell in a Cell Match

Fans will remember this epic battle as the main event on the WWF's June 28, 1998, *King of the Ring* pay-per-view event. Mick Foley was wrestling The Undertaker under his Mankind persona. (Foley also wrestled as Cactus Jack and Dude Love, depending on his mood.) As the match began, Mankind was atop the cage—but The Undertaker soon joined him. Both men were on top of the cage, a full 16 feet above the arena floor. (Distances in wrestling are usually exaggerated, but this figure appeared to be legit.) Then, in a move that put a hush of awe into the crowd, The Undertaker picked up Mankind and threw him off the cage.

The First Fall

Mankind plummeted downward and fell face first through the Spanish-language broadcasters' table. He lay motionless for several minutes. The fall dislocated his jaw and knocked out three of his teeth—one of which later came out his nose. The jaw was put back in place right there in front of everyone, with the cameras rolling. The doctor who was working on Foley was not actually a doctor at all (but he plays one on TV). It was actually Francois Petit, who is the shiatsu masseuse for Vince McMahon and Steve Austin. All three of the teeth were recovered intact and were later surgically put back. One of the teeth cut through Mankind's lower lip. Well, end of match, right? Maybe end of show, call the ambulance. Wrong. They were carrying Foley out

Body Slam

There are certain moments of athletic violence that stick in the mind. Everyone who was watching, for example, remembers the horror of seeing Joe Theisman's leg being broken by Lawrence Taylor on Monday Night Football. The same is true of the Hell in the Cell match. I know wrestling fans who have seen every hardcore angle ever who looked away during this match and who refuse to watch a videotape of the match. "I can't do it," a friend of mine says. "It makes me sick to my stomach!"

Bert's Corner

If you want further insight into just what makes Mick Foley tick, I suggest that you check out the documentary film *Beyond the Mat*.

Captain Lou's Corner

It is hard to shock a wrestling audience these days. They often have a "been there, done that" attitude and are quick to chant, "Boring!" if they aren't excited by what they are seeing. But Mick Foley could shock a wrestling crowd, no matter how jaded it was—and he could do it again and again.

Mick Foley's willingness to sacrifice his body to please his fans turned him into a cult figure.

on a stretcher when he woke up, realized where he was, and climbed off the stretcher. He stumbled back to the ring and climbed back to the top of the cage.

The Second Fall

This time a part of the cage gave away (which was planned), and Foley fell again, this time inside the ring. He finished the match, although he now claims that he doesn't remember much of what happened. The paramedics once again tended to Foley, who was unconscious in the ring. When he regained consciousness, Foley went under the ring, found a bagful of thumbtacks, and dumped them in the ring. Guess who ended up getting the thumbtacks? The Undertaker choke-slammed Mankind into the thumbtacks for the pin and the win. Foley was immediately taken to the hospital.

Goldberg Versus Hollywood Hogan

Hollywood Hogan (the Hulkster in his despicable persona) was the WCW champion, while the challenger, Bill Goldberg, was the undefeated young phenom and former University of Georgia Bulldogs star. Goldberg's alma mater was important because the event, held on July 6, 1998, and shown on *Monday Nitro,* was being held before a sold-out Georgia Dome, filled with fans who were clearing the red clay out of their lungs screaming for Gooold-Berrrgg!

Introduction of the Neck Flip

Goldberg was the United States champion and had held that belt for a while. But Hogan held the real prize, the WCW World Heavyweight Championship belt, and he wasn't above cheating or using his cronies from the New World Order to make sure that the strap stayed around his waist.

Hogan said he'd give Goldberg a title shot on the show that night, but only if Goldberg could first defeat Hogan's partner-in-crime in the nWo, Scott Hall. Goldberg gladly accepted the stipulation. Hogan felt that if Goldberg had to wrestle twice in one night, he wouldn't have enough left to mount a successful challenge to the title.

The match between Goldberg and Hall was impressive enough, and it was only the warm-up. At one point, Hall appeared to be on the verge of victory, about to apply the Outsider's Edge, his finishing move. But then Goldberg did something astonishing. He escaped the move by flipping Hall with his neck alone. The roof practically came off the Georgia Dome.

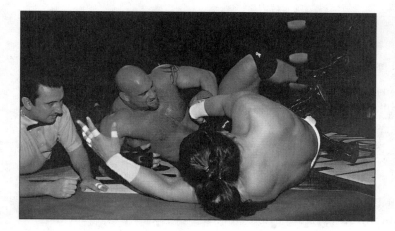

Goldberg's victory over Hogan in the Georgia Dome turned Goldberg into a household name.

The Main Event

Goldberg, of course, went on to pin Hall, setting up the main event. The early action was even-up, with the two exchanging moves in the center of the ring. Things heated up when Hogan took the action outside the ring and belted Goldberg with a chair a few times. Luckily, he hit him in the head. I pity that chair!

Hogan dragged the groggy Goldberg back into the ring and dropped the big leg on him twice—usually a sure sign that Hogan is about to win a match. But when Hogan went for the pin, Goldberg lifted his shoulder just before the referee could count to three—and the match went on.

In Your Face

Some wrestling matches have drawn 40,000 to an arena in the United States, although not many. It happens more frequently in Japan. But never, never before have there been 40,000 wrestling fans who simultaneously counted to three along with the referee the way there were when Goldberg pinned Hogan.

Hogan's Demise

Taken aback by the unexpected development, Hogan was further distracted by Diamond Dallas Page and basketball's Karl Malone, who had come out to watch the match from ringside—and protect Goldberg against an attack by the nWo, should it come. Sure enough, Hogan's pal Curt Hennig came out and moved to ringside. It looked like a gang war might develop—which wasn't that uncommon of an occurrence during the gang-oriented booking of the summer of 1998.

While Hogan tried to sort things out, Goldberg shook out the cobwebs and moved into a corner to launch his final attack. When Hogan finally turned around to face him, Goldberg nailed him with the Spear, followed promptly by a Jackhammer. Hogan was done. Goldberg was the new WCW champ—the first WCW champ ever to be undefeated as a pro.

The Least You Need to Know

➤ Mexican wrestling uses American villains to get crowds worked up.

➤ The *luchadors* invented the acrobatic wrestling moves used everywhere today, and they are still the best at it.

➤ Mick Foley's two falls in the "Hell in a Cell" match are etched into the memories of all who've seen them.

➤ Goldberg went from being an unknown to being a wrestling superstar in a nanosecond.

➤ Goldberg's fame skyrocketed after he defeated Hollywood Hogan for the WCW title.

Part 6

All the Right Moves: Inner (and Outer) Workings of the Ring

Now that we've focused on the action inside the ring, let's take a look behind the scenes at some of the nooks and crannies of the professional wrestling world. First we'll journey into the area I'm the most familiar with: that of managers. From there, we'll take a look a some of the novelty acts that promoters have come up with over the years to keep their product fresh and interesting—things such as midget matches, cage matches, barbed wire matches, and others.

Our focus shifts to the simpatico relationship that has always existed between professional wrestling and television. The grunt-and-groan circuit and the boob tube were made for one another, and that is as true today as it was in the late 1940s when the screen was round and showed a grainy black-and-white picture.

For those readers—and I know you're out there—who want to become professional wrestlers when they grow up, this part includes a chapter on how to choose a wrestling school. For those of you who don't necessarily want to know how to fall from the ring apron to the concrete floor face first without getting hurt but are nonetheless interested in the hows and whys of in-ring action, a chapter on holds and maneuvers follows.

And, to wrap things up, we'll take a look at the origins and current state of the wild world of tag-team wrestling. Proceed at your own risk!

Chapter 25

Managers: Holding the Leash on 300-Pound Pulverizers

In This Chapter

➤ The basic tasks of the wrestling manager

➤ How managers learn the trade

➤ Running the hype, and how it contributes to the gate

➤ Everybody wants to get into the act: managers in the ring

What is a manager? Look it up in the dictionary, and you find something similar to the following: "A person in charge of the training and performance of an athlete or team." Well, that only begins to tell you what we do.

First of all, let me clarify one thing: We are *not* managers in the conventional sense of the word. We do not train the wrestlers the way that a traditional sports manager does. Truth be told, if they didn't already know how to train, wrestlers wouldn't have gotten to the point where we would be interested in representing them as managers. No, we're less manager-trainers than we are business managers. We make the matches, get our wrestlers what we consider their fair share of the gate, and keep them pumped up for the big matches.

And we're part of a team effort. Most times, our wrestlers' performances in the ring are dependent upon our performances outside of it. You've seen us at ringside jumping up and down like Rumplestiltskin, doing anything and everything we can to help our wrestler win—fair or foul.

And, without a doubt, we are—both male and female managers—the most colorful characters in all of professional wrestling. Therein lies our biggest asset: our ability to "hype" or "heat up" a match. So here's the insider information on wrestling's managers.

Management 101

To illustrate what a manager does, and how he or she does it, let me tell you about ol' Captain Lou's own career as manager, and maybe you'll begin to understand.

As a wrestler, I was an also-ran who also ran—away from the likes of Bruno Sammartino, Andre the Giant, and anyone else who looked like they could do me bodily harm. Granted, we sold out all the arenas where I pulled my feet-don't-fail-me-now act, but I was giving my career more than a few second thoughts nonetheless. It was at one of these magic moments of self-doubt that Bruno Sammartino said to me, "You're not a great wrestler, but you never shut up. You'd be a good manager."

Intrigued by Bruno's suggestion, I went to see Vince McMahon Sr. He agreed with Bruno's assessment, saying, "You'd be a natural—you're a good BS-er." Great! But before I realized it, the words were out of my mouth: "What the heck *is* a manager?"

Vince's answer was simple, but to the point: "You do all the hype for your men." That was it. Well, ever since I was a little kid, I've had a motor mouth. In fact, people used to rib me about it, saying that I had a mouth so big I could play the tuba from both ends.

And what better way to use it than as a manager, where I could walk into a room, voice first, and hype my wrestlers until my tongue got tired?

Captain Lou's Corner

One of the wordiest managers I ever knew was Wild Red Berry. Berry studied the dictionary and books like *Bartlett's Familiar Quotations* and would incorporate them into his hype. Once he described a wrestler as having "the sagacity of a chipmunk and the jaws of a lion." Another time he was issuing challenges in the name of his tag team, the Kangaroos, and called on all the "insidious mugwumps" that stood in their path.

Learning the Managerial Ropes

The first wrestler I ever managed was Oscar LeDoux, back in 1969. The kid was a natural for me. He mumbled and couldn't put two words together. So I became his mouthpiece, much like I did for Abdullah the Butcher in more recent times—if you remember, he never uttered a word and had his manager do the talking for him. Anyway, like a kind of dishonest ventriloquist, I represented LeDoux as both a manager and a spokesman. And operating on the theory that you can get anywhere if you keep putting one word in front of another, I was able to maneuver him into the main event at the brand-new Madison Square Garden for its very first wrestling show against Bruno Sammartino—ironically, the man who first suggested that I become a manager.

Wrestle Mania

The Undertaker is Paul Bearer's biggest draw in his stable of wrestlers, but he's not the only one. There's also the Undertaker's brother, Kane. Paul Bearer (a great name for the Undertaker's manager, don't you think?) has a ghoulish face and a fat body. He goes a little too heavy on the eye makeup. Sure, it's part of the total shtick, but let's get real here—I mean, who's going to take Bearer seriously as a man from the Dark Side? Now the Undertaker, *he's* scary. And as comical as Paul Bearer may look, he has done an excellent job of hyping the Undertaker and Kane. He may look silly in his ringside garb, but he draws plenty of press attention, which is a big part of the manager's job.

Paul Bearer, who started his managing career in Mexico as Percival Pringle, now has a gimmick that goes with that of his wrestler, the Undertaker.

I soon found out that if I didn't hype my wrestler well and do well for him and for the promoter at the gate, I would hear Vince saying, "Well, you're not doing your job. Your guys aren't selling out … they're not drawing." So, I'd up my hype to the high-octane level.

Let me tell you about one of those high-octane hypes that worked—too well, it turned out.

Captain Lou poses with the Headshrinkers, one of his WWF champion tag teams. The wrestler second from the left now wrestles solo as Rikishi Phatu, whose large, ugly, exposed buttocks and hot dancing moves have made him popular in the WWF.

Back in the 1970s I managed Ivan Koloff, who was scheduled to take on Bruno Sammartino at the Garden for the world title—or at least the WWF version of it. Figuring that if I put my finger in the ethnic melting pot and stirred, I could build the necessary heat for Koloff, I went on TV to promote the bout. Now, this was back in the days before political correctness became our national virus, so you could say things that you wouldn't dare say today.

Running the Hype

Anyone who knows me knows that I'm proud of my Italian heritage, proud of the fact that my father was born and educated there, and proud that I was born in Rome while he was studying medicine over there. However, my ethnic pride didn't stop me from using hype to build Koloff's match.

I went on television where I played it for all I was worth. With tongue planted firmly in my safety-pinned cheek, I said, "Bruno Sammartino's Italian. I *used* to be an Italian, but I changed my name to Captain Lou Albert. Let's face it, what have 'guineas' ever done?" Here, as they say, I let it all hang out: "All they've ever done is drive garbage trucks. I mean, you take the garbage trucks in New York and you see an Italian driving and a Puerto Rican loading. At midday they switch off …."

Well, that tore it. The hue and cry went up from all quarters. The Young Lords, a Puerto Rican gang, threatened to kill me. My "gumbas" were only a little less incensed. But what the heck, it was only part of my job as manager—to hype the match. Or so I thought.

Wrestle Mania

After he retired as a wrestler, Blassie soon became one of the most hated managers in the WWF lineup, guiding some of the meanest baddies in the ring. He specialized in foreign-invader baddies: Spiros Arion, Victor Rivera, Killer Khan, Mr. Fuji, and The Iron Sheik, to name just a few. In addition to these evil-doers from foreign lands, he had American ne'er-do-wells on his roster, too: Dick Murdoch, Jesse Ventura, Big John Studd, Stan Hansen, and Adrian Adonis were just a few. He's the guy who brought Hulk Hogan into the WWF for the first time, in 1979. Blassie retired from wrestling in the mid-1980s. After that, his biggest claim to fame came when he released the song "Pencil Neck Geek"—a huge novelty hit, named after his phrase for wrestling fans.

The night of the Madison Square Garden bout, I still didn't have a clue. I looked at the capacity house and thought, "What a good manager am I." But Vince had other thoughts. "We're going to have trouble," he kept saying. Even Koloff sensed something and told me not to get too close to him.

They were both right. Almost as soon as Koloff pinned Sammartino to win the belt, someone threw a firecracker from the stands and it went off with a resounding boom! Vince hollered to me, "Don't go into the ring!" But that was unnecessary. I had no intention of doing so, and reverted to my old shtick of running fast, straight out of the Garden. But not before everyone in the capacity crowd had thrown anything and everything that they could lay hands on in my direction: flowerpots, beer cups, and all manner of other unidentifiable fly-bys. It was a wild scene, and my managerial hype had created it.

I sought sanctuary in a nearby restaurant. As I ran in, the bartender yelled, "Captain Lou, you'd better get out of here!" I saw a bunch of young guys, maybe 25 or so, staring menacingly in my direction. So I hollered, "Call the cops," and ran back out into the street to grab a cab. But, as soon as I got in, some of the young toughs started banging on the windows and the roof and rocking the cab. Heeding the driver's pleas to get out, I exited and raced back into the bar. The gang ultimately wrecked the joint, causing $27,000 worth of damage.

Body Slam

Not all interviews go as planned. One time, when I was being interviewed on TV by Vince McMahon Jr., I stood there yammering away and smoking a cigar, spilling ashes all over myself. I didn't realize that my shirt was made of polyester. Suddenly, Vince Jr. looked at me in horror and yelled. I looked down and saw my shirt was on fire! It burned my back and part of my arm—but what the heck, it added to the hype.

Bert's Corner

Conflicts seen around the ring between managers or between managers and wrestlers are often the setup for an upcoming grudge match that has not yet been announced.

Interviews for Managerial Fun and Profit

I've also done interviews that were of a different style altogether—fun and funny. One of them was with my tag team, the Moon Dogs. They would come out and, on camera, eat raw meat, like the Samoans, and let out a howl. Then I'd say something to the announcer like, "Watch it! We have to keep an eye on these Moon Dogs. If they start picking up their legs, you know what's happening—like when a dog lifts its leg? They'll do the same thing to you, so keep an eye on them!"

Perpetual Prankster

You know me, I never met a joke I didn't like—especially one that I could pull on the announcers, the audience, or the wrestlers, including my own. And George "The Animal" Steele was the perfect straight man for such jokes. The Animal was one of the weirdest wrestlers I have ever met, never mind managed. Sometimes I thought he would have been as much at home in a zoo as in the ring.

Anyway, we were both on Vince Jr.'s TV show, and I brought in a third person, introducing him as Doctor Ziff or some such nonsense. And then I added, "He's a psychiatrist and a gynecologist—you know, someone who works both ends." Anyway, the "doctor" (really an actor) sat The Animal down, and George uttered one of his multisyllabic grunts, drooling all over himself. The doctor peered at his head and said, "It's a jungle in there." Then he decided that George needed shock treatments and strapped a metal helmet onto his head and hooked it up to some machine that looked like it came straight off the set of the movie *Frankenstein*. He threw a switch, and all of a sudden George bolted upright in his chair and started speaking in pear-shaped tones: "How now, Brown Cow?" Of course, when the helmet came off, George reverted to The Animal, mumbling unintelligible gibberish, and I slammed into the doctor: "You're nothing but a quack. You're no doctor … you're a veterinarian! "

But fans believe the hype—even hype like that. Later that same week, I was at Kennedy Airport, about to board a plane for the next show. Suddenly this woman came up and hugged and kissed me. She said, "Captain Lou, I want to thank you for sending George Steele to a gynecologist and curing him."

Making the Match

If the manager's first job is to hype the wrestlers, his second is to make the matches. By that, I mean that the manager suggests to the promoter who might make the best-drawing matches.

Wrestle Mania

Jimmy Hart hails from Memphis, Tennessee, and has managed some great wrestlers. Among the wrestlers he has handled, you'll find such big names as Hulk Hogan, Kevin Sullivan, Randy Savage, Lex Luger, and The Giant. He also has handled Brutus Beefcake, The Faces of Fear, King Kong Bundy, Greg Valentine, Earthquake, Honky Tonk Man, The Hart Foundation, Money Inc., and Dino Bravo. Under Hart's direction, Hogan became the WCW World champ. His Hart Foundation and Money Inc. won the WWF tag-team championship. Greg Valentine climbed to the top of the WWF with Hart leading the way, as did the Honky Tonk Man. And Paul Wight, then known as The Giant, won the WCW World Championship with Hart's help.

It's just like boxing—which match will draw the most money? Would you put a Bruno Sammartino in against a Killer Kowalski? Yes. Would you put Bruno in against Charlie Brown? No. You're looking for something that will be very productive for your wrestler—something that suits his talent.

Ringside Antics

This brings us to the most obvious of all the manager's duties. These are the ones *everybody* knows about, the ones everybody sees: our antics at ringside. As a group, managers are among the most colorful to be found in professional wrestling, and I say that with absolutely no humility. We're usually the wildest ones, patrolling the ring apron—often carrying our trademark props such as walking canes, bullhorns, or

even 2x4s—and doing our best to affect the outcome of the match. It doesn't matter how we do it, tripping up the opponent, or even cold-cocking him if the action spills out of the ring.

A Singular Case in Point

I remember one time I entered the ring to help my wrestler, Freddie Blassie. We were somewhere in Pennsylvania, where my charge was scheduled to wrestle Pedro Morales, then the WWF champion. As Morales stood center-ring, bathing in the applause of the crowd, Blassie came out in street clothes, with his arm in a sling.

"I can't wrestle," he told announcer Vince McMahon Jr. "My arm's busted." Then he climbed into the ring to show Morales the note that he had from his doctor. But as he did, I came up behind Morales and hit him with a shot over the head with a chair. Then Blassie ripped off his sling and started pummeling Pedro with his "broken arm." Morales was finally rescued by Gorilla Monsoon and Chief Jay Strongbow, who carried him off to the dressing room, unconscious. When he was revived, he demanded that Blassie be made his top challenger for the WWF title, which was what we wanted all along.

You Win Some, You Lose Some

Sometimes, though, our tricks don't work. Take the time I managed the Wild Samoans, Afa and Sika. On the night they defended their tag-team title against Tony Atlas and Rocky Johnson, I decided that there was no such thing as too little help from the manager. So I brought a solid oak chair with me down to ringside. I hoped that the fans would believe I'd brought it just so I could have the best seat in the house. But I had other plans—it was to be my secret weapon.

The match itself was wild—as anything that features the Samoans tends to be. Finally, all 300 pounds of Afa grabbed Tony Atlas in a full nelson hold. As they struggled, the referee somehow got in the way and was knocked on his keister. This was my chance! With no referee in sight, I climbed into the ring, chair in hand. As Atlas struggled to get out of the full nelson, I brought the carefully aimed chair down, right where his head was. But at the last second he moved, and instead I hit Afa. He went down as if shot, and Tony pinned him. I felt like a total jerk.

Illegal Interference

Most managers find some way to interfere in the progress of a match. One of the most unusual methods I've seen was used by Marlena, who not only managed Goldust, but was also his wife. She once smashed her purse into the face of her hubby's opponent, Brian Pillman. It's just another variation on the gimmick theme.

Call them illegal weapons if you want, but they are *all* gimmicks. They come in all sizes, shapes, and structures. They range from cola cans to ballpoint pens to knives, from pieces of metal to chairs (my favorite). And they are often passed from manager to wrestler at crucial moments in the match.

Probably the best at passing gimmicks was Abdullah Farouk, born Ernie Roth, but better known as the Grand Wizard. He was a master at this trick of the trade. Usually your wrestler can maneuver his opponent over toward where you, the manager, are standing. It's not difficult for a wrestler to get his opponent where he wants him—whether it's a certain point in the ring or, better yet, on the ropes. Brute force works well and so does a baited lure. Experienced wrestlers have many ways of manipulating the position of their opponents so that the manager has a chance to do that voodoo he does so well. A manager and a wrestler working together as a team can achieve rewarding results and wreak disaster on the opponent.

Maybe that's why you see managers mostly in the corners of the heels, not the faces. Maybe the villains need more help. Well, that's what we're there for. So when you see us wandering around ringside, about to inflict all of wrestling's versions of the Biblical plagues on our wrestler's opponent, watch us carefully. Somebody's got to!

Management's Best

Now, I'm good. But there are other good managers out there, too. Otherwise, I'd have nobody to play off of. You've noticed the bios of some of the true greats scattered throughout this chapter. Following are a few more:

Freddie Blassie, I have to admit, was a good manager—that is, if you liked dirty tricks. During his days as a wrestler, he was known as a biter. During interviews, he would always take out a file to sharpen his teeth. As a manager, he was no less scary, in part because he was a little crazy. Even so, I have always respected Blassie. I had to—I had to negotiate contracts with him, pitting my guys against his. But even when negotiating, I always kept my eye on his cane. You never knew when he might try to whack you with it.

And then there was Bobby "The Brain" Heenan, who now works as an announcer for WCW. He still calls himself "The Brain," but he has none. Let me tell you about something he pulled on me back in 1985. I'd just been picked as the WWF Manager of the Year, but Heenan wanted the title, and there was nothing he wouldn't do to get it. So, even after the votes were in, he got other managers—like Blassie, Jimmy Hart, and Johnny Valiant—to give him their votes. It could have worked, but Hillbilly

Bert's Corner

Manager Jimmy Hart, in a previous incarnation, was the lead singer of the rock and roll band The Gentrys. Their hit "Keep On Dancin'" went top 10 in 1965. Today Hart writes many of the wrestlers' theme songs.

Jim gave me his vote, and that secured the award. Heenan was so furious that he hit me over the head with my trophy.

Johnny Valiant is a manager that I respected because of his wrestling reputation. But as a manager, he was a thief. He stole the tag-team title for Brutus "The Barber" Beefcake and Greg "The Hammer" Valentine. And he was a bully, too.

And then there was Jimmy Hart, of the so-called Hart Foundation. He was once a great rock musician, but now he's a sneak. He sent his wrestlers, including Terry Funk, Jim Neidhart, and Bret Hart, out to ruin people in the ring.

As I stated in Chapter 8, "Sexy, Serious, and Supreme in Their Roles," today many of the "managers" in wrestling are women. There are a couple of reasons for this. One is that the managers also tend to be the wrestlers' girlfriends. Because their relationship is two-fold, accommodations on the road can be made more conveniently and economically. The other is that wrestling fans like seeing attractive women at wrestling shows.

Only a few male managers are still working. Jimmy Hart is still in business because he is a friend of Hulk Hogan. As long as Hogan has a job, Hart will too. Another is Lou E. Dangerously, who has a stable of wrestlers in ECW known as the Dangerous Alliance. Dangerously's act is based on that of Paul Heyman, now the head of ECW, who used to manage as Paul E. Dangerously. Lou E., like Paul E. before him, uses a cell phone as his gimmick.

The Least You Need to Know

➤ Managers are the most colorful characters in pro wrestling.

➤ The first job of the manager is to hype his or her wrestlers.

➤ Making the match is part of the job. A good match-up means a great gate and great profits for the wrestlers.

➤ A manager's job is never done. At ringside, the manager is right there in the middle of the action.

➤ A manager usually works the heel's corner rather than the babyface's corner.

Chapter 26

Novelty Acts: What a (One-Ring) Circus!

In This Chapter:

➤ In the cage

➤ Barbed Wire Matches

➤ Pint-sized but pugnacious: midget wrestlers

➤ Crossover dreams: athletes from other sports join the fray

➤ A smorgasbord of wild rituals

Promoters like to keep their wrestling product as wild as possible to keep butts in the seats. Thus, they spice up their shows with novelties, stipulations, unusual competitors, and guest celebrities. And the variety of novelty acts out there is amazing. There's everything from bouts between midgets, such as the Mexican Minis, to putting familiar wrestlers in cages—as when Hollywood Hogan fought it out with Macho Man Savage.

And there are lots of variations on the cage theme—like when Terry Funk, Sabu, and Mick Foley, famous for their "Barbed Wire Matches," replaced the ring ropes with barbed wire. Ouch! That's a tough way to make a living.

Wrestling and Novelty Acts—A Match Made in Promoter's Heaven

It's doubtful that anybody could pinpoint the exact date when all the "wonderful nonsense" of novelty acts first started. But it may have been back in 1877. That's

Captain Lou's Corner

Fred Kohler, wrestling in the 1930s under the name of Fred King, remembers touring the Midwest with a 700-pound bear. He found it something of a challenge. As he told writer Joe Jares, "It kept outthinking me. I finally won a match with it in Dubuque, Iowa, and turned to wrestling more orthodox opponents."

Bert's Corner

Back in the days when many wrestlers were still trying to maintain some credibility for their sport, novelty acts weren't always welcomed by serious wrestlers. Lou Thesz, for example, refused to appear on cards that featured midgets, wrestling bears, or any sort of carnival act.

when Emil Regnier, proprietor of a New York beer parlor, borrowed an idea that goes all the way back to the Middle Ages: He staged wrestling bouts that pitted Greco-Roman wrestlers against bears.

Bear Brawls

The bear most likely "did not understand the fun of the thing," as the *New York Times* reported. It apparently didn't want to be thrown, but it "exhibited no desire to throw his opponent." Still, the spectators *did* understand, and the spectacle soon took off in popularity, spreading to other venues and drawing sizeable audiences wherever it was performed. Regnier even sent the show on the road, touring the United States, but eventually the bears lost patience with the game. One grabbed its human opponent and squeezed him until he collapsed. He later died of internal injuries.

Such acts, however, were more the exception than the rule. The standard form for a novelty act was usually a little more mundane—a wrestler pitted against a boxer fighting for supremacy between the two popular sports. The first such competition pitted William Muldoon against heavyweight champion John L. Sullivan in Sullivan's hometown of Gloucester, Massachusetts, in 1887. But when Muldoon slammed the local favorite to the mat, the fans stopped the show.

Boxers appearing on wrestling shows still generate excitement. Mike Tyson's appearance at the 1998 *WrestleMania* earned that pay-per-view much mainstream publicity and a correspondingly big buy rate.

Depression Era Diversions

The Depression's depressing effect on all forms of entertainment pushed wrestling into desperate straits, and that was the true beginning of an explosion of novelty acts as promoters tried everything they could think of to bring the fans back into the arenas. Masked men, hairy men, hillbillies, midgets, giants, and all manner of sideshow grotesqueries were brought into the act.

Bigger Is Best—for Pulling in Fans

My favorite of this whole clan of hillbilly characters was the legendary Haystacks Calhoun. He was a 600-pound mountain of a man. His wife, Mary, was an impressive 400 pounds herself. Family squabbles in *that* household could get pretty interesting.

He was not just a hillbilly—he personified another category of novelty wrestler, too. You can call them the dreadnaught class—oversized behemoths such as Happy Humphrey (620 pounds), Martin Levy (over 700 pounds), and the McGuire Twins (727 pounds apiece).

Add height to weight, and you get another novelty act: the giants. Andre the Giant (7 feet, 4 inches, 500 pounds) is perhaps the best known. And if you've got giants, you've got to go with the other end of the spectrum as well: Midget wrestlers soon became all the rage, too.

Diminutive, Ain't They? Midgets in Wrestling

The public has always had a strange fascination with midgets, dating back to P.T. Barnum's Tom Thumb—the most famous performer of the nineteenth century. And vaudeville had the Singer Midgets, a troupe of pint-sized acrobats from Germany. So, it was no surprise that wrestling would want to get into the act.

Suddenly midgets were tumbling into the wrestling rings all across America—Sky Low Low, Fuzzy Cupid, Little Beaver, Little Brutus, Pee Wee James, Lord Littlebrook, Billy the Kid (a cowboy), and Gentleman Jim Corbett. They were acrobatic and fun to watch.

Wrestle Mania

Some wrestlers get their uglies from masks or paint, but some come by them naturally. And in the years just after the Second World War, uglies were all the rage. They were usually called "angels" just to be perverse—The Swedish Angel, the Polish Angel—a whole United Nations of angels started popping up in American wrestling rings. And they made wonderful villains. Maurice Tillett is the man who started this whole vogue. His facial features were distorted by some glandular dysfunction, and he had been a circus strongman in England, where he was billed as a "ferocious monstrosity, not a human being." He wrestled as the French Angel, but fearsome features aside, he was a lovely man.

Novelties of Today: Cage Matches

Probably because of TV, today's wrestlers tend to be pretty good-looking. But sidekicks and human mascots are still allowed to be peculiar. Midgets are still used for a joke, and a real giant (Paul Wight) known as the Big Show is one of the WWF's biggest (literally and figuratively) stars.

In Your Face

Lazy or unimaginative promoters can sometimes fall into bad habits, like overworking a gimmick. Cage matches, for example, have been overdone at times—promoters will sometimes use them even when they have no real justification or any story line.

Bert's Corner

The Depression has been over for a long time now, but promoters still find a reason to include novelty acts—usually as the opening match of the card. It's a good way to get the crowd warmed up.

What do you get when you put two wrestlers in a locked cage that stands 15 feet tall and then tell them to fight with no rules? One heck of a sellout crowd, that's what. It might seem inhumane—and if the wrestlers were roosters or dogs, the bout would be illegal. But the cage match serves an important purpose. In wrestling, for the most part, the only way that a title can change hands is through a pinfall—count-outs and disqualifications don't do the trick. But many times, a cowardly champion will take advantage of these stipulations and run away for the count-out or get himself disqualified rather than face a tough challenger in a fair fight. But in a steel cage, the champion can't run away, nor can his allies jump into the melee for the DQ. In other words, the cage match guarantees a clean finish.

Cage matches can be brutal. It's not at all unusual for the wrestlers to get slammed up against the walls, and the rough edges and burrs in the wire can inflict nasty wounds, especially on the face. Not to mention that the wrestlers are just as likely to use the wire as a weapon, shoving their opponent's head into it for a truly bloody effect.

Violent cage matches have a passionate following. Following are a few of the more notorious ones of past years.

The Modern Cage Match

Stipulation matches are at their best when they are used to enhance the story line. A great example of this is the use of a "Cage Match" on the May 1, 2000, episode of *RAW is WAR*. The night before, at WWF *Backlash*, The Rock beat Hunter Hearst Helmsley for the WWF championship. Then on *RAW*, Vince McMahon, incensed by The Rock's victory, came up with what he thought was the perfect plan to get the belt away from him. He would have The Rock face his son, Shane McMahon, in a cage match. The first combatant to set foot on the floor outside the cage would win. McMahon figured that The Rock, trapped in a cage that he would have to scale to get out of, would be more easily contained—thus allowing Shane more of a chance to get out.

Modern-day "Cage Matches" come with a silent guarantee to the fans that the ante of violence will be upped.

McMahon further stacked the deck against The Rock. He hand-picked two of his cronies as the referees, Pat Patterson and Gerald Brisco, to help Shane get out first. Patterson stood in the ring and tried continuously to block The Rock from getting his hands on Shane. Brisco stood at the cage door, opening it for Shane and slamming it in the face of The Rock. Then Triple H, Vince, and Stephanie McMahon-Helmsley all stood outside to keep The Rock inside the cage any way they could.

The Rock fought hard, keeping Shane from climbing his way to the championship and fighting against all the obstacles stacked against him. After The Rock knocked Shane cold, Triple H climbed into the ring. "Renegade" referee Earl Hebner then ran to ringside to help The Rock. Hebner slammed Brisco's head into the door and slammed the door on Triple H. The Rock then executed a Spinebuster on Triple H and scaled the cage wall for the win.

A "Steel Cage Match," therefore, not only provides a dramatic stage for the action, but it also can be a key factor in furthering story lines.

Wrestle Mania

One of the reasons cage matches first came into vogue was that wrestlers started taking advantage of a technicality in the (admittedly very few) rules: You can't lose the belt on a disqualification. And the easiest way to get disqualified was to be counted out of the ring. To keep wrestlers from slipping under the ropes, and to keep outsiders from interfering, promoters started putting cages around the ring. Once inside, the combatants had to stay there until the match was decided with a definite winner and loser.

When Worlds Collide was an event in Los Angeles that combined American and Mexican wrestlers. And it generated a lot of heat. In the main event, Konnan el Barbaro (now known as K-Dogg) was pitted against Perro Aguayo in a cage. As is so typical in cage matches, both wrestlers became bloody quickly.

At one point, it looked like Konnan was a sure thing to win. He had brought Aguayo down, and things looked hopeless for the feisty Mexican. But Aguayo didn't give up, even though Konnan had rammed him into the cage often enough to turn his face into a crimson mask. Aguayo's heart and stamina ruled the cage that night; he turned the tables on Konnan and earned his great victory—and the respect of fans of all nationalities.

Any cage match is a dangerous situation, but when you replace the chain-link with barbed wire, you've moved into a whole new world of potential hurt. Just ask Genichiro Tenryu and Atsushi Onita—they've still got the scars to show for their battle. When Onita and Tenryu got it on in a "Barbed Wire Match" in Japan, they fought in a barbed-wire cage that had the electrifying added attraction of being high-voltage. Talk about extreme!

Tenryu and Onita squared off in the cage, each sizing the other up and looking for an advantage. The atmosphere was tense, and the fans, who'd flocked to the match in hopes of literally seeing sparks fly, were wild with anticipation. The fans got what they came for: Onita found his opening and threw Tenryu into the wire—and sparks really *did* fly. But Tenryu was tough and never gave up. In what must be one of wrestling's wildest matches ever, Tenryu eventually got the better of Onita and emerged from the cage the victor.

Terry Funk is the undisputed master of the "Barbed Wire Match." He seems to spend more time in the cage than outside. And you'd think that, with all his experience, he'd soon run out of challengers. But that's not reckoning with Sabu, who faced him in a bid for the ECW belt and proved to be more than Funk could handle.

Sabu took control early and wrestled like a man possessed. Because it was a title bout, no one was surprised by Sabu's aggressive intensity, but it still seemed unlikely that he could succeed at beating Funk, king of the "Barbed Wire Match," at his own game.

Well, Funk pulled out all the stops to defend his title. As he prepared to bash a chair over Sabu's head, he managed to get his head entangled in the barbed wire. At the same time, Sabu's manager, Bill Alfonzo, got into the act. His interference infuriated Funk, who pulled Alfonzo into the ring, right over the barbed-wire ring ropes.

Countering Sabu's constant and effective attacks, Funk finally managed to get a grip on his opponent and lift him high into the air. The fans were wild, anticipating the next move; everybody thought that a slam of some kind was bound to follow. What really happened was far worse and had every man in the audience cringing in their seats: Instead of running Sabu into the wire as usual, Funk crashed his hapless opponent down, crotch first, on the waiting barbed wire.

That one hard encounter with the wire wasn't enough for Sabu—he went looking for more. Intending to take his revenge, he mounted the top strand of wire and prepared to jump on Funk. But, maybe because of the pain he still felt from his recent confrontation with the wire, Sabu badly misjudged his move, slicing his arm wide open in the process. If the fans had come to the bout looking for blood, they certainly got their money's worth. But even with the injury, Sabu was man enough to put Funk down and take his title belt away from him.

Fighting Words

You don't need high voltage to make a match dangerous. In **Barbed Wire Matches,** just plain ol' barbed wire of the un-electrified variety is more than enough danger for most wrestlers. It's a guarantee that one or both of the contenders will walk away with some serious injuries—which is why they pull in such big crowds.

Captain Lou's Corner

In a "Barbed Wire Match," the most devastating move is to whip your opponent's face into the wire. You can tell "Barbed Wire Match" veterans just by taking a good look at all the scars on their faces.

Body Slam

The gimmicks in novelty matches have grown much whackier during the past five years. When two men were fighting over one beautiful valet, a bottle of Viagra was hung above one corner of the ring and the wrestler to get to it first won the match. Mixed matches are becoming increasingly popular, pitting tag teams comprised of one woman and one man against one another. And there are "Table Matches," in which the winner must put the loser through a table.

Bert's Corner

It's not just football players who wander into the wrestling ring. When stars from other sports step up against pro wrestlers, they create an opportunity for a novelty match.

In Japan nowadays, the ante has been upped further. Japanese cards now sometimes feature "Exploding Ring Matches."

Crashing the Gate: Crossover Wrestlers

How often do athletes from one sport cross over into another? It happens from time to time and has been happening more in recent years. Wrestling attracts a fair amount of crossover traffic, dating back to the early days when collegiate stars of the gridiron flocked to the sport. More recently, many NFL football and NBA basketball stars have tried their hands in the wrestling ring. Some of them try to make a career out of wrestling, and others simply make special appearances.

Dennis Rodman, the colorful ex-NBA star, partnered up with Hollywood Hogan to take on Lex Luger and Paul Wight (the Big Show, then known as The Giant). There would be no slam-dunking here. When Rodman came to the ring, he was wearing an nWo shirt and bandanna. He even had on sunglasses, like Hogan. Just before the match, Macho Man Randy Savage whispered words of advice into Rodman's ear. When the bell rang, all the wrestlers were ready to rumble.

Luger was working Hogan over pretty good at first, but Hollywood turned the tables and Luger lost control. At one point, Rodman rolled out of the ring in search of sanctuary. The Giant took a turn on Rodman while Luger got Hogan in the famous Torture Rack. Hollywood could not work his way loose and submitted to the Rack. Rodman made a fair showing in the ring, and still makes appearances now and again in the ring—if the price is right.

The last big-time celebrity athlete to guest-star in the WWF was Iron Mike Tyson. Wrestling offered Tyson a place to vent his frustrations and to stay in shape. It was fun, and he was paid very well.

Newer Novelties

It should be clear by now: Novelty acts are good for business. For that reason, promoters and managers like them, as do the wrestlers. The more bizarre the matches, the more money they make.

Novelty matches range from "Ladder Matches" to matches where valets are put up for prizes. In some matches, the losing wrestler was forced to cut his hair or retire from wrestling (although he almost always comes back).

With an Emphasis on the Ladder

"Ladder Matches" start by hanging a title belt high above the ring on a cable. Then a ladder is placed in the ring. As you might imagine, the object of the match is to retrieve the belt.

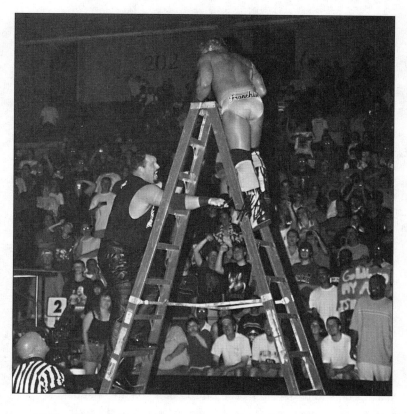

Ladders and fighting get along. Not long after ladders began appearing in martial arts films, they also became a standard prop in pro wrestling.

When two big wrestlers go up a ladder together, one on each side, and meet at the top, anything can happen. The object of the match is to gain possession of the belt and carry it to the mat for a victory. There are variations of "Ladder Matches," but they are all exciting—and dangerous.

Battle Royal

A "Battle Royal" is essentially professional wrestling's equivalent of King of the Mountain, where the last person standing in the ring is the winner. To be disqualified, a wrestler must be tossed over the top rope and fall to the floor. If a competitor lands on the apron, he is not eliminated yet and can climb back in and continue wrestling. Generally made up of 30 combatants, individual entrances are staggered (usually by three-minute intervals) to avoid the confusion of 30 wrestlers charging the ring at once in a wrestling version of a Chinese fire drill.

The Battle Royal generally works better live than on TV because there is a lot of excitement and the event lacks a strong focal point.

The most famous contestant in "Battle Royals" was Andre the Giant, considered the "King of the Battle Royal" because he never lost one. The most famous "Battle Royal" is the *Royal Rumble*, held annually by the WWF a few months before *WrestleMania*, the biggest event on the WWF calendar. The winner of the *Royal Rumble* becomes the number 1 contender for the WWF title and goes on to face the WWF champion in the main event of *WrestleMania*.

Wrestle Mania

During a "Brass Knux Match," brass knuckles are placed on top of a pole in a neutral corner of the ring. It is up to the competing wrestlers to gain possession of them. The first wrestler to acquire them gets to use them. (Sometimes chains are substituted for brass knuckles.) The wrestler gaining access to the weapon has a decided advantage. Putting brass knuckles in the hand of a shooter can result in some serious damage for an opponent.

Three's a Crowd

Sometimes three wrestlers are placed in the ring—and only one gets to leave. More specifically, the first man to win a pinfall is the winner of the match. A couple years back, Raven, Chris Benoit, and Diamond Dallas Page (DDP) were the players in the game. Page's title was on the line.

The match was wild and woolly. Diamond Dallas Page was shoved into a sign behind the audience. This happened not once, but twice. With Page immobilized, Raven and Benoit re-entered the ring and went for the belt. Shortly afterward, an injured Page was seen pulling himself along the runway, trying to get back into the ring. It was a long and painful match, but Diamond Dallas Page finally won and retained his belt.

Novelty matches are limited only by the willingness of wrestlers and the imaginations of promoters and managers.

The Least You Need to Know

➤ "Cage Matches," in which wrestlers fight in a cage, often result in cuts—supposedly due to the burrs on the wire.

➤ Terry Funk is one of the kings of "Barbed Wire Matches."

➤ In Japan, "Barbed-Wire Cage Matches" frequently use electrified wire.

➤ The Mexican Minis are the most popular midget wrestlers in America.

➤ Athletes from other sports and movie actors sometimes step into the wrestling ring for novelty matches.

Chapter 27

TV Wrestling: From the Ring to Your Living Room

In This Chapter

➤ How wrestling developed on the small screen

➤ How announcers fit into the picture

➤ How wrestlers play to the camera

➤ The Monday night ratings war

Does the media have any impact on the success of professional wrestling? Absolutely! Just like all the other major sports, wrestling owes its widespread popularity today to the successful use of television. Of the top 15 shows on cable TV, 8 of them are wrestling. Six of those are in the top 10. In this chapter, you learn all about how modern pro wrestling developed in tandem with the evolution of television, from its early beginnings to the era of cable and pay-per-view.

The Story Line's the Thing

Eric Bischoff, president of World Championship Wrestling, calls it "the soap story line." He's talking about the soap opera-like cliffhanger at the end of every telecast. In days of old, "bookers"—the people responsible for coming up with the story lines—had to worry only about arena shows. Now they have to concern themselves with the unexpected at the end of a televised show. Most shows today end in planned chaos, with the announcer intoning, "We're out of time, but we'll keep the cameras rolling, so tune in next week and make sure you don't miss a thing."

In Your Face

Eric Bischoff said it best: "The only real feud in wrestling is the one between WCW and the WWF."

Captain Lou's Corner

Back in the 1950s in New York, you got *Wrestling from Sunnyside Garden,* with Arnold "Golden Boy" Skaaland, Thomas Marin, and Abe Jacobs. From St. Louis, there was *Wrestling at the Chase.* Cincinnati gave us the Crosley Broadcasting System's studio wrestling. And it was the same all over the country.

Even people who *don't* follow wrestling have heard of the two big Monday night broadcasts: the WWF's *RAW is WAR* on the USA network, and the WCW's *Monday Nitro* on TNT—along with the WWF's *Smackdown* show which helped save the UPN broadcast network with its big Thursday night ratings. The Monday night shows are broadcast head-to-head. Because of the ratings war caused by the shows going head-to-head, the quality of televised wrestling skyrocketed in the late 1990s, with the quality of both the wrestling and the TV production increasing.

RAW and *Nitro* each do a traveling show, with the same ring, stage, and ramp set up in each arena. *Nitro* uses 14 trucks to haul all its equipment from place to place. Only the city changes. .

The Announcers

When it comes to putting together a televised wrestling show, the announcers are every bit as important as the wrestlers. A convincing and informed job of hold-by-hold announcing can do wonders for the believability and the excitement of a TV wrestling match. It's their job to make sure that the audience can sort important information out of the chaos they're watching and follow the story line.

Old-Timers

And just as wrestlers had developed their shtick for the TV audiences, so too did the announcers. Dick Lane was famous for his "Whoa, Nellie!"—a catch phrase later adopted by football announcer Keith Jackson. Dennis James used sound effects to accompany the action, and Guy LeBow donned an air-raid warden's helmet when the action heated up. Paul Boesch, noted for his interviewing technique, once conducted an interview with tag-team partners Ivan Kalmikoff and Karol Krauser while wearing a gas mask to ward off the overpowering smell of garlic that they gave off as a result of their latest meal. And then there was the "Dean of Wrestling Announcers" Gordon Solie, who just recently died. Solie instilled absolute credibility upon the matches he called and was the first to describe a bleeding wrestler as wearing a "crimson mask." All wrestling announcers since have, at least in part, imitated Solie's style.

Bert's Corner

During the early *WrestleMania* era, Jesse "The Body" Ventura (whatever happened to him?) followed the lead of Rowdy Roddy Piper and became a "heel announcer." His comments reflected the attitudes of the villains on the show, thus infuriating whomever the "face announcer" was sitting next to him—usually Gorilla Monsoon or Vince McMahon. The face-and-heel announcing team remains a staple.

Wrestle Mania

New fans of wrestling may be shocked to learn that Vince McMahon Jr. was, for many years, only the announcer on WWF TV shows. It was never acknowledged that he was also the owner of the company. Today's WWF fans find it hard to believe that on the telecast of the first *WrestleMania*, McMahon's name was never mentioned because Monsoon and Ventura were doing the announcing.

Today's Announcers

Today's wrestling announcers are every bit as good at calling the action as their counterparts in the past, and they are even better at helping the audience follow the story lines. The announcers of today are also much more likely to get involved in the action physically. It is no longer a novelty to see the announcer throw a punch or get whacked over the head with a chair. Following are some of the best of the current crop:

Gertner, Joel An ample-waisted heel-announcer/color commentator in ECW who describes himself as the "Quintessential Studmuffin." He perpetually wears a neck brace (a heel cliché, in which the bad guy wears a neck brace or comes out in a wheelchair, to get undeserved sympathy) with a bow tie over it. He's formerly the Dudley Boyz manager.

Heenan, Bobby   One of the best heel announcers of all-time, but a great wrestler and heel manager prior to that. Bobby "The Brain" Heenan's snotty, Beverly Hills commentary has infuriated wrestling fans for years, most recently in WCW.

Lawler, Jerry   Jerry "The King" Lawler is one of the great heel announcers in WWF history. This longtime Memphis wrestler—perhaps best known for his feud with Andy Kaufman—today is known for his quick wit, high-pitched shrieks, and his use of the terms "puppies" and "kitties" to refer to certain parts of the female anatomy.

Okerlund, Mean Gene   One of the all-time great announcers, Mean Gene is one of the best interviewers in the business. A longtime announcer for the WWF where he did locker room interviews for the first *WrestleMania*, he currently works for WCW.

Ross, Jim   The folksy Oklahoman announcer for the WWF. A former football announcer, he loves to brag of wrestlers' pasts on the gridiron. Ross announced for WCW for many years before switching to the WWF. He has worked through serious health problems during the past few years, including Bell's palsy, to remain the best hold-by-hold announcer working today.

Styles, Joey   Bespectacled hold-by-hold announcer for ECW. He is highly excitable, which works perfectly for this stunt-oriented promotion. Every time a wrestler jumps off a balcony and puts his opponent through a table below, Styles can be counted on to exclaim, "Oh … my … *God*! "

Fighting Words

Jim Ross is famous for his colloquialisms, especially his use of the **slobberknocker,** which is defined as a hard-fought, but sloppy, brawl.

Captain Lou's Corner

The legendary Lou Thesz had this to say about TV wrestling phenomenon Hulk Hogan: "On marketing I would give him a 9 or a 10. On wrestling, a 1 or a 0. I had a grandmother who could do a better leg lock."

The Wrestlers

Wrestlers have learned during the years that a televised wrestling match is very different from performing before a live crowd only. At a house show, everything must be done broadly so that it can be seen and heard in the back row.

On TV, with a handheld camera only a few feet away, things have to be done a lot more subtly. Wrestlers have also learned that certain moves should be done while facing or with the back to the camera to make them look more authentic for the TV audience than they would from a side view.

Wrestlers also have learned to use TV to promote future matches and cards. The modern wrestler not only knows where the cameras are, but he also knows what he should say when the red light goes on. Inflammatory remarks are always designed to build ratings points or attendance figures down the road.

The Managers and Valets

I don't have to tell you that I think managers are pretty important in all this, do I? It's our job to use everything we can to hype our charges and get people interested in upcoming matches. And we're not above going to extremes to heat up the fans. That's why you'll see us mixing it up in the ring, if that's what it takes to get the fans to go wild.

The Audience

The TV camera even makes the fans in the audience part of the action. You'll see it panning the crowd all the time, singling out handheld signs and other such. Lots of times the crowd action is completely genuine, but that's not necessarily the case. Sometimes, members of the audience are planted with signs that suit the needs of the wrestlers, the promoters, or even the advertisers. And the camera catches it all.

The Networks

Forget wrestlers versus wrestlers and tag teams versus tag teams—the biggest grudge match out there is the one between Vince McMahon Jr. and Ted Turner, and that match is fought network against network. TNN and USA battle it out for the lion's share of Monday night's ratings. After all, commercial spots on TV are priced according to the ratings, and the winner in the ratings war gets the biggest share of advertising dollars.

Captain Lou's Corner

Lots of wrestlers have made the crossover to the silver screen: Terry Funk, Hulk Hogan, Edge, Steve Austin, Goldberg, Andre the Giant, The Rock, Roddy Piper, Mil Mascaras, El Santo, and yours truly (I was in *Wiseguys*). Others have put in cameo appearances in films: Toro Tanaka played Oddjob in *Goldfinger*, and Lenny Montana played Lucca Brazzi in *The Godfather*.

In Your Face

When Vince Russo took over as the creative director for WCW during the spring of 2000, he said, "The shows have been an embarrassment and disgraceful. I am going to turn World Championship Wrestling completely upside down!"

All in all, television is essential to today's professional wrestling. It provides the outlet for hype, it gives a place where story lines can be developed and, above all else, it makes wrestling available to millions more than could ever fit into all the arenas in the world. In short, it's the driving force behind the power and the money in the industry. It's what brought in the huge audiences, and what made superstars of today's real-life action figures of the ring.

The Least You Need to Know

➤ TV helps wrestling reach millions more people than live shows alone could.

➤ Wrestling announcers make sure that the TV audience knows what's going on.

➤ Wrestlers have learned to be more subtle with their gestures on TV than at a nontelevised show.

➤ The Monday night television ratings war has caused the quality of today's wrestling to skyrocket.

Chapter 28

So You Want to Be a Wrestling Star?

In This Chapter

➤ Breaking into wrestling—the wrestling schools

➤ Choosing a good wrestling school

➤ Requirements for enrollment

➤ Surviving day-to-day training

➤ From student to pro: breaking into pro wrestling

You've heard the old saying about gaining life experience: "I learned it in the school of hard knocks." For most people, that's just a figure of speech—but for pro wrestlers, it's true. Like any other field, professional wrestling's future depends upon its continual influx of talent, especially now that it has exploded into the fastest-growing field in all of sports entertainment. As Pretty Boy Larry Sharpe, owner of the wrestling school The Monster Factory, puts it, "Wrestling needs all the monsters we can get."

During the years, wrestling has conscripted its recruits from other fields of athletics—football, amateur wrestling, and even weightlifting. Those who have crossed over to join its ranks include former football players such as Bronko Nagurski, Leo Nominelli, Lex Luger, Ron Simmons, and—yes—Bill Goldberg. Former amateur wrestlers include Rick Steiner, Big Poppa Pump, and Kurt Angle. Mark Henry came in after a career as a weightlifter. But wrestling still needs many, many more wide-bodies to fill its ever-expanding ranks.

So, what does it take to become a professional wrestler? And where and how does one enlist? This chapter looks into the schools where champions are made and the training regimen that you must go through to become the next Bill Goldberg.

Captain Lou's Corner

Breaking into wrestling is hard. Sometimes it's not what you know, it's who you know. I had help when I was breaking in, and during the years I've helped others—like when I recommended Terry Bollea (Hulk Hogan), Jack Armstrong, and Junkyard Dog as future stars. And I listen to the recommendations of school operators, such as Afa of the Wild Samoan School. So make yourself known to those who can help you.

Training in the Early Days

Back in the days of yore, pro wrestling reached out and took anyone and everyone it could find to fill its talent pool—willing plowboys, farmers, rodeo riders, anyone at all. Most of these early pro wrestlers were skilled in the disciplines of Greco-Roman wrestling. All received their schooling in pro wrestling's world through on-the-job training—learning while earning, if you will.

The College Football Connection

By the third decade of the twentieth century, promoters began scouring the landscape for athletes and, naturally, turned to the gridiron for their recruits. The first was Wayne "Big" Munn of Nebraska. In short order, he was joined in the ranks by Gus Sonnenberg of Dartmouth, Jumpin' Joe Savoldi of Notre Dame, Jim McMillan of Illinois, and Herman Hickman of Tennessee.

Amateur Wrestlers, Weight Lifters, Boxers: Everybody's Welcome

The collegiate amateur wrestlers formed another pool of talent. Verne Gagne won four Big Ten wrestling championships at the University of Minnesota before joining the world of pro wrestling. Jack Brisco—Gerald Brisco's brother—won the NCAA wrestling title in the 191-pound class when he wrestled for Oklahoma State. Bob

Backlund captured the NCAA Division II title at North Dakota State, Kurt Angle won an Olympic gold in 1996, and Allen "Bad News" Coage won a bronze medal in judo at the 1976 Olympics. Weightlifter Ken Patera, who represented the United States at the 1972 Olympic games, crossed over into wrestling, too. Heavyweight boxing champ Primo Carrera switched to wrestling after completing his pugilistic career.

Captain Lou's Story

After I had gotten out of the service, I went to Willie Gilzenberg, who handled boxers "Two Ton" Tony Galento and Red Cochrane, and I told him that I wanted to be a boxer. Gilzenberg said I was too short and suggested that I try wrestling as a career move.

Not incidentally, Gilzenberg was also part of the World Wrestling Federation. He arranged for me to train, one-on-one, with Soldier Barry and Arnold Skaaland. That's how *I* got into wrestling.

Lots of others were discovered from outside the world of wrestling, too. Take Terry Bollea. You know him better as Hulk Hogan. He was playing bass guitar with a Tampa-based rock band when Jack Brisco (who ran wrestling shows in the area) discovered him.

And there are the legacies—wrestlers born to the black and blue—such as Curt Hennig, son of the fabled Larry "The Axe " Hennig. There's also Bret Hart, whose father was the all-time great, Stu Hart. And that's not to mention Dustin Rhodes, formerly Goldust, son of the legendary Dusty Rhodes. And The Rock is a *third*-generation wrestler, the son of Rocky Johnson and grandson of Peter Maivia.

Do You Have What It Takes?

Getting discovered is one way to get into wrestling, but most of today's wrestlers—and yesterday's, for that matter—came to the sport through the wrestling school. And there's no better way to go, really, than to pass through the portals of what can be called Cauliflower State University.

Body Slam

So you wannabe a wrestler? Well, let me tell you, it ain't for wimps. You've got to have athletic ability and some skills, and above all else you've got to be in good shape.

In Your Face

Bill Goldberg never went the route of a formal wrestling school course, but that doesn't mean that he didn't get training. He just trained outside the field of wrestling until he realized where he really wanted to go in his career. "I did my homework," he says. "I studied martial arts. But I had an idea to portray a character that people would like."

Not that you have to be built like a brick skyscraper. But you *do* have to be in reasonably good condition. Otherwise, the school might turn you down. After all, the school officials don't want someone who'll get into their rowing machines and sink them.

Several schools will give you a look-see—a session of rope work, calisthenics, and workouts—to find out if you're in good enough shape to take on their intensive program. They want to know if you can handle their "hard time"—if you've got the ability and agility to see it through without jeopardizing yourself or your health.

So, if you're really, *really* serious about pursuing a career in professional wrestling, and if you're in good shape, you'll want to contact a wrestling school. That's the first step on the ladder to becoming a professional wrestler. (See the card in the front of this book for a listing of some of the current wrestling schools.) When picking a school, check around, do your homework, and find out about school facilities, trainers on staff, and lists of graduates. In other words, check their credentials. Above all else, look for a school that fits both your budget and your schedule.

Choosing Your School

After you've checked a school's credentials, check your schedule. Many would-be wrestlers have day jobs or come from faraway places. Many wrestling schools, such as the Monster Factory, have a four-day-a-week, four-month course for regular students. But if you're a weekend warrior—if your schedule lets you train only on weekends—your program will take eight months.

And you need to consider your budget. The normal price range for most wrestling schools such as the ones on our list runs from $3,000 to $5,000 for intensive training. Some offer a free first session before you go under contract. Many will finance your tuition for a few months, interest-free. And some have a basic charge, with additional set charges per session.

The following is a basic list of the questions to ask while you're checking out your school options:

➤ How long has this outfit been in operation?

➤ Who owns the school?

➤ Does the owner do the training personally, or does the school hire employees as trainers?

➤ What level of experience do the trainers have?

➤ What kind of contract do you have to sign?

➤ Who are some of the pro wrestlers who have attended the school?

➤ Will the school assist you with promotional matters, such as demo tapes?

➤ Will the school help you relocate?

School Days, School Days, Dear Old Golden Rule Days

So you've taken the big step and signed with one of the wrestling schools. Be prepared—it's no walk in the park. Before you even enter the ring, you'll be subjected to a rigorous set of calisthenics to ensure that you're not only fit, but also limber. Fifty push-ups, boom! Boom! Boom! Fifty more. Then another 50. You'll do limbering up exercises until you feel that you can't do anymore and your body's numb, and then there will be more exercises, weight training, and more preparation. And that's all before you enter the ring. After all, any wrestling school worth its salt wants to make sure that you're physically fit to survive what lies ahead of you.

Just like Marine boot camp, sometimes you will doubt that you'll make it. And almost half of those who enroll don't. You might as well shake hands with the guy standing next to you on that first day, because only one of you (according to the odds) is gonna make it all the way.

Body Slam

Wrestling school is *tough*. Champion weightlifter Paul Anderson tried it and quit because it was too hard. But if you make it past the preliminary exercise sessions, hang in there—there's a good chance that you'll make it.

Making Your Moves

Once past the preliminary exercises, it'll be time for your first inside-the-ring instruction. This isn't going to be mano-a-mano—this will be instruction in the finer points of wrestling, such as the holds. You'll learn how to both give and take various moves, suplexes, and various body slams. And you'll learn the most important element in any wrestler's kit bag of tricks: how to fall.

Bert's Corner

Tugboat Tayler, a wrestling teacher in Houston, Texas, teaches his students that there are five rules of wrestling: First, the opponent is in fact your partner. Second, when you hit the ropes, hit all three at once or fly over. Third, make noise. Fourth, when you fall, slap the mat to reduce impact on your back. Fifth, use the headlock as a time to rest.

Taking the Fall

You'll learn how to hit the mat (or your opponent) with your back, your buttocks, or your hands. You'll learn to curl in your shoulders when you hit the ground. And you'll be taught these moves with painstaking care, over and over and over again, rehearsing them to a fare-thee-well. In wrestling, and in any other sport, you can't practice falling too many times. Seriously, WWF superstar Darren Drozdov took a fall wrong on the top of his head during a match in 1999 and has since lost the use of his legs. I can't emphasize enough the importance of learning to fall properly. It's your most basic stock-in-trade.

Inside the Squared Circle

Now you're ready to really get into some ring action, to try out all those moves and falls that you've been practicing by your lonesome. Here's the time when the instructors will separate the champions from the *jibronis*. They'll teach you the margin for safety for each hold and fall, how to look like you're mauling your opponent instead of just gingerly lacing him. And they'll teach you how to take good care of your opponent—remembering that you're only as good as your opponent wants you to look. But all this is only for starters, like an NFL player learning his playbook and going through a few practice sessions against his own teammates. You've still got a long way to go—learning how to perform those moves with verve and application that appeal to the crowd.

Beyond the Basics

Although there are usually no official "chalk talks," no seminars, no classroom discussions, and so forth, your instructor will give you personalized lessons and even recommend that you watch certain wrestlers on TV to pick up pointers from those who've gone before you. Call it post-graduate work, if you will, but it's necessary if you want to make it in the profession.

Moving On Up to the Big-Time

Don't expect a placement service, by the way. But what you can expect is that your instructor is wired into the major organizations and can recommend the students that he judges to be good enough to go on in the sport. For instance, the WWF's Jim Cornette is in regular contact with wrestling school instructors and checks with them to get recommendations of likely prospects—sort of like the scouting process used by major league teams. He asks about the real talent, the wannabes that have well-conceived moves, and pleasing personalities.

And I've got my own sources, too—like Afa of the Wild Samoan School. He'll tout me a graduate who has something special, and his recommendation will give that candidate a start up the ladder to a pro wrestling gig.

Captain Lou's Corner

When you're ready to "graduate," most schools will help you develop a demo tape wrestling against a fellow graduate-to-be. This will be about three minutes long—that's usually all that the major organizations have time to review.

Graduates who aren't picked right off the proverbial vine—who don't get a gig right out of wrestling school—shouldn't despair. If they're really serious about a career in pro wrestling, they can break into the profession by apprenticing, so to speak, at the small shows that have sprung up all over the country. Many of these are staged by instructors who can place their students in them.

The Least You Need to Know

➤ Wrestling gets its talent from many sources, but mostly it recruits from wrestling schools.

➤ The right wrestling school will teach you more than wrestling moves; it will fully prepare you for a wrestling career.

➤ Training schedules are often designed to accommodate wrestlers who also have to hold down full-time jobs.

➤ The most important thing you'll learn in wrestling school is how to fall.

➤ Most wrestling school graduates break into the business by working small, local shows.

➤ Scouts attend small shows, recruiting talent for the major organizations.

Chapter 29

Bone-Crushers and Back-Breakers: All the Right Moves

In This Chapter

➤ Classic wrestling holds

➤ Modern moves and techniques

➤ The favorite moves of top wrestlers

➤ Taking a fall—a wrestler's most important skill

Back in 1948, an article in *Ring* magazine listed "the most effective holds in the history of wrestling." These were Strangler Lewis's headlock, Joe Stetcher's body scissors, Frank Gotch's toehold, and Jim Browning's flying scissors. That was it! Four plain vanilla holds, all of which dated back to the beginnings of the sport—and even before! Four. No more.

But something happened to professional wrestling on its way to television: new holds and moves that went beyond the stalk-your-opponent-to-his-knees variety. Now there were flashy moves, such as Jim Londos's Airplane Spin, Jumpin' Joe Savoldi's Drop Kick, and Gus Sonnenberg's Flying Tackle. And there would be more to come.

In this chapter, you learn the moves of the pros. But before we take you through the recently developed holds and moves, let's run through the classic holds, the ones that are part and parcel of every wrestler's repertoire.

Classic Submission Holds

There are two main types of holds: pins and submission holds. In a pin, a wrestler is put down so that his (or her) shoulders touch the mat. But some holds are so effective that although they don't constitute an actual pin, the wrestler in the hold is in pain and has no chance of extricating himself. The following are a few of the classic submission holds:

Bert's Corner

Lex Luger's famous Human Torture Rack was a really effective variation on the fireman's-carry theme. He lifted his opponent up onto his shoulders, facing upward. Luger then hooked an arm around the neck and the other around the legs—and pressed downward on each side, forcing his opponent's back to bend against his neck.

Body Slam

A full nelson can be a very dangerous hold. If you apply too much pressure, you can break your opponent's neck.

abdominal stretch   Standing to the side of your opponent, you hook one of his legs (you hook his left leg with your right, or his right leg with your left). At the same time, you wrap one of your arms in front of his body and pull his upper arm up behind your head.

back-breaker   After your opponent has been forced to the mat face down, you place both your knees on his back. Put one arm around his neck, the other around one or both of his legs. Lean back until you are lying on your back—your opponent is lifted in the air. Pull back on his neck and legs, forcing him to bend backward.

camel clutch   This is the Steiner Recliner, used by Scott Steiner. With your opponent's face down on the mat, sit on his back and slide your arms under his legs. Apply a chinlock and then pull back.

chinlock   With your opponent either sitting or lying on his stomach and you standing or kneeling above, link your hands under his chin and pull back.

crossface   Wrap one arm across your opponent's face and pull back. This is not a submission hold itself, but it is usually applied in conjunction with one. Bob Backlund is known for his Crossface Chicken Wing submission hold.

figure-four leg lock   While your opponent is on his back, you grab one leg and bend it sideways across the other and behind one of your own—this forms a figure four of your opponent's legs. Holding his straight leg, you fall backward to the mat, securing his bent leg in place by placing your free leg on top of the ankle.

full nelson   Standing behind your opponent, place both your arms under his and lock your hands behind the back of his neck. Apply pressure by pressing down on the neck.

sleeper hold   Place one arm across your opponent's throat and the other up against the side of his head, then lock your hands. This cuts off the supply of blood to your opponent's head and will render him unconscious. (Don't try this one at home, kids.) Complete the move by stepping one leg across your opponent's body to hold it down, while pulling upward on the head. After the hold is completely applied, slowly tighten your grip to the side of your opponent's head.

step-over toe hold   Your opponent is on his back and you're facing him, holding one of his legs. If you've grabbed the right leg, you step around with your own right leg so that you've wrapped *his* around your left leg. You then apply pressure to the knee and leg you're holding. This is usually a set up for the figure-four leglock (above), or you can spin your opponent around for submission.

A Plethora of Pins

Pins are the classic way of winning a wrestling match, as you'll remember from the discussion of the rules in Chapter 5, "Rules? What Rules?" The following are a few of the more common ones:

back slide   This move requires that you get back-to-back to your opponent and hook both of his arms with yours. Drop down to your knees, leaning forward. This drags your opponent up over your back, from which position you can force him to slide over your head to the mat, where you pin his shoulders. When he's pinned down, you brace your legs to keep him there long enough to get that all-important one-two-three count.

cradle   With your opponent on his stomach, you set him up for a camel clutch (see the previous section, "Classic Submission Holds") by putting his arms over your legs. Stand, while simultaneously pushing his head down. You end the move on your knees with your opponent's shoulders pinned to the mat and trapped under your legs.

roll up   There are two versions of this one:

1. In the Bridging Double Leg Pickup version, your opponent is on his back. You grab both his legs and do a forward flip, landing on your feet.

2. In the School Boy version, you kneel down behind your opponent, reach through his legs with one arm, grabbing hold of one leg. Lean in the opposite direction of the leg you've grabbed, pulling your opponent across your body so that he lands on his back, ready for pinning.

sunset flip   Jump over your opponent, grabbing him at the waist on your way down and rolling over his back so that he ends up sitting on the mat. Now, pull him down onto his back, grab his legs, and use them to pin his arms flat.

Captain Lou's Corner

The suplex, which in the old days was pronounced *su–play*, is a very popular move and has been since it was introduced in the 1930s by Sandor Szabo, who wrestled professionally from 1931 until 1963.

Bert's Corner

The modern move called the back-breaker may have the same name as the submission hold (see the previous section, "Classic Submission Holds"), but it's a very different move. In this version, you lift your opponent up and then drop him across your knee, back first.

suplex   Standing behind your opponent, take each of his hands in your opposite hand (that is, hold his left hand in your right, his right hand in your left) so that his arms are crossed in front of his body. Then, using leverage, flip him so that his entire body length crashes to the mat.

victory roll   Jump up to sit on your opponent's shoulders, facing the same way he is. Roll forward, reaching down to grab his legs and hook them over his shoulders, in effect "cradling" him. This pins his shoulders to the mat.

Acrobats and Aerialists

Today many wrestling moves aren't holds at all. Instead, they're a blend of acrobatics and striking blows. Following is a sampling of some of the moves most popular with the fans:

airplane spin   Lift your opponent up by the shoulders. Start spinning around to make him dizzy, and then drop him to the mat with a thud.

arm drag   Also known as the arm whip. Hook one of your opponent's arms and fall to the mat, pulling him down with you.

back drop   As your opponent charges toward you, bend forward. When he reaches your position, grab him, stand erect, and lift him up and over so his own momentum carries him to land on the mat, back first. This is commonly used to counter attacks where the opponent is bent over, say for a piledriver or a powerbomb.

brainbuster   Lift your opponent so that you're chest-to-chest. Now hook both of his legs so that they're up off the ground. Release one leg and, with the arm you've just freed, tuck his head under your armpit. From there, fall backward, driving his trapped head into the mat behind you.

DDT   With a front facelock on your opponent, fall straight down or back, driving his head into the mat.

drop–kick   Jump in the air and kick out with both feet at your opponent. This attack can be focused on your opponent's head, chest, stomach, back, or legs.

elbow drop   This is a simple fall onto your opponent—you just make sure that you land on him elbow-first. This is a finishing move used by The Rock called the People's Elbow.

flap jack   Lift your opponent up into the air as if you're setting up for a back drop. But when you've got his body parallel to the mat, instead of tossing him over, push him straight up into the air. That way, he'll land on his face and chest when he hits the mat.

Other old-time holds include the flying mare, a reverse wrist and arm lock, a double wrist lock and head scissors, and a plain double wrist lock.

Modern wrestlers have designed new and powerful moves based on these simple yet effective holds. Let's examine them next.

Modern Moves

Pro wrestling has become more acrobatic and flashier in an attempt to keep audiences on the edges of their seats. In addition to chair bashing, chain slinging, and the use of chain saws, modern wrestlers have modified proven holds to suit their styles. They have also developed a lot of eye-opening moves of their own. Let's look at a few:

➤ **octopus on your back**   The octopus is a variation of the abdominal stretch. The aggressive wrestler stands to one side of his opponent, grapevines the opponent's leg, bends the opponent's body, and hooks a leg over the opponent's head. In the process, the aggressive wrestler wraps his arms around the opponent's chest. When the move is fully executed, the aggressive wrestler is off the mat completely, clinging to the back of the opponent.

➤ **piledriver**   The piledriver is very popular, perhaps because it's so dangerous. The opponent is picked up with his head down and his feet skyward. The aggressive wrestler drives the opponent into the mat, head first.

➤ **power bomb**   From a bear hug position, slam face down onto back.

➤ **stump puller**   The stump puller isn't pretty, but it's effective. A wrestler gets an opponent into a sitting position and climbs onto his shoulders. Then he grabs his opponent's legs and pulls upward. The pressure on the legs, combined with the weight of the wrestler sitting on the neck area, can result in a quick submission ruling.

Body Slam

Wrestlers have to use their stunt skills to pull off the piledriver without injury. If they attempt a piledriver for real, they could kill their opponents. (Actually, it's impossible to pile drive someone against his will.) With a worked piledriver, the victim's head comes close to the floor without actually touching it.

Winning Moves

Professional wrestlers utilize many moves and holds throughout their careers. During their time in the ring, wrestlers gain confidence in moves and holds that are guaranteed winners. The following list is a run-down of some of today's top wrestlers and the finishing moves and holds that they use time and time again:

Name	Move
Tank Abbott	One-Punch KO
Steve Austin	Stone Cold Stunner
Mike Awesome	Awesome Bomb
Bob Backlund	Crossface Chicken Wing
Buff Bagwell	Buff Blockbuster
Chris Benoit	Crippler Crossface
	Diving Head Butt
Big Show	Choke Slam
Booker T	Axe Kick
Bradshaw	Clothesline from Hell
British Bulldog	Running Powerbomb
D'Lo Brown	The 'Lo Down
Justin Credible	That's Incredible!
Disco Inferno	Last Dance
Shane Douglas	Pittsburgh Plunge
Tommy Dreamer	Spicolli Driver
Dudley Boyz	3-D (Dudley Death Drop)
Spike Dudley	Acid Drop
Edge	Downward Spiral
Ric Flair	Figure-Four
Mick Foley	Mandible Claw
Terry Funk	Moonsault
Gangrel	Impaler
Goldberg	Jackhammer
Grandmaster Sexay	Flying Leg Drop
Juventud Guerrera	Juvi Driver
Eddie Guerrero	Frog Splash
Bad Ass Billy Gunn	Fame-Asser
Jeff Hardy	Swanton Bomb
Matt Hardy	Twist of Fate
Bret Hart	Sharpshooter
Curt Hennig	Hennig Plex
Hulk Hogan	Big Leg

Name	Move
Jeff Jarrett	The Stroke
Chris Jericho	Walls of Jericho
Kane	Tombstone Piledriver
Billy Kidman	Shooting Star Press
Konnan	Tequila Sunrise
Lash LeRoux	Whiplash
Lex Luger	Torture Rack
Dean Malenko	Texas Cloverleaf
Meng	Tongan Death Grip
Rey Mysterio Jr.	Huracanrana
Kevin Nash	Jackknife Powerbomb
Diamond Dallas Page	Diamond Cutter
Raven	DDT
Rhino	Piledriver
Rikishi Phatu	The Phatu Squash
	Stinky Face
Roadkill	Amish Splash
Rock	People's Elbow
	Rock Bottom
Perry Saturn	Rings of Saturn
Randy Savage	Flying Elbow
Scotty 2 Hotty	The Worm
Ken Shamrock	Ankle Lock Submission
Norman Smiley	Norman Conquest
Al Snow	Snow Plow
Scott Steiner	Steiner Recliner
Sting	Scorpion Death Lock
Lance Storm	Piledriver
Tazz	Tazzmission
Triple H	Pedigree
Undertaker	Tombstone Piledriver
Vampiro	Nail in the Coffin
Rob Van Dam	The Vandaminator
Val Venis	The Money Shot
Sid Vicious	Powerbomb
The Wall	Chokeslam
Mikey Whipwreck	Whippersnapper
X-Pac	X-Factor

Remember, the best hold or move is one that *works*—and thrills a wrestling audience. Pro wrestlers experiment to combine effectiveness with crowd-pleasing potential. And no doubt the great moves and holds of the ring will continue to excite viewers and win title belts.

Mistakes and Missed Moves

Not all pro wrestlers have the skills to make their moves convincing. Watch a few matches, and you'll see plenty of action that's as staged as a high school play. But everyone has to learn their trade, and a lot of wrestlers learn theirs in front of the cameras, which aren't too forgiving.

Captain Lou's Corner

Fists are not used as much as forearms. The wrestlers lay them on pretty good. When they whack a guy, the guy's chest becomes black and blue.

Fighting Words

Every once in a while a punch that is supposed to barely miss, or strike a meaty portion of the body where it can cause little or no injury, actually blackens its target's eye or busts his nose because somebody moved or made a mistake. That's called a **potato.**

Convincing Blows

Closed fists are not used too often in the wrestling ring. Why? Knuckles are bony and hard. If you're hit with a fist, there's not a lot of noise, but there could be a lot of pain. Instead of fists, wrestlers tend to use their forearms. The thick flesh makes a slapping sound when it hits, and the flesh softens the blow for both wrestlers.

Pulling Your Punch

When a closed fist is used, the punch is pulled just before impact. Contact is made, but with little power behind the punch. Some wrestlers don't perform this move convincingly. A close inspection of fist punching will sometimes reveal that no contact is really made. The difficulty of faking a fist punch makes the move less desirable than slaps, chops, and forearm attacks. Make a mistake and you'll *potato* your opponent.

Getting Slap Happy

Slapping is another option. An open-hand slap makes a lot of noise and only stings. The slap can turn a wrestler's skin red, adding to the visual excitement of a match. Chops work in a similar fashion. If you keep your eye on a chop right to the end, you may see the edge of the hand being turned at the last moment to result in a slap. It looks like a chop, sounds like a slap, and adds intensity to the match.

How bad does it hurt when a wrestler has his head rammed into a turnbuckle? Not much. The padding on the turnbuckles is very thick; it cushions blows extremely well. It's one of the softest places in the ring. Flexibility and padding make the turnbuckles a safe place to put on a big show. But sometimes the padding slips and part of the turnbuckle is exposed. If a wrestler hits an exposed turnbuckle, real damage can be done.

Wrestle Mania

In a recent match, a wrestler with long hair was on the mat. His opponent grabbed him by his hair with both hands. The downed wrestler reached up and locked his hands with those of his opponent. Then, the long-haired wrestler was lifted, apparently by his hair, and whirled around in the ring. If this move had been legit, the pain would have been excruciating. What was the secret? The wrestler with the hair had his hands locked over the wrists of the other wrestler. It looked as though he was struggling to get free, but he was probably supporting his weight and being swung around by his arms rather than his hair. It was a clean, good-looking stunt—a sure sign of experienced pro wrestlers.

It's a Bird! It's a Plane! No, It's a 350-Pound Flying Wrestler!

At one time the ropes existed to keep wrestlers in the ring. Now the ropes are part of a skilled wrestler's arsenal. The ropes are used for bouncing, throat drops, and most often as a jumping-off spot for aerial acrobatics suitable for a circus.

One wrestler recently managed three complete rotations of his balled-up body between the time he left the top rope and the time he landed—splat—on his challenger, who was flat on the mat at the time. Lying on the mat and seeing some bruiser crashing down on you isn't pretty, but pro wrestlers see it often. How can big men jump on each other from great heights without crushing internal organs and breaking bones? Very carefully.

There are a number of techniques for accomplishing successful jumps. One is the near-miss. This is a landing that is executed to look like a direct hit, but in fact is not. The flying wrestler has landed extremely close to the opponent without hitting his body.

Body Slam

Unlike wrestling rings, boxing rings do not contain springs. This makes it more difficult for wrestlers who perform in boxing rings to execute crowd-pleasing falls and bounces off the rings. There's no bounce, and the fall is going to hurt—a lot.

Bert's Corner

Wrestling has changed throughout the years. Today there's much more choreography in matches. But in the past, most matches were improvised right up until the finish.

Another way to make landings look real but feel (relatively) painless is to land flesh-to-flesh. The jumping wrestler's knees, elbows, and other hard and pointy parts don't lead the way in a flying fall. Instead, the wrestlers go belly-to-belly. When doing this, most of the power of the jump is absorbed by the jumping wrestler as his hands and knees hit the canvas.

A lot of wrestling rings have springs under them, which make it more convincing and makes falls look more devastating. Seeing a wrestler bounce off the canvas is impressive—it looks like the wrestler must have hit really hard to bounce so high. In reality, the spring aids in the illusion and helps to absorb the impact.

Flying wrestlers have to be accurate or someone will get hurt. Remember Yukon Eric's ear. Serious injuries can, and sometimes do, occur when wrestlers become airborne.

Getting a Leg Up

I've said it before: Of all the action in the ring, leg work is likely to be the most real. Legs are a good target for wrestlers. Many submission holds involve the restraint of a person's leg or legs. Wrestlers use their legs as weapons, and their legs are used against them to force submission. When you see a wrestler who has his legs bent backward, you can assume it is real. There are no tricks for leg bending.

The physiology of the legs makes them a great target for impressive moves and crippling holds. For example, the thigh has a lot of meat around the bone, making it a good contact point for a leg drop. The flesh acts as padding and protects both wrestlers. Another way to make impressive leg drops without doing much damage is to land with the back of the knee on the contact spot. The knee can bend seconds before impact to lessen the blow to the wrestler being attacked.

Knee drops can be painful if not executed properly. And the wrestler under attack is not the only one in danger. A wrestler making a knee drop has to be careful; knees can be hurt easily and are extremely painful. The key is to execute a near miss—just like a pulled fist punch.

Kicking Is a Habit

Kicking, which is unheard of in classic wrestling, is common in pro wrestling. Looking at the heavy ring boots worn by most wrestlers, any spectator would agree that a full-contact kick would be, as it says on cigarette packs, hazardous to one's health. Certainly, the wrestlers pack enough power in their lower bodies to do extreme damage with their boots. So how do they kick so hard without hurting anyone? Simple!

Captain Lou's Corner

You usually kick with the inside of your foot, the instep of the foot. Sometimes the toe of the foot is used. Kicking today is much tamer than it used to be. In the old days, guys would get mad and kick hard—and real.

There are a few different kick moves in pro wrestling:

➤ **The near miss**—You'll see plenty of these when inexperienced wrestlers take to the mat—and I mean *see* them if the newcomer is not skilled at making his moves look real. Near-miss kicks aren't particularly impressive, so they're the least effective in terms of crowd appeal.

➤ **Contact, but controlled**—Some kicks actually connect with the opponent's body, but a skilled wrestler does this in such a way that there's little risk and pain.

➤ **Contact, but careful placement**—The third technique is to kick, but to kick in safe locations. For example, kicking someone in the kneecap could easily result in a painful and crippling injury. Kicks to the thighs, biceps, gut, or shoulders—the "meaty" parts—are acceptable.

In conclusion, wrestlers are trained professionals who know just how to make a move appear devastating but in reality allow their opponent to get up and fight another day. If you were to actually piledrive a friend in your backyard, you would take an irresponsible risk of breaking his neck and putting him in a wheelchair. Leave the rough stuff to the pros—and if you want to be a pro, go to school!

The Least You Need to Know

➤ Classic wrestling relies on submission holds, which are still used in modern wrestling.

➤ Modern wrestling has become much more acrobatic than earlier wrestling.

➤ Classic holds include the toe hold, the abdominal stretch, and the camel clutch, among others.

➤ Modern wrestling moves include brainbusters, DDTs, and sleepers.

➤ Some modern moves, such as piledrivers, are too dangerous to use in the ring. These moves are faked as stunts.

Chapter 30

Double Your Pleasure, Double Your Pain: Tag Teams

In This Chapter

➤ How tag-team matches are different from one-on-one bouts

➤ What makes a good tag-team player?

➤ The art of distraction in tag-team matches

➤ Famous tag teams

Wrestling matches in the United States are generally one-on-one. But when tag teams enter the ring, at least four people are prepared to do battle. There is room for both types of matches on the wrestling circuit, and fans like their variety. In fact, their over-the-top theatrics and action make them one of wrestling's most popular features. In this chapter, we show you what tag-team wrestling is all about.

A Brief History of Tag Teams

The very first tag-team match was held in San Francisco sometime in 1901, but it didn't make much of an impact at the time. Wrestling fans usually date the effective beginning of the tag team to three decades later—1937 or 1938, in Houston. That's when a new style of wrestling match—variously called Texas Tornado or Australian Tag-Team matches—began.

Bert's Corner

Tag–team matches were often used as the novelty act to open a show. A famous duo, the Bushwhackers, was the prototype for this kind of act. These New Zealanders were funny-looking, dressed alike, and began a match by licking each others' head for luck. They looked harmless, but they got their start as the Sheepherders—a hardcore blood-and-guts tandem that worked with barbed wire and other foreign objects.

The guy who usually gets the credit for this innovation was Houston promoter Morris Siegel—well, really, his nephew. The story goes that Siegel's nephew was sitting in the john when he was struck by an inspiration—if you can have one-on-one wrestling, why not two-on-two? He shared this bolt from the blue with his uncle, and the rest is wrestling history.

It didn't take long for the concept to spread far beyond Houston—especially because this was the era when promoters were trying *anything* to get Depression-depressed fans back into the arenas. And it expanded—if two were good, why not more? Eventually the "Battle Royal" came into being, where as many as 20 wrestlers would all pile into the ring, and the one left standing in the end would be the winner.

The innovation that really turned tag teams into a keeper of an idea was a simple one: Have one wrestler inside the ropes and one outside at all times. Initially, they were also restricted by being tethered to a turnbuckle, but that particular detail disappeared sometime during the 1990s.

The entire concept of tag-team wrestling changed in the 1950s, when Vince McMahon Sr. came up with the idea of teaming two solo headliners, Antonino Rocca and Miguel Perez, to capture the fancy of Latino fans. From that point on, tag-team matches were no longer thought of as novelty acts, but became a major part of every wrestling show.

The Fabulous Kangaroos

Coming up with just the right mix for a successful tag team isn't easy. Ol' Captain Lou should know—I've managed enough of them in my time. You have to look for the right combination of size, strength, and wrestling styles. And you have to make sure that they have drawing power as a pair. Most of all, the wrestlers have to be able to operate smoothly as a single unit.

One of the best tag teams of the early TV era was known as The Fabulous Kangaroos—Al Costello and Roy Heffernan. They were both very proficient single wrestlers, but their ability to work together made these two Australians *great* as a team. Their superb teamwork combined with their agile wrestling skills made them so great a team that they won the WWWF tag titles on several occasions.

The Need for Speed

Speed is one of the most important elements of a successful tag team. A wrestler has to move fast to get from one side of the ring to the other for a tag with a partner. If a wrestler isn't fast enough, his opponent will prevent him from making a tag. When this happens, the match turns into more of a solo bout.

Granted, in modern wrestling, tagging up is not considered a necessity for a partner to enter the ring. But, by the rules, a tag must be made. However, this is one of those rules that is winked at.

There's another reason why speed is essential in a tag-team match: Fast wrestlers can evade big wrestlers. They can use the ropes to launch flying attacks and can roll with the punches (so to speak) more easily than less agile wrestlers.

The Celebrity Effect

As tag teams grew in popularity, a new gimmick was added to the mix: celebrity guest team members. Mr. T—then riding the wave of his popularity on the hit TV series *The A Team*—was one of the first. His pairing with Hulk Hogan against Rowdy Roddy Piper and Paul "Mr. Wonderful" Orndorff was a big hit at the first *WrestleMania*.

Hogan's celebrity pairings didn't stop there. More recently he partnered up with the bad boy of basketball, Chicago Bull Dennis Rodman, to take on Diamond Dallas Page and his celebrity playmate, Karl Malone of the Utah Jazz.

Road Warriors

Wrestlers take inspiration for their personae from pop culture all the time—so why not tag teams? The Road Warriors (also known as the Legion of Doom in the WWF) were for the better part of the 1980s the biggest and baddest tag team on the planet. They drew their inspiration from the *Mad Max* series of movies. Black leather, mohawks, sinister face paint, you name it—the Road Warriors did whatever it took to make themselves the most frightening tag team in the business. It also didn't hurt that both Hawk and Animal were huge and wore spiked armor shoulder pads into the ring.

Captain Lou's Corner

I look for a certain indefinable "something" in my teams, and I must be finding it because I've had 19 world championship teams. My first was The Mongols, and then there were Tarzan Tyler and Luke Graham, King Curtis and Baron Sciluna, The Lumberjacks, the two Black Jacks (Lanza and Mulligan), The Moondogs, The British Bulldogs, The Headshrinkers, The Wild Samoans, and on, and on, and on ....

Wrestle Mania

The Steiner Brothers, Rick and Scott, both out of the University of Michigan's wrestling program, are a great example of tag teamwork at its best. They've wrestled for the WCW, the WWF, and briefly for the ECW. Now they're back in the WCW, but this time they've split up. Scott has turned evil and now goes by the name Big Poppa Pump. Rick has stayed the same simple soul that he always was and wonders why his brother has turned on him.

Team Players

Tag-team performers must also be able to anticipate the moves and needs of their partners. Learning to time moves, jumps, and tackles is important. The wrestlers on a team must also know how to pace themselves so that they stay fresh in the ring. Tag-team performers must know when to make a tag and when to relieve a partner for a rest.

Captain Lou's Corner

The first tag team to have its own entrance music was The Fabulous Freebirds with the classic tune "Bad Street USA."

Until a team has worked together over numerous matches, the rough edges show during a bout. But wrestlers who wrestle regularly with the same team partners fare much better.

Breaking All the Rules

Another feature of many tag-team matches is their grand tradition of flamboyant rule breaking. It's easier to flaunt the rules in a tag-team match—while the ref is monitoring one dueling duo, the other wrestlers in the ring have a huge chance to cheat. The referee is outnumbered and simply cannot keep an eye on everything that's going on. Wrestlers know this and take advantage of the opportunities afforded by it. Good tag-team wrestlers know that distracting a referee can be crucial in deciding a match.

Distractions work best when a third party can be counted on to make a ruckus to draw away the referee's attention. In this manner, both members of the tag team are free to damage their opponents.

Matching Up the Maniacs

The best tag team wrestlers are matched closely to their partners. Good managers have an ability to put together teams that complement each other. Their wrestling skills, their size, their speed, and their experience are all factored into whether to make them partners in the ring. Sometimes specific wrestlers are brought together as a team for promotional purposes, but the teams that continually finish in the victory circle are carefully crafted.

Now let's take a look at the antics of a couple modern tag teams.

Bert's Corner

Wrestlers are not supposed to enter the ring during a tag match until their partners tag them, but many wrestlers jump into the ring early. It's considered a necessity when wrestling the villains of the sport.

Head Cheese: Al Snow and Steve Blackman

Al Snow is the guy who comes to the ring carrying a mannequin head. Written backward, it says "EM PLEH" (or "HELP ME") both on Al's head and the mannequin head. (In a mirror, get it ....) What a gimmick! So schizo! Fans loved it. Al called his companion "Head," and the fans chanted, "We want Head!" That's Al Snow, a hard-working, credible, hardcore wrestler with a great gimmick.

Then there's Steve Blackman, who is a legitimate as they come. He's a real-life killing machine, but, alas, with the *charisma* of a rock (not the be confused with The Rock). So what does Vince McMahon do? He teams Blackman with Al Snow. Their gimmick is that Al Snow believes that the team needs a gimmick, which looks ridiculous when applied to the wooden Blackman.

Snow tried to call the team the Aliens and hired midgets wearing alien costumes to accompany them to the ring. Then, when Snow wasn't around, Blackman beat up the midgets. Snow thought that it would be funny for Blackman to have a farmer gimmick and tried to teach him how to milk a cow. That turned out to be unfortunate for the cow. Then they were Head Cheese—Al Snow came into the ring carrying

Fighting Words

Some wrestlers have to work harder to be popular than others. The difference is called **charisma.** Some wrestlers just have to show up and the crowd is on its feet (Dusty Rhodes and Hulk Hogan come to mind). Chris Jericho, who has plenty of charisma, likes to purposefully mispronounce the word "charasma," so that it sounds like a lung ailment.

Head, while Blackman looked like he had just rushed in from a Packers game with a big cheese on his head. This was the gimmick that stuck.

And it was at that point that Blackman first became popular with WWF crowds. It doesn't hurt, of course, that Blackman's martial arts moves in the ring are awesome.

The Dudleys

There may have been more dastardly acts in recent wrestling than those perpetrated by the Damn Dudleyz, D-Von and Buh Buh Ray Dudley, upon the women of the WWF, but I don't think so. The Dudleys got their start in ECW. It was very easy to pick a Dudley out of the pack; he was the one with the tie-dyed T-shirt and horn-rimmed glasses held together with white tape.

In Your Face

How do two young and good-looking wrestlers like Edge and Christian get heel heat? They act conceited, of course, so stuck on themselves that liking them is out of the question. These days, before Edge and Christian wrestle, they always pause briefly to pose in the ring. Why? "It's for the benefit of those with flash photography," says Edge.

In their ECW days, there were many Dudleys. Big Dick Dudley was the leader, but he was injury-prone and often absent from the ring. (Big Dick is now wrestling regularly for X-Treme Pro Wrestling, an ECW imitator working in the Midwest.) There was also "Sign Guy" Dudley, who always sat in the front row on the side of the ring facing the TV cameras when the show was taped at the ECW Arena in Philadelphia. Sign Guy held up signs for the TV audience, poking fun at what was going on in the ring, thus starting the sign craze at live wrestling shows. Then there was Little Spike Dudley, the anemic-looking grappler who continually gets the living snot beaten out of him by his much-bigger opponents until, by some miracle, he wins in the end. Spike is still wrestling in ECW, where he is a fan favorite. Only Buh Buh and D-Von made the move to the WWF, where their actions have become as notorious as anything in the history of sports entertainment.

The Dudleys' transition from ECW to the WWF was not a smooth one. Like other wrestlers and tag teams who are new to wrestling's number one promotion, there were adjustments to make. The Dudleys were immediately booked against the toughest tag teams in the Federation—the Acolytes, the Hardy Boyz, Edge and Christian, and the New Age Outlaws. They lost to every one of them. It wasn't until January 2000 that the Dudleys turned the corner. It happened at the *Royal Rumble* in New York's Madison Square Garden. They were slated to wrestle a "Table Match" versus Matt and Jeff Hardy, a pair of youthful, high-flying phenoms. Many, many tables were smashed during the match and, no, the Dudleys did not emerge victoriously—but they did show the teamwork and wild brawling style that has led to their subsequent winning streak. Victories over Edge and Christian, Steve Blackman and Al Snow, and D-Lo Brown and The Godfather followed.

In almost every case, the Dudleys won the match when they put their opponent through a table, their old ECW trademark. Then, on February 27, 2000, at the *No Way Out* pay-per-view event in Hartford, Buh Buh Ray and D-Von Dudley made their way into the record books when they de-feated Road Dogg Jesse James and Bad Ass Billy Gunn, (known as the New Age Outlaws) to win the WWF World Tag Team championship. Since the "brothers" won the gold straps, it has been Buh Buh who has turned into a full-fledged woman-hater. And, knowing the WWF, it will only be a matter of time before the Dudleys get their comeuppance for their evil ways.

Buh Buh puts a table in the ring and then abducts a female, usually one normally protected by the very men whom the Dudleys just destroyed. Buh Buh carries her like King Kong carrying Fay Wray to the top turnbuckle nearest the table. Then he leaps off the turnbuckle and power-bombs his captive through the table to the canvas. They al-ways have to be taken out on a stretcher. Buh Buh first did this to Terri Runnels, the sexy valet who formerly represented Goldust under the name Marlena. Then he power-bombed Lita, valet for Essa Rios. Outrage grew. But then came the day when Buh Buh Ray Dudley, in a woman-hating trance, power-bombed 78-year-old Mae Young.

This must be stopped. What must happen before those Damn Dudleyz get what they deserve? Will they have to power-bomb Stephanie McMahon, the owner's daughter, and send her to the hospital before action is taken? (Although I should note that Buh Buh has been *super* careful to protect the women—especially Mae—when doing these stunts.)

Body Slam

Beware fans and promoters, alike. It never pays to presume how a wrestling crowd is going to react. There was an unexpected side-effect to the Dudleys war on women. They became tremendously popular. Fans couldn't wait to see which of the WWF "babes" was going to be put through a table next. Whether the fans are cheering the Dudleys because they like the misogynistic angle, or be-cause they cheer anything they consider taboo-busting, we don't know. I'd like to think that at least some of them are cheering the women for taking those big bumps.

The Least You Need to Know

➤ Once a novelty act, tag teams became so popular that they've become major attractions in their own right.

➤ The methods used in tag-team wrestling differ from those used in solo matches.

➤ Speed is considered one of the most important qualities for a tag-team wrestler.

➤ People outside the ropes, such as managers and valets, often influence the outcome of tag matches by distracting the referee.

➤ The Dudleys are not nice men—at least, not in the story line.

➤ Wrestling fans love to chant: "We want Head!"

Who's Who in Pro Wrestling

Abbott, Tank   A former professional shoot-fighter who made a successful jump to the WCW. Sporting a goatee and a shaved skull, Abbott drops opponents for the 10-count with an awesome right hand. He wants to duke it out with Goldberg.

Abs, Joey   Born and raised on the mean streets of Greenwich, Connecticut, where he grew up with Shane McMahon, Abs is a member of the Mean Street Posse in the WWF, along with Rodney and Pete Gas.

Acolytes   The WWF tag team consisting of Bradshaw and Faarooq. They love to play cards, smoke stogies, and drink beer. To cover their gambling debts, however, the two have recently hired themselves out as paid protection, dubbing themselves the Acolyte Protection Agency (APA).

Albert   A hairy, body-piercing, bald-headed monster. He recently teamed up with Test and busty valet Trish Stratus to form T&A in the WWF. He's formerly known as Prince Albert, which is street lingo for a particularly icky kind of body piercing.

Alfonso, Bill   Calling himself the "Manager of Champions," Bill Alfonso has managed a number of ECW strap-holders throughout the years, most notably Sabu and his current charge, Rob Van Dam. Always with a whistle in his mouth, the hyperactive Alfonso is not afraid to zip quickly into the ring and interfere on behalf of his wrestler.

Anderson, Arn   One of the original Four Horsemen and one of the best ever, Arn "The Enforcer" Anderson is now a front office character for WCW.

Anderson, C.W.   Half of the Dangerous Alliance tag team with "Beautiful" Billy Wiles in ECW, Anderson is a young, old-school up-and-comer known for his spinebuster finisher. He's managed by Lou E. Dangerously.

Angel A member of The Baldies of ECW, along with Grimes and Devito, Angel claims to be the "King of the Streets." He and the other Baldies are feuding with the "Original Gangsta," New Jack.

Angle, Kurt A former Olympic gold medallist in wrestling, Angle's wrestling skills are matched only by his ego. "Your Olympic Hero," as he likes to call himself, is a proponent of the "Three I's"—integrity, intensity, and intelligence—although it's more a case of "Do as I say, not as I do." Angle loves to insult wrestling audiences and then add enthusiastically, "It's true! It's true!"

Kurt Angle won a gold medal at the 1996 Summer Olympics in Atlanta.

Artist FKAPI, The The Artist Formerly Known as Prince Iaukea is a Samoan warrior in the WCW who has enlisted the valet services of the lovely Paisley.

Asya Originally a female bodybuilder, Asya was brought into the WCW by Ric Flair. Relatively new to the world of wrestling, Asya has developed amazing wrestling skills in the short time she has been wrestling. In fact, she can hold her own with the toughest men in the WCW.

Austin, Steve Stone Cold Steve Austin, one of the most popular wrestlers of all time, is a bald-headed, denim-clad, working-class grappler who has carried on incredible feuds in the WWF with Shawn Michaels, The Rock, and Vince McMahon, to name but a few. Some of his catch phrases—for example, "whoop-ass"—have entered the popular vocabulary. He has been sidelined with a neck injury but returned recently to help The Rock win the title.

Awesome, Mike An ECW champion before making the jump to the WCW, Mike Awesome has amazing agility for a man of his mammoth size. He is currently feuding with Hulk Hogan and Kevin Nash of the Millionaire's Club as a member of the New Blood.

Mike Awesome held the ECW Heavyweight Championship when he left that organization to join the WCW. Emergency ECW matches had to be booked to explain the sudden change in title.

B. B.   A busty valet who appeared on the scene in the WWF first as an EMT, where she quickly became a fan favorite.

Bagwell, Buff   A pumped-up pretty boy who loves to pose and dance for the crowd. Buff coined the phrase "Buff's the stuff" and currently wrestles in tag competition with Shane Douglas as members of the New Blood in WCW.

Baldies, The   A trio of street thugs in the ECW consisting of Angel, Devito, and Grimes, who have declared all-out war on the "Original Gangsta" New Jack.

Bearer, Paul   The freakish mortician manager of Kane and The Undertaker. Bearer claims to be Kane's father. He is easily recognized by his bloated frame, pasty-white complexion, and unnerving voice.

Benoit, Chris   "The Crippler," perhaps the best technical wrestler in the business, Benoit appeared on the WWF scene as one of the Radicalz. Since then he has won the Intercontinental belt and has amazed everyone with his Diving Head-Butt finisher.

Berlyn   An avant garde German with a black mohawk and goatee, Berlyn came to the WCW to prove the superiority of his German fatherland over the United States. Originally accompanied by The Wall, the two have since gone their separate ways.

Big Boss Man   A WWF heel who was a tough prison guard before turning to wrestling. He loves to administer nightstick beatings on his opponents. He recently teamed up with Bull Buchanan.

Big Show   A huge 500-pound, 7-foot, 4-inch goliath in the WWF. After a bitter feud with the Rock in which he allied himself with Shane McMahon, the Big Show turned over a new leaf—or went a little crazy—when he began mimicking other wrestlers and coming to the ring in their outfits, using their catch-phrases.

Big T   Grew up in the "da Hood" with Booker and Stevie Ray. He debuted in the WCW to violently remind Booker of his roots. Since then, he formed Harlem Heat 2000 with Stevie Ray and manager J. Biggs.

333

Big Vito   One of the Mamalukes, a WCW tag team hailing from Bensonhurst, Brooklyn, with supposed ties to the Mafia. He is managed by Disco Inferno.

Bigelow, Bam Bam   Dubbed "The Beast from the East," Bam Bam's huge frame and tattoo-laden skull have intimidated opponents for years. Currently wrestling in the WCW, Bam Bam is known especially for his hardcore wrestling.

Bischoff, Eric   Half of the regime at the WCW. Bischoff teamed with Vince Russo to "save" the WCW. He allied himself with the younger wrestlers—the New Blood— against the older stars—the Millionaire's Club. He is currently carrying on an epic feud with Hulk Hogan.

Blackman, Steve   Dubbed the "Most Dangerous Man Alive," Blackman's knowledge of self-defense, particularly the martial arts, is second to none. He reluctantly teamed with Al Snow to form Head Cheese.

Blue Meanie, The   A tubby 300-pounder, The Blue Meanie's psychotic get-up un- nerves many of his WWF opponents. He sports a blue mohawk and has painted on a pair of shades around his eyes. This crazy ECW alum is allied with Stevie Richards.

Booker T   Formed the legendary tag team Harlem Heat with his brother, Stevie Ray. However, Stevie Ray kicked him out with the aid of WCW counsel J. Biggs and re- placed him with Big T to form Harlem Heat 2000. Booker is intent on evening the score.

Bradshaw   A member of the Acolytes along with Faarooq in the WWF. Bradshaw loves to smoke cigars, play cards, and kick butt. He often hires himself out as paid protection with Faarooq as the Acolyte Protection Agency (APA).

Brisco, Gerald   A tag-team champ in his day, Brisco is now a corporate flunkie of Vince McMahon.

British Bulldog   Davey Boy Smith, a superstrong muscular Brit in the WWF known best for his devastating power slams.

Brooklyn Brawler   A Brooklyn street tough and perennial jobber, the Brawler has been around for years and hasn't won too many matches.

Brown, D'Lo   A gifted technical wrestler, D'Lo Brown is known for his unique saunter and his 'LoDown finisher. After a great deal of singles success, D'Lo has teamed up with the Godfather in the WWF.

Buchanan, Bull   A relative newcomer to the WWF, Buchanan is a thug through and through. Teaming up with the Big Boss Man, Buchanan displays remarkable agility for a man of his size, executing leg drops off the top rope and other acrobatic maneu- vers.

Buzzkill   A persona of Brad Armstrong, Buzzkill is a WCW competitor who preaches peace, love, and all that appeals to your typical flower child. Far out.

Candido, Chris   A WCW cruiserweight contender who originally made his name in the ECW. Accompanied by valet/wife Tammy Lynn Sytch, he is dubbed "Hard Knox" Chris Candido in the WCW.

General Rection   The new persona of the crazy Hugh Morrus of the WCW. General Rection (first name, Hugh; middle initial, G.) is a 300-pounder who leaps from the turnbuckles like a *luchador*. He is known for his squeaky laugh and his Last Laugh moonsault finish. He's managed by Jimmy Hart.

The Cat   The Cat Ernest Miller is a pimpin' martial arts expert in WCW who loves to "get on the good foot" in his flashy red dancing shoes. He's a great self-promoter.

Christian   Half of the tag team Edge and Christian, the WWF champs. Christian was a member of Gangrel's Brood but has since split off with his brother, Edge. An adherent to Goth culture, Christian has nevertheless developed a swelled head after winning the tag straps.

Chyna   The Ninth Wonder of the World, Chyna is the first woman to compete in the WWF's men division, at one point holding the Intercontinental title. The leather-clad Amazon recently hooked up with the Latino Heat, Eddie Guerrero.

Chetti, Chris   Chetti is a handsome Italian with an outwardly nonthreatening, laughable demeanor. But in the ECW ring, Chetti is all business. He is presently allied with Nova, forming one of the top tag teams in ECW.

Corino, Steve   Corino describes himself as an old-school wrestler and objects to all the hardcore aspects of the ECW. He feuded with Dusty Rhodes. This smart-mouthed heel has a number of allies, such as Rhino and Jack Victory, who cater to his every whim.

Credible, Justin   A member of the Impact Players with Lance Storm and Jason, Credible is one mean S.O.B. He recently captured the ECW title from archenemy Tommy Dreamer. He finishes off his opponents with a spinning tombstone piledriver. Credible started his big-league wrestling career as the masked Aldo Montoya in the WWF.

Justin Credible, ECW Heavyweight champion, not only has one of the best names in wrestling, but he's also one of the best wrestlers as well.

335

Crowbar   A long-haired psycho, Crowbar currently teams with David Flair in the WCW. The two are accompanied by the equally crazed Daffney Unger.

Cyrus the Virus   The long-haired spokesman for the Network in ECW. Cyrus is a spiteful heel intent on pulling the plug on ECW broadcasting.

D-Generation X   The poorly behaved WWF clique consisting of Triple H, X-Pac, Road Dogg, and Bad Ass Billy Gunn, along with their valets, Stephanie McMahon-Helmsley and Tori.

Dangerous Alliance, The   The tag team of C. W. Anderson and "Beautiful" Billy Wiles, managed by Lou E. Dangerously. The Dangerous Alliance spurns the hardcore edge of ECW and are adherents to the old school style of wrestling. They're escorted to the ring by the lovely Elektra.

Dangerously, Lou E.   A cell-phone carrying manager in the ECW. Lou E. once was a sidekick of Paul Heyman, the ECW's promoter, but he felt that he wasn't getting the credit he deserved. Since then, Lou E. does whatever he can to thwart Heyman. He manages the Dangerous Alliance.

Dawn Marie   Also referred to as Dawn Marie Bytch. She's a lovely but devious brunette valet who accompanies the Impact Players and who is romantically connected with Lance Storm in the ECW.

A wiggle here, a giggle there, and Dawn Marie has become one of the most popular women in all of wrestling.

Debra   A blond bombshell of a valet in the WWF whose ample bust was the inspiration for the term "puppies."

Demon, The   Inspired by the demonic Kiss outfit of Gene Simmons, the Demon leaves his coffin for one thing only: to kick butt in the wrestling ring. His monstrous appearance is more than enough to unnerve most competitors.

Devito, Tony   A Bronx-born, cigar-chomping street thug and a member of The Baldies. Devito and his Baldie cohorts are out for New Jack's blood.

Diamond, Simon   Technically skilled but arrogant to the extreme, Simon Diamond can't help but incur the hatred of ECW fans with his conceited "Simon says" commands.

Disco Inferno   Nobody had better tell this rassler that disco is dead—he loves it that much. Self-proclaimed "Manager of Champions," Disco appointed himself manager of the reluctant Mamalukes and continues to leech himself onto the WCW tag team. (It's been said that he is thinking of updating his image by calling himself "Hip-Hop Inferno.")

Disco Inferno is hopelessly —and lovably—stuck in the '70s.

Dog, The   A WCW wrestler "walked" to the ring by Fit Finlay and Brian Knobs. The Dog wears a leash and enjoys sticking his head out the car window when traveling from show to show. But when he steps into the ring, this Dog sure can bite.

Doring, Danny   "Dastardly" Danny Doring's massive ego displays itself in both his arrogant strut and the "Muffin Ass" logo on the backside of his trunks. He teams with Roadkill, a 300-pound Amish grappler.

Dreamer, Tommy   "The Innovator of Violence," Dreamer has been one of the mainstays of ECW for years. Recently his long time lady friend Francine left him for his archenemy, Raven, setting off a new chapter in the epic Raven-Dreamer feud. He won the ECW title but was defeated in his first title defense by Justin Credible after Francine interfered.

Dudley Boyz   The "bruthas with different muthas," these ECW alums have made a successful transition to the WWF. Buh Buh Ray and D-Von are hardcore competitors who love to power-bomb women through tables. They're famous for their 3D (Dudley Death Drop) finishing move.

Dudley, Spike   Not your typical wrestler, Spike Dudley is super small at well under 200 pounds. Nevertheless, dubbed "The Giant Killer" of the ECW, Spike, in his tie-dyed shirt and denim overalls, has more than held his own against some awesome competition. His finish, the Acid Drop, is one of the most exciting finishers in wrestling.

Duggan, Hacksaw Jim   A long-haired, bearded competitor in WCW who comes to the ring armed with a 2 x 4 and the Stars and Stripes. He's known for his "Hooo!" battle cry and his tremendous clothesline that explodes from a three-point football stance.

Edge   A blond-haired Adonis who, along with Christian, holds the WWF Tag Team titles. A gothic warrior, Edge, along with his brother, Christian, has become an over-confident jerk.

Elektra   The sensuous valet for the Dangerous Alliance of ECW, Elektra was connected with Doring and Roadkill before deserting them for Lou E. Dangerously and company.

Elizabeth   Originally the valet for Randy Savage back in the 1980s, now a member of Team Package with the Total Package and Ric Flair. Elizabeth and the Package are romantically linked, but the conniving Vince Russo has dragged Liz away against her will through contractual means, igniting a bitter feud.

Fabulous Moolah   One of the great woman wrestlers of all time, Moolah has been wrestling for countless decades. She's often seen with Mae Young in the WWF.

FBI   The Full Blooded Italians, an ECW tag team made up of the outrageously obese Sal E. Graziano and the technically brilliant Little Guido.

Finlay, Fit   The "Belfast Bruiser" of the WCW, this Irish street fighter defines hardcore wrestling. He recently feuded with the disgusting Brian Knobs in a hardcore war.

Flair, David   The son of wrestling great Ric Flair, David currently teams with Crowbar and is managed by the mysterious Daffney Unger. He turned against his father and joined the New Blood.

Flair, Ric   The "Nature Boy," perhaps the greatest ever. Recognized by his bleached-blond mane, Flair is superb on the mic and in the ring. He currently wrestles with the Total Package in the WCW as Team Package and is a member of the Millionaires Club. He recently was stabbed in the back by his son, David, who has allied himself with the New Blood. Flair is known for his Figure-Four Leg-Lock finisher.

Flynn, Jerry   A master of the martial arts who has taken his butt-kicking skills into the WCW. With each passing success, he moves higher in the ranks.

Foley, Mick   A legendary brawler whose personae have included the deranged Mankind, the violent Cactus Jack, and the flaky Dude Love. Mick Foley is renowned for taking some crazy bumps, especially in the famous "Hell in the Cell" match with the Undertaker.

Francine   An ECW valet who has appeared alongside a number of wrestlers, most notably Tommy Dreamer. However, she has recently incurred Dreamer's hatred after running off with Raven.

Funaki   Half of the tag team Kaientai with Taka Michinoku. He's a tough, high-flying competitor who came to the WWF by way of Japan.

Funk, Terry   Hailing from the Double-Cross Ranch in Amarillo, Texas, the Funker is one of the greatest hardcore wrestlers in history. Funk continues to compete in the WCW Hardcore division, although he is well into his 50s.

Gangrel   A vampire-like wrestler in the WWF who founded the now-inactive Brood. Gangrel loves to drink blood from a wine glass and spit it at his opponents.

Gas, Pete   A childhood friend of Shane McMahon's from Greenwich who is a member of the Mean Street Posse in the WWF along with Rodney and Joey Abs.

Godfather   The pimp of the WWF, the Godfather is always accompanied to the ring by a train of "hos." He recently teamed up with D'Lo Brown.

Goldberg   A man of few words and one of the world's most popular wrestlers, the bald, goateed Goldberg is all business in the ring. His intensity is his only gimmick. The Spear and the Jackhammer, his finishing moves, are two of the most devastating maneuvers in wrestling.

Graziano, Sal E.   A member of the FBI (the Full Blooded Italians) with Little Guido. At 600 pounds, Sal E. is the brawn of the FBI and can easily squash most opponents.

Grimes   A member of the street-tough triumvirate that is The Baldies of the ECW along with Angel and Devito. He is carrying on a bitter feud with New Jack.

Guerrera, Juventud   A "Young Warrior" in the WCW and a member of the Filthy Animals division of the New Blood. Juventud's lucha libre agility and "Juvy Driver" finish have made him a force to be reckoned with.

Guerrero, Chavo Jr.   A *luchador* out of Mexico, Chavo is truly crazy—he used to enter the ring accompanied by Pepe, his wooden horse. He's known for his Swinging DDT finish.

Guerrero, Eddy   A wrestler of Latino ancestry who entered the WWF as one of the four Radicalz. He makes use of negative Latino stereotypes to draw heel heat. He used his self-described "Latino Heat" to capture the heart of Chyna.

Eddy Guerrero has delighted wrestling fans throughout the years playing a variety of roles, ranging from the evil to his current fun-loving "Latino Heat."

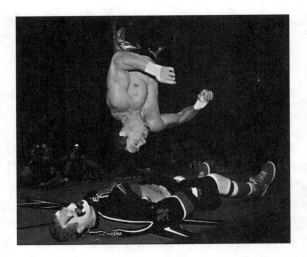

Gunn, Billy   D-Generation X member Bad Ass Billy Gun, often called Mr. Ass, is a true narcissist. He held the tag title with Road Dogg as the New Age Outlaws. He has been sidelined recently due to an injury.

Hall, Scott   An Outsider and one of the founders of the nWo with Nash, Hall is one cool character both on the mic and in the ring. His "Outsider's Edge" finisher is one of the more electrifying finishes in wrestling.

Hancock, Ms.   A leggy blonde, this valet initially appeared on the WCW as a Nitro girl and then as a member of Standards and Practices. Her stunning looks won the hearts of wrestling fans, and since then she has been a mainstay of the WCW.

Hardy Boyz   Matt and Jeff. Known for their high-flying and truly psychotic stunts, the Hardys put it all on the line every time they step in the ring. Recognized by their multicolored hairdos and sharp outfits, the Hardys are one of the top tag teams in the WWF.

Harlem Heat   Originally the team of Stevie Ray and Booker T, until a disagreement led to Booker being fired from the duo and replaced with Big T—and J. Biggs as manager.

Harris Brothers   Bald-headed heel twins with a vicious mean streak. Close allies of Jeff Jarrett, the Chosen One, and members of the second incarnation of the nWo.

Hart, Bret   "The Hitman," one of the best technical wrestlers. A proud Canadian from Calgary, he learned to wrestle in his family's "Dungeon." He's known for his submission hold, the Sharpshooter.

Hart, Jimmy   "The Mouth of the South" has managed wrestlers for years. His fast talking and tacky suits have made him a fan favorite in the WCW.

Hayashi, Kaz   A technically gifted wrestler who came to the WCW by way of Japan. Perhaps the most gifted member of the Jung Dragons, Kaz finishes off his opponents with an amazing Senton Bomb.

Headbangers   Mosh and Thrasher form one of the more bizarre tag teams in wrestling. With shaved skulls and skirts, these guys look more like a rock band than a tag team. They're known for their Stage Dive finisher.

Helms, Shane   A member of Three Count, with Evan Karagias and Shannon Moore. Helms is intent on pursuing a career as a pop star, a dream that has proven problematic, at best.

Hennig, Curt   A seasoned ring veteran and legendary wrestler known for his technical ability and Hennig-plex finishing move. He has currently aligned himself with the Millionaires Club in the WCW.

Henry, Mark   See *Sexual Chocolate*.

Hogan, Hulk   One of the all-time greats. Hogan is known for his Superman comeback, his boot to the face, and his awesome leg drop. Now a member of the Millionaires Club in the WCW, Hogan is warring with the New Blood, especially Billy Kidman, Mike Awesome, and Eric Bischoff.

Holly, Hardcore   A blond-haired competitor who will do whatever it takes to win. Hardcore is the cousin of Crash Holly but doesn't quite take his relative seriously.

Holly, Crash   Hardcore Holly's little cousin, Crash Holly claims to weigh several hundred pounds more than he actually does. As Hardcore champ, Crash must defend his title 24-7. Despite taking vicious beatings, he somehow manages to defy the odds and retain his belt.

Hunter Hearst Helmsley   See *Triple H*.

Ivory   A beautiful brunette who knows how to handle herself in the ring—she's a two-time WWF Women's champion.

Jacqueline   Although she is perhaps the bustiest of all the WWF ladies, Jacqueline brings more to the ring than just her looks. She's a terrific wrestler and has twice won the WWF Women's belt, one time even defeating a man, Harvey Whippleman.

Jami San   A member of the Jung Dragons with Kaz Hayashi and Yang.

Jarrett, Jeff   Dubbed the Chosen One, Jeff Jarrett is best known for shattering guitars over his opponents' heads, a gimmick lifted from the Honky Tonk Man. A member of the New Blood, Jarrett has captured the WCW title on several occasions. He is currently feuding with Diamond Dallas Page.

WCW Heavyweight champion Jeff Jarrett's gimmick is smashing guitars over people's heads.

Jason   The manager of the diabolical Justin Credible and a member of the Impact Players. He describes himself as the "Sexiest Man on Earth."

Jazz   A lady wrestler in the ECW, formerly aligned with the Impact Players. Jazz became disgusted with the arrogance of Credible and Jason and turned against them. She recently teamed up with Chetti and Nova.

Jericho, Chris   Y2J, the "Ayatollah of Rock'n Rollah," is an electrifying performer and a fan favorite. He has two finishers, the Lionsault and the Walls of Jericho submission hold.

Johnny The Bull   A member of the Mamalukes along with Big Vito. An Italian-American from Bensonhurst managed by Disco Inferno.

Jones, Judge Jeff   The manager of Mike Awesome when he was in the ECW, Judge Jeff Jones comes to the ring attired in judicial robes.

Jung Dragons   The trio of Kaz Hayashi, Yang, and Jami San, these Japanese Musketeers have astounded WCW with their aerial wrestling skills.

Kaientai   The acrobatic WWF tag team consisting of Taka Michinoku and Funaki, two terrific competitors out of northern Japan.

Kane   "The Big Red Machine," the brother and sworn enemy of the Undertaker. He wears a mask to cover the awful burns he received in a fire. He rarely speaks but uses a "voice box" when he does. He is feuding with X-Pac and DX over Tori. He's managed by Paul Bearer.

Kane wears a mask because he was burned in a fire as a child or so they say.

Kanyon, Chris   Chris "Champagne" Kanyon was a member of the Jersey Triad with Diamond Dallas Page. Now an ally of the Millionaires Club in the WCW, he is known for his "That's a Rap" finishing move.

Karagias, Evan   A member of Three Count in the WCW, along with Shannon Moore and Shane Helms. Although he may not have the talent to be a pop star, Karagias, with his Tidal Wave finish, is one heck of a wrestler.

Kat, The   A buxom valet in the WWF who briefly held the WWF Women's title. However, she is perhaps best remembered for baring her "puppies" on a live pay-per-view. She is currently feuding with Terri Runnels.

Kid Kash   Kid Kash is money! An up-and-comer in the ECW, Kid Kash puts it all on the line every time he steps into the ring. Not even a broken jaw could stop him from performing in the squared-circle. He teamed briefly with Nova while Chris Chetti recovered from an injury.

Kid Romeo   A product of the Powerplant wrestling school, the WCW's in-house training outfit, Kid Romeo is an exciting and hungry up-and-comer who is ready to steamroll his way to the top.

Kidman, Billy   A superb wrestler, Kidman is one of the top members of the WCW's New Blood as well as the Filthy Animals. He has carried on an intense feud with Hulk Hogan and is known for his heart-stopping Shooting Star Press finisher. He's often accompanied by his hot valet, Torrie Wilson.

Kimberly   The valet/wife of Diamond Dallas Page. Their relationship has had its ups and downs, such as when she turned on him during a match with Jeff Jarrett for the WCW title, costing him the belt.

Knobs, Brian Originally one of the Nasty Boys, Brian Knobs is an overweight head-banger with poor hygiene. Nevertheless, he is one of the best brawlers in WCW.

Konnan A Cuban-born, bald-headed *luchador* and a member of the Filthy Animals faction of the New Blood with Rey Mysterio, Kidman, and Juventud Guerrera. He's known for his Tequila Sunrise finisher.

La Parka Clad in a skeleton suit, La Parka is one mysterious character. A true hard-core competitor, few can handle a chair better than La Parka. Don't let his size fool you—this big guy has all the agility of a *luchador*.

LeRoux, Lash A ragin' Cajun from the bayous of Louisiana and an acrobatic cruis-erweight in the WCW. He also goes by the moniker Corporal Cajun.

Lita The lovely valet of Essa Rios, Lita is not above getting involved in a match, often performing death-defying moonsaults on Essa's opponents.

Little Guido A Full-Blooded Italian in the ECW, Guido's amazing technical prowess is superbly complemented by the huge size and strength of his partner, Sal E. Graziano.

Lynn, Jerry Known for his amazing ECW matches with Rob Van Dam, Lynn was dubbed the "New F'n Show." Sidelined by injury, Lynn became angry over the lack of attention that he received compared with Van Dam. Lynn now wants to show the world that he is every bit the man Van Dam is.

Madusa A talented lady wrestler and valet in WCW, Madusa once captured the Cruiserweight title. She feuded recently with Oklahoma but has yet to align herself with the New Blood or the Millionaire's Club.

Maestro, The A flamboyant musician and pianist in the WCW who is obsessed with his trade—so obsessed, in fact, that he takes his wrath out upon his opponents. He is accompanied by the lovely Symphony.

Mahoney, Balls A big, bearded, self-described "chair-swinging freak" in the ECW. Balls Mahoney, from Nutley, New Jersey, is known for his tremendous brawling skills.

Malenko, Dean "The Man of 1,000 Holds." A technically brilliant cruiserweight who first appeared in the WWF as one of the Radicalz. He's a former WWF light heavy titleist.

Mamalukes The WCW tag team consisting of Johnny the Bull and Big Vito, two Italian street thugs from Bensonhurst with supposed Mafia ties.

McMahon, Linda The wife of Vince and mother of Stephanie and Shane, Linda McMahon appeared on the WWF scene with a bang. In fact she sponsored Mick Foley's entrance into a four-way championship match, angering her family to no end. Recently her backing of The Rock over Triple H has further infuriated her spouse and children.

McMahon, Shane   Brat offspring of Vince McMahon. Shane has consistently sought to keep The Rock from attaining preeminent status in the WWF.

McMahon, Stephanie   The spoiled daughter of Vince McMahon and a member of D-Generation X. She eloped with Triple H and now wields vast influence within the WWF.

McMahon, Vince   The head honcho, the CEO of the WWF. He is not afraid to use his power to maintain order in his federation. The all-time heel-promoter, Vince is currently warring with The Rock.

Mean Street Posse   From the Mean Streets of Greenwich Connecticut, Pete Gas, Joey Abs, and Rodney are flunkies of Shane McMahon who took their street smarts into the WWF.

Meng   Hailing from Tonga, Meng is a martial arts master in the WCW who, at 300 pounds, can also make use of ample size and strength. He subdues opponents with his Tongan Death Grip finisher.

Michaels, Shawn   "The Heartbreak Kid" Shawn Michaels is one of the best in-ring performers in recent WWF history. His narcissistic antics endeared him to the ladies but infuriated many others. He is the founder of D-Generation X.

Michinoku, Taka   Half of the high-flying Kaientai with Funaki. He came to the WWF by way of northern Japan.

Mideon   Ever since his soul was sacrificed by the Undertaker in the WWF, Mideon has turned into a disturbing weirdo. With an eye drawn in the middle of his forehead and tattoos crisscrossing his body, Mideon has a truly frightening appearance. He is known for his Eye Opener finisher.

The Millionaires Club   One of two major factions at war in WCW. The Millionaires Club consists of the older stars who feel that they are being unfairly victimized by WCW bosses Bischoff and Russo, as well as the younger wrestlers in the New Blood.

Moore, Shannon   One of the talented wrestlers in Three Count who dreams of becoming a pop star despite an obvious lack of talent. The guy can't even lip synch, let alone sing.

Morrus, Hugh   See *General Rection*.

Mosh   Half of the mysterious and zany Headbanger tag team in the WWF. He has a shaved head and is fond of wearing skirts, pointed falsies, and eye makeup.

Mysterio, Rey Jr.   The son of legendary wrestler Rey Misterio, Mysterio Jr. is considered one of the most technically skilled acrobatic wrestlers in the world. He currently wrestles in the WCW as a member of the Filthy Animals faction of the New Blood.

nWo   The New World Order, founded by Nash and Hall upon their debut in the WCW. The nWo sought to consolidate all the power in the WCW within their own clique. The nWo was defunct for a while but re-emerged with Jeff Jarrett as the most prominent member. However, the genesis of the Millionaires Club/New Blood feud has eclipsed the nWo lately.

Nash, Kevin   Dubbed Big Sexy, Nash is a 7-foot monster whose Jackknife Power-bomb is one of the most devastating moves in wrestling. A founder of the nWo, Nash is a member of the Millionaires Club and is struggling against the New Blood, particularly Mike Awesome.

Kevin Nash is seven feet tall and good-looking. He would remain a top star among female fans even if he never slapped on another hold.

New Blood   One of the two major factions currently at war in the WCW. The New Blood is made up of young, up-and-coming wrestlers who feel that the older stars—the Millionaires Club—are standing in their way. WCW bosses Vince Russo and Eric Bischoff have offered the group their full support thus far.

New Jack   "The Original Gangsta" of the ECW. He's known for his tremendous hardcore attacks, especially his insane dives off of balconies. New Jack's ultraviolence has horrified fans for years. New Jack has been a marked man lately, having incurred the enmity of The Baldies.

Nova   Originally a flamboyant and gimmicky wrestler in the ECW who wore elaborate capes and costumes into the ring, Nova recently shelved all his gimmicks and got back to the basics. This has caused some tension with his tag partner Chris Chetti, but the two remain one of the teams in the ECW.

Oklahoma   A hat-wearing hickish cowboy and front office stooge in WCW who was put in charge of the women's division. His sexist attitude, however, earned him the hatred of the women competitors.

Outsiders, The   The name given to Scott Hall and Kevin Nash when they debuted in the WCW.

Page, Diamond Dallas   This no-nonsense New Jersey native has been a major force in the WCW for years. Currently a member of the Millionaire's Club, DDP is feuding with the New Blood—Jeff Jarrett and Eric Bischoff in particular.

Paisley   A voluptuous WCW valet who has joined forces with the Artist Formerly Known as Prince Iaukea.

Patterson, Pat   A former WWF Intercontinental champ who has become one of Vince McMahon's corporate stooges.

Piper, Rowdy Roddy   A Scottish, kilt-wearing, bagpipe-playing, microphone master. One of the all-time greats, he still wrestles sporadically with the WCW.

Psychosis   A tough *luchador* in the WCW who originally donned a mask until it was removed by Billy Kidman during a match. However, Psychosis quickly won over the ladies as he turned out to be quite handsome. He uses a guillotine leg drop finish.

Pump, Big Poppa   Scott Steiner has the biggest muscles in wrestling. All this guy ever does is lift weights, hang out with the ladies and square off in the wrestling ring. His finisher, the Steiner Recliner, displays his awesome power, causing all his opponents to scream for mercy. He is the brother of Rick Steiner, the Dog-Faced Gremlin.

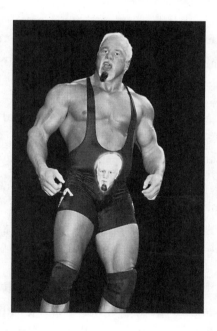

Big Pappa Pump, formerly known as Scott Steiner, has muscles on muscles. Perhaps one day he'll pump so much he pops.

Raven   A dark, brooding head-banger in ECW. He carried on a legendary feud with Tommy Dreamer that is still going strong following a brief partnership that ended with Raven stealing Dreamer's long-time girlfriend, Francine.

Rhodes, Dustin   The son of Dusty Rhodes, the "American Nightmare" portrays a cold-blooded heel in the WCW. He feuded with Hardcore champ Terry Funk in the WCW.

347

Rhodes, Dusty "The American Dream," a legendary wrestler in his day. After making an appearance for the ECW, Dusty was verbally assaulted by Steve Corino, and a bitter feud erupted that shows no signs of letting up. He is famous for his Bionic Elbow.

Roadkill A 300-pound Amish rassler, Roadkill comes to the ring dressed in formal Amish attire. Dubbed the "Angry Amish Chickenplucker," Roadkill forms a formidable tag team with Danny Doring. Agile for his size, Roadkill is capable of executing splashes from the top rope.

Rhino Rhino is the handpicked ECW TV champion of Cyrus and the Network. The Rhino is a brutal wrestler who has fallen in with Steve Corino and Jack Victory. He is known for his Gore finishing move.

Richards, Stevie A nutty WWF performer who believes that imitation is the highest form of flattery. He comes to the ring dressed in the ring regalia of other WWF performers to gain acceptance. Thus far it has not worked.

Rikishi A huge bleach-blond Samoan known for his grossly revealing outfit, his dancing skills, and, most of all, for his infamous Stinky Face finishing move.

Rios, Essa An acrobatic cruiserweight in the WWF. He teamed up with Eddy Guerrero before the two turned on one another. He's accompanied by his valet, Lita.

Road Dogg The Road Dogg Jesse James, half of the tag team the New Age Outlaws and a member of D-Generation X. He is known for his braided hair and for his long, catchy speeches when making his ring entrance.

Rock, The One of the most popular wrestlers in recent history. The Rock is best known for his great mic skills featuring such catch phrases as "If you can smell what The Rock is cookin'?" He currently is involved in a bitter feud with Triple H, D-Generation X, and the McMahons.

Rodney A member of the Mean Street Posse. He is a friend of Shane McMahon's from Greenwich who is now trying his hand as a grappler in the WWF.

Runnels, Terri A buxom valet who has been with both the Hardy Boyz and Edge and Christian, and has turned on both teams. She recently feuded with the Kat.

Russo, Vince One of the two top dogs in the WCW, Russo, along with Eric Bischoff, runs the show in the WCW, where he is trying to push the young stars—the New Blood—over the Millionaires Club. Russo wars with Team Package in particular, having pried Elizabeth away from the Total Package and driven a wedge between Ric Flair and his son.

Sabu A truly psychotic wrestler who has no qualms about sacrificing his own body to get the win. His aerial attacks are heart attack-inducing. Known mostly for his stints in ECW, Sabu currently wrestles for XPW (X-Treme Pro Wrestling).

Sandman, The   A chain-smoking, beer-drinking brawler in the ECW who carries a Singapore Cane with which to beat his opponents. Known for his long and raucous ring entrances, he feuds with Raven and the Impact Players.

Saturn, Perry   Saturn entered the WWF as one of the four Radicalz. His bald head and beard give him a sinister aspect that intimidates fans and opponents alike. However, Saturn is the only Radical who has not yet won a WWF strap, although he has recently set his sights on the Hardcore title.

Sexual Chocolate   Mark Henry, a former Olympic weightlifter, uses his ample frame to squash his opponents. He carried on a torrid love affair with Mae Young, who was at least 50 years his senior. He is dubbed the "World's Strongest Man."

Shamrock, Ken   An Ultimate Fighting champion who made a successful transition to the WWF. He is known for his no-nonsense style in the ring as well as his submission holds.

Sid   See *Vicious, Sid.*

Sinister Minister   A mysterious character in the ECW who reads tarot cards and has cast some sort of spell over Mikey Whipwreck, turning the formerly affable Whipwreck into a paranoid looney.

Smiley, Norman   Known for his crazy and erratic behavior, Screamin' Norman Smiley is also one of the top hardcore wrestlers in the WCW. Norman loves to dance. He often enters the arena dressed in the uniform of the local sports team.

Snow, Al   A crazed mad man, Snow is often accompanied to the ring by Head, a mannequin head that he carries around and often talks with. He recently teamed with a reluctant Steve Blackman to form Head Cheese.

Steiner, Rick   An amazing technical wrestler who learned his trade grappling at the University of Michigan and who often wears a collegiate wrestling helmet into the ring. Rick turned on his brother Scott, a.k.a. Big Poppa Pump, starting a family feud.

Steiner, Scott   See *Poppa Pump, Big.*

Stevie Ray   A member of Harlem Heat with his brother, Booker T, in the WCW until Stevie Ray turned on him. With the help of J. Biggs and Big T, Stevie Ray kicked out Booker and formed Harlem Heat 2000 with Big T and J. Biggs as manager.

Storm, Lance   From "Calgary, Alberta, Canada," as this obnoxious egomaniac constantly reminds us, Storm is a member of the Impact Players along with Justin Credible and Jason in the ECW. He is the longtime beau of Dawn Marie.

Sting   A face-painting WCW superstar, Sting is renowned for his Stinger Splash and Scorpion Death Lock. As a member of the Millionaire's Club, Sting is currently involved in a feud with New Blood member Vampiro.

Stratus, Trish   The busty valet of T&A, the tag team consisting of Test and Albert. She was one of the first ladies to be power-bombed through a table by the Dudley Boyz.

Super Crazy   A high-flying Mexican *luchador* in the ECW who always puts on a show with his unbelievable aerial assaults.

Sytch, Tammy Lynn   The curvaceous valet and fiancée of "Hard Knox" Chris Candido. Tammi is known for her seductive poses as well as her loyalty to Candido.

Tajiri, Yoshihiro   "The Japanese Buzzsaw" of the ECW spits green mist into the faces of his opponents. He is known for his Tarantula submission hold. He fell in with Cyrus and Steve Corino but was betrayed by them and has apparently turned on them.

Tanaka, Masato   A native of Japan, Tanaka occasionally represents the Japanese FMW promotion in the ECW. He is known for his impressive wrestling technique, especially his finishing moves the Roaring Elbow and the Diamonddust. He is also quite handy with a chair.

Tazz   An ECW alum who made the transition to the WWF. Built like a bulldog and known as the "Human Suplex Machine," Tazz finishes off opponents with his Tazzmission submission hold.

Team Package   The team of the Total Package and Ric Flair, along with their valet, Elizabeth. Members of the Millionaires Club in the WCW, Team Package has dealt with much adversity lately due to Vince Russo's abduction of Elizabeth and his manipulation of David Flair, pitting the youngster against his father.

Test   A big, blond wrestler who is quite agile for his size. At one point, he was engaged to Stephanie McMahon before she ran off with Triple H. Test now teams with Albert as T&A, managed by Trish Stratus.

Thrasher   Half of the Headbangers of the WWF along with Mosh. He is known for his shaved skull and strange outfits.

Three Count   The WCW team of Evan Karagias, Shane Helms, and Shannon Moore, a band of wannabe pop stars who are using their WCW exposure to jumpstart their music career. Their horrible lip-synching and lame dancing have incurred the enmity of wrestling fans the world over.

Too Cool   The WWF tag team of Scotty 2 Hotty and Grandmaster Sexay, two hip competitors who are well known for their dancing.

Tori   The valet of X-Pac and a member of D-Generation X. She is perhaps best known for her double-crossing of Kane when she dropped him like a sack of bricks and went off with his archenemy, X-Pac.

The Total Package   The narcissistic Lex Luger just loves to show off his muscular physique. A member of the Millionaires Club and Team Package with Ric Flair and Elizabeth, he was incensed over the kidnapping of Elizabeth by Vince Russo.

Triple H   Raised on the unforgiving streets of Greenwich, Connecticut, Hunter Hearst Helmsley has become the top heel in the WWF. The Game, as he is often called, carried on epic feuds with Steve Austin, Mick Foley, and The Rock. The leader of D-Generation X, Triple H is married to Stephanie McMahon, Vince's daughter.

350

Undertaker   Brother and nemesis of Kane, one of the WWF's top heels, although injuries have plagued him lately. A huge, pale-faced, black-wearing monster known for his Tombstone Piledriver, he is accompanied to the ring by Paul Bearer, who controls him with an urn.

Vampiro   A Gothic warrior with an eerily painted face. He carried on a bitter feud with Sting and is known for his Nail in the Coffin finishing move.

Van Dam, Rob   Dubbed Mr. Pay-Per-View, Mr. Monday Night. Managed by Bill Alfonso, Rob is one of the best acrobatic wrestlers in the world. He was forced to relinquish his TV title after Cyrus and the Network threatened to cancel the ECW on TNN.

Rob Van Dam is ECW's most popular wrestler. He can talk, is good-looking, and flies with the best of the aerial corps.

Venis, Val   A self-absorbed porn star who turned to wrestling in the WWF. He finishes off his opponents with his specialty move, the Money Shot.

Vicious, Sid   A big, blond-headed monster. Sid is best known for his awesome power moves. He carried on a feud with Jeff Jarrett for the WCW title.

Victory, Jack   A cold-blooded mercenary in the ECW who will do anything for a buck. This 320-pound bully is now a stooge for Steve Corino.

Viscera   A mammoth 500-pound monster in the WWF with bleach-blond hair and scary eyes who can squash his opponents.

Wall, The   Originally appeared in the WCW as the bodyguard for Berlyn. He then developed his own gimmick: choke-slamming opponents through tables. He is a member of the New Blood.

Whipwreck, Mikey   A perennial underdog, Mikey Whipwreck at one point held the ECW triple crown, thanks to some amazing luck. Since then, however, the normally upbeat Whipwreck has fallen under the spell of the Sinister Minister and has apparently gone insane.

351

Wilson, Torrie   A stunning blond WCW valet who grew up on a farm near Boise, Idaho, and is currently dating Billy Kidman.

X-Pac   A great acrobatic wrestler, X-Pac currently belongs to D-Generation X and is romantically involved with Tori, whom he stole from his former tag-team partner, Kane.

Yang   A member of the Jung Dragons out of Japan, along with Jami San and Kaz Hayashi.

Young, Mae   An old-timer who still wrestles well into her 70s. She had a brief romance with Mark Henry and shocked the world by flashing her chest at a pay-per-view event. She is often seen with the Fabulous Moolah.

 # Title Histories

Undisputed Champions

1908	Frank Gotch
1914	Charley Cutler
1915	Joe Stetcher
1917	Earl Caddock
1920	Joe Stetcher
1921	Ed "Strangler" Lewis
1921	Stanislaus Zbyszko
1922	Ed "Strangler" Lewis
1925	Wayen "Big" Munn
1925	Stanislaus Zbyszko
1925	Joe Stecher
1928	Ed "Strangler" Lewis
1929	Gus Sonnenberg
1931	Ed "Strangler" Lewis
1931	Henri DeGlane
1931	Ed Don George
1932	Ed "Strangler" Lewis
1933	Jim Browning
1934	Jim Londos
1935	Danno O'Mahoney
1936	Dick Shikat

1936	Ali Baba
1936	Dave Levin
1936	Dean Detton
1936	Everett Marshall
1936	Lou Thesz
1938	Steve "Crusher" Casey
1939	Lou Thesz
1939	Bronco Naguski

NWA/WCW World Title History

NWA (National Wrestling Alliance) World Title

October 1948   Orville Brown

Brown was recognized as the first champion.

November 27, 1949   Lou Thesz

Thesz (National Wrestling Association champ) was awarded the belt after Brown was injured in an automobile accident (November 11) before their unification bout scheduled for November 25, 1949.

March 15, 1953   Whipper Billy Watson   Toronto, Canada

Won by count-out. Special referee: Jack Dempsey.

November 9, 1956   Lou Thesz (2)   St. Louis, Missouri

On June 14, 1957, Edouard Carpentier defeated Thesz when the champion could no longer continue due to injury. NWA later ruled that the title cannot change hands due to injury and reinstated Thesz. Carpentier's claim served to legitimize other NWA title lineages.

November 14, 1957   Dick Hutton   Toronto, Canada

January 9, 1959   Pat O'Connor   St. Louis, Missouri

June 30, 1961   Buddy Rogers   Chicago, Illinois

Killer Kowalski defeated Rogers on November 21, 1962, in Montreal, Canada, after Rogers's ankle broke during the first fall. Because it was billed as a three-falls match, the NWA didn't recognize the title change.

January 24, 1963	Lou Thesz (3)	Toronto, Canada
January 7, 1966	Gene Kiniski	St. Louis, Missouri
February 11, 1969	Dory Funk Jr.	Tampa, Florida

In 1972, Lord Al Hayes defeated Funk, but the decision was later ruled a DQ due to interference from Dory Funk Sr.

May 24, 1973	Harley Race	Kansas City, Missouri
July 20, 1973	Jack Brisco	Houston, Texas
December 2, 1974	Giant Baba	Kagoshimi, Japan
December 9, 1974	Jack Brisco (2)	Tokyo, Japan
December 10, 1975	Terry Funk	Miami, Florida
February 6, 1977	Harley Race (2)	Toronto, Canada

On February 27, 1979, in Auckland, New Zealand, Peter Maivia defeated Harley Race (via DQ) but refused to take the belt, giving it back to Race.

August 21, 1979	Dusty Rhodes	Tampa, Florida
August 26, 1979	Harley Race (3)	Orlando, Florida
October 31, 1979	Giant Baba (2)	Nagoya, Japan
November 11, 1979	Harley Race (4)	Amagaseki, Japan
September 4, 1980	Giant Baba (3)	Saga, Japan
September 10, 1980	Harley Race (5)	Otsu, Japan
April 27, 1981	Tommy Rich	Augusta, Georgia
May 1, 1981	Harley Race (6)	Gainesville, Georgia
June 21, 1981	Dusty Rhodes (2)	Atlanta, Georgia
September 17, 1981	Ric Flair	Kansas City, Missouri

On February 9, 1983, the masked Midnight Rider (Dusty Rhodes) defeated Flair, but he gave back the belt when he refused to identify himself to NWA president Bob Geigel. On Jan. 6, 1983, WWC champ Carlos Colon defeated Flair in San Juan, Puerto Rico, but Flair retained the NWA title.

June 10, 1983	Harley Race (7)	St. Louis, Missouri
November 24, 1983	Ric Flair (2)	Greensboro, North Carolina
March 21, 1984	Harley Race (8)	Wellington, New Zealand

Not acknowledged in North America.

March, 23, 1984	Ric Flair (3)	Kallang, Singapore

Not acknowledged in North America.

May 6, 1984	Kerry Von Erich	Dallas, Texas
May 24, 1984	Ric Flair (4)	Yokosuka, Japan

On November 28, 1985, Dusty Rhodes defeated Flair in Atlanta, Georgia, but the decision was later changed to a DQ, and Flair retained the title.

July 26, 1986	Dusty Rhodes (3)	Greensboro, North Carolina
August 9, 1986	Ric Flair (5)	St. Louis, Missouri
September 25, 1987	Ron Garvin	Detroit, Michigan
November 26, 1987	Ric Flair (6)	Chicago, Illinois
February 20, 1989	Rick Steamboat	Chicago, Illinois
May 7, 1989	Ric Flair (7)	Nashville, Tennessee

World Championship Wrestling

July 7, 1990	Sting	Baltimore, Maryland
January 11, 1991	Ric Flair (8)	East Rutherford, New Jersey
July 1, 1991	Vacant	

Flair left WCW for the WWF, fired by WCW after a no-showing scheduled defense against Barry Windham and was stripped of the title.

July 14, 1991	Lex Luger	Baltimore, Maryland

Luger defeated Barry Windham to win the title.

February 29, 1992	Sting (2)	Milwaukee, Wisconsin
July 12, 1992	Vader	Albany, New York
August 2, 1992	Ron Simmons (Faarooq)	Baltimore, Maryland
December 30, 1992	Vader (2)	Baltimore, Maryland
March 11, 1993	Sting (3)	London, England
March 17, 1993	Vader (4)	Dublin, Ireland
December 27, 1993	Ric Flair (9)	Charlotte, North Carolina

On April 17, 1994, the belt was held up after a match with Rick Steamboat. Flair won the rematch on April 24, 1994, in Atlanta, Georgia.

| July 17, 1994 | Hulk Hogan | Orlando, Florida |
| October 29, 1995 | Vacant | |

Hogan lost by DQ to The Giant (Big Show) in Detroit, Michigan, in a match where Jimmy Hart agreed that Hogan would lose the title if he lost by DQ. WCW refused to recognize the title change and declared the title vacant.

| November 26, 1995 | Randy Savage | Norfolk, Virginia |

Savage won a three-ring Battle Royal, eliminating Hogan.

December 27, 1995	Ric Flair (10)	Nashville, Tennessee
January 22, 1996	Randy Savage (2)	Las Vegas, Nevada
February 11, 1996	Ric Flair (11)	St. Petersburg, Florida
April 22, 1996	The Giant (Big Show)	Albany, New York
August 10, 1996	Hulk Hogan (2)	Sturgis, South Dakota
August 4, 1997	Lex Luger (2)	Detroit, Michigan
August 9, 1997	Hulk Hogan (3)	Sturgis, South Dakota
December 28 1997	Sting (4)	Washington, D.C.

On December 29, 1998, Sting's title was held up after a match against Hogan in Baltimore, Maryland. On February 22, 1998, Sting won a rematch in San Francisco, California.

April 19, 1998	Randy Savage (3)	Denver, Colorado
April 20, 1998	Hollywood (Hulk) Hogan (4)	Colorado Springs, Colorado
July 6, 1998	Goldberg	Atlanta, Georgia
December 27, 1998	Kevin Nash (Diesel)	Washington, D.C.
January 4, 1999	Hollywood Hogan (5)	Atlanta, Georgia

Nash allowed Hulk to pin him, to reunite the two factions of the nWo.

| March 14, 1999 | Ric Flair (12) | Louisville, Kentucky |
| April 11, 1999 | Diamond Dallas Page | Tacoma, Washington |

Diamond Dallas Page defeated Sting, Hogan, and Flair in a Four-Way match.

| April 26, 1999 | Sting (5) | Fargo, North Dakota |
| April 26, 1999 | Diamond Dallas Page (2) | Fargo, North Dakota |

Diamond Dallas Page defeated Sting, Kevin Nash, and Goldberg in a Four-Way match.

May, 9, 1999	Kevin Nash (2)	St. Louis, Missouri
July 11, 1999	Randy Savage (4)	Ft. Lauderdale, Florida

Savage defeated Nash in a tag-team match with Savage and Sid versus Nash and Sting.

July 12, 1999	Hulk Hogan (6)	Jacksonville, Florida
September 12, 1999	Sting (6)	Winston-Salem, North Carolina
October 25, 1999	Vacant	

Sting was stripped of the title for hitting referee Charles Robinson on October 24, 1999.

November 21, 1999	Bret Hart	Toronto, Canada

Hart defeated Chris Benoit in the tournament final. His title was held up on December 19, 1999, after a match against Goldberg in Washington, D.C. Hart won a rematch on December 20, 1999, in Baltimore, Maryland.

January 2000	Vacant	

Hart was unable to defend his title due to injury. The WCW stripped him of the title.

January 16, 2000	Chris Benoit	Cincinnati, Ohio

Benoit defeated Sid Vicious to win the title. Vicious's foot was on the rope.

January 17, 2000	Vacant	

Benoit left to join the WWF, without losing his belt.

January 24, 2000	Sid Vicious	Los Angeles, California

Vicious defeated Kevin Nash to win the title.

April 10, 2000	Vacant	

Eric Bischoff and Vince Russo declared all titles vacant. New titleholders were to be determined at Spring Stampede PPV.

April 16, 2000	Jeff Jarrett	Chicago, Illinois

Jarrett defeated Diamond Dallas Page in the finals of the tournament and Spring Stampede.

April 24, 2000	Diamond Dallas Page (3)	Rochester, New York
April 26, 2000	David Arquette	Syracuse, New York

Arquette pinned Eric Bischoff in a tag-team match, with DDP and Arquette versus Jeff Jarrett and Bischoff.

WWF World Title History

WWWF Title

| May 1963 | Buddy Rogers | |

Rogers was awarded this title by promoters (Vincent J. McMahon and Toots Mondt) who were breaking from the NWA, allegedly because they did not recognize Rogers's loss to Lou Thesz (January 24, 1963).

May 17, 1963	Bruno Sammartino	New York, New York
January 18, 1971	Ivan Koloff	New York, New York
February 8, 1971	Pedro Morales	New York, New York
December 1, 1973	Stan Stasiak	Philadelphia, Pennsylvania
December 12, 1973	Bruno Sammartino (2)	New York, New York
April 30, 1977	Billy Graham	Baltimore, Maryland
February 20, 1978	Bob Backlund	New York, New York
1979	The WWWF was renamed the WWF	

WWF Title

| November 30, 1979 | Antonio Inoki | Tokushima, Japan |

Inoki was not acknowledged in North America.

| December 6, 1979 | Vacant | |

Bob Backlund pinned Inoki in Tokyo, Japan. WWF President Hisashi Shinma declared it a no-contest due to outside interference from Tiger Jeet Singh. Inoki refused the belt.

| December 7, 1979 | Bob Backlund (2) | |

Backlund wrestled as champion upon returning to North America.

December 26, 1983	Iron Sheik	New York, New York
January 23, 1984	Hulk Hogan	New York, New York
February 5, 1988	Andre the Giant	Indianapolis, Indiana
February 1988	Vacant	

Andre gave the belt to Ted DiBiase. WWF officials decided that he could do this, and stripped him of the title.

March 27, 1988	Randy Savage	Atlantic City, New Jersey

Savage defeated Ted DiBiase in the tournament.

April 2, 1989	Hulk Hogan (2)	Atlantic City, New Jersey
April 1, 1990	Ultimate Warrior	Toronto, Canada
January 19, 1991	Sergeant Slaughter	Miami, Florida
March 24, 1991	Hulk Hogan (3)	Los Angeles, California
November 27, 1991	Undertaker	Detroit, Michigan
December 3, 1991	Hulk Hogan (4)	San Antonio, Texas
December 4, 1991	Vacant	

The belt was held up after controversy for the winner of Royal Rumble.

January 19, 1992	Ric Flair	Albany, New York

Flair won the Royal Rumble by eliminating Sid Justice (Sid Vicious).

April 5, 1992	Randy Savage (2)	Indianapolis, Indiana
September 1, 1992	Ric Flair (2)	Hershey, Pennsylvania
October 12, 1992	Bret Hart	Saskatoon, Canada
April 4, 1993	Yokozuna	Las Vegas, Nevada
April 4, 1993	Hulk Hogan (5)	Las Vegas, Nevada
June 13, 1993	Yokozuna (2)	Dayton, Ohio
March 20, 1994	Bret Hart (2)	New York, New York
November 23, 1994	Bob Backlund (3)	San Antonio, Texas
November 26, 1994	Diesel (Kevin Nash)	New York, New York
November 19, 1995	Bret Hart (3)	Landover, Maryland
March 31, 1996	Shawn Michaels	Anaheim, California
November 17, 1996	Sycho Sid (Sid Vicious)	New York, New York
January 19, 1997	Shawn Michaels (2)	San Antonio, Texas
February 13, 1997	Vacant	

Shawn Michaels was injured.

February 16, 1997	Bret Hart (4)	Chattanooga, Tennessee

Hart defeated Undertaker, Vader, and Steve Austin in Four-Way match.

February 17, 1997	Sycho Sid (Sid Vicious) (2)	Nashville, Tennessee
March 23, 1997	Undertaker (2)	Chicago, Illinois
August 3, 1997	Bret Hart (5)	East Rutherford, New Jersey
November 9, 1997	Shawn Michaels (3)	Montreal, Quebec

Vince McMahon had referee Earl Hebner call for the bell prematurely. Bret Hart did not submit, but the victory and title were given to Michaels.

| March 29, 1998 | Steve Austin | Boston, Massachusetts |

Special referee was Mike Tyson.

June 28, 1998	Kane	Pittsburgh, Pennsylvania
June 29, 1998	Steve Austin (2)	Cleveland, Ohio
September 27, 1998	Vacant	

Austin was pinned by Undertaker and Kane simultaneously. The belt was held up.

| November 15, 1998 | The Rock | St. Louis, Missouri |

The Rock defeated Mankind (Mick Foley) in the finals of the tournament.

| December 29, 1998 | Mankind (Mick Foley) | Worcester, Massachusetts |
| January 24, 1999 | The Rock (2) | Anaheim, California |

The Rock won an I Quit match when a tape of Mankind saying "I Quit" was played.

January 26, 1999	Mankind (2)	Tucson, Arizona
February 15, 1999	The Rock (3)	Birmingham, Alabama
March 28, 1999	Steve Austin (3)	Philadelphia, Pennsylvania
May 23, 1999	Undertaker (3)	Kansas City, Missouri
June 28, 1999	Steve Austin (4)	Charlotte, North Carolina
August 22, 1999	Mankind (3)	Minneapolis, Minnesota

Mankind pinned Austin in Three-Way match with Hunter Hearst Helmsley. Special referee was Gov. Jesse Ventura.

| August 23, 1999 | Hunter Hearst Helmsley | Ames, Iowa |
| September 14, 1999 | Vince McMahon | Las Vegas, Nevada |

September 26, 1999	Vacant	

McMahon gave up the belt.

September 26, 1999	Hunter Hearst Helmsley (2)	Charlotte, North Carolina

Triple H defeated The Rock, Kane Mankind, Big Show, and British Bulldog in a Six-Way Challenge match.

November 14, 1999	Big Show (Paul Wight)	Detroit, Michigan

Wight won a Three-Way match between Helmsley and The Rock.

January 3, 2000	Hunter Hearst Helmsley (3)	Miami, Florida
April 30, 2000	The Rock	Washington, D.C.
May 21, 2000	Hunter Hearst Helmsley (4)	Lexington, Kentucky

ECW World Title History

Eastern Championship Wrestling

April 25, 1992	Jimmy Snuka	Tabor, Pennsylvania

Snuka defeated Wildman Sal Bellomo (Salvatore Bellomo) after they each won a Battle Royal to determine the match participants.

April 26, 1992	Johnny Hot Body	Philadelphia, Pennsylvania
July 14, 1992	Jimmy Snuka (2)	Philadelphia, Pennsylvania
September 30, 1992	Don Muraco	Philadelphia, Pennsylvania
November 16, 1992	Sandman	Philadelphia, Pennsylvania
April 3, 1993	Don Muraco (2)	Radnor, Pennsylvania
August 8, 1993	Tito Santana	Philadelphia, Pennsylvania
September 18, 1993	Shane Douglas	

The title was awarded when Santana was no longer available in ECW.

October 2, 1993	Sabu	Philadelphia, Pennsylvania
December 26, 1993	Terry Funk	Philadelphia, Pennsylvania
March 26, 1994	Shane Douglas (2)	Valley Forge, Pennsylvania

Douglas pinned Funk in an eight-man War Games match (Douglas, Mr. Hughes, and Public Enemy versus Funk, Kevin Sullivan, and Tazmaniac [Tazz]).

August 30, 1994, Eastern Championship Wrestling Renamed Extreme Championship Wrestling

April 15, 1995	Sandman (2)	Philadelphia, Pennsylvania
October 28, 1995	Mikey Whipwreck	Philadelphia, Pennsylvania
December 9, 1995	Sandman (3)	Philadelphia, Pennsylvania

Sandman defeated Mikey Whipwreck and Steve Austin in a Three-way Match.

January 27, 1996	Raven	Philadelphia, Pennsylvania
October 5, 1996	Sandman (4)	Philadelphia, Pennsylvania

Sandman pinned Stevie Richards (substituting for Raven) in a Tag match.

December 7, 1996	Raven (2)	Philadelphia, Pennsylvania
April 13, 1997	Terry Funk (2)	Philadelphia, Pennsylvania
August 9, 1997	Sabu (2)	Philadelphia, Pennsylvania
August 17, 1997	Shane Douglas (3)	Ft. Lauderdale, Florida

Douglas defeated Sabu and Terry Funk in a Three-Way match.

October 16, 1997	Bam Bam Bigelow	Queens, New York
November 30, 1997	Shane Douglas (4)	Monaca, Pennsylvania
January 10, 1999	Taz (Tazz)	Kissimmee, Florida
September 19, 1999	Mike Awesome	Villa Park, Illinois

Wins Three-Way over Taz and Masato Tanaka.

December 17, 1999	Masato Tanaka	Nashville, Tennessee
December 23, 1999	Mike Awesome (2)	White Plains, New York
April 13, 2000	Tazz (Taz) (2)	Indianapolis, Indiana
April 22, 2000	Tommy Dreamer	Philadelphia, Pennsylvania
April 22, 2000	Justin Credible	Philadelphia, Pennsylvania

Rasslin' Resources

Official and Fan Web Sites

Andre the Giant:

www.albany.net/~hit/puroresu/hallfame/andre (bio, title history, and links)

www.andrethegiant.com or www.obeygiant.com (The "Giant has a Posse" campaign)

www.dory-funk.com/andre.html (Dory Funk recalls a memory of The Giant.)

Kurt Angle:

www.goldwrestler.com (Coming soon)

www.kurtanglewwf.com (Official site)

Stone Cold Steve Austin:

www.stonecold.com (Official site, through the WWF)

www.tuscws.com (Unofficial Stone Cold Web site, with news, polls, chat, and more)

www.zapnow.com/sports/stonecold (Austin's Lair fan site, with old news, photos, sounds, and more)

Buff Bagwell:

www.geocities.com/houseofbuff (The House of Buff, with news, a bio, and pictures)

Chris Benoit:

www.chrisbenoit.com (Official site)

olympia.fortunecity.com/bischoff/63 (Fan site, with history, facts, and a bio)

Big Show:

www.paulwight.com (Coming soon)

Steve Blackman:

www.lethalblackman.cjb.net (The Lethal Site fan site)

British Bulldog:

www.geocities.com/jfjwrestling/bulldog (Biography, PPV history, and title history)

Chyna:

www.freeyellow.com/members2/kpac (Fan page with pictures)

chynahq.hypermart.net (Chyna Headquarters site, with pictures and news)

www.wdass.net/chyna/Welcome.html (The Chyna Shrine site, with photos and information)

Faarooq:

www.geocities.com/Colosseum/Arena/6536 (Fan site with photos, tale of the tape, and information)

Ric Flair:

www.ricflair.com (Unofficial site, with news, history, merchandise, and more)

Mick Foley:

www.mickfoley.com (Official site, through the WWF)

www.geocities.com/Colosseum/Lodge/8068 ("Foley Is God" fan site, with photos, news, video, injuries list, and more)

www.geocities.com/Colosseum/Dome/1289/foleyisgood.htm ("Foley Is Good" fan site, with photos (Japan, ECW, WWF), match information, and more)

www.wwf.com/subsites/cactusjack (The WWF's Cactus Jack site)

Four Horsemen:

www.geocities.com/Colosseum/Bleachers/4825 (History and photos of the legendary tag team)

Dory Funk Jr.:

www.dory-funk.com (Official site)

Goldberg:

www.amigonet.org/goldberg.htm (Goldberg's fan page with news, commentary, sounds, and links)

Chavo Guerrero Jr.:

www.chavojrfan.com (Chavo fan page)

Scott Hall:

saturn.spaceports.com/~outsider (The "Outsiders Empire" fan site, with news, bios, photos, and more)

Hardy Boyz:

www.mattandjeffhardy.com (Official site)

Bret Hart:

www.brethart.net (Official site)

www.geocities.com/Colosseum/Park/4011 (Sharpshooter Central)

www.geocities.com/Colosseum/7700/hitman.html (A tribute to The Hitman)

www.hitman.faithweb.com (The Dungeon)

Owen Hart:

www.pulpwrestling.com/owen (Fan memorial site)

www.geocities.com/Colosseum/Slope/9955/index.html (Fan memorial site)

www.canoe.ca/SlamWrestling/ohart.html (Slam! Wrestling's Canadian Hall of Fame)

Hunter Hearst Helmsley (Triple H):

www.angelfire.com/me3/HHH (The Pedigree Zone fan page, with history, a bio, and photos)

Curt Hennig:

www.geocities.com/Colosseum/7692/main.html (Tribute to Mr. Perfect, a fan page devoted to his WWF career)

www.curthennig.com (Coming soon)

Hulk Hogan:

www.hulksterrules.com (The Hulkamaniac's fan site; it even has a pop-up window reminding you to take your vitamins.)

www.wrestlingmuseum.com/pages/bios/hogan2.html (History of Hogan, including older photos)

Chris Jericho:

www.chrisjericho.com (Official site)

www.angelfire.com/al/DestroyersofLight/index.html (Jericho-holics Anonymous fan site)

Junkyard Dog:

webster.unh.edu/~gwd/jyd.html (In memory of Sylvester Ritter, the Junkyard Dog)

Konnan:

www.konnan.com (Official site, with photos, videos, links to fan pages, and more)

members.aol.com/virgpp/konnan.html (Ultimate Konnan Page fan site, with a bio, photos, and more)

Jerry Lawler:

www.kinglawler.com (Official site; also the home page of Memphis Championship Wrestling and the Kat)

www.geocities.com/Colosseum/Field/7818 (Quotes from the King)

Legion of Doom:

www.lod2000.com (Official site)

Rey Mysterio Jr.:

www.bruce-lee.demon.co.uk/reysmain.html (Career history, photos, and more)

zone.rowdygirl.com/reyphoto.htm (Photos of Rey Rey)

www.reymysteriojr.com (Coming soon)

Shawn Michaels:

twodudes.simplenet.com/shawn.htm (A bio, multimedia, and lots of photos)

www.showstoppa.com (More than 500 photos, articles, PPV history, and news about HBK)

Kevin Nash:

www.kevinbigsexynash.com (Official site)

Diamond Dallas Page

www.ddpbang.com (Official site of Page and Kimberly)

www.geocities.com/jfjwrestling/ddp (Fan site with photos, history, and images)

Roddy Piper:

rowdygirl.simplenet.com/RowdyGirlsWCWZone/piper.htm (Piper's Pit fan site, with a bio, history, photos, multimedia, and more)

users.ipa.net/~yuchtar/Piper.html (Piper site by a non-wrestling fan; contains movie information mostly)

Raven:

members.tripod.com/~RAVEN__316 (The Raven's Nest fan site, with photos, a message board, and more)

www.scottlevy.com (The Raven's Crucifix fan page)

The Rock:

www.therock.com (Official site through the WWF)

www.geocities.com/Colosseum/Rink/5026/splash.html (Know Your Role Blvd fan site, with news, sounds, and more)

www.therockbottom.com (The Rock Bottom fan site, with a message board, and news)

brahmabull.cjb.net (The Rock Site fan site, with photos, sounds, links, and such)

www.angelfire.com/tx/wrestletainment (The Rock's Corner fan site, with history and embedded links)

Sandman:

hak.chriskanyon.com (Fan page with bio, TV results, and multimedia)

Randy Savage:

www.machoman.com (Official site; coming soon)

Scott Steiner (Big Poppa Pump):

www.zoomnet.net/~bucky

www.bigpoppapump.com (Fan "shrine" to Scott Steiner with news, bio, match results, photos, and video segments)

Sting:

www.geocities.com/jfjwrestling/sting (Powerslam Sting page, with a bio, career history, photos, and more)

members.xoom.com/stingfansite/index.html (Sting Fan Site, with photos, a guest book, chat area, and more)

ladysting.homestead.com (Lots of Sting photos, including projects by Steve Borden)

www.geocities.com/Colosseum/Field/3994/MAIN.HTM (This is Sting fan page, with a bio, career information, photos, links, and more.)

Tazz:

www.tazzmania.com (Fan site, with news, photos, a bio, and more)

Vampiro:

www.vampiro.net (Official site of Ian Hodgkinson)

Rob Van Dam:

www.robvandam.com (Official site)

Ultimate Warrior:

www.ultimatewarrior.com (Official site)

rohit.8m.com (The Ultimate Site; under construction)

The Undertaker:

www.geocities.com/Colosseum/Mound/7686/wwfpage.html (The Undertaker and Kane stats and history)

welcome.to/thelordofdarkness (Death Valley fan site, with a bio, photos, history, and more)

www.rraz.co.uk/alexs/UnderTaker.htm (Wrestling record for The Undertaker)

www.geocities.com/Colosseum/Dome/2535/index.html (History and links)

www.undertaker.com (Link to the WWF's home page)

General Web Sites

www.1wrestling.com (Wrestling news)

www.2xzone.com (News, interviews, results, book reviews, and columns)

www.albany.net/~hit/puroresu (Site devoted to Japanese pro wrestling. Includes title histories, news, and more.)

www.bruisermania.com (Wrestling news and results)

www.eyada.com (Wrestling insider Dave Meltzer's show on Monday through Friday 6 P.M. to 8 P.M.)

www.geocities.com/jfjwrestling (Power Slam, with wrestlers' bios)

www.iwrestling.com (Headlines, news, results, and links)

www.latestwrestlingnews.com (Wrestling news—mostly results)

www.lethalinjection.com (Wrestling humor, columns)

www.lordsofpain.net (Lords of Pain news and results page)

www.prowrestle.about.com (About.com's pro wrestling home page. Includes stories, results, and links.)

www.prowrestlinginsider.com (Pro Wrestling Insider news and results)

www.pwbts.com ("Pro Wrestling's Between the Sheets" columns and links) www.slam.ca/SlamWrestling/home.html (SLAM! wrestling page, with news, reviews, and a column by Bret Hart)

www.thebizarr.com (Wrestling news and columns)

www.therocksays.com (News, results, transcripts, and more)

www.tpww.net (The People's Wrestling Web site. Includes news, results, and columns.)

www.users.aol.com/Solie/index.html (Solie's Vintage Wrestling site, with everything from latest results to old NWA images. Posts a newsletter, available only online, every Saturday.)

www.wrestlefan.com (The Pain Clinic: call-in talk show with wrestling guests. Posts the transcripts of past shows. Slam line: 716-234-7526.)

www.wrestlingallstars.com (Home page for *Wrestling All Stars* magazine, along with *Ringside Wrestling, Superstar Wrestlers,* and *TV Wrestlers*. Includes news, images, results, and feature stories.)

www.wrestlingmuseum.com (Pro Wrestling Online Museum, with photos, bios, real names, and more)

Suggested Reading

Anderson, Arn. *Arn Anderson 4 Ever: A Look Behind the Curtain*. Minneapolis, Minnesota: Stephen Barlow Distribution, 1998.

Dibiase, Ted. *Every Man Has His Price: The True Story of Wrestling's Million Dollar Man*. Sisters, Oregon: Multnomah Publishers, Inc., 1997.

Duncan, Royal, and Gary Will. *Wrestling Title Histories, 4th Edition*. Waterloo, Ontario: Archeus, 2000.

Foley, Mick. *Have a Nice Day: A Tale of Blood and Sweatsocks*. New York: Regan Books, 1999.

Hart, Bret. *Bret "Hitman" Hart: The Best There Is, the Best There Was, the Best There Ever Will Be*. North York, Ontario: Stoddart Publishing, 2000.

LeBell, "Judo" Gene. *Gene LeBell's Grappling World*. Los Angeles: Gene LeBell, 1999.

Lentz, Harris M. III. *Biographical Dictionary of Professional Wrestling*. Jefferson, North Carolina: McFarland & Company, Inc., 1997.

Page, Diamond Dallas. *Positively Page: The Diamond Dallas Page Journey*. Owings Mills, Maryland: Positive Publishing Ltd., 2000.

Rock. *The Rock Says: The Most Electrifying Man in Sports-Entertainment*. New York: Regan Books, 2000.

Sugar, Bert Randolph, and George Napolitano. *The Pictorial History of Wrestling: The Good, the Bad, and the Ugly*. New York: Smithmark Publishers, 1984.

Thesz, Lou. *Hooker*. Online at www.twc-online.com/thesz; to order an autographed copy, mail to Lou Thesz Book, 7647 Granby St., Suite #22 (Dept. WS), Norfolk, Virginia 23505.

Von Erich, Fritz. *Von Erichs: Triumphs & Tragedies of Wrestling's First Family*. Dallas, Texas: Taylor Publishing, 1987.

Fighting Words Glossary

angle   A technique used by promoters and managers to create a feud or a grudge match. It may involve only one match or continue over several matches.

At Show   Short for "Athletic Show." A regular feature of carnivals in the nineteenth century that showcased athletic prowess.

babyface   See *face*.

Battle Royal   A match that involves 30 or more wrestlers who enter the ring one at a time at regular intervals. It's every man for himself, and anyone thrown over the top rope is eliminated. The last wrestler in the ring wins the match.

blading   A practice in which wrestlers hide blades on their bodies and cut themselves during a match to create a dramatic gush of blood.

blow up   To become weary or depleted of energy. Some wrestlers blow up on the entry ramp.

booker   The person in charge of planning a match. Promoters hire bookers to create just the right combination of talent, angles, and finishes for an exciting card.

Brass Knux match   A match in which brass knuckles are placed on top of a corner pole in the ring. The first wrestler to get to them can use them.

bump   A fall or a hit that literally knocks the victim down hard; usually this is the high point of a match. Wrestlers, referees, managers, valets, and other participants can all suffer from bumps in the ring.

cage match   A match in which the ring is surrounded by a metal cage to keep competitors in and interference out. The cage can be climbed or rigged with an electrical current to keep the wrestlers off.

card   A list of wrestling matches occurring at a specific place and time.

carney   Term used to refer both to carnivals and to carnival operators and employees.

count-out   If a wrestler is knocked out of the ring, he has 10 seconds to get back in without help. The opponent must back off in a neutral corner. If he interferes in any way, the count starts over. This practice is worked into matches to allow wrestlers some breathing time. If both men are out of the ring for a 10 count, the match is over. This is called double disqualification via countout because "the ref called for the bell."

cycle   Steroids are prescribed in cycles, so the building up or shrinking down of muscles as a result of the drug is called a cycle.

disqualification   Losing a match for breaking the rules or leaving the ring rather than by being pinned or forced into submission.

do the job   Getting pinned in the ring. It's a thankless job, but someone has to do it.

DQ   See *disqualification*.

draw   A wrestler's public image, carefully created by promotion and performance, which is awesome enough to bring fans into the arena.

dud   An extremely dull or boring match.

exposing the business   Giving away wrestling secrets, either on purpose or accidentally.

face   A hero or good guy, also known as a babyface. Faces can be very unpopular when they always follow the rules and are promoted as wimpy goody-goodies.

fall   One contest to a conclusion. Most U.S. matches are only one fall in length. In Mexico, two out of three is the norm.

Falls-Count-Anywhere match   To win a match, you must pin your opponent for a three count. In a Falls-Count-Anywhere match, the pin can occur anywhere in the arena, even in the aisles.

feud   Matches that are scheduled between wrestlers who hate each other, usually with the good guys versus the bad guys.

finish   The final moves that signal who will win or lose as the match draws to a close.

First Blood match   A match in which the first man to juice is the loser.

getting heat   The role of the bad guy to get the crowd to boo or react with hostility to him. An enthusiastic cheer or boo means that the match is successfully getting heat.

getting over   Connecting with the crowd by making the fans accept and react to your wrestling persona.

gimmick   A prop used as a wrestler's trademark and also often as a weapon. Also, a wrestler's persona.

Greco-Roman wrestling   An old form of wrestling, developed in France in the 1860s. This type of wrestling requires a wrestler to throw an opponent so that both shoulders touch the mat simultaneously. Tripping and holds below the waist are not allowed.

green   An unseasoned wrestler who makes mistakes early in his career.

Hair versus Hair match   In these matches, the loser gets his head shaved as a humiliating punishment (but often escapes before he can be touched). A popular variation is the Mask versus Mask match, in which the loser must reveal his face.

ham 'n' egger   A professional opponent—one who hasn't yet made it to a high level of fan-recognition, so he (or she) is cast as the loser in bouts. Also known as a *jobber*.

Handicap match   A match that is booked two-on-one or three-on-one to introduce a vicious new heel. He takes on two or three undersized jobbers who get completely destroyed.

hardway juice   Blood drawn during a match without the use of blading.

heat   The audience's excitement and anticipation of a match. "Face heat" means cheering. "Heel heat" means booing.

heel   A bad guy who doesn't follow established rules; the opposite of a face.

hook   Illegal tricks, moves, or gimmicks used to win a bout underhandedly.

hooker   A wrestler who employs hooks to take out a challenger.

hot tag   A tag-team strategy often used in matches between heels and faces. The heels pulverize the smallest face, angering his partner, who is unable to get into the ring until he is tagged. The ref is distracted from the action by the gyrations outside the ring. Then, beaten nearly unconscious, the lesser face leaps across the ring to tag his partner. The partner proceeds to clean house in a triumphant victory.

house   The spectators at a match.

jabroni   See *jobber*.

job   A wrestler's defeat in a planned match. A clean job means to beat a wrestler with a legal pin or submission.

jobber   A wrestler who loses on purpose to make other wrestlers look good. New wrestlers just breaking into the business almost always spend some time as jobbers until they build a fan following.

juice   Blood or to bleed.

kayfabe   A private language used in wrestling, originated by carneys. Like "pig Latin," it allows people who use it to speak in public about secrets or tricks of the trade without worrying that anyone who overhears them will understand what's being said.

kill   When the fans lose enthusiasm for a wrestler, the heat dies down. Wrestlers who do a lot of jobs suffer from this loss of drawing power. Also, if matches constantly have endings that are unclear in who won or lost, people will not be drawn to matches, and the industry loses money.

Ladder match   A specialty match in which the championship belt is dangled above the top of a ladder and the wrestlers must compete to climb up and grab it in order to win.

legit   The real thing, or reality in general. Opposite of a work. A match is legit if there are no tricks involved. When shooters wrestle, the action is legit.

loaded   Everyday items that have supposedly been altered for use as weapons in the ring—for example, a loaded tennis racket that could fell a 350-pound man, or a loaded briefcase used to smash in an opponent's face.

Lumberjack match   A match designed to finalize a feud that fails to come to a conclusion due to frequent disqualifications via count-out. The ring is surrounded by neutral wrestlers who are instructed to throw anyone who comes out of the ring back in again.

mark   A fan who believes that everything he sees, both in and out of the ring, is real.

No Disqualification match   A match in which the winner must pin his opponent or make him submit by any means possible (even cheating is allowed).

Nontitle match   A match in which a champion wrestler can lose without affecting his future prospects.

paper   Free tickets given to fans for a match; usually done to fill an arena before a television taping. This doesn't happen nearly as often as it used to because now tickets sell.

pin   Forcing an opponent's shoulders to the mat and holding them there for a three count by the referee. Matches can be won by pinning the opponent.

pinfall   A fall that ends in a pin.

pop   The sudden rush of enthusiasm as a popular wrestler enters the ring or when a dramatic move is made.

post   To slam into the ringpost.

potato   A head injury caused either by a direct hit or a crash. It usually results in a black eye, so jobbers have to be careful not to potato the main face accidentally.

potato shot   A blow that causes a potato.

ref bump   A planned strategy that eliminates the ref by knocking him out when he accidentally gets in the way. While the ref is unconscious, all kinds of hijinks could happen in the ring without being regulated.

ringboy   A punk.

ringrats   Wrestling groupies.

ringpost   The posts at the four corners of the ring.

run-in   What happens when wrestlers, managers, or others who are not part of a match jump in to join the fight.

save   A run-in to stop any action that erupts between foes after a match is over.

Scaffold match   A match that takes place on various contraptions up in the air and in which wrestlers have to climb, fight, and sometimes fall to their doom.

schmazz   Everybody fighting everybody. Climactic chaos to end a show or a segment of a show.

scientific wrestling   Old-style wrestling simulating a sport, rather than purely done for entertainment. Scientific matches are those that are based on the legit use of standard holds and moves, and are conducted strictly according to Greco-Roman rules. They involve no flamboyant tricks or gimmicks.

screw-job   A match fought outside the rules of wrestling.

sell   To convince the crowd of the superiority of an opponent. A jobber does this by reacting to moves with the proper enthusiasm and pain. A wrestler can have big problems if his opponent does not sell for him when he is supposed to.

shoot   A legitimate fight, or anything legit.

shooter   A wrestler who is skilled at making matches seem legit even if they are not. The term originally meant a wrestler who wrestled only on the "up and up." The word derives from the phrase "straight-shooter."

Shooting match   A clean, legit match.

squared circle   Another term for the wrestling (or boxing) ring.

Squash match   A match between a superstar and a jobber. The jobber is completely dominated by the star.

stiff   Hitting hard even when the match is worked. Jobbers do not expect to be hurt much, and they hate it when they are stiffed.

strap   A championship belt.

Strap match   A match in which the opponents are strapped, chained, or roped together; this usually evolves into a juice match.

stretch   A type of shoot in which one wrestler dominates rather than injures another wrestler.

Texas Death match   A match with no rules; however, the booking might include some previously agreed-upon rules such as what gimmicks are allowed. For example, both wrestlers may be allowed to wear cowboy boots, but the heel's boot (not to mention the boot's heel) might be loaded. The match goes until one wrestler is unable to continue.

turn   To change from a bad guy into a good guy or vice versa. Angles are often set up by turns.

turnbuckle   The padded buckles on the four ringposts to which the ropes are attached.

work   Any practice that is not legit. An injury can be worked in order to give a wrestler some time off.

work rate   An approximate ratio of good wrestling to rest holds in a match or in a wrestler's overall performance.

Lucha Libre Glossary

espaldas planas   Lateral press.

foul   Low blow.

guillotina   Leg drop.

martinete   Piledriver. This move means an instant DQ in Mexico.

mortal   High-risk maneuver.

palmoteo   Chop.

patata   Kick.

patata voladora   Flying drop-kick.

plancha   Crossbody block. Leaping onto one's opponent to knock him down.

quebradura   Back-breaker. Sometimes used to mean Torture Rack.

rana   Any move that uses the legs to scissors the opponent's head.

salto mortal   High-risk move that involves a midair somersault, like a moonsault.

senton   Leap on an opponent back first.

silla   To use your butt as a weapon. To sit on your opponent.

tope   Flying head butt.

tope suicidi   Flying head butt in which the *luchador* leaps from inside the ring to nail his opponent outside the ring, going either through or over the ropes.

Collectibles Price Guide

Here's an idea of what some of the neatest wrestling collectibles are worth on the open market. (Source: *Professional Wrestling Collectibles,* by Kristian Pope and Ray Whebbe Jr.)

"Superfly" Jimmy Snuka's ring attire	$150
Terry Funk's Double-Cross Branding Iron	$150
Singapore cane signed by Sandman	$150
Buddy Rogers trading card	$150
Pat O'Connor trading card	$100
Lou Thesz trading card	$95
Verne Gagne Trivia Game	$60
1954 NWA calendar	$45
Jesse Ventura action figure	$40
Roddy Piper action figure	$35
WrestleMania I Official Program	$30
1953 edition of *NWA Official Wrestling* magazine	$30
1963 edition of *Wrestling World* magazine	$25
Captain Lou Albano action figure	$10 (cheap at any price)

Autographs

Karl Gotch	$150
Gorgeous George	$150
Bruiser Brody	$110
Antonino Rocca	$100
Ed "Strangler" Lewis	$100
The Sheik (Ed Farhat)	$50
Ric Flair	$50
Kerry Von Erich	$45
Hulk Hogan	$40
Dick the Bruiser	$25

Index

Caddock, Earl, 353
Cage Matches, 54, 288
  barbed wire, 290
Calhoun, Haystacks, 287
California audiences, 212
Callas, Mark, 160
camcorders, 235
camel clutch, 312
cameras, 235
Can-Am Connection, 204
Candido, Chris, 84, 89, 175, 212
Capitol Wrestling, 28
cards, 248
carnivals, 38
  women, 84
  wrestling, 14-15
Carpentier, Ed, 74
Carpentier, Edouard, 77, 96, 354
  Thesz, Lou, match with, 261-263
Casey, Steve "Crusher," 66, 354
catch phrases, 132
  Austin, Steve, 141
  Rock, The, 134
cauliflower ear, 45
Chainsaw Charlie, 195, 214
  New Age Outlaws, rivalry, 257-258
Chainz, 132
champions
  ECW, 362

NWA (National Wrestling Alliance), 354
  undisputed champions, 353
  WCW, 356
  WWF, 359
  WWWF, 359
Chandler, Happy, 70
characters
  introduction of, 21
  moral ambiguity, 9
charisma, 327
Chetti, Chris, 35
Chief Chewchki, 44
chinlocks, 312
chops, 39
choreography, 38-46
Christian, 33, 92
Chyna, 33, 154, 157-159, 213-215
  acting career, 159
  cosmetic surgery, 158
  crossover appeal, 24
  Web sites, 366
Clary, Dennis, 10
clotheslines, 38
Cochrane, Red, 305
Cole, Michael, 91
collar and elbow style wrestling, 14
collectibles, 379-380
college football, 304
collegiate wrestling, 3
Colon, Carlos, 355
Colossal Connection, 207

Connery, Sean, 4
Coolidge, Calvin, 16
Corbett, Jim, 287
Corino, Steve, 35
corner posts, 39
Cornette, Jim, 214
Corporal Kirchner, 203
Corporation, The, 134
Count Dracula, 44
count outs, 52
Covert, Jim, 203
cradles, 313
Credible, Justin, 35, 363
  finishing move, 316
Crockett, Jim, 253
crossfaces, 312
crossover acts, 24, 292
crossover competitions, 286
Crowbar, 33
Crush, 130, 210-211, 213
Crusher, 110
Curley, Jack, 21
Cutler, Charley, 62, 353
Cyrus the Virus, 35

D

Dallas Sportatorium, 231
Damn Dudleyz, 328
Dangerous Alliance, 35
Dangerously, Lou E., 35
Dangerously, Paul E., 34, 139
David Letterman Show, 83

Valiant, Johnny, 201, 284

Vampiro, 33, 169-170
finishing move, 317
Web sites, 369

Van Dam, Rob, 35
finishing move, 317
Web sites, 370

Vega, Savio, 131

Vegas, Vinnie, 117

Veloz, Ciclone, 259

Venis, Val, 33, 163, 215, 250
finishing move, 317

Ventura, Jesse, 24, 77, 139, 154, 279
crossover appeal, 24-25

venues, 232-233

Vicious, Sid, 33, 171-172, 358, 360-361
finishing move, 317

victory rolls, 314

Victory, Jack, 35

viewers, 8-9

vignettes, 185

villains, 50

Vinny, 215

violence, 9

Virgil, 208-209

Viscera, 33, 218

Volkoff, Nikolai, 201, 203-205, 207

Von Erich, Chris
suicide of, 107

Von Erich, David, 106, 241
death of, 106

Von Erich, Fritz, 105-107, 372
gimmick, 106
iron claw grip, 106

Von Erich, Kerry, 107, 208, 356
drug arrest, 107
Flair, Ric, rivalry, 240-241
foot amputation, 107
motorcycle accident, 107
suicide of, 107

Von Erich, Mike
drug problem, 106
suicide of, 106

Von Erich, Waldo, 79

Von Erichs: Triumphs & Tragedies of Wrestling's First Family, 372

W

Wagner, George. *See* Gorgeous George, 67

Wall, The, 33, 177
finishing move, 317

Wallstreet, Michael, 92

Wannamaker, John, 10

Ware, Koko B., 204-205, 207

Washington, George, 16

Watson, Billy, 66

Watts, Bill, 106

WCW (World Championship Wrestling), 4, 27, 31-34
champions, 356
current roster, 33

factions, 240
nWo, 243
WWF
defections from, 32
ratings, 194

weapons, 44
fans, 232

Weaver, Johnny, 84

Web sites, 7
fan sites, 365
general wrestling sites, 370

Wells, George, 203

Weston, Mae, 85

Whebbe Jr., Ray, 379

Whipwreck, Mikey, 35, 164
finishing move, 317

Whistler, Clarence, 16

White, Vanna, 4

Wight, Paul "The Big Show," 362

Wild Samoan School, 304

Will, Gary, 371

Willard, Jess, 28

Williams, Steve, 137

Wilson, Torrie, 33, 90, 170

Windham, Barry, 138, 201, 213, 356

Wippleman, Harvey, 209

Wolfe, Billy, 85, 87,

Wolfe, Buddy, 96

women, 84
Burke, Mildred, 8, 85-86
carnivals, 84
Chyna, 157-159

X-Y-Z